Digital Freedom

In the present age of the digital era, the terms digitalization, emerging technologies, and social media have become buzzwords. Among all the innovations in our history, digital technology has advanced the fastest. With the freedom of digitalization, emerging technologies, and high-speed internet, computing devices may now work remotely. Every industry, including banking and finance, healthcare, agriculture, logistics, academia, government sectors, and businesses, has recognized the need for innovative digital technologies for their development, boosting efficiency and speed and cutting costs. Digitalization has also converted non-digital applications into digital ones to make things easier for people, at the same time that social media has an increasingly significant impact on human lives and industries. Consequently, the primary goal of this book is to explain to readers how newly emerging digital technologies and social media have significantly altered and aided in the growth of today's organizations and how the freedom of using these technologies has proved to be beneficial, particularly during the COVID-19 pandemic that has affected the entire world.

This book demonstrates its argument by providing real-world cases from both established and developing nations, particularly India. The book also investigates how digital transformation may help every industry and organization be more agile and efficient. Readers will learn about the main goals of digital initiatives that have been launched to create a digitally empowered society worldwide. In this book, the benefits and challenges of digitization, digital tools, and other technologies in diverse fields are also examined.

Digital Freedom

Faizur Rashid and Sadaf Rashid

CRC Press
Taylor & Francis Group
Boca Raton London New York

CRC Press is an imprint of the
Taylor & Francis Group, an **Informa** business

First edition published 2024
by CRC Press
2385 NW Executive Center Drive, Suite 320, Boca Raton FL 33431

and by CRC Press
4 Park Square, Milton Park, Abingdon, Oxon, OX14 4RN

© 2024 Faizur Rashid and Sadaf Rashid

CRC Press is an imprint of Taylor & Francis Group, LLC

Library of Congress Cataloging-in-Publication Data
Names: Rashid, Faizur, author. | Rashid, Sadaf, author.
Title: Digital freedom / Faizur Rashid and Sadaf Rashid.
Description: First edition. | Boca Raton : CRC Press, 2024. |
Includes bibliographical references and index. |
Identifiers: LCCN 2023012724 (print) | LCCN 2023012725 (ebook) |
ISBN 9781032517506 (hardback) | ISBN 9781032517520 (library binding) |
ISBN 9781003403784 (ebook)
Subjects: LCSH: Telecommuting. |
Electronic commerce. | Flexible work arrangements.
Classification: LCC HD2336.3 .R44 2024 (print) |
LCC HD2336.3 (ebook) | DDC 658.3/123–dc23/eng/20230711
LC record available at https://lccn.loc.gov/2023012724
LC ebook record available at https://lccn.loc.gov/2023012725

ISBN: 9781032517506 (hbk)
ISBN: 9781032517520 (pbk)
ISBN: 9781003403784 (ebk)

DOI: 10.1201/9781003403784

Typeset in Times
by Newgen Publishing UK

Dedication

To my parents, spouse, children, brother, sisters, and friends for their emotional support and encouragement.
Faizur Rashid

To Faizur, Shifa, Reyan, friends, and family for your love and inspiration.
Sadaf Rashid

Contents

Foreword

We are surrounded by technology in utilizing mobile devices, computing devices, automated machines, smart agriculture, smart townships and homes, smart offices, and smart hospitals. This is the concept of digitalization which reaches every corner of our lives. It provides comfort, ease, and utility in our lives and professions. The potential scope for writing a book about digitalization is so vast because it appears everywhere in society and integrates all modern technology.

Today, every field of our daily activity is surrounded by digital devices which offer freedom of uses, access, and the ability to connect. Certainly, there is a need to highlight visionary pros and cons, the effectiveness of digitalization for students, academics, and society, and the uses and misuses of digital devices by the political inter-folio.

We are not certain about the end of freedom; rather, digital freedom gives us views and vision worldwide. There are several new digitized technologies like AI, AR, VR, and sensing capacity: the self-learning capacity of devices integrating into machines. We are fortunate to have all these modern conveniences, and we have much still to learn about them.

Digitalization is evolving very rapidly, but this book gives a broad overview of digitalization in and around us happening today. There will undoubtedly be even more information to consider in the next edition of this book. I found it very broadly informative and believe you the reader will too.

Prof. (Assistant) Tilahun Shiferaw
Director, Library and Information Science
Haramaya University, Ethiopia

Preface

Digital Freedom is primarily intended for younger students who are glued to modern digital technology and who have grown up in a digital world. They should read it to learn more about the freedom to use sophisticated digital technologies, as well as their role, importance, and implications in numerous industries. This book offers the most recent and up-to-date information available.

The scope of this book is to look into how the freedom of advanced digital technologies will improve the economy and society as a whole. The benefits of digital technologies are not limited to technology-based businesses but may also be used in many sectors of the economy, be it education, business, agriculture, banking, health, and so on. The emerging advanced technologies such as Artificial Intelligence (AI), blockchain, Internet of Things, etc. are all promising technologies for the growth of businesses, the economy, and for the country as a whole.

The main benefit of this book is its focus on how increased digital technological independence can benefit the economy and society as a whole, as we are living in a world where people are growing increasingly dependent on their smart digital devices, whether for work or pleasure.

Another key purpose of the book is to investigate how improved digital technology freedom will benefit the economy and society in general. Digital technologies have numerous applications outside of technology-based industries, including education, business, agriculture, banking, health care, and so on. This book will also address how the COVID-19 pandemic, in particular, has underlined the global need for digitalization.

The major motive of this book is to show how emerging advanced technologies like AI, blockchain, the IoT, and social media platforms are all promising for business, economics, and overall country progress.

The book is designed to demonstrate how digital technologies are currently used for a wide range of reasons, ranging from personal to political. The first illustration of everyday digitalization freedom is social connectivity. Connecting with our loved ones who live far away has become incredibly simple and quick. The freedom of digitization has made it easier to communicate. Digital payment mechanisms are the second common illustration of the freedom allowed by digitalization. Digital payments are favored because of their reduced reliance on cash, rapid transfer speeds, and convenience of use. Digitalization-related freedoms can be seen in everyday activities such as online shopping, food ordering, and so on.

Organization of the Book

This book includes the following ten chapters:

Chapter 1 Digitalization: This chapter offers a thorough introduction to digitalization, digitization, and some of the key terms used in the internet and networking. This chapter covers advances in digital technology and how these technologies are evolving. This chapter also discusses our digital rights and how vital they are to us as digital citizens. Also discussed is how digital freedom is generating a surge in internet users and smartphone usage, as well as its influence on the economy worldwide. The chapter also highlights topics like digital democracy and E-Governance and how they affect modern society.

Chapter 2 Social Media and Digital Freedom: This chapter discusses how social media has become a vital aspect of our lives in the digital age. This chapter also explains how social media may have both beneficial and harmful effects on society. The number of social media users and the most popular social media platforms that now dominate the Asia-Pacific markets and other developed and developing countries are also discussed in this chapter. Toward the end of the chapter, the role of social media in politics is also explored.

Chapter 3 Cyber Laws: This chapter examines how the misuse of social media contributes to the growth of e-violence, hate speech, and various cybercrimes on social media, as well as the societal consequences of these crimes, and the different cyber laws that governments across the world have enacted to curb crimes and activities on social media and cyberspace. Towards the end of the chapter, we will also discuss some of the most important social, ethical, and technological challenges that users and LGBT (Lesbian, Gay, Bisexual, and Transgender) individuals around the world are currently facing.

Chapter 4 Pros and Cons of Digitalization: The main objective of this chapter is to explore both the positive and negative sides of utilizing modern digital tools, platforms, and technologies in the digital age in several different fields.

Chapter 5 Digital Education and Digital Library: The first part of this chapter examines how advanced digital technologies have influenced the global educational system, as well as the impact of the COVID-19 pandemic on the educational system. Different trends in the digital education system are also presented. And the second part of this chapter discusses the concept of digital libraries, their benefits, and their challenges. In this part of the chapter, students are given the keys to the information resources.

Chapter 6 Digital Healthcare: This chapter focuses on the number of developing digital technologies, both novel and advanced, that have all contributed to the development of the digital global healthcare industry. The chapter also provides advanced digital technologies application and their impact on the healthcare industry. It also examines several government initiatives for the global expansion of healthcare sectors.

Chapter 7 Digital Agriculture and Digitalization in Food Industries: This chapter explains how modern and innovative digital technology has the potential to transform the agriculture economy in a variety of ways. Also discussed is how digital adoption has supplied farmers with better answers and lessons in the agricultural sector's evolution. The second part of this chapter gives an overview of the digital transformation occurring in food industries.

Chapter 8 Digital Banking and Finance: This chapter discusses how digital technology has impacted the banking and finance sector as well as the government's various initiatives in this sector and its role in pushing the banking and finance industry into digital operations. The chapter introduces digital payment methods adopted worldwide to speed up payments and improve the country's economy.

Chapter 9 Digital Logistics: This chapter presents the importance of digitization in the logistics business, as well as how various initiatives and others have aided in the improvement of the logistics sector and government investment.

Chapter 10 E-Commerce Digitalization: This chapter discusses how crucial digitization is in today's digital environment for integrating the economy through the creation of digital markets. The chapter also discusses how internet and smartphone penetration in various countries around the world has aided the expansion of E-Commerce business. Besides, the chapter provides the relationship between logistics and E-Commerce.

TEACHERS, STUDENTS, AND NON-ACADEMIC PERSONS

The readers of this book may come from academic, non-academic, and informatics backgrounds. The book is aimed at pupils of the younger generation who are already accustomed to modern digital technologies and who have grown up in a digital environment. They should read this book to gain a better understanding of the freedom of using advanced digital technologies, their role, importance, and implications in various fields.

Today, in this digital era, around 80–90% of teachers are using advanced digital tools and technologies to improve the classroom experience. This book's major aim is to provide a thorough overview of the applications of digital tools and technologies. As today's teenagers are more active users of digital technologies, it is essential to make them aware of and educate them about the positive and negative outcomes of digital technologies at the school level itself. Thus, this book can be used to teach at both intermediate levels and undergraduate levels.

Individual chapters in this book can also be used as tutorials for digital education, digital banking and finance, and digital healthcare. Each chapter ends with a set of exercises for readers to test their knowledge. Some exercises can also be used as research discussion topics. The reference lists at the end of each chapter are provided to enable readers to find the research literature that contains the origin of the concepts and techniques presented.

Acknowledgments

Writing a book is similar to going on a journey. Not only do you face numerous challenges but also you gain valuable experiences as well. It takes a significant amount of time and effort to write a book and it would be impossible to achieve without walking on the tough path.

First and foremost, I sincerely thank my wife and co-author, Mrs. Sadaf Rashid who worked hard day and night without feeling any exertion. Next, thanks to my growing children Shifa's and Reyan's patience of uncountable days and nights where I was unable to mingle with them in their activity of games and watching television. Also, my brother Aadil indirectly gave me the power to continue the work in all situations. I am grateful for all support of my co-workers' motivation in the department of computer science and the college at Haramaya University. I would like to express my gratitude to everyone from whom I learned something new and useful. Thank you so much to everyone who has been so visionary.

It would be incomplete not to thank Ms. Gabriella Williams, the editor of information science at T&F and her colleagues Borkakoti Jubi and Khushbu, who helped me move towards stronger writing. I cannot forget Mr. Sanjay Jain, CEO of MICA Ranchi, who shaped me in professionalism and hard work.

My father and mother are my backbone during hard times. Their support, encouragement, motivation, and inspiration continued throughout my life and provided the fuel to accelerate the journey.

Finally, the Almighty is permitting me the breath, health, strength, patience, and bravery to pursue my dream of publishing this book.

Author Biographies

Faizur Rashid has worked within the academic industry for over twenty years, of which fifteen years of experience was gained in university settings. He developed a wide range of skills in teaching, research, and administration that meet, and exceed, expectations. A village boy journeyed from a small village to abroad. Growing up in an area with low literacy levels required him to prove himself, every step of the way. He achieved his success when he received his first award of excellence among hundreds of teachers in PGTs from MICA Ranchi in India, in 2004.

In his teaching career, he passed through various roles as a teacher, coordinator, and vice-principal that helped students succeed. As a teacher, he realized his duty to apply himself to every situation, including assignments, delivering lectures, discipline, managing the expectations of the students, answering questions, practice stages, work plan implementation, methods, or research, and adoption of an environment that fosters and encourages learning.

As far as school, NGO, college, and university experiences are concerned, he has enjoyed teaching and learning at all levels related to his research interests. Hundreds of the students were inspired by him to pursue the course of computer science. He relishes the opportunity to bring bright ideas and a new level of success to all organizations he is a part of. He has published a few research papers, successfully designed and developed curriculums adopted by his current university, and was most recently motivated to write his first book *Digital Freedom* with his wife and co-author Sadaf Rashid. Together they've endured sleepless nights after working long hours and being parents to two children, to write this book.

Sadaf Rashid was born in the district of Warangal and bought up in Maharashtra, India. She completed her Master's Degree in the field of Computer Science and later completed Microsoft Certification in .NET. She worked in a small company as a software developer after receiving her professional certification in .NET and C# and has developed customized software for the health domain. She started to assist Faizur after their marriage and while taking care of the family.

Author: Faizur Rashid (Ph.D.)
Co-author: Sadaf Rashid (MCA)

Abbreviations

3D	Three Dimensional
5D	Fifth Dimension
2FA	Two-Factor Authentication
3FA	Three-Factor Authentication
5G	Fifth Generation
ABDM	Ayushman Bharat Digital Health Mission
ADHA	Australian Digital Health Agency
ADHD	Attention Deficit Hyperactivity Disorder
ADL	Activities of Daily Living
AES	Advanced Encryption Standard
AI	Artificial Intelligence
AIDS	Acquired Immunodeficiency Syndrome
AIel	AI-Supported E-Learning
ANN	Artificial Neural Network
ANPD	National Data Protection Authority
ANVISA	Brazilian Agency for Health Regulation
AP	Advanced Placement
APAC	Asia-Pacific
API	Application Programming Interface
AR	Augmented Reality
ATM	Automated Teller Machine
BBNL	Bharat Broadband Network Limited
BCT	Blockchain Technology
BDA	Big Data Analytics
BFS	Breadth-First Search
BNPL	Buy Now, Pay Later
BPPS	Bharat Bill Payment System
BTRC	Bangladesh Telecommunications and Regulatory Authority
CAD	Computer-Aided Diagnosis
CAPTCHA	Completely Automated Public Turing Test to Tell Computers and Humans Apart
CARD	Computer-Aided Administration and Registration Department
CAST	Computer-Aided Simple Triage
CBSE	Central Board of Secondary Education
CCLA	Covenant on Civil and Political Rights
CDS	Clinical Decision Support
CIET	Central Institute of Educational Technology
CMC	Computer-Mediated Communication
CNN	Convolutional Neural Network
CoAP	Constrained Application Protocol
COD	Cash On Delivery
COVID-19	Coronavirus Disease 2019

CSL	Cybersecurity Law
CSP	Cloud Service Provider
DAISY	Digitally Accessible Information System
DB2	Database 2
DDoS	Distributed Denial of Service
DDS	Data Distribution Service
DEIT	Department Of Electronics and Information Technology
Demat	Dematerialized
DFS	Depth First Search
DFS	Digital Financial Services
DigiLEP	Digital Learning Enhancement Program
DIKSHA	Digital Infrastructure for Knowledge Sharing
DL	Deep Learning
DLI	Digital Library Initiative
DOC	Document
DTH	Direct to Home
DVD	Digital Versatile Disk
EA	Enrolled Agent
ECHR	European Convention on Human Rights
ECS	Electronic Clearing Service
EFTPOS	Electronic Funds Transfer At Point-Of-Sale
eHealth	Electronic Health
EIT	Electronic Information and Transactions
EMR	Electronic Medical Record
EU	European Nation
FAP	Family Acceptance Project
FBI	Federal Bureau of Investigation
GDP	Gross Domestic Product
GDPR	General Data Protection Regulation
GPS	Global Positioning System
GUI	Graphical User Interface
HER	Electronic Health Record
HIS	Health Information System
HIV	Human Immunodeficiency Virus
HTML	Hypertext Markup Language
ICCPR	International Covenant on Civil and Political Rights
ICT	Information Communication Technology
ID	Identifications
IDE	Integrated Development Environment
IFF	Illegal Financial Flows
IGNOU	Indira Gandhi National Open University
IIoT	Industrial Internet of Things
IIT	Indian Institutes of Technology
INSNA	International Network for Social Organization Analysis
IoMT	Internet of Medical Things
IoT	Internet of Things

IPS	Indoor Positioning System
IPC	Indian Penal Code
IS	Information System
ISL	Indian Sign Language
ISP	Internet Service Providers
IT	Information Technology
ITES	Information Technology Enabled Services
ITS	Intelligent Tutoring Systems
KITE	Kerala Infrastructure and Technology for Education
KNN	K-Nearest Neighbors Algorithms
KPI	Key Performance Indicators
KR	Knowledge Representation
KYC	Know-Your-Customer
LAN	Local Area Network
LFG	Liberalization, Privatization, and Globalization
LGBT	Lesbian, Gay, Bisexual, and Transgender
LIFO	Last-In-First-Out
M2M	Machine to Machine Communications
MAN	Metropolitan Area Network
MFA	Multi-Factor Authentication
mHealth	Mobile Health
MHRD	Ministry Of Human Resource Development
MICR	Magnetic Ink Character Recognition
ML	Machine Learning
MOM	Management-Oriented Modeling
MOOCs	Massive Open Online Courses
MPHS	Multi-Purpose Household Survey
MPI	Master Patient Index
MSME	Micro, Small, and Medium-Sized Enterprise
MVA	Medical Virtual Assistants
NCERT	National Council of Educational Research and Training
NCFS	National Cybersecurity Framework
NCI	National Cohesion and Integration
NDHB	National Digital Health Blueprint
NEFT	National Electronic Fund Transfer
NFC	Near-Field Communication
NIOS	National Institute of Open School
NIST	National Institute of Standards and Technology
NLP	Natural Language Processing
NPTEL	National Programme on Technology Enhanced Learning
NWP	National Writing Project
OERs	Open Educational Resources
OTP	One-Time Password
P2M	Person to Merchant
PCIDS	Payment Card Industry Data Security

PCM	Precision Crop Management
PDA	Personal Digital Assistant
PHCs	Primary Healthcare Centers
PIN	Personal Identification Number
PIPEDA	Personal Information Protection and Electronic Documents Act
POCD	Point-Of-Care Tests
POS	Point of Sale
PROLOG	Programming Logic
PSVR	Play Station Virtual Reality
QR Code	Quick Response Code
RAS	Robot-Assisted Surgery
RFID	Radio Frequency Identification
RPM	Remote Patient Monitoring
RTC	Record of Right, Tenancy, and Crops
RTGS	Real-Time Gross Settlement
SA	Standalone
SAAS	Software as a Service
SEO	Search Engine Optimization
SFIO	Serious Frauds Investigation Office
SGML	Standard Generalized Markup Language
SNA	Social Network Analysis
SPSS	Statistical Package for Social Science
SQL	Structured Query Language
SVM	Support Vector Machines
SWAYAM	Study Web of Active-Learning for Young Aspiring Minds
TD	Temporal Difference
Telehealth	Telephonic Health
ToS	Terms of Service
UDHR	Universal Declaration of Human Rights
UGC	University Grant Commission
UK	United Kingdom
UN	United Nation
UNESCO	United Nations Education, Scientific, and Cultural Organization
UPI	Unified Payment Interface
URL	Unified Resource Locator
US	United States
USD	United State Dollar
VLEs	Virtual Learning Environments
VPN	Virtual Private Network
VR	Virtual Reality
WAN	Wide Area Network
WECITI	Wed-Based Citizen-IT Interface
Wi-Fi	Wireless Fidelity
WPAN	Wireless Personal Area Network
WWW	World Wide Web
XML	Extensible Markup Language

1 Digitalization

SUMMARY

In this chapter, readers will learn about emerging digital technology and the numerous elements that influence its use in their daily lives. We will also look at what our digital rights and responsibilities are and how important they are as digital citizens in expanded digital technology. We'll discuss digital freedom and its importance in this digital age and how in developing countries India is causing an increase in internet users and smartphone usage, and its impact on the Indian economy. Further, we will also explore the concept of digital democracy and look at several E-Government initiatives that have been introduced over the past ten years. Finally, we'll examine how digital democracy boosts the effectiveness and openness of public administration and better communication with citizens and also its challenges.

1.1 INTRODUCTION

The terms "digitization" and "digitalization" are closely related and frequently used interchangeably in various publications. The term "**digitization**" means the conversion of data into a string of 0s and 1s also known as "**binary digits**." The widespread adoption of advanced and innovative digital technology to produce, process, and disseminate information has resulted in a socio-economic transformation known as "digitization" (Abd-El-Barr and El-Rewini, 2005).

The term "**digitalization**," on the other hand, is defined as "an organization's, industries, or country's adoption or increased use of digital technology" (Hacker and Van Dijk, 2000). The effects of digitalization on society have been at the forefront of debate since the term was coined. The term "digitization" was first used in connection with computerization in a 1971 essay published in the *North American Review*. In it, Robert Wachal (Gorensek and Kohont, 2019) explored the social consequences of the "digitization of the society" while taking computer-assisted humanities research critics and potentials into account.

Digitalization is a part of digitization, and digitalization is the first step towards realizing digitization. The twenty-first century has been regarded as the "golden age of technology," and digitalization has had a significant impact. With the rapid development that occurs each year, smartphones and the freedom of digitalization are the most valuable things that the present generation possesses. Therefore, every sector in this century is undergoing a digital transition and implementing smart solutions.

People who use digital services gradually alter their lifestyles and become a part of the evolving information society. The freedom of digitalization is used in a variety

DOI: 10.1201/9781003403784-1

1

of industries where success would have been impossible without digital technologies, such as education, banking and finance, health, agriculture, and so on.

The freedom of digitalization has played an important role in the growth of the economy and, in many ways, in the growth of employment globally. The emergence of digital freedom has successfully contributed to the simpler and more convenient use of digital technology for humans. This has helped make our lives simpler, safer, and much quicker. It has modified and strengthened our lifestyles dramatically. Indeed, the freedom of digital technology has improved our quality of life, with 70% of the world's population now accepting and adopting digital advancement technology.

1.1.1 WHAT IS "DIGITAL"?

The word "**digital**" is a universal language of information, whether it's text, pictures, or video images. It implies that the information in the computational devices by the variables that takes a limited number of discrete values. The day digital computation started, the new form of terms began, such as "digital computers." It serves as a common denominator for signals from digital devices, telephones, televisions, radios, cameras, and computers.

A string of 0s and 1s is the formation of a combination of binary digits like 10010101 that can be converted into numbers of its type. Various types of number systems represent binary combinations like binary number systems, decimal number systems, octal number systems, and hexadecimal number systems. Each of the number systems with base values 2, 10, 8, and 16 consecutively are converted to the other format.

Digitalization can be stabilized with the combination of digital devices and software. Every system and implication needs its component to revive and function. The matter of revival depends on the functional and structural level of the elements.

Elements to Structure the digital system need common "feel and use" components that are mentioned in Table 1.1.

Functional Elements help to perform the computations with the help of hardware and software. Four basic functions can be performed by digital devices that are given in Table 1.2.

There are the few key terms of digitalization that are defined in Table 1.3, and we will use few of them throughout this chapter.

1.1.2 WHAT IS DIGITAL FREEDOM?

The word "digital freedom" emphasizes the freedom to have access not only to information and digital technology internationally but also to freedom of speech, viewpoint, freedom to express opinion, experience, and the right to privacy.

Our era is rich in novel digital technologies, and the freedom of digitization facilitates the exchange of data and information globally. The freedom of digitalization has profoundly changed our society and has made its way directly into our homes, personal lives, and daily routines. The "Digital India" initiative was started in 2015 to digitalize India and increase the country's economy. It accelerated the revolution and altered nearly every aspect of business. This has also resulted in a greater

TABLE 1.1
Structural Components

Structural Elements	Descriptions
Storage	It includes primary and secondary memory and is installed into the system according to the features and prices.
Processors	It has a big role to translate and execute the instruction and transfer it back to the requester.
Motherboard	It is the design of logical gates connected with sockets, processor(s) memory, and chips that integrate all the other components of the computing system and link to each other.
Register	Category of computer memory used to store and transfer information that is being used by the processor.
Input-output Devices	It helps the digits in and out through certain sources like Input (keyboard, joysticks, microphone, touchpad, mouse, scanners, etc.), Output (monitor, printers, Xerox, speakers, projector, Faxes, etc.).

Source: Table developed by the authors.

TABLE 1.2
Functional Components

Functional Elements	Descriptions
Data Processing	Data has a wide variety of forms of text, audio, video, games, images, graphs, etc. It takes the data from input sources, processes it by the processor, and gives the fundamental result as output in the digital system.
Data Storage	Computation devices store the data either temporarily or permanently as required by the user. This is one of the important features of the digital device. There are many storage devices {(RAM, ROM, buffer, Register, etc.) (Hard Disk, Magnetic Disk, Magnetic tape, CD, DVD, flash, etc.)}.
Data Movement	Data is sent and received among the peripheral devices which are also known as input-output devices. Serving the data from the source to the destination.
Controls	The control unit manages the computer's resources and hyper control the instruction to the functional parts. There are two basic controls including the arithmetic logic unit (ALU) and memory unit (MU).

Source: Table developed by the authors.

rise in the number of internet and smartphone users in India alone than in any other developing country (Digital India Mission, no date).

It has been demonstrated that people feel more vivid, simpler, autonomous, and knowledgeable because digital freedom has made their lives a lot easier. The flexibility of digitalization has altered our lives to a far greater extent. In this digital age,

TABLE 1.3
Important Terms of Digitalization

Term	Description
Digit	Here, 0 and 1 are the digits used which only the whole computation system understand.
Binary Digits	The meaning of the binary is two (2). It relates to the basic function of the binary number system that every alphanumeric character will be converted into a stream of 0s and 1s. A binary digit is called a bit.
Circuit	A component through which electricity flows.
Microchip	A unit of integrated circuitry of thousands of register capacity manufactured at the microscopic level.
Register	A CPU register is a small set of data holding memory.
Interpretation	Translation of code within the computer system. It could be translating from programming language to machine language understanding.
Data	The raw fact which exists in every activity of life.
Processing	Execution of the data in a machine.
Digital Computing	Composite of electronic and electrical that understands the data in discrete form.
Digital Device	A piece of physical equipment that uses digital computing. For example, Desktop, Laptops, Palmtop, Wrist Top, etc.
Digital Freedom	The freedom to access information and express viewpoints without hesitation.

Source: Table developed by the authors.

digital media allows us to contact and engage with our friends and relatives in a variety of ways, even if they are quite far away from us.

1.2   DIGITAL TRANSFORMATION

Digital transformation is the engineering to integrate any organization through technology to increase efficiency and performance; in other words, the process of transformation of analog data into digital form like the storage of images in the computing system.

Each industry functions on a different level of structure and system that makes the journey of the organization unique in transformation. It needs a new mindset and tech capacity for operational changes. It provides the capacity to analyze, monitor, secure, authenticate, and enjoy for any organization or social level. Digital transformation needs advanced embedded technologies like Artificial Intelligence, the Internet of Things, and a supportive virtual or real environment.

1.2.1   TECHNOLOGICAL ADVANCEMENTS

A wide range of projects technology has been successfully carried out during the past ten years all over the world. ICTs can help to identify and minimize corruption and bribery, improve academic research, health, and defense in a variety of ways:

- Governments can use technological advancements to increase the effectiveness and transparency of public administration and to better communicate with their citizens.
- Citizens can make use of ICTs to raise awareness about the problem of corruption, report abuses, collect data, and monitor government activities.
- Through the phenomena of "hackathons," the use of ICTs to combat corruption has increasingly functioned as a means of bringing the tech community and activists, and civil society closer together.

A hackathon organized by the most recent International Anti-Corruption Conference sought to use emerging technologies in creative ways to combat corruption.

E-Government development is supported by the fight against corruption. Therefore having access to digital technologies gives the average person awareness of public affairs and digital transactions, which fosters an open and clear society. Because of its automated processes and ease of access to information, technology can play a significant role in reducing corruption. Effective E-Government transparency initiatives must be implemented to fight against corruption.

1.2.2 ARTIFICIAL INTELLIGENCE (AI)

AI is a set of characteristics of the mind. These characteristics help to plan, evaluate, and solve problems. Simply, intelligence can be defined as the ability to make the right decision based on a given set of inputs and a variety of possible actions.

The right decision can not only be applied to humans but also to animals that exhibit rational behavior. But the intelligence that is exhibited by human beings is much more complex than that of animals. Like humans can communicate with language some animals can also do the same. Humans and animals can solve some problems to a limited extent. The only difference is that humans have more intelligence and adaptability than animals.

Beginning of AI: The 1950s marked the very early days of AI. Alan Turing raised whether the machine could think and introduced the Turing machine in 1950 which was able to solve the mathematical problem with simplicity. Turing proposed a minimum thinker agent for a particular domain (Jones, 2008).

Problem-Solving, Games, AI: Early on in the development of intelligent machines and intelligent applications, scientists focused on mathematical solvency and games. The search problem of chess was introduced by Claude Shannon while some of the logic and algorithm was not applicable at that period. A heuristic search was able to apply faster and more efficient moves between the cells to play the game of chess. Scientists invented various algorithms and ideas that they coined according to the uses of the application area of AI which is detailed in Table 1.4.

The computer scientist, Arthur Samuel in 1959 extended the learning checkers program; he allowed two copies of the program to play offender and defender. Both of the players were learning from each other during play (McCarthy, no date).

Results-Oriented Applications: In the 1970s, the development of AI continued and moved onto a more focused area of an expert system. The first expert system architecture

TABLE 1.4
List of AI Years, Algorithms, and Scientists

List of AI Algorithms Introduced in Different Years

Year	Name of Program	Developers/ Scientist Group	Purpose
1950s	Game-playing programs	UK at Oxford University	Two-people complex games
1952	Checkers playing program	Arthur Samuel, Christopher Strachey	Checkers program for playing on the Ferranti Mark I
1955	Artificial Intelligence	John McCarthy and Team	Attributed the word
1956	General Problem Solver (GPS)	Simon and Newell	End analysis through GPS to solve problems but it was restricted to toy problems
1957	The Logic Theorist	Allen Newell, Herbert Simon, and J.C. Shaw	To find proofs for equations
1958	Lisp	John McCarthy	Programming language for artificial Intelligence research
1959	"Machine Learning" term Coined	Arthur Samuel	Wrote a program to play a game of chess better than humans.

Source: Data developed by the authors.

was developed as rule-based called MYCIN by Ted Shortliffe in 1974 at Stanford (Jones, 2008). The expert system, MYCIN, was operating in the domain of medical diagnosis and represents the inference of knowledge. Other applied areas operated in natural language understanding. The vision of AI was able to answer the questions like enquiries from customers. A general model of and its connectivity is shown in Figure 1.1.

Searching and AI

Most of the solution to the problem of AI is fundamentally search algorithm. It can be defined as a technique that encapsulates the problem from its starting state to its goal state. The way to decide to reach the goal is either through an algorithm or a strategy. The efficiency of achieving the goal depends on the efficiency of the algorithm and functionality. Table 1.5 describes the characteristics of the search algorithms.

Importance of Search Algorithms: Search algorithms enhance accuracy through logical search mechanisms and solve the problem in order to reach the final goal.

Search Programming: Algorithms solve the problem through the formulation of the particular area using the entity of that field.

Goal-Based Agents solve problems using the most ideal series of actions through integrated components and provide direction of error or perfection.

Business Growth supports the growth of business production through rules and procedures of algorithms that result from the desired action.

Neural Network System: Algorithms connect various nodes in different levels of hierarchy. The level is also called a layer and is divided logically into a hidden layer,

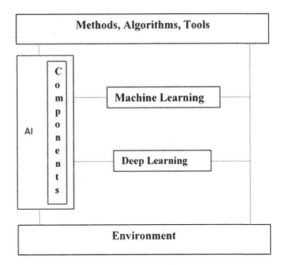

FIGURE 1.1 Common architecture of AI application.

TABLE 1.5
Types of Search Algorithms

Characteristics of Search Problem	
Characteristics	**Description**
Completeness	A complete search algorithm provides the minimum solution to the problem for a given input.
Optimality	The best solution is given by the algorithms with a low cost for the search path.
Depth of a Problem	Length of the shortest path from the initial state to the end state.
Time Complexity	The time is taken to solve the problem
Space Complexity	The memory required during the search or execution of an algorithm. It depends on the type /size of the problem.
Admissibility	An algorithm to find the optimal solutions.

Source: Table developed by the authors.

an input layer, and an output layer. These systems are used for training, learning, and input–output mapping.

There are several search algorithms in the programming language. Each and every search algorithm has a parameter of efficiency that is measured by time, space, quantity, and goal. The details of the search are outside the scope of this book and are not covered briefly here. We studied the search algorithm starting from junior standards like a linear search and binary search among a list of values. The efficiency also called the complexity of algorithms is measured using different Omega values which depend on the size of inputs and the capacity of the machine. Overall, the search algorithms are categorized into uninformed search and informed search.

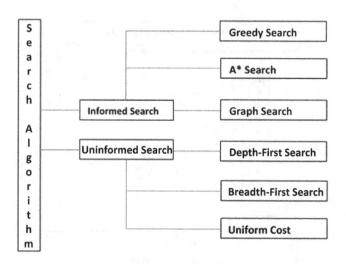

FIGURE 1.2   Classification of algorithms of AI.

The classification of the search algorithm is shown in Figure 1.2.

Uninformed search algorithm: These algorithms do not have enough information that can drive to the end goal other than the information given in the problem. These are categorized into breadth-first search (BFS), depth-first search (DFS), and uniform cost search.

Breadth-first search: Data that is classified in graph or tree structure are utilized by this algorithm. It starts searching from the root node of the tree/graph and traverses all the neighbor nodes. It uses the technique of traversal pre-order, in-order, or post-order at each level.

The **depth-first search** algorithm is used to search the data in the structure of a graph or tree. It begins from the root node and traverses to the next level of leaves of roots then backtrack the previous level. It uses the logic of Last-In-First-Out (LIFO) from the data structure.

Uniform cost search differs from both DFS and BFS in that it takes the least cost path.

Informed search algorithm: These categories of algorithms have enough information on data and problems. It achieves the goal on the basis of information and better performance and complexity.

Greedy search is the nearest node to the goal node which is expanded and the factor is calculated using the heuristic function h (d). The distance between a node and the goal node is taken as h (d). The closer node to the endpoint presents a lower heuristic value. The best path to the goal node is achieved by taking the lowest possible value of the node.

* tree search is a combination of the uniform cost algorithm and the greedy algorithm. The cumulative cost greedy search cost h (d) and cost of the uniform cost algorithm g (d) is searched using f (d). The cost of the distance between the current nodes to the goal node is estimated using h (d), also called forward cost.

The cost g (d) is also known as a backward cost which is used to estimate the overall cost between a node and the root node. The optimal algorithm's forward cost (h (d) of the A* tree is less than or equal to the actual cost (h*(d)) for all nodes. The technique to select the node is the lowest total cost value (f (d)).

A* graph search: The negativity of the A* tree algorithm wastes time in the back search of branches which already been searched and were overcome in the A* graph search algorithm. The consistency property of this algorithm is the achievement of the optimal solution of the forward cost of two successive nodes is less than or equal to the backward cost.

Knowledge Representation (KR)

In relation to AI, knowledge is given to the machine to solve the problem of a particular area. The knowledge expressed using a proposition is called declarative knowledge and the knowledge which is used to achieve some goal (task or job) is also called procedural knowledge. Logics are used to represent declarative knowledge. It is simpler, easier, and more flexible to use but loses the potential of real vision.

The primary goal of knowledge representation is to enable an intelligent entity (program) with a knowledge base to allow it to make intelligent decisions about its environment. The popular knowledge base platform to make an expert system is PROLOG. Prolog functions on the basis of propositional logic, predicate logic, and ontology. The detail of logic is outside the scope of this book.

Machine Learning

Machine learning allows a computer to learn through a variety of computing algorithms and methods. It finds the relationship between a given set of data and produces information. Machine learning is categorized into supervised learning, unsupervised learning, semi-supervised learning, and reinforcement teaching (Russell, 2010).

Supervised learning algorithms use data for training that classified each training vector. The goal of learning is to predict using the trained data sets to classify correctly through the unseen vector. The types of supervised learning problems include regression, classification, and problem models.

- Nearest Neighbor
- Naive Bayes
- Decision Trees
- Linear Regression
- Support Vector Machines (SVM)
- Neural Networks

Unsupervised learning is helpful to find the pattern in the given set of data. It makes classes by segmenting and reducing the size of the data and training without any category. This learning is used to find the pattern, mining category, and finding centroid which helps to drive meaningful insights to the user. It includes Clustering and Association algorithms.

- k-means Clustering,
- Association Rules
- Markov Model
- KNN

Semi-supervised learning lies between supervised and unsupervised learning. It is best to find the model of data sets.

Reinforcement learning is achieved only at the end of the event or game. For example, you learn many tricks and techniques (rules) after losing the game. Games are events that play with an unknown number of steps till one player wins or loses. The end of the learning is called reinforcement. Yet, this is hard to take a sudden decision for an agent at risk like the "driverless car," "flying chopper," etc.

It allows machines and software agents to automatically determine the ideal behavior within a specific context, to maximize its performance. An agent needs to make a decision based on his current state also known as Markov Decision Process if the problem is repeated. Reinforcement learning passes through the following steps to produce an intelligent agent.

- Agent observes the input state.
- Agent takes an action on the basis of decision making.
- Agent receives reinforcement from the event after the action is performed.
- Reinforcement is stored to state the action of information.

Common Algorithms are:

- Q-Learning
- Temporal Difference (TD)
- Deep Adversarial Network

1.2.3 INTERNET OF THINGS (IoT)

The IoT refers to the collective network of technologies, sensors, and software facilitates to make communication between and within the devices. Nowadays, in day-to-day life, a variety of devices like cars, toys, live cameras, vacuums, and machines can collect data through sensors and respond intelligently to the user. It grew rapidly due to the achievement of high speed and the new generation of processors, smaller sizes, and high-speed networks. The functionality depends on smart devices, IoT, and GUI (Graphical User Interface) which is shown in Figure 1.3.

Smart devices are eligible to connect with computer systems effectively like security cameras, television, barcode, drone with sensors, etc. with computing capability. The pattern or data is transferred to the IoT application while it collects from the sources.

IoT applications are the software that receives the data from various IoT devices. The collected data is analyzed through AI applications and techniques.to make the appropriate output. This output helps to make decisions.

Graphical User Interface (GUI): The GUI is used to manage IoT devices such as websites and mobile applications.

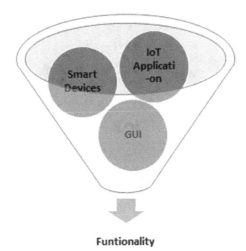

Funtionality

FIGURE 1.3   Functionality of IoT.

IoT Technologies

Edge Computing technologies support the transfer of data from a source to a real platform and improve the computing capacity at the edge of the IoT network. The performance improves by reducing the latency and response time.

Cloud Computing helps to store the data remotely. The security of the cloud is not high due to the distributed technology. It allows the accessibility of the data from the devices connected through the network.

Machine Learning and Analytics gives real-time output on the basis of data using methodologies and algorithms of machine learning. A large volume of data stored in the cloud is analyzed through the deployed algorithm of machine learning.

AWS IoT is the cloud vendor that provides easy-to-use services like access control, encryption, and security for a large volume of data.

IoT Features

The IoT ecosystem is becoming an important part of organizations. Modern devices are equipped with several features to connect with each other. For example, mobiles can be connected to the TV, printers, faxes, copiers, computers, etc. All the features of IoT are represented in Figure 1.4 and described briefly in Table 1.6.

IoT Improves Life

People's everyday life and work depend on technology and technology devices. Ranging from entertainment to day-to-day useful devices in homes, offices, markets, and everywhere else. People have become used to it. It makes our lives easier, more productive, and more comfortable. From morning remote operation to smart ovens and refrigerators, sensing bathroom system, sensing doors, sensing cars, and auto-scheduling the day with alarms in watches. The twenty-first century has become the

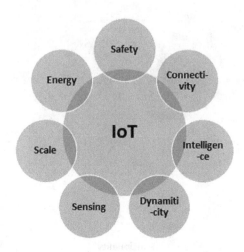

FIGURE 1.4 IoT features.

TABLE 1.6
IoT Features with Description

List of IoT Features with Description	
Features	**Description**
Safety	The application should have safety, security, and a firewall for data to keep away from misuse.
Connectivity	The communication among interrelated components of IoT like sensors blue tooth, Wi-Fi, Radio waves, etc. is important to pass the data.
Intelligence	Intelligent models are designed to get an insight into the data to see the output.
Dynamic Nature	Decisions are taken on collected and processed data using components of IoT that change the state dynamically. Like Assessing weather status change continuously.
Sensing	There are components to gather data through sensors, GPS, RFID, etc. for a specific task. It helps to model the learning for decision.
Scale	The parameter is fixed to take the decision for a specific area. For example, an automatic taxi start or end point is fixed. The hurdles of road and other symbolic entities are scaled.

Source: Table developed by the authors.

smart and digital century that gives us freedom to live our lives connected to everywhere from anywhere.

IoT Protocols

The data is shared between two connected devices with optimum security provided by a certain model in IoT protocol. It gives voice to the voiceless devices.

Bluetooth is a short-distance wireless technology. It helps to pair and connect two smart devices and a small amount of data can be transferred easily and accurately. The latest version of Bluetooth core with 2.4 GHz has a range of 50 to 150m with a speed of 1 Mbps (Singh, Sharma and Agrawal, 2011).

Wi-Fi is the modern technology that permits accessibility with authenticity and security. Wi-Fi 6 connects to the internet wirelessly with a speed of 9.6 Gbps in multiple channels. It transfers data with the help of Radio waves (Yinan, Shuguo and Dawei, 2012).

Z-Wave is a wireless protocol that helps to connect with smart devices in a low-cost structure. The rate of transfer of data is 100kbps. Its category is Bluetooth, Wi-Fi, GPS, etc.

Cellular can transfer a high volume of data at a low cost with applications of IoT. It functions in GSM, 2G, 3G, 4G, and 5G. It can transfer 21000 MHz in the range of 200 KM.

Similarly, there are various protocols like 6LoWPAN, RFID, Zigbee, LiteOS, OneM2M, DDS, and CoAP with their capacity, scale, and ranges to assist the IoT technology and share the data.

1.2.4 AUGMENTED REALITY

Tomas Cloud introduced the word "Augmented Reality" in 1990 by looking at the electrical wiring procedure. Augmented reality (AR) is a technique through which users can view magnified images in a composite manner (Furht, 2011). This technology helps users to visualize the data using AI as an algorithm. AR can be used to create virtual environments in simulators for various reasons like cities, streets, boards, game spaces, etc. to train for navigation of the robotic machines.

AR Benefits: The future of AR is to assist in real activities of life to make it more efficient in a trustworthy way. The environment of users can be integrated with digital information like virtual reality (VR), which creates an artificial environment. For example, it gives a better understanding of the molecule's structure and its interaction with other molecules. The perceptual information can be generated using a real-world virtual environment.

It idealize the information of the real-world using three-dimension (3D) components for any perception. It provides a more accurate situation of the real world for a particular case to deploy the AI system. It connects the smart devices of the users to share voice, image, data, or information to give a feeling of the natural environment.

Area of AR to Use: The first application came using AR which televised football games in 1998. Now almost all the virtual environments delivered in smartphones, tablets, and glasses, for the virtual design of vehicles, aeronautical, defense, consumer products, and medical, etc. are tested without failure of real environment to the attraction of users.

All the mentioned areas can be trained and tested to apply the real-world scenario in AR without risk and real ground. It helps to design, produce, test, and apply to get a better outcome for the users. Sensors, GPS, accelerometer, accumulator, glasses, and compass are a few of the required components used for AR.

Augmented Reality (AR) vs. Virtual Reality (VR)

The real-world and natural environments can be seen in the designed software of the virtual world. The head-mounted display with sound creates a full immersion in the virtual world. Other advanced VR systems are google daydream, Oculus rift, Gear VR, VIVE, Sony PSVR, Microsoft Hololens, etc. The AR systems available are Target App, Apple measure App, U.S. Army, Pockman Go, Google Glass, etc.

VR systems are developed for different areas of the environment. AR is the environment that provides the basis of information while VR involves a completely simulated environment. VR uses head-mounted sets with sound. AR is not limited and uses glasses, phones, and projection, it can be viewed on mobile devices with the generated environment while AR users realize the real environment within the environment.

1.2.5 REAL-WORLD CASES (1–2)

REAL-WORLD CASE 1 (IoT USE)

India is becoming a hot place for IoT device and application developers. The government is incorporating almost all the sectors like banking, finance, industries, manufacturing, consumer, retail, agriculture, IT, law, real estate, and others through digital India Planning which is discussed in later chapters. The challenge is to reach to the remote people in India and crisis of important components like chips, processors, and related integrating electron and computational part are under question for manufacturer which depends mainly on imports.

REAL-WORLD CASE 2

India has had a lot of success with E-Governance initiatives and ICT projects in terms of increasing accessibility and lowering corruption. Innovative digital technologies and E-Government platforms have been implemented to reduce corruption in government services and to promote greater transparency (Payne, 2006).

Its goals include lowering corruption, bringing public delivery services to the doorsteps of the underprivileged, and empowering people in areas like health, education, agriculture, and commerce, among others. The plan consists of several initiatives that will concentrate on enhancing national internet connectivity, knowledge, and governance. The initiative also aims to change governance from electronic to mobile governance, or "M-Governance." It is also undeniable that India has been on a growth path for the past two decades. The global survey also reported recently that not only young people but also adults have become so digitally savvy that they can't even imagine living or breathing without these tools (El-Darwiche, et al., 2013).

1.3   WHY IS DIGITIZATION IMPORTANT?

The term "digitization" has become fashionable nowadays. Advanced digital technologies have progressed faster than any other breakthrough in history. Any industry may benefit from digitization since it improves process efficiency, uniformity, and quality. There are several examples (discussed in the real-world case) of digitalization that have existed and continue to exist in all aspects of life and business. Digitization accelerated for businesses and organizations around the world, and this digital adoption has resulted in significant changes in all industries and sectors. Networking and software are at the heart of digitization. Important software terms are summarized in Table 1.7 and networking terms are introduced in Table 1.8.

1.3.1   DIGITAL USERS

Users who are engaged to access content from the web and social media using digital devices are also known as digital customers. Digital sources help both the way to the customers and organizations. The organization may reach the customer with their offering, discounts, and availability of products for the customers. The users also have knowledge of the latest trend in the market and products without moving here and there. The number of digital users around the world is increasing every minute, hour, and day due to the feasibility and availability of the information at hand. Worldwide internet users are shown in Figure 1.6 on the basis of the data published by Ani Petrosyan on February 13, 2023 and available at Statista.com. Mobile phone users are shown in Figure 1.5 below of selected countries. Basically, four types of digital users exist: *tech-oriented, tech-active-users, tech-knowledgeable-users, and tech-relax-users.*

TABLE 1.7
Software Terms

Important Terms of Software

Program	A set of instructions that produce meaningful output.
Module	A piece of a small set of programs. A unit from a big project is divided into subsections to solve and distribute the problem easily.
API	Intermediation of two software that helps to talk two software from each other.
Testing	The mechanism to check the expectation and objective of any software.
Load Balancing	Distributing the module of the project among the team of developers.
CI / CD	Continuous integration and continuous development are used to deploy and deliver projects.
Environment	The scenario created by developers before delivering to the end users. It is further divided into the production environment, development environment, and staging environment.

Source: Data developed by the authors.

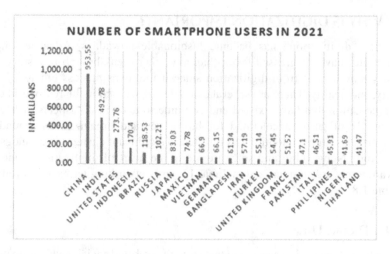

FIGURE 1.5   Number of mobile users worldwide 2020–2021.

Source: (Laricchia, 2022) newzoo.

Tech-oriented: This category is technically sound and adopts the latest technology quickly. Exploring the application and techniques is easy for them. All the areas are reached easily by them. Digital services are a blessing for them as they like to feel digitized freedom. It is easy for any government or non-governmental organization to reach them.

Tech-active-users: The mid-range of people who are active in the use of mobile apps. They want to achieve everything in their hand online sitting at home or in the office.

Tech-knowledgeable-users: Above mid-range of age people like to establish using computing systems. They are eager to acquire knowledge. These users are equipped with computers and spend time interacting digitally.

Tech-relax-users: Connect to all age people who are not affected by technology or non-tech objects. Their interactions with technology are very limited. Uses of digitization are the most compulsory zone for offices or personnel that matter to their livelihood. For example, banking, payment of various bills, government forms, etc. The Features of IoT are described in Table 1.6 above.

Devices and applications are used efficiently by successful users. The use of the functionality of the application and software properly increases the user's interest. The structure of the network and internet support the users to access the information needed. It improves the authenticity, applicability, and friendliness of the users.

Two or more interconnected computing devices that can share resources like faxes, printers, and the exchange of files are called networks. The computers on the network are linked through satellites, telephone lines, radio waves, cables, or infrared light beams. There are common types of networks in architecture. Local Area Networks (LAN), Metropolitan Area Networks (MAN), and Wide Area Networks (WAN) are important divisions of networking. The differences in architecture, characteristics, property, speed, and distance are basically among them. The connection is made either through wire or wireless. The client sends the request to the server and gets back the response after the evaluation of the server.

Local Area Networks are bound to a small range of limited distances. Connected network devices are called servers and workstations are also called clients. Servers provide services to the user of workstations. The configuration of servers like processor, memory, and speed, is higher than workstations. Installation of servers is made through network professionals and managed by network administrators. The new form of LAN is called a personnel area network (PAN) that connects using Bluetooth or Wi-Fi.

Metropolitan Area Network covers the distance of a city to another city limited to a single geographical area. A variety of organized technology is used to establish backbone connections like Ethernet, fiber cables, radio and microwave, etc.

Wide Area Network connectivity is wider than LAN. It can connect from country to country and the world with a global network. Routers, switches, multiplexers, and brides are used to connect LAN and MAN to the global network that becomes a form of internet.

The important terms of "internet" and "networks" are explained in Table 1.8.

Internet

The internet is a computer network system connected and linked worldwide. The United States Department of Defense introduced the internet in the 1960s. Later in the 1970s ARPANET served as a resource and in the 1980s they allowed commercial extension (Leiner et al., 2009).

Users can deploy the information anywhere through the domain of the server and access information from the server under authenticity. The popular proverb "network

---

TABLE 1.8
Networking Terms

Important Terms of Networking

Network	Two or more interconnected computing devices that can share resources.
Internet	A connected network of computing and smart devices worldwide.
Server	A computer device with special configuration and installation of a program that provides services to the client. Strong web servers are Microhost, Atlantic, Cloud, etc. and Server devices are Dell EMC, HPE, Lenovo, Fujitsu, etc.
Workstation	The location of the computer from where users work.
Node	Similar to the client that link one to other and extends the network.
Connection	The act of joining or joined two objects.
Link	Established connection between two objects that form a relationship.
Speed	Worldwide traveling of data from one to other computing devices.
Load Balancing	Distributing traffic of the network equally across a pool of resources that support an application.

Source: Table developed by the authors.

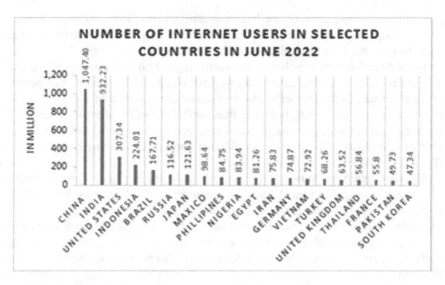

FIGURE 1.6 Worldwide internet users.

Source: (Petrosyan, 2023) Statista.com.

of networks" is also mentioned for the internet. Its usability is huge and facilitates the world's users to access the content and link through using hyperlinked documents, www, chatting and video calls, file sharing, etc. Figure 1.6 shows the internet users in the world.

1.3.2 Rise of Smartphone Use

The majority of the digital population worldwide are using their smartphones to access the internet. More than any technology in human history, mobile communication had greater impact on humanity in a very short amount of time. Today, with the freedom of digitalization, smartphones and the internet have removed isolation, and have proved to be the greatest revolutionary technology of economic development. Smartphones have evolved from a simple speaking device to a multimedia device capable of video and audio calling, downloading and uploading videos and songs, and much more. In addition to this, smartphones have other features like calculators, alarm clocks, address books and high-quality digital cameras.

Today, in this digital era, smartphones have a greater influence on social, economic, and political activities. People across the world are using smartphones for many reasons. For example, in Africa, farmers are using smartphones for text messaging to get the latest pricing information and also to improve their knowledge of where to sell goods to increase their incomes. Many housewives are using smartphones to order groceries, to shop apparels etc.; students are using smartphones for getting easy notes or any important information about their studies. With the use of smartphones, election campaigns are also observed. With the prevalence of smartphones and internet, texting, tweeting and trolling are becoming commonly used terms in this digital age. Thus, smartphones with internet connection have become a primary mode of communication around the world.

1.3.3 REAL-WORLD CASES (1–2)

REAL-WORLD CASE 1 INDIAN SCENARIO

As a result of digital freedom and India's ongoing digital push, the number of people using the internet is expected to double year by year. India is also undergoing a digital revolution as a result of the government of India's "Digital India" initiative, with Internet users expanding their horizons beyond search and social networking sites to include more sophisticated practices such as online shopping, education, banking, and social schemes.

In reality, India was ranked as the world's second-largest online market in 2019, trailing only China. Both urban and rural areas are likely to see an increase in internet and smartphone users, indicating a dynamic increase in internet usage. India, with over 900 million internet users, is the world's second-largest online economy, behind only China. Despite a large number of internet users, the country's internet penetration rate was estimated to be about 50% in 2020. This meant that roughly half of India's 1.37 billion people had access to the internet (Keelery, 2020).

REAL-WORLD CASE 2

RISE IN SMARTPHONE USE DURING COVID-19 IN INDIA

Advancements in digital technology and innovations are extremely important in our daily lives and society because they have been so powerful that they have helped us to save both time and money. Advances in mobile phone technologies have resulted in significant changes in almost every aspect of our lives in recent years. Office work, shopping, music, movies, hospitals, education, travel, transportation, marketing, banking, and long-distance communications are examples of fields that have dramatically transformed the globe at very different levels.

Smartphones have always played an important role in keeping us connected and in touch with our families and friends, and their significance was emphasized as much as anything else during the COVID-19 pandemic. According to a study by GlobalData, telecommunications companies are expected to do well in the post-COVID-19 world. According to experts, the pandemic's consequences, although temporary, have resulted in a change in consumer behavior. Millions of users around the world would be more integrated and up to date with digital tools as reliable communication becomes more important. As the mobile consumer prioritizes connectivity and collaboration, businesses can gain a greater understanding of the difficulties that come with working from home (GlobalData, 2020).

In certain ways, the pandemic has changed the way we shop, function, and interact with others compared to before. During the lockdown, we video-called our friends and family, attended various important Zoom meetings, attended online classes, played endless hours of games, and streamed movies on these devices.

Thanks to the arrival of the latest "5G age," Smartphone companies that lead in the IoT and 5G spaces play a critical role in bringing people together and making lives simpler.

1.4   WHAT IS A DIGITAL RIGHT?

The rights and freedoms to use and access all sorts of digital technology reasonably and suitably are defined as "digital rights and responsibilities." As a digital technology user on the internet, you have the right to privacy and freedom of expression.

Human and legal rights that allow individuals to access, use, create, and publish digital content on devices such as computers and mobile phones, as well as in virtual spaces and communities, are referred to as digital rights (Pangrazio and Stefton-Green, 2021).

Digital rights are extremely significant in today's digital era. In the digital age, digital rights are simply human rights: the right and freedom to access all sorts of digital technology. In reality, digital rights are human rights and freedoms that allow people to access, use, build, and publish digital media, or to access and use computers or other digital communication networks.

When it comes to the use of emerging technology, digital rights specifically deal with freedom of speech and the right to privacy.

In today's digital age, privacy is a matter of personal knowledge, judgments, and profiling. As it has become very difficult to protect and safeguard our privacy in this digital age, people across the world are becoming increasingly aware of their digital rights and privacy and are becoming more concerned.

As our daily lives rely heavily on online activities such as information of shopping, working, socializing, and sharing. Our digital rights, especially the rights to privacy and freedom of speech, have become an issue of global concern. It is very important to consider how various businesses and governments use and manage our data and documents. It is very important to understand how various businesses, government sectors, and commonly used social networking platforms such as Facebook and other common social media such as WhatsApp and Instagram are using and processing our information and records.

1.4.1   IMPORTANT OBJECTIVES OF DIGITAL RIGHTS

Equal and universal Internet access for all: The internet has created new opportunities as well as challenges for free expression. People should have the equal and universal right to access the internet, irrespective of their income, geographical location, or their disabilities. The UN Human Rights Council recognizes in a report that the right to access is essential to freedom of opinion.

It is already stated in Article 19 of the ICCPR from 1966 and implicitly in Article 10 of the ECHR from 1950, and the Court's subsequent jurisprudence demonstrates the Court's openness to technological and social innovation.

An Internet activist named John Perry Barlow issued a declaration on the independence of the internet in 1996, emphasizing the open and free nature of the internet.

Freedom of speech, expression, and association: These fundamental human rights are jeopardized on the internet when governments block websites or social media platforms, violating the right to communication and free association, censoring material, and restricting freedom of expression and information (Barlow, no date).

As the world has become an amalgamation of various rich cultures and diversities, a new right has emerged with the right to cultural diversity. It poses new challenges to the media and business ("creative industries"), challenges that UNESCO has taken up in particular (Frau-Meigs, 2011). Cultural expression is classified as free thought, expression, and information under the 2005 UNESCO Convention on the Protection and Promotion of the Diversity of Cultural Expressions. It expressly refers to the rapid development of information and communication technologies, which allows for greater cultural interaction, as well as UNESCO's mandate to promote the free flow of ideas through word and image. The Convention seeks to promote and respect cultural expression as a result of the creativity of individuals, groups, and societies but warns that the exercise of cultural expression, including by cultural industries, must not violate human rights and fundamental freedoms (Cf. UNESCO, 2005).

Privacy, oversight, and encryption: Citizens must be able to choose who stores their personal information and erase it at any moment. Theft of credentials, appropriation of personal data, and use for financial advantage are all threats to the right to privacy on the internet.

Right to anonymity is a crucial concept in the defense of free expression and the right to privacy. The right to anonymity and communication encryption is particularly violated in nations that prohibit the transmission of encrypted messages and communications, which is required for safe and secure online transactions. Problems can arise from anonymity, such as defamation or cybercrimes. Some attempt to address anonymity by imposing registration requirements or the use of specialized software. Governments all over the world attempt to restrict anonymity and the use of encryption tools for a variety of reasons, ranging from enabling illegal activities to facilitating terrorism.

In May 2015, the Special Rapporteur on Freedom of Expression published his report on encryption and anonymity in the digital age (Kaye, 2015). The report emphasized the following issues in particular:

The Special Rapporteur stated unequivocally that an open and secure internet is now one of the prerequisites for exercising free expression and must thus be protected by governments. Encryption and anonymity must be strongly protected and promoted because they provide the privacy and security required for the meaningful exercise of the right to free expression and opinion in the digital age. The

Special Rapporteur emphasized the importance of anonymous speech for human rights defenders, journalists, and protestors. Any attempt to prohibit or intercept anonymous communications during protests, he said, was an unjustified restriction on the right to peaceful assembly guaranteed by the Universal Declaration of Human Rights (UDHR) and the International Covenant on Civil and Political Rights (ICCPR).

Right to be forgotten: This is the right to have private information about a person removed from internet searches, databases, and directories. The EU has recognized it as a "right to erasure" in the GDPR, and it has already been used in nations such as Argentina, the United States, South Korea, and India.

1.4.2 RESPONSIBILITIES IN DIGITAL RIGHTS

Every citizen around the world has fundamental rights. These rights include freedom of speech and expression, freedom to vote, freedom to practice any religion, etc. Likewise, every internet user around the world has the right to freedom of speech and the right to access the internet without outside interference.

It is very important to know and understand our rights and responsibilities, especially when we are online. The freedom of digitalization has given every internet user the right to freedom of speech or expression, freedom to express an opinion, etc. In this digital world, every internet user should also understand how to use their digital rights and responsibility.

Because the freedom of digitalization today has provided many schools with the opportunity to use digital devices such as tablets and laptops, teachers now have a great opportunity to guide and educate students about the digital world around them and how to be good digital citizens through the appropriate and proper use of digital technology. With advancements in digital technology and an increase in internet users, particularly among young people, teachers must be responsible for ensuring that students of all ages are aware of and educated about their digital rights and responsibilities as good digital citizens. The students should also take the necessary steps to protect their technology and themselves from external threats or harm.

Over the past few years, there have been too many cases of cyberbullying in the media, mainly through texting, sexting, Facebook, and other social media, and it needs to stop. Unfortunately, these things have horrible effects and major consequences. Students should be aware of these dangers and educated that they should not post any unsuitable content, especially about sensitive topics like religion, as there have been many big controversies over the past few years regarding these topics. They should also use appropriate and fair language and behavior when interacting with others, i.e., there should be no cyberbullying. They should respect others' opinions and knowledge. They should learn to obey all intellectual property laws.

The students should realize and understand that they are not behaving professionally and respectfully, but unlawfully. They need to be informed and educated that this kind of conduct is unethical, and if found, they will be reprimanded and punished. The illegal downloading of music and videos has also been an ongoing problem in our digital world. Students should be educated and made aware that what they are doing is illegal and offensive.

In today's digital world, when someone posts, comments, pokes, shares, and so on, others should move on without abusing or harming them with their controversial comments or remarks.

Thus, understanding all these digital rights and responsibilities will encourage everybody to maintain healthy, peaceful, and secure relationships in this digital world.

1.4.3   What is "Digital Citizenship"?

The term "digital citizenship" means how to make proper use of digital technologies, how to socialize or interact with others when you are online, and what needs to be learned to help make better stewards of this technology for the next generation.

The term "digital citizenship" also means knowing and understanding how to make proper use of digital technology appropriately and responsibly in this digital world.

The rise of the internet has increased opportunities for civic, social, and political participation. Thus, digital citizenship is simply defined as "the right to participate in society online" (Mosserberger, Tolbert, and Mcneal, 2007).

A digital citizen also contributes his or her abilities and experiences in school and personal settings by making appropriate use of the internet and various digital technologies.

Important Elements of Digital Citizenship

With the increased freedom of digitalization, we have become more and more active in the digital world. As digital citizens, we have many digital rights and responsibilities that we have to learn, understand, and obey to maintain a friendly digital environment.

Because students are said to be the foundation of our society, they must be educated and taught how to interact, communicate, and overcome various technological challenges. Every student must contribute adequate and relevant content to the online environment that can have a positive impact on society and recognize that their behavior as digital citizens has various consequences. Students should also be trained on how to make appropriate and effective use of technology to ensure the safety of the internet world.

When debating and teaching digital citizenship, there are nine elements to deal with. As technology becomes more accessible to students, these are pillars of information that teachers, administrators, parents, students, and every individual as a digital citizen need to be aware of. Some of these elements are directly related to student's lives outside of school, while others are specifically related to how they use digital technology in schools.

Digital Access: While we live in a digital world, technology is not accessible to all. Because not every child will have a personal computer or internet at home, teachers should be aware that they need more technology for students to use and that every student should have equal access to the internet.

Today, due to the freedom of digitalization in schools across the world, teachers can inspire their students by using advanced digital technology in their classes.

Digital Commerce: The term "digital commerce" refers to the online sale and purchase of goods or products, as well as how to handle money safely in the digital world. Teachers should also educate and inform their students about E-Commerce concepts as part of their learning course. This is a very important aspect that all teachers should share with their students because their future careers will be influenced by it.

Digital Communications: Communication is a very important aspect of a healthy and safe digital relationship. To maintain a fair and long-term digital relationship, teachers must guide and educate their students on how to interact, socialize, communicate, and respond politely and respectfully with others on the internet, as part of good digital citizenship.

Digital Literacy: The term "digital literacy" refers to the ability to use and understand how emerging digital technologies and the latest digital media like tablets, smartphones, and PCs function, which has given people the freedom to actively participate in the digital world.

A digital literacy is defined as "knowledge assembly," which includes "how to assimilate the information, evaluate it, and reintegrate it" (Pool, 1997). However, as digital spaces, texts, and tools evolve and become more complex, so does what it takes to be considered literate.

Digital literacies is defined as "semiotic activity mediated by electronic media," without elaborating on the more specific skills and practices required (Thorne, 2013).

Communication is a very important aspect of digital literacy. Students should understand how to communicate, interact, and work ethically in the internet world without creating any negative consequences for society. Smoothly and respectfully, they should communicate or connect in the digital environment. They should also be guided and directed so that no controversial statements on the internet should be made.

Students should also learn to differentiate between real and fake content, which, on the other hand, can hurt their lives. To live a healthy life, they should know what content is good to post on the internet and what content should be avoided in the digital world.

Digital Etiquette: The term "digital etiquette" refers to the method of using digital technology and its advantages for internet users. Teachers should educate their students on how to positively react to any posts or comments on the internet rather than behave negatively, which will help students protect themselves from any future conflicts. Therefore, students should make better decisions in the digital environment and become more fluent in it.

Digital Laws: Digital law discusses the legal rights and responsibilities that regulate the use of digital technology. There are different laws to safeguard internet users who use digital devices like laptops, smartphones, etc., and digital media like Facebook, Instagram, etc. In this digital age, there have been many cases of various illegal activities and crimes like cyberbullying, hacking someone's emails, falsifying documents, and illegally downloading music and videos. As a result, students should be educated about digital laws and regulations to avoid committing crimes and engaging in illegal activities.

Digital Rights and Responsibilities: Digital Rights and Responsibilities are a set of rules and regulations that every internet user should follow. In this digital society, students should learn about their digital behavior and relationships. They should be educated on how to behave properly in an online world. They should be educated and guided on how to create a digitally friendly environment in this digital world. They should understand the consequences and risks of all their activities and actions on the internet. Their responsibility is to understand the difference between their personal and private lives. Their responsibility is to know what should and should not be posted online. Every citizen across the world has their fundamental rights in the real world; likewise, in the internet world, every internet user, as a digital citizen, has their digital rights and responsibilities.

Today, with the freedom of digitalization, the internet is not only used for personal benefits but also for various negative purposes. In schools, teachers should discuss this subject with their students, make them aware of and take responsibility for their actions, and identify and report any wrongdoings on the internet as well.

Digital Health and Wellness: Our existence in the digital world is the same as in the real one, so the individual's demands and freedoms in real life need to be applied to the digital world. Trust is a very important aspect of the well-being of digital health and wellness. Therefore, to maintain healthy digital relationships in the digital world, every internet user as a digital citizen needs to build trust and gain trust in a digital environment. It is also important that teachers educate their students on how to protect themselves from any threats or harm to achieve good digital health and wellness.

Digital Security and Privacy: The term "digital security and privacy" not only deals with protecting digital technology from viruses or bugs but also with safeguarding our personal and sensitive information from various threats. In addition, teachers should educate and inform their students about the consequences of potential threats while using digital devices at home or school.

1.5   CORE ELEMENTS OF DIGITAL FREEDOM

Freedom of Speech and Expression: Every individual around the world has the right to freedom of opinion, speech, and expression; this right includes freedom without interference from the outside world. Freedom of expression means the ability to express one's opinions and to seek, obtain, and share knowledge and ideas through any medium, regardless of borders, caste, religion, or nationality, and whether one's ideas are expressed orally, in writing, or print, visually, or through any other medium of one's choice.

Privacy: Today, in this digital age, privacy is a very important factor because the internet contains the personal information of millions of users around the world. Therefore, privacy aims to keep all the personal information and records of every individual private so that their data or records remain undisclosed. Privacy also means protecting your personal information or details from theft or other threats.

When so much of our communication, media, and exchange of information has moved online, privacy has become a major concern. A significant element of human autonomy is privacy. Privacy protects the information that we do not want to be shared publicly, like our health or personal finances. So privacy is also considered a fundamental human right by the UN Declaration of Human Rights, the International Covenant on Civil and Political Rights, and many other international and regional treaties.

Security: Privacy and security are interrelated. Your right to control your personal information and how it is used is referred to as "privacy." On the other hand, security refers to how your personal information is safeguarded. Computer and network security have evolved as the freedom of digitalization has become a forum for financial and other sensitive transactions. Early on, we advocated the legal use of encryption to safeguard personal and financial data, which has become a big concern today.

Transparency is especially vital given the government's increasingly clandestine use of new technology for law enforcement and national security purposes. Without accountability, it's difficult to hold the government to account and safeguard digital rights.

Freedom to Access Information: Every individual should have the freedom or right of access to information or data around the world, irrespective of caste, creed, religion, color, etc. Everyone should have the freedom to access the internet without outside interference.

1.5.1 FREEDOM OF COMMUNICATIONS

Freedom of expression, both verbally and in writing, has never been greater than it is now. Freedom of digitization has opened new doors for communications, providing a plethora of chances for freedom of expression. The democratization of the public realm has immense potential to enrich the public discussion. However, the new technologies come with their own set of issues, not least in terms of the limits of freedom of expression.

Freedom of expression and speech in today's digital age offers an enormous amount of information and knowledge tools that open up new possibilities and challenges for speech and participation. The concept of freedom of speech and human rights must be extended not only to conventional media but also to the internet and all types of new media outlets, contributing to progress, democracy, and dialogue.

Article 19 of the Universal Declaration of Human Rights (UDHR) and the International Covenant on Civil and Political Rights (ICCPR) both guarantee freedom of expression. According to the Universal Declaration of Human Rights, "Everyone has the right to freedom of opinion and expression; this right includes the freedom to hold opinions without interference and the freedom to seek, receive, and impart information and ideas through any medium and regardless of frontiers."

According to the ICCPR, "Everyone should have the right to freedom of expression," and this right shall include the freedom to seek, receive, and impart information and ideas of all kinds, regardless of frontiers, orally, in writing, or print, in the form of art, or through any other medium of his choice.

When a sacred value like freedom of expression collides with revolutionary technological progress, as digitization does, we get into trouble. The degree to which new technologies may cause changes that impair the core principles entrenched in current fundamental laws relating to conventional media is a critical subject. It's especially difficult to strike a balance between freedom of expression and personal privacy (Ellul, 1964; Von, S. and Bjorn, 2016; Winston, 1998).

The norms and criteria required for freedom of expression in traditional media have attracted a lot of attention throughout the years. Some limitations on freedom of expression have been deemed necessary when regulating communication, and these restrictions are enforced by national or international courts.

The Internet has evolved as a medium that has altered mostly local communication capabilities into a worldwide phenomenon that spans everything from personal one-to-one emails and social networks to reaching out to enormous audiences globally in the digital era. The expansion of advanced digital technologies has not only enabled unprecedented access to information; it has also revolutionized the environment by introducing new sorts of information such as speech, audio, video, image, text, and code, which may be accessed via a variety of devices and technologies. By lowering obstacles to entry and enabling new spaces for publishing and peer-to-peer cooperation, these networks and services democratized communication. Users can take on the role of writers, broadcasters, or publishers on the internet, bypassing the conventional gatekeepers of previous forms of media and opening up a world of possibilities for generating, sharing, and trading all types of material.

According to this perspective, the internet has emerged as a globally accessible method of communication free of traditional restrictions on free speech and expression. However, the government has imposed certain limitations and regulations on content regulation as online content has become increasingly contested and confined in a nationalized domain that challenges the free flow of information and freedom of expression.

1.5.2 Freedom of Expression in a Digital Age

Every individual should have freedom of speech and expression. This right includes the freedom to hold views, thoughts, and opinions and to obtain and impart knowledge and ideas, irrespective of boundaries and without outside intervention by public authorities.

With increased freedom of digitization and commercialization around the world, there is a growing convergence of media that has transformed communication networks in terms of time and geography, as well as in terms of content and social etiquette.

When a growing amount of news reporting takes place on Facebook and other social media platforms, which compete for the advertising money that has sustained traditional media, the future of the news industry is increasingly questionable (Carlsson, 2016).

As a result of the freedom of digitization, the traditional media system has become fractured, not only in terms of structure and use but also in terms of legal issues. Many social networks and platforms available on the internet in India are not subject to the same constitutional safeguards as traditional media. Simultaneously, the internet, and particularly social media, have offered a window through which thoughts and opinions can reach a wider audience than ever before. It has also become more difficult to distinguish between public and private ideas when they border on hate and harassment, as well as to distinguish truth from lies.

1.5.3 Digital Freedom in the COVID-19 Pandemic

COVID-19 became a global pandemic unlike any other, with comparisons to the Great Depression and the 1918 Spanish Flu in terms of human behavior. People all over the world have been affected by the global coronavirus pandemic. Since its discovery in December 2019, the virus has infected millions of people all around the world. To curb the COVID-19 pandemic, social distancing protocols, nationwide lockdowns, and quarantine measures were imposed across the world.

The interaction between human beings and emerging digital technologies has been thoroughly noticed in recent decades, but it has yet to be examined in the context of the worldwide pandemic.

To achieve this requirement, various sorts of human behavior such as shopping, education, working, meeting, etc. switched from offline to online, resulting in faster adoption of advanced digital technologies among ordinary people all around the world. On the other side, the digital divide between citizens also widened. But fortunately, the digital technology used during the pandemic dramatically increased the ability of the health system to diagnose, track, and contain patients with a probable infection. Not only in the healthcare sector, where computerized tomography machines are used, but also in education, the workplace, banking, and every aspect of daily life where computers, smartphones, and video-based communication platforms are used, the technology represented by computers, smartphones, and video-based communication platforms has brought tremendous change to our lives.

1.6   DIGITAL DEMOCRACY/E-DEMOCRACY

In the present age of digitization, the use of innovative digital technologies has changed the way we live and work in society today. Every activity in and around our life is dependent on technologies and applications. The use of activity using freeware applications without any disturbance is also called e-democracy. It transformed many industries as diverse as health, banking, education, agriculture, and finance. Right from the beginning, digital media has made a strong motive for people who want to improve democracy.

The global impact of the digital revolution may be seen in the tremendous shifts it has enabled, including greater public access to information, the creation of new gateways to goods and services, and more chances for civic engagement and social networking with larger communities. More significantly, information and communication technologies are considered to heavily influence and mediate political institutions and activities, technology for new media (Loader and Mercea, 2011).

It is widely acknowledged that new media technologies have a significant impact on the public's access to information and government documents, political campaign tactics and messages, voter attitudes, and preferences, activist efforts to spread their messages, and how issues enter the public discourse (Loader and Mercea, 2011).

1.6.1   WHAT IS DIGITAL DEMOCRACY?

Digital democracy is defined as "A Collection of attempts to conduct democracy without the constraints of time, space, and other physical limitations, using ICT or computer-mediated communication (CMC) instead, as a supplement, not a substitute, for traditional ('analog') political practices" (Hacker and Van Dijk, 2000).

The pursuit and practice of democracy from any point of view using digital media for both online and offline political communication is known as "digital democracy."

The distinction between online and offline should be made because political activities take place both offline and online, including at physical gatherings or virtual meetings when various digital devices are employed as support.

In the area of digital democracy, there is comparatively little research on how our democratic institutions can use digital technologies and how citizens can participate in day-to-day democratic activities like voicing particular concerns, creating and evaluating legislative proposals, making decisions, or holding public officials accountable.

Three justifications for digital democracy (Tsagarousianou, 1999):

- The retrieval and interchange of political information between governments, public agencies, representatives, political and community organizations, and individual citizens is improved through digital democracy.
- Community building, public discourse, and deliberation are supported by digital democracy.
- Citizens' participation in political decision-making is increased through digital democracy. In nations with strong internet penetration, nearly all national and international governments and their public administrations, as well as the majority of political parties, political organizations, and political groups, have now developed websites with political and other public information. We are in a phase of transition from a democracy based on the press or television to one based on the internet, where the role of the internet for political campaigning is rapidly growing (Davis et al., 2009).

E-Participation

E-participation is currently a highly well-liked concept in connection with the growth of Web 2.0 and user-generated content. E-Democracy or digital democracy are just two names for this idea. The final two terms are about political matters and the interaction of citizens with governments or political figures. Policy concerns in general and citizens' interactions with both governments and public administrations are what e-participation stands for. The use of digital media to mediate and alter how citizens interact with governments and public administrations to increase citizen engagement is known as "e-participation" (Van and Jan, 2010).

E-participation can be compared to the well-known steps in the policy-making process, including defining the agenda, developing the policies, making decisions, implementing the policies, and evaluating the policies. The stages of agenda setting, policy preparation, and policy evaluation have seen the highest e-participation to date.

Agenda setting: Governments occasionally allow citizens to respond or provide feedback with their ideas, proposals, or complaints on government websites in addition to informing citizens about their policies. The most popular e-participation application is information provision.

Policy development: During the peak of the internet craze, numerous Western countries established official online consultations with the public to discuss already prepared policies. Their main aim was to involve more residents in the planning process than just those who attended formal meetings and were seen as more or less professional lobbyists. The same types of lobbyists continued to participate, and governments refused to accept the findings because they were believed to be unrepresentative, which generally led to unsatisfactory results.

However, in the present age of digitization, as the number of internet users increases and technology advances, there are greater prospects for online plan consultations as more people can participate and as many improvements in plan consultations, like the visualization and simulation of plans, are presented (Botterman et al., 2009).

Making a decision: Computer networks provide new ways to participate in voting during elections, referendums, and official opinion polls. Between electronic distance voting and electronic voting machines, a differentiation should be drawn. Here, we talk about the final form of voting. For those who are unable to vote in person because of their disability, lack of time, or location, it provides new opportunities. However, the overwhelming majority of data in the rare cases where online e-voting is being performed by the citizens who are living out of the country reveals that these changes do not, or only hardly, result in a higher voter turnout.

Policy execution: Governments make considerable use of digital media to monitor illegal activity and violations of laws and regulations. However, the government may benefit from more sets of eyes to monitor social developments. This is unquestionably a form of involvement in the implementation of policy. We're talking about municipal and police websites where people can report all kinds of crimes, from seeing someone using a hands-free device while driving to seeing child pornography. These snitching websites are becoming more and more well-liked. They can also be used to file complaints against actions taken by governments and to report offenses committed by civil officials.

Still, a strong supply-side focus dominates the delivery of E-Government services. The intention is to deliver as many government services as feasible online and in the most cutting-edge formats available, including full electronic transactions.

Online government services that are more user-focused and demand-driven undoubtedly fall under the umbrella of e-participation programs. Citizens can speak out in favor of better government services in this way. Trust in government services is a crucial foundation for overall trust in the government, and it has political implications.

Policy evaluation: To improve the quality of their online public services, some governments have set up online quality panels or individual feedback systems. This enables citizens to provide feedback and review the quality of service being provided. Governments now have the chance to continuously enhance their services. However, the e-participation apps that are expanding the fastest are all the citizen information and control sites that let people assess the outcomes of government policies daily and use that knowledge to make their own decisions in daily life, like where to live.

E-Governance

Although the phrase "E-Government" has become more commonplace recently, it still lacks a standard meaning. This term is defined by various governments and groups to fit their purposes and goals. Here are a few often-used definitions:

The term "E-Governance" refers to the use of Information and Communication Technology (ICT) in government organizations, the public sector, and other areas for the improvement of governance and communication with business and industry. With freedom of digital technology, E-Governance is a trending concept after E-Commerce and e-learning. There are four steps in the E-Government process (Shah, 2007):

- Information on the policies that govern the provision of various services will be published on websites for citizens to access.
- Clients can also download programs to use when getting services.
- Document delivery via electronic means.
- Services delivered electronically.

As digital tools provide an effective method of governance, digitalization makes daily administration simpler. Therefore, E-Governance makes use of modern digital technologies and electronic media to strengthen and expand good governance.

According to the World Bank, the term "E-Government" refers to the use of information technologies by government organizations that have the potential to revolutionize interactions with citizens, enterprises, and other branches of government, such as Wide Area Networks, the internet, and mobile computing (Sudan et al., 2015). These technologies can be used for a variety of purposes, including better citizen service delivery, improved interactions with business and industry, citizen empowerment through information access, or more effective government administration. Less corruption, greater transparency, greater convenience, income growth, and/or cost savings may result better.

E-Governance, as defined by UNESCO in 2005, "is the use of information and communication technology in public administration to enhance information and public service, promote citizen engagement in decision-making processes, and make the government more accountable, transparent, and efficient" (Budd and Harris, 2009). E-Government is the practice of this governance through an electronic medium to enable an effective, quick, and transparent method of communicating information to the public and other agencies as well as for carrying out administrative tasks for the government.

Thus, E-Governance can be simply defined as the electronic transmission of government services and information to the general population.

1.6.2   ICT AND CORRUPTION

Information and communications technologies (ICTs) are becoming more widely recognized by governments as important instruments for promoting efficiency, accountability, and transparency, as well as for identifying and decreasing corruption. Many recent studies have been made on the connection between ICT-related e-government and corruption in many developing nations. Case studies from this research have demonstrated that corruption is rife in these nations and that it may be reduced through good governance policies and initiatives. Recent case studies of nation-specific policies and initiatives have also been published, for instance in

China LAN (2004), ZHANG and ZHANG (2009) and MISTRY (2005) note that the public sector in poor countries is frequently characterized by low institutional capacity, limited stakeholder involvement, high levels of corruption, and informality in a valuable overview of the literature on public sector performance measurement (or lack of formal rules and procedures).

The following are some potential areas in which ICTs can help in the fight against corruption, according to the Swedish Program for ICT in Developing Regions (Gronlund, 2010).

- **Automation,** which can lessen the potential for fraud in routine tasks.
- **Transparency,** which can limit discretionary behavior;
- **Operational anomalies,** outliers, and underperformance detection;
- **Preventive detection** through network and person monitoring;
- **Educating** the public about its right to protest arbitrary treatment and empowering it;
- **Reporting** to establish channels for complaints that can result in effective action, penalize transgressions, and close loopholes;
- **Deterrence,** by publicizing information about reported examples of corruption; promoting moral behavior through participation in public discourse and internet forums.

1.6.3 REAL-WORLD CASES

Digital India initiatives: The "Digital India" program has been launched by the government of India, which is led by Prime Minister Mr. Narendra Modi. However, the UPA government of India claimed that the visionary schemes of the UPA government were renamed from the old plan name "National e-Governance" to the new name "Digital India" (U.C Meena, no date). The UPA government Mr. Shashi Tharoor claimed the several plans that have been changing to the new name from the old name. For Example, new name "Skill India" renamed from "National Skill Development Program (2010)," "Make in India" renamed from "National Manufacturing Policy (2011)," "Swachh Bharat Mission" renamed from "Nirmal Bharat Abhiyan (2013)," and "PAHAL" renamed from "Direct Benefit Transfer for LPG (2013)" (Vivek, 2017).

These aim to shift India to digital efforts to make the country a digitally empowered society. To benefit the power of modern digital technology and to make the use of these technologies more accessible, this effort was started. India is a nation that is rich in cultural, linguistic, geographic, and traditional diversity. Many people were left living below the bare minimum of socio-economic standards as a result of the British occupation. The requirement of the hour is good governance or offering the greatest number of services to people in the shortest amount of time possible (Sudan, 2015). E-Government, which offers "direct democracy," is what can make the dream of good governance a reality (Tauseef and Sulayman, 2014). As a part of their online digital transformation, governments all over the world aim to increase their effectiveness and transparency. Digital services and online platforms have greatly increased as a result of this.

E-Governance projects have been implemented globally over the past few years. India has implemented numerous E-Governance projects to enhance the quality of communication between the public and the government.

India has introduced the "Digital India" program and E-Government with a vision to provide a strong digital democracy. E-Governance unquestionably introduces the automation needed to root out corruption. The government can communicate with citizens more easily, quickly, and smoothly, which improves good governance. As a result, the Indian government has taken several initiatives.

INITIATIVES FOR E-GOVERNANCE IN INDIA

In India, several E-Governance initiatives have already been implemented by the government. Projects like UMANG (Unified Mobile Application for New Age Government) for bill payment services, DigiLocker to provide paperless availability of public documents, UPI (Unified Payment Interface) for digital payment platform, MeriPehchan for citizen ease to access government, MyGov, MyScheme launched in July 22 for eligibility based services (PIB, 2022), MPHS (Multi-purpose Household Survey), e-SEVA (Electronic Sources), CARD (Computer-aided Administration and Registration Department), and Saukaryam (Civic Services in Vishakapatnam) have proven to be very helpful in Andhra Pradesh. Khajane and Bhoomi (Earth) in Karnataka, Gyandoot and Maiti Shakti in Gujarat, and similar initiatives in other states. Gujarat's interstate transportation system has undergone a revolution thanks to the installation of automated interstate checkpoints that have reduced harassment for transporters and eliminated the arbitrary excise duty imposition that once existed.

- **Bhoomi Project (Online Delivery of Land Records)–Karnataka:** The Karnataka state-run BHOOMI project is a land records computerization system. It allows land records to be updated online. Farmers are the primary beneficiaries of the BHOOMI initiative. They are no longer subjected to harassment when obtaining a copy of the RTC (Record of Right, Tenancy and Crops) from the information kiosk at the sub-district offices. You can track the status of the mutation application and apply to change a mutation in the RTC. Farmers who update their records using a biometric authentication system are no longer concerned about possible record tampering by dishonest police. Courts could use a database of land records to decide on a variety of civil disputes involving possession, ownership, and agriculture (E-Governance Project Lifecycle, no date).

- **AARAKSHI–Jaipur:** The Jaipur City Police uses the intranet-based Aarakshi system to facilitate FIRs, criminal records, vehicle thefts, missing person records, etc. It is similar to a closed, private user group that is only accessible to approved personnel. All of the city's field-level personnel, including police stations, circle officers SP, and even district collectors, could make use of it.
- **SARITA (Stamps Registration and Archiving):** One of the major revenue generators for every government is normally the state's department of stamps and registration. The Stamps and Registration activity can make more money because of the effective government–citizen interface provided by the program. The Registration and Valuation module is the brains of this application. Other modules include networking and scanning tools that facilitate secure departmental information sharing as well as "electronic copying" of registered papers that allows for the return of the original document shortly after the presentation (Karyemsetty and Prasad, 2016).
- **WEBCITI–Punjab:** An E-Government project called WEBCITI (Web-based Citizen-IT Interface) aims to provide a citizen–IT interface for district administration services in Fatehgarh Sahib, Punjab. It is a system for disseminating information that makes it easier for the public to learn about different government programs, including eligibility requirements, steps to follow, contact information, and forms that can be downloaded, among other things. These include granting licenses such as those for carrying arms, granting authorization for conferences and rallies, etc., as well as providing certificates for events such as births, deaths, caste, rural region, etc. The web interface accessible at the intranet counters at the development block/revenue tehsil and other locations where the information is available can be used to find out about various schemes and procedures, the status of an application, etc. (Karyemsetty and Prasad, 2016).
- **AKSHAYA–Kerala:** The Akshaya project was launched in November 2002. In the native language it means "perpetuating wealth." Akshaya e-Centers are being built throughout Kerala as part of that state's extensive effort to promote e-literacy. In the beginning, these centers will act as ICT diffusion nodes, teach one member of each household how to use computers, and every community has an ITeS (Information Technology Enabled Services) delivery point. All Akshaya e-Centres will be networked with a single operations center and have Internet connectivity (Naik, 2021).
- **The e-SEVA project-Andhra Pradesh (Front-end Citizen Service Delivery):** Government to citizen and e-business to citizen services are the goals of this project. The word "SEVA" describes the concept of "service." The e-SEVA project's standout feature is the online delivery of all services to customers and residents, who are connected to the appropriate government agencies and given access to online information at the point of service delivery. The e-SEVA project can access 30 different services through

a single window. These include paying electric, water, phone, or property tax bills, applying for or renewing or applying for a new driving license, getting the information you need, and applying for a passport for all its attributes. The services include e-forms, certificate issuance, and license and permit issuance, online utility bill paying, and more. Cash, checks, money orders, credit cards, and the Internet are all acceptable forms of payment (E-Governance Project Lifecycle, no date).

- **GYANDOOT-Madhya Pradesh:** The word "Gyandoot" is taken from Hindi language which means a "Messenger of knowledge." Gyandoot was launched in January 2000 and is an intranet that links rural Cyber cafes that provide for the necessities of the people in Central India's Dhar tribal district. It is a community-based, extremely cost-effective, and self-sufficient method of bringing the advantages of information technology to tribal villagers' front doors. The project uses a cutting-edge G2C methodology to address the social, economic, and development requirements of the people of 1,600 villages of Dhar district. There are around 25 to 30 communities served by each kiosk. There are a number of services provided by this project, such as income certificates, domicile certificates, caste certificates, employment news, rural newspapers, rural markets, e-education, etc. (Jafri et al., 2002).
- **Media Lab Asia:** According to Section 25 of the Companies Act, the Department of Electronics and Information Technology (DeitY), Ministry of Communications and IT, and Government of India established Media Lab Asia in 2001 as a not-for-profit corporation to carry out innovation-driven research and development and develop ICT-based products, solutions, and services that are scalable and have a lasting impact on the lives of the average person. A full-scope program for Media Lab Asia was approved by the government in 2003 after an initial one-year timeframe. The project aims to eliminate the digital divide between those who have and those who do not. Its main goal is to develop tools that will make it possible for someone illiterate to utilize computers. The project's focus areas are micro-entrepreneurship, employment, education, and healthcare (Annual Report, 2011–2012).

Efforts were taken to fulfill the goals of E-Governance in India (Jalta, 2012)

- Redefining the responsibilities, structure, functioning, and improvements in administrative procedures.
- Data and IT infrastructure standardization.
- Improvement of Governmental Literacy (Citizens and Employees).
- Creation of a portal for national, state, local, and municipal governments.
- The digitization of data in the public domain.
- Offer facilitation counters and public information.

- Establish the foundation of communication with fiber connections and trust-worthy media.
- The simultaneous globalization of all departments and organizations.
- The horizontal and vertical integration of different government functions.
- The E-Government framework should be scalable and flexible to meet the needs of society.

1.7 CHALLENGES AND DIFFICULTIES (NAGARAJA, 2016)

There are still many barriers to E-Governance despite numerous initiatives in this direction, including the digital divide between urban and rural areas, poverty, illiteracy, security and privacy concerns, maintenance costs, etc.

- **Interoperability:** One of the most important aspects of electronic governance is interoperability. Ministry and department cooperation is challenging, and it has become a barrier to processing and exchanging data. In other words, the acquisition of web-based data and the format in which it should be stored appear to be the main problems with E-Governance.
- **Security:** In the present age of digitization, the security of online transactions is a major concern; E-Governance is used for services like insurance, banking, and utility bill payment. In reality, citizens are still unhappy with using government services because of a lack of security.
- **Privacy**: Privacy is also one of the major concerns with E-Governance. Government should guarantee the accuracy of any information submitted by citizens. Otherwise, any organization or person could misuse confidential and personal data.
- **Authentication:** It is crucial to identify the correct use of the services to prevent private competitors from abusing them. In the meanwhile, the digital signature is crucial in ensuring authenticity. In actuality, it is costly and necessitates frequent upkeep.
- **Not Cost-effective:** It is one of the economic issues – implementation of E-Governance operations and maintenance of services fetch huge costs to government.
- **Reusability:** Any models developed by the government, must be reusable. E-Governance is a national plan that incorporates any software or modules that should be used by other administrations.
- **Maintenance issues:** Maintenance should be given due importance because the IT ministry has been continuously developing new software to fill the current needs of citizens. Consequently, the government has launched new projects like digital India.
- **Portability**: The primary requisite for portable applications is the independence of components from hardware and software platforms in possible reuse by administrations.
- **Accessibility:** In the era of digital technology, most are using the internet via computers and smartphones. In the context of India, there is still a gap arising between users and nonusers; it is because of the language barrier, most of the

people are digitally illiterate, and inadequate infrastructure in rural areas such as poor internet connections, electricity issues etc.

- **Usability:** Users of E-Governance may be literate or illiterate. Any technology or software should be user-friendly; only then, can citizens use it as smoothly as possible.

1.8 CHAPTER CONCLUSION

Thus with the freedom of digitization and with the rapid advances of digital technology, such as ICT for monitoring, big data for capturing, data mining for identifying mobile applications for promoting accessibility, and forensic tools for minimizing corruption in a country getting breakthrough. But "Digitalization and e-governance," however, cannot promise that corruption will completely disappear. It can only offer a good foundation for decreasing societal corruption levels. To increase public confidence in effective democratic E-Governance, the government should invest more in these projects to make them transparent, effective, safe, and citizen-friendly.

EXERCISES

1. What do you mean by digitalization?
2. What is the difference between the terms "digitalization" and "digitization"?
3. What is digital transformation and why is it important in today's digital era?
4. What are two benefits of digital transformation?
5. Explain the transformation of AI and list three benefits of AI search algorithms?
6. What is smartphone penetration and what factors influence the demand for smartphones?
7. What are the four main reasons for how popular smartphones are becoming in India?
8. What are digital rights and what are our responsibilities in digital rights?
9. What is the role of Right of Information in the world of digitalization?
10. Explain the term "digital literacy"?
11. What is the meaning of digital freedom?
12. What is freedom of speech in a digital age?
13. Define the term "E-Governance"?
14. What steps should be taken to adopt E-Governance successfully?
15. Are advanced digital technologies like ICT helping in the victory of the war against corruption?
16. What is "Digital India Initiatives" and what are its key objectives for the country's development?
17. What are challenges to E-Governance implementation in the country?

REFERENCES

Abd-El-Barr, M. and El-Rewini, H. (2005) 'Fundamentals of Computer Organization and Architecture'. ISBN 0-471-46741-3, John Wiley & Sons.

Annual Report (2011–2012) *'Media Asia Lab'*. Available at: https://dic.gov.in/images/annual/annual_report_english.pdf (Accessed: 11 October 2022).

Barlow, J.P., (no date) *'A Declaration of the Independence of Cyberspace'*. Available at: www.eff.org/cyberspace-independence (Accessed: 11 May 2020).

Botterman, M., Millard, J., a.o. (2009) *'Value for Citizens, A vision of public governance in 2020'*. Report for the European Commission, Information Society and Media. Luxemburg: European Communities, DOI: 10.2759.

Budd, L., and Harris, L. (Red.). (2009) *E-governance: Managing or Governing?* New York, NY: Routledge.

Carlsson, U. (2016) 'Freedom of expression in the digital transition'. *Journal of Media Business Studies* 13(3) 187–197.

Davis, R., Baumgartner, J., Francia, P.L., and Morris, J.S. (2009) 'The Internet in US election campaigns'. In: A. Chadwick & Ph. Howard (Eds.). *Routledge Handbook of Internet Politics*. London and New York: Routledge.

Digital India Mission, (no date). Available at: https://indialends.com/government-schemes/digital-india-mission (Accessed: 10 September 2020).

El-Darwiche, B. et al. (2013) *'Digitization for Economic Growth and Job Creation'*. Available at: https://www3.weforum.org/docs/GITR_Chapter 1.2_2013.pdf (Accessed: 13 October 2020).

Ellul, J. (1964) *The Technological Society*. New York: Knopf.

Frau-Meigs, D. (2011) *Media matters in the cultural contradictions of the information society-Towards a human rights-based governance*, Council of Europe, p. 189.

Furht, B. (2011) *Handbook of Augmented Reality, Science and Business Media*, Springer, LLC, DOI:10.1007/978-14614-6-1.

GlobalData (2020) *'Telecom sector will shine in post Covid-19 era, says GlobalData'*, March 27. Available at: www.globaldata.com/media/coronavirus/telecom-will-shine-in-post-covid-19-era-says-globaldata/ (Accessed: 13 May 2020).

Gorensek, T. and Kohont, A. (2019) 'Conceptualization of Digitalization: Opportunities and Challenges for Organizations in the Euro-Mediterranean Area', *International Journal of Euro-Mediterranean Studies* (IJEMS), vol. 11, no. 2.

Gronlund, A. et al., (2010) *'Increasing transparency and fighting corruption through ICT: empowering people and communities'*, SPIDER ICT4D Series No. 3. Available at: http://upgraid.files.wordpress.com/2010/11/ict4d_corruption.pdf (Accessed: 20 December 2022).

Hacker, K.L and Van Dijk, J. (2000) 'What is digital democracy?' in K.L. Hacker & J. van Dijk (eds.), *Digital Democracy*. Issues of Theory and Practice (London, Sage). pp. 1–9.

Indian National Congress, (no date) *'CONGRESS SCHEMES RENAMED BY BJP'*, *CONGRESS SCHEMES RENAMED/REPACKED BY NDA*. Available at: www.inc.in/congress-schemes-renamed-by-bjp (Accessed: 5 December 2022).

Jafri, A. et al., (2002) *'Information Communication Technologies and Governance: The Gynandoot Experiment in Dhar District of Madhya Pradesh, India'*, April. Available at: https://assests.publishing.service.gov.uk/media/57a08d384f0b652dd00182a/WP 160.pdf (Accessed: 28 December 2022).

Jalta, N. (2012) *'Eclipse Based Framework for e-Governance'* JP Publications.

Jones, M. Tim. (2008) *Artificial Intelligence: A System Approach* (Accessed: 17 February 2020).

Karyemsetty, N. and Prasad, K.L. (2016) 'A Study on e-Governance Initiatives in India', *International Journal of Innovative Research in Science, Engineering and Technology*, ISSN (Online) – 2317–8753, vol. 5, no. 5, May 2016.

Kaye, D. (2015) *'Report of the special Rapporteur on the promotion and protection of the right to freedom of opinion and expression'*, A/HRC/29/32, 29 May. (THE 2015 Report of the SR on FOE), paras 12, 16 and 56.

Keelery, S. (2020) *'Number of internet users in India 2015–2025'*, October 16. Available at: www.statista.com/statistics/255146/number-of-internet-users-in-india/ (Accessed: 13 December 2022).

Lan, L. (2004) 'E-Government: A catalyst to good governance in China', *Knowledge Management in Electronic Government*, vol. 3035: pp. 317–324.

Laricchia, F. (2022) *'Smartphone Users by Country worldwide 2021'*, Newzoo.com. Available at: www.Statista.com (Accessed: 22 December 2022).

Leiner, B.M. et al. (2009) 'A Brief History on the Internet', October, *ACM SIGCOMM Computer Communication Review*, 22, vol. 39, no. 5.

Loader, B., Mercea, D. (2011) 'Networking Democracy?' *Information, Communication and Society*, 14: 757–769.

McCarthy, J. (no date) 'Arthur Samuel: Pioneer in Machine Learning', Available at: http://info lab.stanford.edu/pub/voy/museum/Samuel.html (Accessed: 22 February 2021).

Meena, U.C. (no date) *'Digital India: A program to transform India into a digitally empowered society and knowledge economy'*. Available at: www.itu.int/en/ITU-D/Regional-Prese nce/AsiaPacific/Documents/Events/2017/Sep-SCEG2017/SESSION-2_India_Mr_Ut tam_Chand_Meena.pdf (Accessed: 12 March 2020).

Mistry, J.J. (2005) 'A conceptual; framework for the role of government in bridging the digital divide', *Journal of Global Information Technology Management*, vol. 8, no. 3: 28–46.

Mosserberger, K., Tolbert, C. J., and Mcneal, R.S. (2007) *Digital Citizenship: The Internet, Society and Participation,* The MIT Press. Available at: https://doi.org/10.7551/mitpr ess/7428.001.0001

Nagaraja, K. (2016) 'E-governance in India: Issues and Challenges', *Journal of Economics and Finance (IOSR-JEF)*, vol. 7, no. 5, Ver. IV, pp. 50–54.

Naik, K.S. (2021) 'E-governance success projects in Kerala: a study of Ahshaya', *International Journal of Multidisciplinary Educational Research*, ISSN: 2277- 7881, 10 December 2021.

Pangrazio, L. and Stefton-Green, J. (2021) 'Digital Rights, Digital Citizenships and Digital Literacy: What's the difference?', *Journal of New Approaches in Educational Research*, vol. 10, no. 1, 15–27, e-ISSN: 2254-7339. Available at: https://doi.org/10.7821/ near.2021.1.616

Payne, J. (2006) *'E-Government: A Critical Anti-Corruption Tool'*. Available at: https://pdf. usaid.gov/pdf/Pnadm957.pdf (Accessed: 7 November 2023).

Petrosyan, A. (2023) *'Global Number of Online Users, by Country'*, February 13, 2023. Available at: https://www.statista.com/statistics/271411/number-of-internet-users-in-selected-countries/

PIB, (2022) *'E-governance'*, Ministry of Electronics & IT, Government of India, 03 Aug, Available at: www.E-governance (pib.gov.in).

Pool, C.R. (1997) 'A new digital literacy'. *Educational Leadership*, 55(3), 6–11.

Shah, M. (2007) 'E-Governance in India: Dream or Reality?' *International Journal of Education and Development using ICT*, vol. 3, no. 2.

Singh, P., Sharma, D. and Agrawal, S. (2011) 'A Modern Study of Bluetooth Technology', *International Journal of Computer Science, Engineering and Information Technology*, August, vol. 1, no. 3.

Stallings, W. (2016) *'Computer Organization AND Architecture: Designing for Performance'*.

Sudan, R. et al. (2015) *'e-Government'*, May 19. Available at: www.worldbank.org/en/topic/ digitaldevelopment/brief/e-governmnet (Accessed: 19 December 2022).

Sudan, R. (2015) 'Towards SMART Government: The Andhra Pradesh Experience', XL VI *India Journal of PA* 300.

Tauseef, S. and Sulayman, M. (2014) '*E-Government Strategy- A Proposed Infrastructure*', Faculty of Applied Science International Islamic University Islamabad.

Thorne, S.L. (2013) 'Digital literacies'. In M. Hawkins (Ed.), *Farming Languages and Literacies* (pp. 192–218). Routledge.

Tsagarousianou, R. (1999) 'Electronic democracy: Rhetoric and reality'. *Communications: The European Journal of Communication Research*, 24 (2), pp. 189–208.

UNESCO (2005) '*Convention on the Protection and Promotion of the Diversity of Cultural Expressions*, Preamble, Article 1 and 4'.

Vivek, V., (2017) 'Modi has Merely Renamed 19 out of 23 Congress Schemes', 24 June, Available at: www. Shashi Tharoor says BJP renamed 23 Congress schemes. He's right about 19 I Latest News India–Hindustan Times.

Von, S. and Bjorn (2016) '*The importance of freedom of speech in a free society*', in Fritt, Stockholm: Sveriges Riksday.

Van, D. and Jan, A.G.M. (2010) 'Participation in Policy Making. In: Study on the Social Impact of ICT'. *Report for European Commission, Information Society, and Media Directorate-General*, pp. 30–70. Luxemburg: European Communities DOI. Available at: http://ec.europe.eu/information_society/eeurope/i2010/docs/eda/social_impact_of_ict.pdf. (Accessed: 20 December 2022).

Winston, B. (1998) *Media Technology and Society. A history from the Telegraph to the Internet*. London: Routledge.

Yinan, G., Shuguo, Z., and Dawei, X. (2012) 'Overview of Wi-Fi Technology', *The 2nd International Conference on Computer Applications and System Modelling*.

Zhang, J. and Zhang, Z. (2009) 'Applying E-government information system for anti-corruption strategy', *Proceedings of the 2009 International conference on management of e-Commerce and e-government*: 112–115. http://dx.doi.org/10.11 09/ICMeCG.2009.40

2 Social Media and Digital Freedom

SUMMARY

In this chapter, we will discuss how social media in today's digital age has become an integral part of our lives and how every user has become increasingly reliant on social media. Also, we will discuss how, with the freedom of digitization in the digital age, people's right to freedom of speech has been strengthened by the use of social media, which has enabled individuals to communicate their information, thoughts, and opinions. This chapter also provides an overview of the key issues concerning restrictions on freedom of expression and describes how the government has approached them. Further, we will also study how social media can be influential on society in both positive and negative ways. We will also learn about the number of social media users and the most popular social media platforms that are today dominating the market in various countries. At the end of this chapter, we will discuss the role of social media platforms in politics.

2.1 INTRODUCTION

The term "social media" refers to a collection of resources for exchanging information that is largely focused on the internet and smartphones. It is a platform that combines technology, telecommunications, and social interaction to allow people to communicate using words, images, films, and music. Web-based and mobile technology is used in social media to transform contacts into open conversations.

Social media is a platform that provides for sharing and exchanging ideas and information over the internet and on mobile devices. It enables everyone to interact or communicate through videos, images, messages, and music. Users can interact and communicate quickly through computers, laptops, smartphones, and social media networks like Facebook, WhatsApp, and Instagram. Some of the most popular social media websites are Facebook, TikTok, WeChat, Instagram, Twitter, WhatsApp, YouTube, and LinkedIn.

Another type of social media is mobile social media, which is defined as social media that is utilized in conjunction with mobile devices.

2.1.1 ACADEMIC OPINIONS ON SOCIAL MEDIA

According to Andreas Kaplan and Michael Haenlein (2010), social media is "a group of internet-based applications that build on the ideological and technological foundations of Web 2.0 and allow the creation and exchange of user-generated content." "Web 2.0" refers to internet platforms that allow users to participate interactively.

According to Lusk (2020), social media is the use of Facebook, blogs, Twitter, Myspace, and LinkedIn for communication, photo, and video sharing.

According to a survey by Moran, Seaman, and Tinti-Kane (2020, p. 5), Facebook, Twitter, and YouTube were the social media sites most frequently used by academic employees.

According to Boyd (2010), social networking sites have been welcomed by teenagers and young people in particular as a method to interact with their peers, share information, reinvent their personas, and highlight their social life.

Social networking sites have changed how we connect in person, how we obtain information, and how our friendships and social groupings function (Asur and Huberman, 2010).

2.1.2 SOCIAL MEDIA VS. OTHER MEDIA

Social media and traditional media both share the same idea of spreading information and data, but they do so in very different ways. The features of social media make it a digital environment, where users not only create content but also enrich it with information like tags, posts, labels, and other classifications. The ability to contextually combine social media sites with other websites allows for the creation of user-developed widgets.

- **Easily accessible:** Social media websites are easily accessible to the general public and are either free or nearly free. Users can easily create accounts on different social media platforms of their choice and thus can access information easily. On the other hand, industrial media is typically privately held and not publicly accessible.
- **Convenience:** Social media platforms are always subject to change. Every time, people can change their profile pictures, blogs, preferences, etc., while industrial media cannot be changed once it has been made; for example, a published magazine article cannot be changed immediately.
- **Two-way communication:** The similarity between traditional and social media is that both disseminate information. But one-way communication is solely supported by traditional media. Social media, on the other hand, enables two-way communication. It indicates that, in contrast to traditional media, users of social media can post comments, reactions, etc.
- **Reach:** With the freedom of digitization, social media platforms today have a mass audience globally, just like commercial media.
- **Supports all file formats:** Traditional media typically only come in one format. Newspapers and books, for instance, are unable to display a video while all file types, including text, graphics, video, and documents, are supported by social media. Therefore, social media in this digital world is also known as "digital media."
- **Usability:** The majority of social media platforms don't demand any specialized knowledge to produce content. Websites for social media provide technologies with practically no operating expenses. Industrial media, on the other hand, need certain expertise and training.

- **Time consumption:** Compared to traditional media, social media is very instant and fairly quick as it is the faster means of producing and spreading information. On the other hand, in other media like magazines and books, information is published over a longer time period.
- **Center of attraction:** Disseminating information to large audiences is a characteristic of both media types. But the main focus of social media is to enable users to communicate with both known and unknown individuals. The focus of conventional media, in contrast, is on keeping the public informed about a variety of topics, including politics, world affairs, etc.

2.1.3 TYPES OF SOCIAL MEDIA

There are different types of social media, as shown in Figure 2.1 below.

The following categories can be used to categorize social media:

Social networking: The term "social networking" refers to an internet service that allows users to form virtual networks with others. It has features such as chat, instant messaging, photo and video sharing, updates, and so on. Facebook and LinkedIn are the most popular social networking sites.

Blogs: Individual users produce and maintain descriptive content in the form of blogs, which can include text, photos, and links to other websites. The potential for blogs to be interactive is one of their most appealing features. Readers are encouraged to submit comments, and the trail of comments can be tracked.

Microblogs are similar to blogs in that they allow users to write and share content in a limited number of characters (typically 140 characters or less). Twitter is a microblogging service that allows users to send, post, and receive "tweets," or short messages.

Vlogs and video-sharing sites: Video blogs (Vlogs) are blogging sites that primarily use video as the main form of content, with text supporting it. The most popular video-sharing website on the internet today is YouTube. YouTube allows users to watch, upload, share, subscribe, and even comment on videos.

Wikis: Wikipedia is a collaborative website that allows multiple users to create and edit pages on a variety of topics. While a single page is referred to as a "wiki page," a "wiki" refers to the entire associated content on that topic. These many pages are linked together by hyperlinks, allowing users to interact in a complex and non-linear way.

Social bookmarking: People can use bookmarking and content curation networks to find, store, share, and debate new and popular material and media. Also people use bookmarking sites like Pinterest to find, save, and share visual material.

Social news: These services enable you to upload a variety of news items as well as links to external articles. Voting and commenting on the items are used to facilitate interaction. The most crucial element is voting because the items with the most votes are displayed first. The most popular are Digg, Reddit, and Propeller.

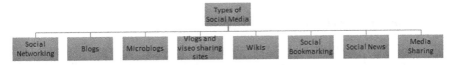

FIGURE 2.1   Types of social media.

Media sharing: This also allows the user to upload and share photos or videos. These sites, like the other networks, are important for brand awareness, lead generation, audience engagement, and a variety of other social marketing objectives.

2.2 THE ART OF SOCIAL NETWORKING

As already discussed in Chapter 1, today, with the freedom of digitization, every sector of society is using communication mediums or social network mediums like Twitter, Facebook, Telegram, WhatsApp, and other wired resources. The advancement of these societies' ability to use advanced technologies has resulted in vertical growth, which connects anyone from a known or unknown node (user or group). The analysis of connected nodes and users for optimum purposes in social media is called social network analysis (SNA). Communication mediums are commonly used for influencing areas like academics, healthcare, finance, banking, shopping, food, and entertainment (Stockman, 2004). These communication mediums assist society in both negative and positive behavior. A variety of applications are being used to communicate purposefully between the users which are also called node (n) in the domain of networking (n to n).

Advances in digital technology and its applications have pushed the boundaries of society from the ground up. Society forms a group of people, which establishes the word "social network (SN)."

Social network analysis (SNA) is figuring out the linkages among social elements and the ramifications of these linkages (Stockman, 2004). It has advanced because people have collaborated. These people were shaped by the endeavors of a sociometrist group that dealt with little gatherings. The fundamental objective of SNA is to inspect connections among people; for example, impact, correspondence, counsel, companionship, trust, and so forth. As specialists keen on the advancement of these connections and the general construction, in addition to their effect on both individual conduct and group execution, they led an exploration to quantify the development of the SNA field for the time frame (1963–2000). They counseled three information bases that identified three parts of science (specifically, humanism, medication, and brain research). Among their discoveries were that the field's genuine development began in 1981 and showed no signs of slowing and that the turn of events in the field occurred faster in social science than in medicine and brain science. They saw that SNA's success in the 1980s was due to the standardization of interpersonal organization research since the late 1970s, as well as the new accessibility of reading material and programming. Today, informal organization experts have a worldwide association called "The International Network for Social Organization Analysis," or INSNA, which holds yearly gatherings and also issues various expert diaries. Furthermore, numerous locations for network research and preparation have opened.

2.2.1 BENCHMARKS OF SOCIAL NETWORKS

The communication between the vertices (nodes) v is linked through edges e. The vertex of a graph can be denoted as v(g), and the edges of the graph can be denoted as e(g). Graph g is forming a network of society. Sub-graph of a graph g is assumed g`, if exists from g to g`.

Data set d = {G_1, G_2, ..., G_n}, of different sets of subgraphs (subgroup) in a social network. Frequently appearing nodes in a social network is no less than the minimum support threshold.

Twitter is a worldwide popular medium in technology to air any opinion with a limitation of 140 characters. Other media are also used, in individual countries for their interest.

Twitter is one of the "micro-blogger" platforms, where users can post and receive messages. Users can link to any unified resource locator (URL) of their choice in their blogs. Aired messages in a blog are referred to as "tweets." Node to node are connected from one to other for personal interest or organization's choices whose tweet is visible in the "timeline." The same tweet can be tweeted by others.

The popularity of tweets depends on the interest, purpose, and uses of another node. Generally, Twitter and blog followers are not visionary. A variety of microblogs are used worldwide like Sina Weibo in China, Twitter in Western countries, etc.

Twitter users are connected from node to node randomly in a spider-web fashion. It might create a variety of logical diagrams of connectivity from one node to another. A user can tweet any message to the next node, which can be retweeted to the other node. There is a chance that a message will be returned to the same node from which it was sent. This situation creates a clique (overlap) of messages to the various nodes. The flow of tweets, retweets, and cliques was shown in a hexagonal Twitter network with 3 degrees of separation in Figure 2.2.

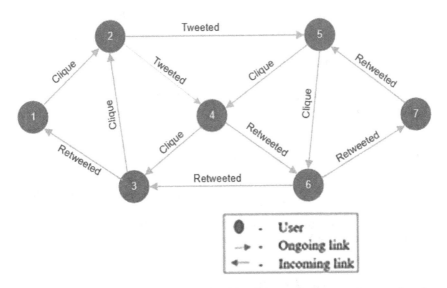

FIGURE 2.2 Hexagonal Twitter network with minimum 3 degrees of separation from nodes 1 to 7.

2.3   ROLE OF SOCIAL MEDIA IN THE DIGITAL AGE

Social media plays a very significant role in the digital world. The rapid growth of social media suggests that India's media will become "all-digital" in the future.

The most important thing is that social media platforms have allowed people all around the world to express their opinions, raise their voices, and share their emotions. A social media user is rewarded with a sense of participation and immediate feedback from a "community" of friends. In other words, social media channels allow the thoughts of people to be open to a large and diverse audience.

For building good human relationships, the majority of companies are now using social media to their advantage. They understand how important social media sites like Twitter, Facebook, LinkedIn, YouTube, Instagram, WhatsApp, and Google+ are for reaching out to prospects, clients, and partners.

Social networking will help you develop and maintain stronger consumer relationships. According to studies, Twitter is the most effective networking tool because it provides real-time updates about what is happening in the world.

Social media was created to enable users to socialize and interact with family and friends, but it was later adopted by various companies looking to expand their businesses and use advanced communication methods to reach out to customers.

Today, because of digital freedom, many big and small companies are using social media to benefit their human relationships. They know the importance of social media platforms such as Twitter, Facebook, LinkedIn, YouTube, Instagram, WhatsApp, and Google+ in reaching prospects, customers, and partners. The key to every successful business is to adopt a fully digital strategy for your company.

2.3.1   JUSTIFICATIONS FOR USING SOCIAL MEDIA IN THE DIGITAL AGE

Marketing: Advertising on popular social media platforms like Twitter, Facebook, Google +, LinkedIn, and YouTube goes viral every day, and it helps a lot with marketing worldwide.

The ability to communicate and connect with your customers is what makes digital marketing so appealing. You learn about their likes and dislikes, as well as gaining information about their daily lives and requirements.

Brand recognition: Social media also helps promote your company and lets you reach out to both existing and future customers. Because the success of your company is also measured by how good you are at raising the visibility and recognition of your brand, products, or services among targeted customers. In short, social media marketing will assist in rising brand recognition and driving traffic to your websites.

Brand loyalty: Today, in this age of digitization, social media marketing is necessary for all organizations, but it's also just the beginning of the process of building brand loyalty. A great digital marketing plan includes having website content that generates sales, a strong SEO strategy, and products that customers genuinely want to buy. Social media marketing will at the very least enhance brand awareness and website traffic.

Search engine optimization (SEO): When someone searches for your company on Google, social profiles are likely to be the first results.

Customer support: Today, we see many people using social media to express their dissatisfaction with organizations. Customers ask questions, offer feedback to a company's customer service team, and seek help.

If there is any problem with your product or service, your company should immediately respond to it. With the feedback of every customer, your company can easily find where the problem arises and will be able to take prompt action to fix it. Today, many major organizations have noticed this and have recruited social media customer support agents to personally communicate on sites like Twitter and Facebook.

Competitors' engagement: The earlier you begin your digital marketing campaigns, the sooner you'll be able to observe the expansion of your business. It is preferable to invest in your internet presence early rather than wait until the last minute and spend a fortune trying to catch up with your rivals.

Increase sales: For a rapid increase in our sales, you need to be very active on social media every day. You can actively connect with your customers by creating campaigns or Facebook contests and offering them a reward, such as a discount coupon. Many big companies offer various discounts on various brands to be successful in a highly competitive world and to run their businesses in the long term.

2.3.2 Freedom of Expression, Speech, and Social Media

The internet and social media have evolved into vital communication tools, allowing people to exercise their right to free expression and exchange information and ideas. In the last year or so, there has been a growing global movement of people advocating for change, justice, equality, accountability of the powerful, and respect for human rights.

The term **"freedom of speech and expression"** means every individual has a fundamental right to express and share their feelings, ideas, opinions, and knowledge freely on the internet without any interference and the fear of threats or harm.

Social media platforms have transformed our way of connecting across social, political, and geographical boundaries. This transformation has created great opportunities for freedom of expression and speech worldwide.

Social media platforms have also evolved as an important source of self-expression. In the current digital age, social media platforms have become such a powerful tool that they have allowed millions of internet users around the world equal access and the freedom to share their thoughts, feelings, and perspectives.

Some of the most widely accepted definitions of freedom of expression that are accepted as genuine international norms are as follows:

- "Everyone has the right to freedom of opinion and expression; this right includes freedom to hold opinions without interference and to seek, receive, and impart information and ideas through any medium and regardless of frontiers." [Article 19, Universal Declaration of Human Rights, 1948 (UDHR)]
- "Everyone shall have the right to hold opinions without interference." "Everyone shall have the right to freedom of expression; this right shall include freedom

to seek, receive, and impart information and ideas of all kinds, regardless of frontiers, either orally, in writing or print, in the form of art, or through any other medium of his choice." [Article 19(2), International Covenant on Civil and Political Rights, 1966 (ICCPR)] (CCLA, 2015).

- "Any restrictions on the operation of websites, blogs, or other internet-based, electronic, or similar information dissemination systems, including systems to support such communication, such as internet service providers or search engines, are only permitted to the extent that they are consistent" with paragraph 3 [Article 19]. In general, legal prohibitions must be content-specific; paragraph 3 is incompatible with general bans on the functioning of particular websites and computer systems. General Observation No. 34 on Freedom of Expression by the Human Rights Committee.

Similarly, citizens of India have the right to "freedom of speech and expression" under Article 19 (1) (a) of the Indian Constitution. The right to freely express one's convictions and beliefs by voice, writing, printing, photographs, or any other method is known as freedom of speech and expression. It also includes the ability to propagate or publish the thoughts of others.

Thus, under the Indian Constitution and other international documents, freedom of speech and expression is recognized as a fundamental right in whatever medium it is exercised. And, given the increasing use of the internet and social media as a medium for exercising this right, access to this medium has also been recognized as a fundamental human right.

Hence, social media is a powerful tool for exercising one's right to free speech and expression, but it's also increasingly being used for illegal security regulations. However, freedom of speech and expression does not guarantee people the right to speak or publish without risk, and the legislature can enact legislation to limit the right to speech and expression for a variety of reasons, because many cybercrimes may be easily committed through social media.

Restrictions on Freedom of Speech and Expression

Freedom of expression is a critical driver of many other human rights. However, as the internet is an important element of human rights it also causes violations and increases their potential harm. Therefore, the law and practice of restrictions must also be implemented accordingly.

Freedom of speech and expression does not mean that any citizen can hold the right to speak or publish without responsibility. It is not an unrestricted permission that grants protection to every imaginable use of language and shields those who abuse this freedom from penalty.

The following grounds constitute limits under Article 19(3) of the ICCPR:

- To respect the rights and reputations of others.
- To safeguard morality, public health, public order, or national security.

The legislature may enact laws restricting the right to free speech and expression on the following grounds, according to Article 19(2) of the Indian Constitution:

- India's sovereignty and integrity
- Security of the state
- Friendly relations with foreign states
- Public order
- Decency or morality
- Contempt of court
- Defamation
- Incitement to an offense

2.3.3 SOCIAL MEDIA CENSORSHIP

In today's world of digitization, it is critical to keep up with the progressive trends. A technologically digitized world with an increasing capacity for communicating, simplifying, and storing information at breakneck speed has placed information at the heart of development (Vyas, 2008). There can be no democratic participation in decision-making without transparency and information sharing. Social media can reach the masses and disseminate information, which has resulted in everyone acting as a watchdog, scrutinizing the powerful, and exposing mismanagement and corruption.

Unlike traditional mass media, which requires permission from media owners like newspaper editors or television stations, social media platforms also enable people to interact with others. Also, states that have long restricted their media have found it more challenging to control the information that is communicated due to the growth of social media. In contrast to visual and print media, information can emerge and spread more quickly on social media without being as easily influenced and banned by governments. Therefore, today with the advent of social media and its immense power to deliver information to the masses, governments are facing big challenges and are working hard to regulate them. As a result, social media platforms have made it easier for people to protest, leak information, plan protests, and criticize governments.

Furthermore, social media platforms have become the foundation of modern civilization due to their limitless possibilities and widespread reach. It has a unique role in the functioning of democracies all over the world due to its importance in the storage and dissemination of information and opinion. Using social media and the internet, citizens can unite across borders. Even though everyone is not physically present, the protest is not diminished in any way. As a result, it is understandable why governments all over the world want to censor the internet.

External Instigation for Censorship

The majority of the main social networking sites have made a public declaration endorsing the principles of transparency and openness. Twitter pledged to promote "the unrestricted flow of knowledge." Facebook also states that its "aim is to offer individuals the power to share and make the world more open and connected," claiming that this will "promote greater understanding" and reduce violent conflict on a global scale. The most repressive and authoritarian countries, especially those ruled by a Communist party or a theocracy, are those that put external pressure on social networking services to censor material or prevent access.

Facebook access has been temporarily restricted or banned in many nations. In other nations, access to the website has also been constrained in many ways. China, Russia, Iran, North Korea, and Syria are the only countries that continue to impose a total ban on access to social networking sites as of July 2022. The only nations where access to Facebook is deliberately prohibited in this way are China, Russia, and Iran, while it is still feasible to access the website through onion services in North Korea because the majority of its citizens do not have access to the internet.

The same kind of pressure has also been applied against democratic countries. For instance, the Indian government has recently made multiple attempts to censor content on social networking sites, urging these companies to do so if users formally report that the content is "disparaging" or "harassing" or if it offends Indians' cultural "sensibilities." Additionally, political and governmental pressure to control the content on social networking sites has been seen in the United States.

2.3.4 REAL-WORLD CASES (1–6)

REAL-WORLD CASE 1 (CHINA)

Under authoritarian systems, social media are much more strictly regulated than in democratic countries. China is particularly aggressive in blocking social networking websites and restricting internet content. China is a country with strong internet and social media restrictions. Therefore, China was ranked as the worst nation in the world in terms of access to the internet and digital media by the NGO Freedom House in 2015. Expression in the nation is severely regulated and controlled because of measures like keyword banning and website censorship implemented by "The Great Firewall of China" (King, Pan and Roberts, 2013).

REAL-WORLD CASE 2 (INDIA)

India has experienced a sharp rise in Internet censorship over the last few years. India updated the IT Act 2000 with the new "IT Rules 2011" in 2011. Internet intermediaries were required by these regulations to delete offensive content within 36 hours of receiving a complaint. The government received criticism in 2011 for requesting that big websites like Google, Facebook, and Yahoo "pre-screen" content and remove any problematic or libelous material before it went live. It was claimed that the government advised internet service providers to employ people rather than machines to complete necessary tasks. (Section 66A of the Information Technology Act, 2000)

In 2012, when two ladies were detained for posting complaints about the disruption of Bal Thackeray, the head of the right-wing Hindu party Shiv Sena, funeral services Facebook, there was a great deal of outrage in India. They were taken into custody by the notorious India IT Act (2008), which makes it illegal to send "grossly offensive and menacing messages sent by electronic means, as well as false messages meant to defraud, deceive, mislead, or irritate, taking online censorship beyond offline regulations" (Section 66A of the Information Technology Act, 2000).

REAL-WORLD CASE 3 (IRAN)

Facebook was prohibited in Iran following the 2009 election over concerns that opposition movements were forming there (Taylor, 2013). However, as of September 2013, it was believed that both Twitter and Facebook had been unintentionally unblocked after four years of the website being blocked for Facebook. The following day, Iranians lost unrestricted access to Facebook and Twitter, leading many to speculate as to whether the opening was intentional or the consequence of a technical error.

REAL-WORLD CASE 4 (RUSSIA)

On February 24, 2022, when Russia invaded Ukraine, it had dramatic consequences for the whole world. This invasion has resulted in the biggest refugee crisis in Europe since World War II and tens of thousands of deaths on both sides. The Russian invasion of Ukraine resulted in a Facebook ban on Russian official media from monetizing material. Russia consequently decided to block access to Facebook and Twitter. The limits, according to the regulatory body Roskomnadzor, were put in place to limit content on Facebook and Twitter that disagreed with the opinions of the Russian government (Emerson and Nieva, 2022).

REAL-WORLD CASE 5 (SYRIA)

According to the Syrian government's justification for the closure, the website encouraged attacks on officials. Israeli penetration of Syrian social networks on Facebook was another concern for the regime. Syrian residents also utilized Facebook to criticize the government of Syria because doing so in public used to be a crime that might result in jail time. All ISPs stopped blocking Facebook in February 2011, and the website is still available (JPOST.COM STAFF, 2007).

REAL-WORLD CASE 6 (NORTH KOREA)

According to The Associated Press, North Korea began censoring Facebook in April 2016, which was "a move highlighting its concern with the proliferation of online information." Without prior approval from the North Korean authorities, anyone attempting to access it risks punishment (Talmadge, 2016).

Internal Instigation for Censorship

Additionally, social networking sites are under internal pressure to restrict their material or deny access to certain members. A few valid and generally apolitical goals may be served by certain kinds of this censorship, with relatively minor negative effects on legitimate First Amendment concerns:

- First, social networking companies may block communications to stop convicted criminals from taking advantage of accusers, witnesses, or victims, or to stop specific individuals from intimidating or harassing other users.
- Second, the removal of pornographic or violent content may contribute to the creation and maintenance of a setting that is appropriate for users of all ages and sensibilities, thereby expanding the site's capacity to act as a forum for public communication and discourse, and boosting its appeal to advertisers.
- Third, such filtering might be required to stop the website from being harmed by phishing and hacker assaults.
- Fourth, such censoring might be required to abide by copyright, trademark, and publicity laws. A certain level of this form of censorship would seem to be necessary to preserve the ambiance that draws users to such sites in the first place, although it does have the potential to be abused or applied too broadly. Social networking services, however, might block content for unsettling reasons.

2.4   ONLINE HATE SPEECH ON SOCIAL MEDIA

Online hate speech is a kind of speech, communication, or behavior that takes place on the internet in the form of speech, messages, or comments, written to target an individual or a community based on their caste, race, color, religion, ethnic origin, sexual orientation, disability, or gender. Hate speech leads to hatred, violence, physical attacks, discrimination, and even deaths within the community or country.

The most common causes of hate speech around the world are religion, caste, or race. With its rich diversity of language, caste, ethnicity, faith, community, and beliefs, India poses a unique case for hate speech regulation.

Hate speech is also categorized as follows:

- Defamation
- National security
- Privacy and security
- Hate speech
- Copyright
- Religious offence
- Fraud
- Obscenity/nudity
- Violence
- Bullying/harassment
- Government criticism
- Suicide promotion
- Other

2.4.1   HATE SPEECH

Thus, "hate speech" is defined as any statements, comments, or remarks that are made either in writing or orally to defame, humiliate, or attack any religion, caste, or cultural group.

Online hate speech is a real-time example of how the internet offers various threats and challenges regarding the freedom of speech and expression while still protecting our human dignity.

Social media platforms like Facebook, Twitter, etc. make it easier to share knowledge and information while also improving accessibility and civic participation. At the same time, they are exposed to fake information and hateful speech, fake memes of politicians, and illegal material or content being posted across the channels by various users.

REAL-WORLD CASE (HATE CRIME IN INDIA)

It can be seen from Table 2.1 that most of the hate crimes reported in India were targeted toward Dalits and Muslims between September 2015 and December 2019 (Bhat, 2020). In 2018, the bench of Chief Justice of Supreme court of India Deepak Mishra, D.Y. Chandrachud, and Ajay Manikrao Khanwilker, warned against India turning into "mobocracy" (Poonawalla, 2018). A total of 902 crimes were reported because of alleged hatred, ranging from caste and religion to killing and love jihad (Kanwal, 2021).

2.4.2   Impact of Social Media and Hate Speech

Today, as a result of digital freedom, social media has become both a blessing and a curse for humans. The freedom of digitalization has made our lives very easy and fast. Despite being so useful and relevant in our lives, many social media platforms today have attacked our privacy and given rise to hate speech.

Misuse of social media has many negative and positive consequences. It has given rise to many consequences like sexual harassment, criminal offenses, hate speech,

TABLE 2.1
Incidents of Hate Crimes in India from 2015 to 2019

Community Targeted	Number of Hate Crime Incidents
Dalits	619
Muslims	196
Others	35
Adivasi	31
Transgender people	29
Christians	18

Source: Kanwal, (November 22, 2021).

violence, illegal discrimination, and invasions of individual privacy. There are both illegal and serious activities that occur as a result of social media abuse.

YouTube, one of the most popular social media platforms, has had a difficult time developing and implementing a clear strategy for deleting and removing hateful content and posts from its platform. According to teachers and many officials, YouTube has quickly become a viral sensation for the videos that provoke "anti-Semitism, bigotry, and homophobia" on the internet as it allows any individual to upload and post hateful or offensive content, which results in various crimes and violence and harms a nation's peace and harmony. In reality, the comment section on YouTube is full of hate speech and derogatory remarks or comments.

Therefore, many countries around the world prohibit hate speech on the internet through various acts and laws under the Criminal Code. The main objective of such laws is to maintain peace and harmony around the world.

Social media platforms like Twitter, Facebook, YouTube, and LinkedIn have developed strict standards and guidelines for the regulation of hate speech on the internet. They have also imposed strict action if they used any of these platforms for fake news or misinformation and provoked violence around the world.

2.4.3 GLOBAL HATE SPEECH

Nearly every continent has reported incidents of hate speech on social media platforms. Nowadays, nearly one-third of the world's population uses Facebook alone as a means of communication. According to experts, as more and more people use the internet, those who are homophobic, sexist, or racist have discovered online communities that can validate their beliefs and incite violence. Social media sites also give violent actors a chance to advertise their performances. Over the past few years, in many countries around the world, lynch mobs and other forms of communal violence have been increasing widely, with several cases stemming from rumors spread through WhatsApp groups.

2.4.4 REAL-WORLD CASES (1–3)

REAL-WORLD CASE 1 (GLOBAL HATE OF INDIA)

Facebook is one of the most powerful and widely used social media platforms in India. However, in recent months, many governments have started to scrutinize the website for what they say is its lax approach to hate speech.

Facebook India has been widely criticized for how it treats and marks hate speech on its website. In order to maintain its relationship with India's ruling party and administration, Facebook is charged with refusing to restrict the unlawful hate speech of Hindu nationalist leaders (Frayer, 2020).

In the context of content limitation, Facebook limited access to 878 contents in response to Ministry of Electronics and Information Technology directives for violating Section 69A of the Information Technology Act of 2000. Nine of them were put on hold for the time being. In response to private allegations of defamation, Facebook also limited access to 143 contents. The business has a limited number of accounts on Instagram (Ajmal, 2021).

In 2021, Facebook said that it is taking steps in India to fight hate speech and misinformation. In terms of users in India, Facebook is the most dominant market. It's WhatsApp messaging program is one of the most popular in the country. Facebook has been chastised around the world for allegedly allowing hate speech to flourish.

The Indian Cyber Crime Coordination Center was established in recent years to speed up investigations. The expansion of the country's cyber security business is another area that could help reduce cybercrime statistics. With the launch of the 5G network and the establishment of the 5G network, more investments in the industry might combat growing dangers (PIB, 2019).

REAL-WORLD CASE 2 (GLOBAL HATE—UNITED STATES)

The Pittsburgh synagogue gunman in 2018 was a user of the social media network Gab, whose weak policies have drawn extremists barred by more established platforms. Before murdering eleven worshipers during a Shabbat service with a refugee theme, he preached there the conspiracy theory that Jews wanted to bring immigrants to the country and make white people a minority. This "great replacement" cliché, which was used at the white nationalist gathering in Charlottesville, Virginia, the year before and which has its roots in the French extreme right, reflects demographic concerns about non-white immigration and birth rates. (Roose, 2018)

REAL-WORLD CASE 3 (GLOBAL HATE—SRI LANKA)

As a result of some extreme Buddhist groups accusing Muslims of forcing people to convert to Islam and vandalizing Buddhist ancient sites, inter-communal hostilities have risen over the past year in Sri Lanka.

Angered by the murder of a driver, Sinhalese Buddhists attacked mosques and Muslim-owned homes in the central Kandy district, a famous tourist destination, resulting in violence that claimed at least two lives. The government of Sri Lanka claims that some of the violence was sparked by Facebook posts threatening additional attacks on Muslims. As a result, Facebook, Viber, and WhatsApp were blocked in March 2018 (Aneez and Sirilal, 2018).

2.5   SOCIAL MEDIA USERS IN ASIA-PACIFIC COUNTRIES

The global freedom of digitization has provided us with an excellent opportunity to welcome the internet with open arms. Google, Facebook, and Twitter, in particular, have become integral parts of the daily lives of millions of users in Asia and the Pacific. Further, the number of social media users in Asia-Pacific (APAC) regions has been steadily increasing as the country's internet penetration has increased. As a result, the development of social media in the Asia-Pacific region has been accelerated by improved internet infrastructure. It can be seen from Table 2.2 that the number of social media users in India is rising with every passing year.

Figure 2.3 shows in the number of social media users who are active is highest in the Eastern Asia region, followed by Southern Asia.

TABLE 2.2
Number of Social Media Users (India) in Percentage Across Demographics

Year	Percentage (%) Users
2015	19.13
2016	22.99
2017	29.49
2018	35.44
2019	46.44
2020	50.44
2021	54.58
2022	58.31
2023	61.66

Source: Basuroy, 2022b.

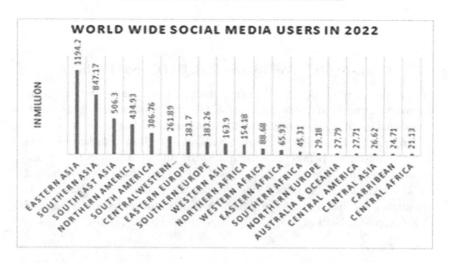

FIGURE 2.3   Worldwide social media users in 2022.

Source: (Dixon, 2023b) Statista.

2.5.1   WHATSAPP USERS IN INDIA AND THE WORLD

WhatsApp is one of the most popular social networking platforms. It was launched in 2010. India is the largest market for WhatsApp, with millions of rising users. You can use WhatsApp to chat, share photos, make voice and video calls with your family and friends, update your status, and even send documents and attachments. WhatsApp has evolved into a convenient way to communicate with those in your social network, and it can also be used by companies to provide fast and easy customer support.

In India, the smartphone and low-cost mobile internet connection have changed many aspects of life, redefining society, culture, politics, commerce, and the media landscape.

In January 2021, Union Minister of India, Mr. Ravi Shankar Prasad, while announcing new social media rules, revealed that WhatsApp is the most used app in India. He revealed the complete statistics on the use of social media apps in India: WhatsApp was the most popular, followed by YouTube, Facebook, Instagram, and Twitter (Chrakravarti, 2021).

According to report of App Annie shared with Mobile Marketer, WhatsApp surpassed Facebook last year as the social network's most popular app by monthly active users on smartphones. According to the survey, WhatsApp outperformed Facebook because of its widespread use in developing nations like Singapore, Russia, Hong Kong, and Malaysia, where owning a mobile device is expensive relative to the average income (Troise et al., 2020).

2.5.2   FACEBOOK USERS IN ASIAN COUNTRIES

Facebook was launched in 2004. With over two billion monthly active users, Facebook is without a doubt the most popular social networking app in the world and is among the most commonly used social networking sites.

In several countries, such as the United States, it is said to be extremely popular, as well as in those in Asia. Facebook is one of the most popular social media networks in Asian countries, including India. India had 314.6 million users in 2023, followed by many other top countries around the world (Dixon, 2023a).

Table 2.3 shows the top ten countries in the world with the most Facebook users, five of which are in Asia. India tops the list, followed by Indonesia, which had a range of 119.9 million Facebook users in 2023.

2.5.3   MOBILE PLATFORMS IN ASIA

Mobile internet is the most common way for consumers in Asia Pacific to access digital services. For people to be able to engage effectively in society, access to quick, dependable, and continuous connectivity has become essential. In Asia Pacific, more than 130 million people signed up for mobile internet services for the first time in 2020 and 2021.

TABLE 2.3
Facebook Users in Asian Countries

Country	Facebook Users 2023 (in Million)
India	314.6
Indonesia	119.9
Philippines	80.3
Vietnam	66.2
Thailand	48.1
Bangladesh	43.25
Egypt	42
Pakistan	37.3
China	3.4
Singapore	3.3

Source: (Dixon, 2023b), Statista.com.

REAL-WORLD CASE: MOBILE-FIRST, PLATFORM-DOMINATED MARKET: INDIA

According to the Reuters India Digital News research, smartphones are the primary device for getting online news for 68% of respondents. Surprisingly, 31% of respondents stated that they only use mobile devices to access internet news (Aneez et al., no date).

According to the Reuters survey, Facebook and WhatsApp are particularly popular, with 75% of respondents using Facebook and 82% using WhatsApp to acquire their news. Instagram (26%) is the most popular social media platform for news, followed by Twitter (18%) and Facebook Messenger (16%) (Aneez et al., no date).

In less than a decade, India has transformed into a mobile-first, platform-dominated media market. In other words, following print, television, and the Internet, social media is the fourth generation (4G) of media. Moreover, the popularity of regional language programming has exploded, with Hindi, Marathi, Tamil, Telugu, Kannada, and Bengali topping the lists. In India, three out of every four users make use of social media in their native language. Mobile internet tariffs in India are among the cheapest in the world, which is a significant element in this regard.

As a result of this, rural areas have a higher percentage of mobile internet users than urban areas. This has also helped to bridge the gap between the digital divide and the control of a small English-language elite over content development, distribution, and consumption.

Connectivity

The foundation of a fully developed digital society is connectivity. Both 3G and 4G networks have had 100% population coverage in the city-state since 2013, and 71% of people will have access to 5G networks by the end of 2020. The introduction of 5G networks and improvements to the current 4G infrastructure are significantly affecting network performance. For instance, Singapore's average download speed rose by 15% in 2020, hitting 60 Mbps. Singapore is one of only four nations in the Asia Pacific region to have a commercial 5G standalone (SA) network, the others being Australia, South Korea, and Thailand (GSMA, 2021).

The deployment of the latest network generation has advanced for other Asia Pacific 5G leaders. For instance, by the end of 2020, South Korea will have 98% of its population covered by 5G. This has encouraged the uptake of 5G services, with 5G already accounting for more than 25% of all mobile connections in the nation (GSMA, 2021).

2.5.4 CURRENT TRENDS IN MEDIA AND SOCIAL CHANGE

Nearly half of the world's population is connected to social media. It allows people to make their voices heard and to communicate in real-time all around the world. Social media has also played a very significant role by enabling people to connect and exchange information and ideas very quickly. We share our feelings by sending or receiving photos and videos with our family and friends because social media has become such an important part of our daily lives.

The mass media is an essential institution of society that meets the social and economic demands of larger social groupings. Developing nations like India have relied heavily on the mass media for years. The media, in particular in the post-globalization period, must educate people on how to adapt their traditional attitudes to new progressive requirements.

Social movements are partly on the decline in the age of globalization since everything is viewed from a materialist point of view. The remark that "Movements also critically build upon existing human and material resources" has been made with good reason (Mcquail, 1980). Such resources are scarce, and issues are more complicated in developing nations. Regarding social movements in the age of globalization, it has been noted that "the term globalization has become dominant in discourses about social, economic, and cultural processes in contemporary society" (Berger, 2012). In a nation like India, the globalization process has had an impact on rural groups in addition to metropolitan ones.

Sociological perspective: The media is a force for change (Mcquail, 1980). The issue of whether or not the media is indeed a force for social change is raised. Infotainment syndrome in media needs to end.

Socialization is facilitated by the media. "What is essential about informal socialization is that people generally do not perceive that they are being taught what roles to play and how to play them, what values to espouse, what attitudes to have, what aims to strive for, and so forth" (Berger, 2012). It is very possible to explore the special role that the media may play in a nation like India. Value erosion is a significant issue in the post-globalization period. Media can withstand the collapse of values in a capitalist society. Media critics "must be aware of the values represented by the characters portrayed in mass-produced media and should assess what these values say about society," according to a statement made in the field (Gisbert, 2011).

In today's multicultural and multidimensional society, media can strengthen moral and spiritual values. As Berger correctly noted, "Media analysis ought to bear in mind that they are concerned with works of art when they evaluate sitcoms." The public arts serve as the foundation for media content. TV shows in India have a huge impact on societal mindset, also known as social milieu and cultural ethos, whether directly or indirectly. Institutions are typically defined as some permanent and recognized norms of procedure managing the relations between individuals and groups (Gisbert, 2011). The media is a type of social institution that is important, current, and effective today. Traditional media and mass media are closely related to each other. The issue of folkways and mores is said to be intimately tied to traditions and institutions, with which we have been dealing thus far. Folk media can be incorporated with contemporary electronic media to promote societal change.

Media and social change (future challenges): To affect societal change today in this digital age, the media must overcome numerous obstacles. "Globalization's spread has increased interest in sustainable development and the eradication of poverty" (Basudeb, 2013). In India's agro-based society, the media may inform citizens about sustainable development. However, when excellent governance is achieved, the media's role can be productive and supportive. Although there are more socioeconomic development programs in India, their quicker execution alone can effect change.

India's mass media must close the gap between urban and rural areas because villagers do not always benefit equally from progress. Media can be a tool for bringing about social and cultural change. "Socio-cultural language is the purpose of development communication" (Nair and White, 1996).

Changing media priorities: In the process of bringing about societal transformation, mass media should present fresh opportunities. Receiving feedback is crucial for improving accuracy (Joseph, 1997). The media currently receives relatively little feedback. According to additional research, "the term mass communication must suggest at least five characteristics: (a) reasonably large audiences (b) fairly unequal audience composition (c) some form of message reproduction (d) rapid distribution and delivery (e) and (e) low consumer unit cost." The media is a purely urban phenomenon in India in this perspective. If media is accessible to the underprivileged at a lower cost, it can be mass-produced. To improve stimulus responses, media mechanisms need to be modified.

Thus, the media and society do not always communicate well with one another. Increasing awareness at different levels is more crucial. India demands more equitable communication because it is morally just and practically more useful. As a result, bringing about social change in India is fraught with difficulty. Numerous people can be engaged in social change through media. By fostering an information community that is technologically advanced and rich in information, it can eventually influence progressive principles and change Indian culture from one that is rooted in tradition to one that is modern. Only the use of mass media and digital freedom may lead to a change in the future.

2.5.5 REAL-WORLD CASES

India is currently the world's second-most populous nation after China, with a population of over 1.1 billion people. Nearly 70% of the population is active on social media. The users of social media have been steadily increasing by double digits every year.

India is the second-largest international market after China. It can be seen that the number of social media users in India and the world is rapidly growing, and it is estimated that there will be tremendous growth in the future. One of the most important reasons for this growth is the Indian government's "Digital India" initiative.

The number of people using social media in India is increasing rapidly due to the availability of low-cost prepaid connections, such as the free Jio Sim launched by the Reliance Industries and low-cost internet-enabled handsets in the beginning and JioFi in 2021. Competitors like Vodafone and Airtel India also launched many plans. Almost all the service providers are giving 1 GB of data each month free, which is helping people with digital freedom.

Several internet-based firms, like Zomato, cab aggregator Ola, UrbanClap, and many more, had their growth spurred by the widespread internet access, and the development of this ecosystem facilitated the delivery and cashless transactions throughout the pandemic. Mobile data revolution can also be credited with the emergence of OTT platforms in India like Netflix and Amazon (Sharma, 2021).

According to the data in Table 2.4 below, when the researcher looked into the demographics of Indian users, he discovered that the most influential, nation-building college students are actively devoting their time to social media, accounting for 33% of all users, followed by young men at 27% (Nasir, Khatoon, and Bhardwaj, 2018).

TABLE 2.4
Percentage of Social Media Users Across Demographic Groups

Category	Number of Users in Percentage (%)
College students	33%
Young men	27%
Non-working women	11%
Older men	10%
School kids	12%

Source: Table developed by the authors.

2.6 THE RISE OF E-VIOLENCE AND CYBERCRIMES ON SOCIAL MEDIA

The role of social media is very influential in our society, in both positive and negative ways. No doubt, digital freedom has made social media a critical component of today's digital society. Using numerous social media platforms such as Facebook, Twitter, Instagram, and others, networking and engaging with friends and family has grown faster. However, the misuse of social media has had a severe impact on our society. This has given rise to e-violence and cybercrime in many ways.

Because it is an easy, cheaper, simpler, and faster way of communicating and disseminating ideological views, executing hidden plans, and promoting terrorist organizations, social media platforms have also given rise to terrorism, abuse, E-violence, and crimes in today's digital world.

Social media has given rise to different illegal and criminal activities, which has forced the government to impose certain regulations on social media users. As a result, legal censorship and the installation of strong cyber laws have become critical to secure all of our sensitive information from cybercriminals on social media.

2.6.1 DIFFERENT TYPES OF CYBER CRIMES

The National Cyber Crime Reporting Portal highlights the following cybercrimes (Puroshothaman, 2019):

Identity theft: This is becoming increasingly common in social networking. Identity theft is the attempt to access a person's data for illegal purposes. In this type of crime, criminals obtain personal information about the victim from social media sites. It is used to steal someone else's identity to commit fraud or steal their money. Criminals utilize their stolen identities to purchase unlawful items, commit crimes, etc.

Scam or fraud on the internet: Another type of internet fraud is the cloning of a person's account to obtain personal information. The offenders use the images and photographs to create a new account and then cheat friends and relatives into providing bank account details or other important information. They may also send obscene content to create disrespect.

Phishing and email scams: Phishing is another type of cybercrime that occurs when a false email purporting to be from a specific organization requests confidential personal and financial information. Cybercriminals used this to commit various crimes and unlawful activities such as espionage to steal personal information such as passwords, usernames, credit card details, bank details, and so on. As a result, the user is duped into providing their personal information, which they then use to their advantage.

Cyberbullying: Social media has also rapidly increased the risk of cyberbullying. The basic platform for such issues is social media networking on sites like Facebook and WhatsApp. Furthermore, cyberbullying and cyber theft are very common among teenagers on social media. Because of the lack of privacy in social media, the chances of a third party misusing a person's private information are very high. The main reason for this problem is social media because it is simple and fast. Most internet users upload vulgar pictures or videos, make derogatory comments, spread fake news or information, send abusive messages, and post various content related to religion, caste, etc., which would later become a major subject of worldwide controversy. Over the past few years, for instance, intolerant and extremist terrorists are pushing all sorts of racism in society, causing horrific harm to several families around the world, whether through their hate speech online or online calls for infiltration and violent campaigns.

Malware attacks: Cybercrime manifests itself in a variety of ways, such as the use of sophisticated tools like malware to attack our social media identities, or they can easily access our personal information on social networking sites and shopping websites. Another method is to create a fake account on social media to defame another person or steal our private data on social networking sites and E-Commerce platforms. Another significant type is a gender-based attack or an attack on minors. Child pornography is also increasing at a fast rate in cyberspace, and women and minor children are the primary victims because the offender's identity is unknown.

2.6.2 MOST COMMON TYPES OF CYBER CRIMES

Hacking is the illegal use of numerous social media networks to gain unauthorized access to computers or other digital devices. The hackers, who are commonly associated with cyber criminals, send messages to social media users. This happens when the user clicks on those malicious links and gets compromised by thieves. Cybercriminals can access a targeted user's digital device via many different techniques (Alferidah, Khalid, and Jhanjhi, 2020). Victims may get malicious links from the attackers that, when clicked, take users to other pages with harmful outcomes.

Spamming: Social media forums may be used by cybercriminals to spread unlawful information through the use of information that is typically sent in writing as a message to users of social media. Spam was initially more prevalent through emails, but it has recently become more prevalent through social media forums. It happened via the distribution of communications with harmful links that are unlawful. A spammer can direct undesired mass communications by posting a large number of links in the form of advertisements or personal messages using a fictitious identity (Patel, 2017). Attackers may send hazardous links to their intended victims, and when they are clicked, the users are taken to other pages with harmful outcomes.

Cyberstalking is defined as the intentional and hostile use of the internet and other cutting-edge technology to hurt others. It may also use email threats with inappropriate content such as naked pictures, films of abuse or obscenity, and sending derogatory remarks that may be used and leave the victim feeling irritated, violated, and emotionally depressed.

The most widely used stalking tactic for both male and female victims is receiving unwanted phone calls, voicemails, and texts.

Malware attacks can destroy the security of data protection. Three types of malware exist for social networking websites: Trojans, clickjacking, and cross-site scripting (XSS) (NW3C, 2013). Criminals can employ cross-site scripting to spread malicious malware on social networking platforms to collect user data. When employed against web applications, XSS is a threat that attackers or cybercriminals can use to download malware, steal cookies, or take over a user's account on a social network.

A Trojan is a virus that contains a secret code and is used to steal someone's private information. This type of malware threat is fairly widespread on social media networks. It is used as a fraud method by criminals to gather confidential data and steal cash from bank accounts (Fughani, Matrawy, and Lung, 2012). The Clickjacking worm is an additional variety of social networking malware. In click-jacking, the cybercriminal builds a website to attract social media users. Users who click on that link will have secret links that will redirect them to another page. Upon clicking on the links, the users find it on the walls of their friends, and they often press on that page and become infected.

2.6.3 CYBERCRIMES ON SOCIAL MEDIA

In the same way that technological improvements can be used to manage, deter, prevent, and prosecute crime, in the same way, a criminal utilizes social media to commit a crime, technological improvements can be used to control, deter, protect, and prosecute crimes. It is important to include security precautions, like using the current and latest versions of antivirus software, keeping all software up-to-date, learning the fundamentals of security, and using protected and strong passwords.

Below are the common cybercrimes and the potential security measures to stop them in detail.

For spamming:
- Filter for spam
- Tools for identifying different kinds of spammers
- Internal defense systems
- Test with the "Completely Automated Public Turing Test to Tell Computers and Humans Apart" (CAPTCHA) every time
- Enabling verification

For hacking:
- Offering appropriate security tools
- Enabling authentication
- Making use of firewalls
- Anti-virus protection software

For malware attacks:
- Antivirus and anti-malware software
- An index of threat-reduction tactics
- Virus gateway
- IPS Systems for protecting against or recognizing interruptions
- Threats involving emails are lessened by the whole protection stack
- Firewalls

- A security program for email
- Avoid clicking on suspicious messages
- Programs for XSS and SQL injection should be carefully implemented to avoid attacks
- Detection of malware with a signature
- Anomaly-based malware detection

For phishing:
- CAPTCHA
- Electronic certifications or digital certificates
- Using genetic- and attribute-based anti-phishing algorithms
- Methods like the IREP, C4.5 algorithm, and neural network
- Anti-phishing software
- One-time password (OTP)
- Do not click on suspicious links or visit suspicious websites
- Users should be educated about cybercrime, particularly phishing

For online identity theft:
- 3FA (three-factor authentication)
- Use of biometrics
- Methods such as outlier identification, logistic regression, genetic algorithms, SD and CD algorithms
- Identity theft prevention software, such as Symantec's LifeLock
- Refrain from communicating any personal information to strangers by email or verbally
- Limit the quantity of personal data you post online,
- Using authentication techniques such as CAPTCHA and multi-factor authentication (MFA)

2.6.4 PREVENTION AND SECURITY MEASURES

Other than the above-mentioned security and prevention methods, there are some other security rules and procedures like passwords and backup data, as well as hardware and software technologies like fault-tolerant computers and security monitors. At many businesses today, all are part of an integrated security management effort.

Strong passwords: For each account, use a different username and password combination and avoid writing them down. For security management, a layered password scheme is typically employed. An end user must first provide their identifying code, or user ID, to access the computer system. The end user is then required to enter a password to access the system. Passwords should be regularly updated and contain uncommon combinations of upper- and lower-case letters and numerals. Third, a distinct file name must be entered to access a specific file. In certain systems, a different password is needed to read a file's contents than to write to it.

Secure your monitors: System software packages known as "system security monitors" may be used to secure a network. Programs called system security monitors to keep an eye on how computers and networks are used while guarding against fraud, unauthorized usage, and destruction. These tools offer the security controls required to restrict network access to authorized users. Passwords and identifying codes, for instance, are widely used in this manner. The utilization of a computer system's hardware, software, and data resources is also governed by security monitors. For instance, access to particular hardware, software, and data files may be restricted, even for authorized users.

Protect your mobile phones: Many individuals are unaware that unwanted software, such as computer viruses and hackers, can also infect their mobile devices. Make sure to only get the software downloaded from reliable sources. It's also crucial to keep your operating system updated. Always install anti-virus software on your mobile phones. Use a secure lock screen as well, just to be safe. Otherwise, anyone could see all of your private information if you lose your phone or simply leave it on the table for a short period. Even worse, someone might infect your computer with malicious software and utilize your GPS to follow your every move.

Create backup files: Duplicate data or program files are known as backup files, and it is important to always create backup copies of your important files to lower your risk of losing them due to a virus, computer failure, theft, or tragedy. Keep all of your important files in one location on the hard disk of your computer so that you can quickly make a backup copy. Save duplicates of your files on a CD, the internet, or a USB disk. To prevent theft or fire, keep your backup media in a safe location away from the computer. Periodically check the backup media to ensure that the files are usable.

Additionally, there is a file retention method, which entails keeping copies of files from earlier times and can also protect files. If the current files are destroyed, the files from earlier times can be used to create new current files. For control purposes, multiple generations of files may occasionally be retained. Therefore, master files from various recent processing periods (also referred to as child, parent, and grandparent files) may be stored as a backup.

Online identity protection: It is preferable to be overly cautious when it comes to online identity protection. You must be extremely cautious while disclosing personal information online, such as your name, address, phone number, or financial information. Always check that the websites are secure before making any online purchases or other activities. As the number of cybercrimes increases day by day, a user must enable their privacy settings when using or logging onto social networking sites.

Blacklisting: "Blacklisting" is monitoring all sources trying to connect to and exchange data with a certain system. Many organizations now use blacklistings to safeguard themselves against phishing emails and websites. Each source's standing is evaluated, and the information it provided is examined for evidence of harmful code or content. Any sources identified as malicious are subsequently added to a "blacklist" and barred from the network. Software like Symantec's LifeLock and McAfee collects information from a variety of sources to assess if a website, file, or other computer system poses a security risk and, if so, whether it should be blacklisted. To restrict illegal content on the internet, the governments of various countries, like Australia, have already taken steps to establish a network blacklist (Australian Bankers Association, no date).

Controlling computer failure: There is a range of controls that can stop or lessen the effects of computer failure. Power outages, electrical circuitry issues, telecommunications network issues, hidden programming flaws, computer infections, operator errors, and electronic vandalism are only a few of the causes of computer system failure. Computers can be maintained remotely and automatically. Programs for managing software upgrades and preventive hardware maintenance are commonplace. It is possible to set up a backup computer system using disaster recovery companies. To prevent issues, major hardware or software modifications are typically meticulously planned and carried out. Finally, to maintain a company's computer systems and networks, highly educated data center staff as well as the use of performance and security management tools are essential.

Error-tolerant system: Many companies today utilize error-tolerant computer systems, which feature backup processors, peripherals, and software and offer fail-over functionality to support individual components in the case of system failure. If there is a significant hardware or software failure, this system might include a fail-safe feature that allows the computer system to keep running at the same level. However, many error-tolerant computer systems provide a fail-soft feature, allowing the system to continue functioning at a reduced but acceptable level in the event of a significant system failure.

Disaster recovery system: Disasters can be both natural and man-made. The computing infrastructure of an organization can be seriously harmed by fires, earthquakes, floods, terrorist attacks, criminal activity, and human error. Losing even a few hours of processing power can destroy a lot of businesses, especially online E-Commerce shops and wholesalers, airlines, banks, and Internet service providers. Without computing resources, many businesses could only last a few days. For this reason, businesses create disaster recovery processes and formally document them in a disaster recovery plan. It details the personnel who will assist in disaster recovery and their responsibilities, as well as the facilities, equipment, and software that will be used, the order in which applications will be handled, and the personnel who will use the facilities. Effective disaster recovery plans also include agreements with other businesses for the use of alternate premises as a disaster recovery site and off-site database storage.

Information system controls: Information system controls are techniques and tools that make an effort to guarantee the reliability, legitimacy, and propriety of information system operations. It is necessary to create information system (IS) controls to guarantee accurate data entry, processing, storage, and output. The quality and security of the input, processing, output, and storage operations of any information system are therefore monitored and maintained by IS controls.

Secure wireless fidelity (Wi-Fi) and network connections: Unsecured Wi-Fi networks in various locations provide additional assistance to cyber criminals. These Wi-Fi connections may pose as trustworthy Wi-Fi networks or may have already been compromised by malicious parties before other users connected to them. Even when using a Virtual Private Network (VPN), the link ultimately establishes a connection to a hacked Wi-Fi network. Therefore, organizations should develop strong information security rules, including extensive logging and monitoring procedures and data access control. Every remote connection should have the proper configurations in place at both ends to avoid malicious use. Additionally, employees shouldn't be granted administrative privileges on systems that belong to their employers.

Stay away from unknown emails: Even when a questionable email appears to be from a friend, avoid clicking any links from unknown sources or websites. The most common online hazard for identity theft is email-borne malware and viruses. Consider how many emails you received in the last year that appeared to be from friends but were sent by strangers.

Protect personal information: Always be alert and understand how to spot phishing. For example, your bank will already have your sensitive account and personal information, such as your password and personnel identification number (PIN), so it won't send you an email informing you that your account has been compromised and requesting that you update it. Never answer emails that request personal information. Also, do not disclose your OTP (one-time password) to anyone; even your bank will not request it. These are phishing attempts. Don't post your complete date of birth, including the year, on Facebook.

Parental guidance and supervision: Today, in this world of digitization, it is the responsibility of parents to always keep an eye on their children's online activities and behaviors. Parents should also constantly guide and educate their children regarding the pros and cons of using digital tools and technology, social media, and the cybercrimes that are increasing on the internet. Parents should always keep an eye on all browser and email activities, and children should only have access to one computer that is centrally located in their house. Using parental control software that restricts the kinds of websites a user can access is a smart move.

2.6.5 ADVANCED TECHNOLOGIES TO STOP CYBER ATTACKS

Effective anti-cybercrime measures are frequently more successfully implemented in conjunction with the application of new digital technologies. To pinpoint these key nodes within the ecosystem of cybercrime, existing and new technologies may be very helpful. Therefore, security and risk management leaders must fully engage with the most recent technological advancements.

Big data analytics (BDA): To detect and stop financial crimes like illegal financial flows (IFF), BDA serves as a significant and increasingly effective method (Tropina, 2017). BDA is becoming the tool of choice for those fighting financial crime as a result of the exponential expansion of electronic transactions and the rising volumes of unstructured data. It gives users the ability to handle enormous volumes of data, look at nonlinear datasets, uncover or foresee crime trends, and connect seemingly unrelated pieces of information. Additionally, it enables users to recognize possible unlawful behavior, comprehend it better by examining the connections between parties, and form predictions. Additionally, BDA is also quite effective in spotting new forms of growing payment fraud, such as cryptocurrency.

Artificial intelligence (AI) and machine learning (ML): AI and ML play a significant role in the current cybersecurity environment, and both can be utilized to implement various cybersecurity measures. Machine learning is being used more and more to combat E-Commerce fraud. Many pieces of information regarding suspected fraudsters are presently available, including their purchase history and profile, online surfing habits, social media usage, and the false identification they present to have their orders accepted.

Blockchain technology: Blockchain is a digital ledger that stores transactions as blocks and is openly accessible and decentralized. This ledger's ability to be immutable and to restrict access to authorized members helps in the transparent storage of information. By using public key infrastructure to authenticate participants and encrypt their communication, blockchain improves user confidentiality. Blockchain can provide sophisticated security measures. Data is stored safely and securely because of the blockchain's main nature of immutability and the recording of any changes. Due to the decentralized nature of blockchain systems, a single node failure does not affect the network as a whole. Since a history of each transaction is kept, it is always possible to search for it. The Blockchain Network's participants digitally sign the transaction data to guarantee transparency.

Cloud computing: A branch of cybersecurity focused on protecting cloud computing systems is called "cloud security," also referred to as "cloud computing security." The security measures in place maintain regulatory compliance, safeguard data privacy, offer governance, manage data retention, and regulate authentication and access to data.

Black hole and sink hole: Black hole and sink hole routing are two distinct methods for rerouting and preventing harmful online traffic, especially distributed denial of service (DDoS) assaults. Black hole routing is the technique of routing all communication intended for a computer that is being attacked to an inactive, void router known as a "black hole." The harmful components in this internet traffic eventually run out of places to stop.

Sinkhole routing is the technique of sending all web traffic to a machine that is under attack through a router called a "sinkhole" that analyzes the traffic. It allows web traffic to proceed to its destination as the sinkhole router examines, blocks, and tracks any malicious activity.

Biometrics: Today, in this digital world, biometric security is becoming a rapidly expanding field of cyber security around the world in all spheres of life. The term "biometrics" is a combination of the Greek words "bios," which means "life," and "metrics," which means "measuring." It is described as automating the analysis of biological and behavioral traits to identify individuals. These are security measures offered by computer systems that analyze genetic patterns, facial identification, voice recognition, fingerprints, hand geometry, retina scans, signature dynamics, keystroke analysis, and other physical characteristics that make each person unique. To measure and digitize a biometric profile of a person's fingerprints, voice, or other bodily characteristics, biometric control systems employ specialized sensors. The digitized signal is processed, and its results are compared to an individual's previously processed profile that is kept on the magnetic disk. If the profiles match, the person is granted access to secure system resources and is permitted admission into a computer network.

Smart cards are used to prevent online fraud and identity theft. Smart cards are small cards that fit in your pocket that include a microchip inside that allows them to store a lot of data, encrypt data, and connect to other devices. A smart card may resemble a credit card or an identity card, among other things. In terms of cybersecurity, smart cards can be used to authorize and carry out financial transactions online by inserting them into a reader. Smart cards can provide additional sources of verification, such as encrypted card identifiers and unique PINs, to make it more difficult to commit fraud and identity theft by identifying and blocking transactions coming from suspicious locations. Smart cards can automatically and randomly encrypt the data transferred in an online transaction to prevent tampering by cyber criminals. As a result, numerous financial institutions have already adopted smart card technology in many countries.

The Fourth Industrial Revolution: Several social, political, cultural, and economic revolutions are occurring in the twenty-first century, and the Fourth Industrial Revolution signals these developments (Schwab, 2016). The biggest aim of the Fourth Industrial Revolution is to increase income levels and enhance living standards for people all around the world. High-speed internet access, cloud technologies, data science, and other technologies are the driving forces behind the envisioned fourth industrial revolution's emerging technologies. It will also extensively rely on robotics engineering and technologies, augmented reality technology, additive manufacturing, AI technologies and their sub-fields, the Internet of Things (IoT), and Industrial Internet of Things (IIoT) devices. This also has important implications for cybersecurity due to the complexity of cyber-attack landscapes brought on by bio-inspired and AI-based cyber-attacks.

2.6.6 COMBATING CYBERCRIME: CHALLENGES

Cybercrime poses a multifaceted threat to society, with a growing number of attacks on individuals, companies, and governments. Security is directly threatened by the use of cybercriminal technologies, which are becoming more and more crucial in the facilitation of terrorism and the majority of organized crime.

Loss of data and evidence: As the world becomes more and more digitalized, electronic evidence might displace traditional kinds of evidence as the foundation for the investigation and prosecution of any type of criminal conduct. As all the data is frequently erased, loss of evidence is a very frequent and visible issue. Further data collection outside of the territorial area paralyzes the system for investigating cybercrime.

Encryption: It has been acknowledged as a significant obstacle in the global fight against cybercrime that criminals are misusing encryption techniques to conceal their conversations or stored data, conceal their financial transactions, and evade detection due to weak passwords. There must be strong encryption tools, as they ensure the protection of our most fundamental human rights and the security of our digital economy. However, the usefulness and efficacy of these technologies also provide considerable opportunities for illegal activity.

Encryption is now a standard feature in the services offered by an increasing number of electronic service providers. Tools that enable personal encryption and/ or anonymization of communications and other data are widely available and being marketed at the same time. As a result, current investigation methods, like the legal interception of communications, are losing their effectiveness or even becoming technically impractical. The documented increasing and expanding adoption of operational security measures, such as the use of multi-layered encryption by terrorists, cybercriminals, and other serious organized criminal organizations, significantly impedes investigations. A major challenge for the identification and removal of online child sexual exploitation material is the fact that child sex offenders, for instance, are continuously and increasingly using online anonymity and encryption tools, including end-to-end encrypted apps, to store and share material with lower risks of being discovered (CSEM).

Cryptocurrencies are considered an essential element for carrying out many of the crimes committed online. Cryptocurrencies continue to be the mainstream of illegal digital transactions and make it possible to plan, carry out, and profit from cybercrime because of their pseudonymization and decentralized architecture. Criminals are increasingly focusing on customers and intermediates, such as wallet owners, currency exchanges, and mining firms, as the price of some of the most well-known cryptocurrencies, such as Bitcoin, Ethereum, or Monero, rises. Consequently, a lot of investors are attempting to profit from its rising costs. More than 300,000 transactions per day are now being made using Bitcoin. For example, an international organized crime group obtained login information from hundreds of banking institution customers in 2018 and then used the information to steal €1 million in cash (Europol 2018, p. 55).

The prospects for detection and asset recovery, as well as the prevention of fraudulent transactions, are complicated by the growing criminal usage of decentralized crypto-currencies, along with the increased abuse of tumbler/mixer services and crypto-currency exchangers. Cybercrime investigations are made more difficult by the absence of norms for due diligence and know-your-Customer (KYC).

Cybercriminals continue to take advantage of cryptocurrencies, with Bitcoin serving as the preferred medium of exchange on illegal markets and as payment for online extortion schemes like ransomware and DDoS attacks. As a result, when conducting criminal investigations, law enforcement generally uses Bitcoin as a kind of cryptocurrency. The use of Bitcoin ATMs by criminals, which is continuously expanding, is one of the more recent phenomena. On the other side, as access to anonymous cards was restricted in early 2018, the misuse of bitcoin-topped-up debit cards significantly declined. According to recent trends, respectable cryptocurrency users and businesses are increasingly becoming victims of cybercrime.

Rise of illicit financial flows (IFF): Money that has been earned, moved, or utilized outside of legal channels is referred to as an IFF (World Bank 2017, p. 36). In this digital world, IFFs harm national economies, particularly in developing nations. As a result, cybercrime and IFFs are increasingly intertwined, resulting in a growing illegal digital economy.

All IFF-related operations can be dramatically impacted by emerging digital technologies. These technologies are increasingly being used by criminals as "cross-cutting variables" to support other criminal activities. An organized group of criminals increasingly use the internet to perform illegal activities like fraud, phishing, online theft, corruption, tax evasion, and other crimes, both in developed and developing nations. Criminals profit from the digital world's anonymity, complexity, and frequent lack of adequate regulations, as evidenced by illegal activities such as Darknet, cryptocurrencies, gambling, and others. These factors make it possible to transfer money, engage in money laundering, and trade in illegal goods (Tropina, 2016).

Loss of location and legal issues: Loss of location may also lead to ambiguity regarding the jurisdiction for the execution of procedural rules. The rise in criminal use of crypto-currencies and encryption tools has also created circumstances in which law enforcement is no longer reasonably able to pinpoint the location of the offender, the criminal enterprise, or the electronic evidence, In these circumstances, it is frequently unclear which nation has jurisdiction as well as the legal framework that governs the gathering of evidence in real-time or the employment of unique investigative capabilities, such as tracking criminal activity online and using a variety of undercover tactics. Additionally, because cloud-based services and storage are becoming more popular, the actual locations of the data kept there may vary.

It is increasingly clear that "conventional" instruments of cooperation, such as mutual legal aid regimes, are inefficient in the digital age. As a result, the international community must search for new assistance mechanisms.

Jurisdictional challenges: It can be challenging and time-consuming to determine the correct jurisdiction in an international setting to control the preservation and gathering of evidence from Electronic Service Providers, who are frequently based in multiple nations. The task is centered on achieving effective international legal cooperation. The majority of the time, victims and perpetrators are situated in various legal jurisdictions. Therefore, those cases can only be resolved if national legal systems are in line with one another and efficient methods for cooperation exist. Therefore, a comprehensive worldwide effort to combat cybercrime entails harmonizing the relevant portions of local criminal laws and establishing robust procedural powers (World Bank 2017, p. 26).

Inadequate strategic approaches and poor legal systems: According to expert research, to effectively combat cybercrime, strategic and legal frameworks are crucial. National cybersecurity strategies have not been adopted by many developing countries. Unfortunately, as many developing countries lack appropriate legal frameworks for electronic evidence and cybercrime, It is estimated that more than two-thirds of nations in Africa, the Americas, Asia, and Oceania believe their cybercrime laws are only partially sufficient or nonexistent (UNODC, 2013). As a result, when choosing a site to operate from, organized criminal groups take a lot of things into account. The quality of the rule of law is one of the most crucial elements. Cybercriminals always choose safe locations, thinking that poor regulations and poor law enforcement will make it more difficult for them to be caught and convicted and reduce the expected punishment (Kshetri, 2010).

Emerging technologies: With the freedom of digitalization, technological advancement provides a plethora of continually changing tools for cybercrime. This becomes more challenging because new technical developments, uses, and upcoming technologies provide more challenging situations. Law enforcement and the court must constantly improve their procedures and invest in information, equipment, and skills to keep up with technological advancements. This requires time and resources that public bodies frequently lack, especially in developing nations. Keeping up with technology developments results in operational complications and makes it tough to address basic security issues. The technologies that promote innovation and benefit society frequently hinder law enforcement authorities' efforts.

Development of digital infrastructure: Cybersecurity will be significantly impacted by how digital infrastructure develops in emerging nations. Technically speaking, older wireless network generations that are extensively utilized in developing nations are more vulnerable to cyberattacks. To prevent becoming the targets of and tools for attacks on the global digital infrastructure, developing nations must improve and strengthen their systems.

Human rights challenges: There is a need to strike a balance between security and citizen rights and freedoms, particularly the right to privacy and freedom of expression. Governments must design and implement strong legislative safeguards and standards to deal with this area (World Bank 2017, pp. 171–177). It is crucial to note that, contrary to common belief, security measures do not always infringe on people's freedoms. On the contrary, they could greatly help to protect those rights if done correctly and by legal protection.

Role of the private sector: The growing importance of the commercial sector in countering cybercrime is another obstacle since many cases cannot be resolved without the participation of the private sector. Private businesses rule the digital world; they own and run infrastructure, offer goods and services to customers, and manage databases. They frequently have exclusive access to the information and potential evidence needed for an inquiry. Therefore, law enforcement agencies rely on partnerships with businesses, many of which are international. Governments must consequently create effective public–private cooperation channels by initiating, fostering, and advancing global initiatives.

Insufficient funds: Cybersecurity initiatives must be as efficient and cost-effective as possible because developing countries frequently have extremely few resources. These nations don't have enough money to support programs that would cover the basics of cybersecurity. Security is frequently not the first choice for expense allocation for the majority of businesses. Decisions must therefore be carefully considered and prioritized by region. As a result, businesses also don't seem to be very interested in spending money on or putting cybersecurity safeguards in place.

2.6.7 Initiatives for Combating Cybercrimes

As the number of cybercrimes increases at an alarming rate, numerous national organizations and international networks have introduced a wide range of initiatives to fight cybercrime and ensure internet safety globally.

Research and observation: Observing the problem's scope is essential for determining the breadth and depth of the sites covered, the forms used, and the groups addressed, but it's also crucial for deciding how to approach the issue. At least one organization that tracks the scope of the issue appears to exist in many European nations; however, this "observation" typically consists of nothing more than gathering user complaints, which, while better than nothing, does not provide an accurate picture of the problem's scope.

Getting complaints and looking into them: Many organizations that combat cybercrime allows users to lodge complaints about specific websites via phone or, more commonly, an online form. Other organizations offer links to official or unofficial organizations, such as the police or other NGOs that will help with or investigate concerns.

The straightforward blog "Stand up to Hate" offers a helpful and comprehensive list of the kinds of details the police will need, and it offers advice on how to take screenshots or download content in case these are taken down before the complaint can be investigated. It offers its online form for reporting as well as links to online forms in many other nations and other organizations that deal with racism or intolerance (Titley, Keen, and Foldi, 2014).

The Canadian website "Stop Racism and Hate Collective" has many excellent initiatives to fight online hate, such as numerous online campaigns, resources on racism, an online form for submitting complaints, and detailed information on how users can directly complain to various sites hosting racist content. Because this increases the likelihood that those in charge will take notice, and because many social networking sites or blog hosting sites have terms and conditions that prohibit racist or abusive language, they encourage people to file complaints directly with websites or hosting companies (British Institute of Human Rights, 2012).

Awareness-building, education, and training: The primary long-term goal of anyone concerned with issues of racism, bigotry, hate speech, or other forms of intolerance is to educate and raise awareness among children. Various educational and awareness campaigns are carried out to reduce cybercrime around the world.

Data governance: Data governance is a global concern in this digital world, as data has become a vital component of all actions by major actors in the digital economy. Data controls and data strategies that are adopted to meet business objectives are also referred to as "data governance." Data security, usability, consistency, integrity, and availability are important areas of concern for data governance. Cybersecurity is a branch of information security and data governance that deals with safeguarding digital data (Vaughan, 2020).

2.6.8 REAL-WORLD CASES (1–3)

REAL-WORLD CASE 1 (ISSUE OF CYBERCRIME IN CANADA LITERACY)

Anti-Hate Network for Canadians: The increase in hate crimes across the nation, which is having terrible effects on victims, families, and communities, is being addressed by the Canadian government. The Canadian Anti-Hate Network is an independent, non-profit organization that tracks, investigates, and confronts hate groups by educating the public, the media, researchers, courts, law enforcement, and community organizations about hate groups. The Anti-Racism Action Program has committed $35 million to 175 anti-racism projects since October 2020 to eliminate systemic discrimination against Indigenous Peoples, racialized communities, and religious minorities (Canadian Heritage, 2022).

REAL-WORLD CASE 2 (INCREASE IN CYBERCRIMES IN INDIA)

The developing digital village included India, which has the world's second-largest internet population. While growing internet connectivity benefits everyone, it also exposes our digital society to new dangers. Cybercrime is growing at an exponential rate with no bounds, evolving at the same rate as new technologies.

The number of cybercrimes reported in India continues to rise at an alarming rate each year. To combat cybercrime, the Indian Cyber Crime Coordination Center was established in recent years with a four-billion-rupee investment by the government to speed up investigations. Also, with the introduction of the 5G network and the construction of smart cities in the country, more investments in the industry may be able to combat rising dangers. In 2019, India saw a significant spike in cybercrime reports in some states. From Table 2.5, it can be seen that over 44.5 thousand cybercrime incidents were reported in that year. According to research organizations and experts, attacks could affect all industries, including manufacturing, services, education, and healthcare (Basuroy, 2022a).

REAL-WORLD CASE 3 (INCREASE IN RACISM IN THE US ON SOCIAL MEDIA DURING THE COVID-19 PANDEMIC)

The first reports of COVID-19 infections were made in December 2019 in several patients from Wuhan, Hubei Province (China). On March 17, 2020, former US President Donald Trump posted the following tweet: "The United States will be powerfully supporting those industries, like airlines and others,

TABLE 2.5
Number of Cybercrimes in India from 2012–2019

Year	Number of Cybercrimes (in Thousands)
2012	3,477
2013	5,693
2014	9,622
2015	11,592
2016	12,317
2017	21,796
2018	27,248
2019	44,546

Source: (Basuroy, 2022a) Statista.com.

that are particularly affected by the Chinese virus." "We will be stronger than ever before!" He supported the use of the term "kung flu" and described the COVID-19 pandemic as a "Chinese virus" in one of his Twitter posts on social media. The phrase "Chinese Virus" created many debates, and among Donald Trump fans, hashtags like "Chinese Virus" and "Wuhan Virus" began to trend on different online social networking platforms, with Twitter being the most well-known of them (Scott, 2020).

Since the COVID-19 outbreak began, anti-Asian discrimination has increased. There was an increase in racism against ethnic Asians after the pandemic outbreak in 2020. In the same year, a post on Instagram encouraged "shooting any Asian we see in Chinatown." There were many offensive words used to describe ethnic Asians as "ethnic Chinese." In eight weeks, Asian Americans from all around the country reported 18,00 cases of discrimination connected to COVID-19 to the Asian Pacific Policy and Planning Council. Examples include Asian Americans being subjected to property destruction, physical assault, verbal harassment, being coughed on, eviction from stores and restaurants, and employment discrimination. Asian Americans are frequently called "foreigners" and told to "go back to [their] country" in xenophobic remarks, despite having American citizenship and lineage (Scott, 2020).

These all became possible to reach quickly to the people and administrator through digital tools.

2.7 SOCIAL MEDIA AND POLITICS

As we have already discussed, in the digital age, social media is a very powerful and effective platform for connecting people and allowing users to exchange thoughts, ideas, and other data. Social media is also helpful in politics. Social media has changed politics in the same way that it has changed our social lives. The use of social networking sites for political campaigning, protest organization, political expression, and discussion has grown both domestically and internationally. Social media can be used to practice democracy and political engagement in the context of politics. All of this directly affects how politically motivated individuals behave in politics. Political parties have successfully managed the election campaign using social media platforms. Social media also enables them to disseminate important information to voters and engage them in political campaigns.

The message, morals, political corruption, and dynamics of political conflict can all be strongly influenced and changed by social media. There are several well-known social media platforms, such as Facebook, Twitter, Instagram, YouTube, Linked In, Pinterest, and others. Political parties, organizations, corruption in politics, and international politics can all use these mediums. Social media has a significant impact on messages and can alter values, political corruption, and the dynamics of political conflict.

Facebook, the most prominent social media platform, helps political marketing campaigns by providing access to a variety of channels for communicating with the target demographic. Because of this, politicians are experts at promoting themselves and their candidates on social media. Additionally, it helps in creating a favorable impression of their candidate and disseminating crucial facts to the public to spur political change and win over more supporters.

Social media helps in political activity: Users can create groups of people who share common interests by sharing content like articles, photographs, videos, and documentaries on all the well-known social media platforms, Because there are fewer restrictions on how information may be shared on social media, it is becoming more important in political activity. Social media plays an important role in the two-way contact between politically motivated people and politicians, whereas the majority of mainstream media simply offers users a one-way communication capacity. Social media is important in the decision-making process since it allows a group of individuals to communicate opinions with one another and come to an informed choice. Therefore, using social media in politics offers a useful means of managing, controlling, and communicating about political activity. As a result, social networking sites have undoubtedly developed into a strong tool for political organization and mobilization, as well as a significant platform for political speech and debate globally.

2.7.1 POLARIZATION THROUGH SOCIAL MEDIA

Both elections and political campaigns have been significantly impacted by social media platforms, especially Facebook and Twitter. Political parties have utilized social media platforms on a global scale to spread their views, influence voters, conduct political campaigning, and organize their supporters.

Social media has impacted elections and campaigns in the following ways:

- **Direct contact with the electorate:** Politicians can avoid the conventional strategy of contacting voters through paid advertising or earned media by using social media.
- **Free marketing:** Political campaigns now frequently create advertisements and post them for free on YouTube instead of, or in addition to, paying for airtime on television or radio.
- **Viral marketing:** They make it possible for activists and voters with similar viewpoints to readily exchange news and details about upcoming elections.
- **Addressing the audience with the message:** Political campaigns have access to a lot of data or analytics on their social media followers and can tailor their messaging to certain demographics.
- **Donations:** Social media is used by campaigns to request that their supporters donate money.
- **Examining popular opinion:** Campaigns can instantly assess how the public is reacting to a problem or controversy using both Twitter and Facebook. Without the need for costly consultants or polling, politicians may then immediately modify their campaigns to reflect the results.
- **Comments or feedback:** Inquiring about the opinions or comments of voters can be beneficial.

2.7.2   REAL-WORLD CASES (1–3)

REAL-WORLD CASE 1 (UNITED STATES OF AMERICA)

The world first saw how social media platforms may be helpful to win elections in the United States in 2008. Obama's campaign expertly "extended his reach, increasing voters, as well as reinforcing his pre-existing fan base" through the use of social media platforms. The selection of the first African-American President of the United States was also employed to coordinate volunteer campaign staff and collect financial support from supporters. The 2008 US presidential election was another step toward democratic discourse made possible by social media platforms, according to a study on the role of social media in the 2008 US presidential elections. This Barack Obama campaign demonstrated how social networking sites allow politicians to communicate with millions of their supporters in a single day and allow those supporters to connect and form online groups that can be used to help plan rallies or support get-out-the-vote campaigns (Gerodimos and Justinussen, 2015; Ott, 2017).

REAL-WORLD CASE 2 (INDONESIA)

As there was tremendous growth in the number of internet users and mobile internet users in Indonesia between 2018 and 2019, social media is viewed as a strong electoral force in Indonesia due to the country's high social media usage and the significant number of young voters.

The 2014 elections in Indonesia marked the first time that the internet, mobile devices, and social media were significant factors. Social media was utilized by all major parties to engage voters. Numerous election-related articles from traditional media outlets were posted on social media. NGOs and election watchdogs also gathered public reports of vote buying and other electoral crimes via social media (Thornley, 2014).

REAL-WORLD CASE 3 (INDIA)

In India, opinions on the influence of social media on elections have changed from optimistic to pessimistic.

In the 2014 Indian elections, as described by CNN:

Many politicians are using social networking sites to connect with tech-savvy first-time voters, even though they initially appear out-of-touch and conventional in their flowing kurtas (Indian traditional shirts) and Gandhi hats.

Nowadays, having a Facebook page or official YouTube channel is just as significant as hosting large rallies and putting up billboards with candidates' faces on them. (Khullar and Haridasani, 2014)

2.8 CHAPTER CONCLUSION

The advancement of digital media has given rise to new challenges and opportunities. Access to all kinds of emerging technologies has allowed everyone to participate in public discourse. Because of this, threats to freedom of expression or speech are becoming more evident, and this has also given rise to cyber violence worldwide. Therefore, in this digital age, the most widely used social media platforms like Facebook, Instagram, Twitter, YouTube, etc. have not only gained worldwide popularity but also generated a great deal of controversy. Therefore, it is very important to educate and instruct internet users, particularly teenagers, on the consequences and proper usage of social media, as well as what is and isn't appropriate behavior on such large-scale networks. Also, the users must be taught the difference between private and public information, how to handle sensitive data and the consequences of misusing social media. One of the major issues in the world of social media is the rapid growth of cybercrime around the world. The above-mentioned challenges have led everyone to study the various cyber laws that are introduced by the governments of various countries worldwide and are intended to regulate social media directly or indirectly (see Chapter 3).

EXERCISES

1. What is social media? Describe the different types of social media.
2. What is the difference between social media and other media?
3. Describe the term "freedom of speech and expression."
4. What are the restrictions on the right to free speech and expression according to Article 19(2) of the Indian Constitution?
5. Describe hate speech in short, and list the classifications of hate speech.
6. Asia's market is dominated by social media platforms. Give reasons?
7. What are the various types of cybercrime?
8. What is spam?
9. What are the protective measures used for phishing?
10. What are biometrics? Explain what they are used for.
11. What modern technologies can protect against cyber attacks?
12. Distinguish between black hole and sink hole routing.
13. What are the advantages of using smart cards?
14. What is the Fourth Industrial Revolution's main goal?
15. What are the difficulties in combating cybercrime?
16. What is meant by the term "crypto-currencies"?

17. What kinds of illegal activities involve the use of cryptocurrencies?
18. What exactly does IFF stand for?
19. Which cryptocurrency is commonly used by cybercriminals?
20. What are the ways in which social media helps with political campaigns and elections?

REFERENCES

Asur, S. and Huberman, B.A. (2010) 'Predicting the Future with Social Media.' Social Computing Lab: HP Labs, Palo Alto, California. pp. 1–8.

Aneez, S. and Sirilal, R. (2018) 'Sri Lanka to lift social media ban: minister', March 13. Available at: www.reuters.com/articles/us-sri-lanka-clashes-socialmedia/sri-lanka-to-lift-social-media-ban-minister-idUSKCN1GP2LO (Accessed: 4 January 2021).

Aneez, et al., (no date) 'India Digital News Report', Available at: www.reutersinstitute.politics.ox.ac.uk/our-research/india-digital-news-report (Accessed: 10 May 2021).

Ajmal, A. (2021) 'Facebook Restricted access to 878 pieces of content between July and December last year, says report', May 20. Available at: www.timesofindia.indiatimes.com/india/facebook-restricted-access-to-878-pieces-of-content-between-july-and-december-last-year-says-report/articleshow/82799769.cms (Accessed: 10 August 2021).

Alferidah, Khalid, D. and Jhanjhi, N.Z. (2020) 'A Review on Security and Privacy Issues and Challenges in Internet of Things', International Journal of Computer Science and Network Security IJCSNS, No. 4, pp. 263–286.

Australian Bankers Association (ABA) (no date), Submission 7.1, p. 2 Sophos Private Limited, Submission 66, p. 5.

Basuroy, T. (2022a) 'Number of Cyber Crimes Reported across India from 2012–2021', Oct 13, Available at: www.India: number of cyber crimes 2021 I Statista.

Basuroy, T. (2022b) 'Social Network Penetration India 2015–2025', Sep 29, Available at: www.India: social network penetration 2025 I Statista.

Basudeb, S. (2013) 'Globalization, Liberalization and economic development', New Century Publications, New Delhi, p. 113.

Bhat, M.M.A. (2020) 'Hate Crimes in India'. Jindal Global Law Review, 11, 1–5, https://doi.org/10.1007/s41020-020-00119-0, 04 August 2020.

Berger, A.A. (2012) Media analysis techniques, Sage Publications, New Delhi, pp. 122–23.

Boyd, D. (2010) Taken Out of Context: American Teen Sociality in Networked Publics Berkeley, CA: University of California, 2008. Available at: www.danah.org/papers/TakenOutOfContext.pdf (Accessed: 19 February, 2020).

British Institute of Human Rights (2012) 'Mapping study on projects against hate speech online', Council of Europe, 15 April.

Canadian Heritage (2022) 'Government of Canada and the Canadian Anti-Hate Network Launch Anti-Hate Toolkit for Canadian Schools', June 29. Available at: www.canada.ca/en/canadian-heritage/news/2022/06/government-of-canada-and-the-canadian-anti-hate-network-launch-anti-hate-toolkit-for-canadian-schools.html/ (Accessed: 03 January 2023).

CCLA (2015). 'Summary: International Covenant on Civil and Political Rights (ICCPR)', October 27, Available at: HTTP://ccla.org/privacy/surveillance-and-privacy/summary-international-covenant-on-civil-andpolitical-rights.iccpr/ (Accessed: 23 January 2020).

Charkravarti, A. (2021) 'Government reveals stats on social media users, WhatsApp leads while YouTube beats Facebook, Instagram', (Last updated: February 25, 2021).

Available at: www.indiatoday.in/technology/news/story/government-reveals-stats-on-social-media-users-whatsapp-leads-while-youtube-beats-facebook-instgram-1773021-2021-02-25 (Accessed: 06 April 2021)

Dixon, S. (2023a) *'Leading countries based on Facebook audience size as of January 2023'*, We are Social, Meltwater, February 24, Available at: www.statista.com/statistics/268136/top-15-countries-based-on-number-of-facebook-user (Accessed: 25 February 2023).

Dixon, S. (2023b) *'Number of worldwide Social Media Users 2022, by Region'*, February 13, Statista, Available at: www. Global social media users by region 2022 | Statista. (Accessed: 25 February 2023).

Emerson, S. and Nieva, R. (2022) *'Facebook and Twitter has been blocked in Russia'*, March 4. Available at: http://buzzfeednews.com/article/sarahemerson/russia-blocks-facebook-twitter (Accessed: 12 September 2022).

Faghani, M.R., Matrawy, Lung, C.H. (2012) *'A Study of Trojan Propagation in Online Social Networks'*, in *5th International Conference on New Technologies, Mobility and Security (NTMS)*, pp. 1–5.

Frayer, L. (2020) *'Facebook Accused of Violating Its Hate Speech Policy in India'*, November 27. Available at: www.npr.org/2020/11/27/939532326/facebook-accused-of-violating-its-hate-speech-policy-in-india (Accessed: 06 February, 2021).

Gerodimos, R. and Justinussen, J. (2015) 'Obama's 2012 Facebook Campaign: Political Communication in the Age of the Like Button', *Journal of Information Technology & Politics*, 12, 2, pp. 113–132.

Gisbert, P. (2011) *Fundamentals of Sociology*, (New Delhi, Orient BlackSwan), p.34.

GSMA Intelligence (2021) 'Consumer Survey'.

Joseph, J.C. (1997) *Mass Media and Rural Development*, (New Delhi, Rawat Publishers), p.16.

jpost.com Staff (2007) *'Syrian gov't blocks use of Facebook'*, November 24. Available at: www.jpost.com/Middle-East/syrian-govt-blocks-use-of-facebook (Accessed: 12 September 2020).

Kanwal, S. (2021) *'Halt the Hate'*, haltthehate.amnesty.org, November 22. Available at: www.statista.com/statistics/980033/identity-of-hate-crimes-victims-india (Accessed: 12 September 2022).

Kaplan, Andreas M. and Heinlein, Michael (2010) 'Users of the World, Unite! The Challenges and Opportunities of Social Media', *Business Horizons*, vol. 53, 2010, pp. 59–68.

Khullar, A. and Haridasani, A. (2014) *'Politicians slug it out in India's first social media election'*, April 10. CNN. Available at: https://edition.cnn.com/2014/04/09/world/asia/indias-first-social-media-election/index.html (Accessed: 09 June 2020).

King, G., Pan, J., and Roberts, M. (2013) *'How Censorship in China Allows Government Criticism nut Silence Collective Expression'*, *America Political Science Review,* vol. 107, no. 2, 2013, p.3.

Kshetri, N. (2010) 'Diffusion and Effects of Cyber-Crime in Developing Economies.' *Third World Quarterly*. vol. 31, no. 7, pp. 1057–1079. doi/abs/10.1080.01436597.2010.518752

Lusk, B. (2020) 'Digital Natives and Social Media Behaviors: An Overview'. *The Prevention Research,* vol. 17, pp. 3–6.

Mcquail, D. (1980) *Mass Communication Theory*, (London: Sage Publications), p. 90.

Moran, M., Seaman, J., and Tinti-Kane, H. (2020), 'Teaching, learning, and sharing: How today higher education faculty use social media'. Babson Survey Research Group. Available at: https://files.eric.ed.gov/fulltext/ED535130.pdf (Accessed: 20 January 2021).

Nair, K.S. and White, S.A. (1996) *Perspectives on Development Communication*, (New Delhi, Sage Publications), p.56.

Nasir, J.A., Khatoon, A. and Bharadwaj, S. (2018) 'Social Media users in India: A Futuristic Approach', *International Journal of Research and Analytical Review*, vol. 5, no. 4, ISSN 2349-5138.

NW3C (2013) *'Criminal Use of Social Media'*, NW3C.

Ott, B.L. (2017) *'The age of Twitter: Donald J. Trump and the politics of debasement'*, Critical Studies In Media Communication, vol. 34, no. 1, pp. 59–68, Communication & Mass Media Complete.

Patel, et al. (2017) *'A theoretical review of social media usage by cyber-criminals'*, *International Conference on Computer Communication and Informatics* (ICCI), IEEE.

PIB (2019) *'Indian Cyber Crime Coordination Center (I4C)–A-7 Pronged Scheme to Fight Cyber Crime'*, July 17. Available at: www.pib.gov.in/pressreleaseshare.aspx?PRID= 1579184 (Accessed: 10 June 2020).

Poonawalla T.S. Vs Union of India and Others (2018) *'Cow Vigilantism and Lynching'*, 9 Supreme Court of India, 501.

Purosothaman, U. (2019) *'Impact of social media on youth'*, RESEARCH GATE, October, Available at: www.researchgate.net/publication/336716719 (Accessed: 02 June 2020).

Roose, K. (2018) *'On Gab, an Extremist-Friendly Site, Pittsburgh Shooting Suspect Aired His Hatred in Full'*, October 28. Available at: www.nytimes.com/2018/10/28/us/gab-robert-bowers-pittsburgh-synagogue-shootings.html (Accessed: 04 September 2021).

Schwab, K. (2016) *'The fourth Industrial Revolution: what it means, how to respond'*, World Economic Forum [online], Available at: www.weforum.org/agenda/2016/01/the-fourth-industrail-revolution-what-it-means-and-how-to-respond/ (Accessed: 04 October 2021).

Scott, D. (2020) *'Trump's new fixation on using a racist name for the coronavirus is dangerous'*, March 18. Available at: www.vox.com/2020/3/21185478/coronavirus-usa-trump-chinese-virus (Accessed: 12 April 2021).

Section 66A of the Information Technology Act, 2000.

Sharma, N. (2021) *'Reliance Jio's cheap data turned India's internet dreams into reality'*, September 7. Available at: www.qz.com/india/2055771/relaince-jios-cheap-data-turned-indias-internet-dream-into-reality (Accessed: 11 December 2021).

Stockman, F.N. (2004) *'What binds us when with whom? Context and structures in social network analyses'*, *Extended version of keynote at the SUNBELT XXIV*. International social network conference, Portoroz (Slovenia).

Taylor, C. (2013) *'Iran Unblocks Twitter and Facebook'*, September 16. Available at: http://mashable.com/archive/twitter-facebook-iran (Accessed: 12 April 2021).

Talmadge, E. (2016) *'North Korea blocks Facebook, Twitter and YouTube'*, April 4. Available at: http://globalnews.ca/news/2616449/north-korea-blacks-facebook-twitter-and-youtube/ (Accessed: 12 April 2021).

The Mobile Economy Asia Pacific 2021, GSMA, 2021.

Troise, et al., (2020) 'Perspective of the App Economy: Tenets of Innovative Phenomenon' *International Business Research: Canadian Education of Science and Education*, vol. 13, no. 3, ISSN 1913-9004.

Tropina, T. (2016) *'Do Digital Technologies Facilitate Illicit Financial Flows? The World Development Report 2016'*. Digital Dividends. Background Paper. Available at: http://pubsdocs.wprldbank.org/en/396751453906608518/WDR16-BP-Do-DigitalTechnologies-Facilitate-Illicit-Financial-Flows-Tropina.Pdf (Accessed: 11 January 2023).

Tropina, T. (2017) *'Big Data: Tackling Illicit Financial flows'*. In Atlantic Council & Thomson Reuters(Ed.). Big Data: A twenty-First Century Arms Race. Available at: www.atlanticcouncil.org/wp-content/uploads/2017/06/Big_Data_A_Twenty-First_Century_Arms_Race_web_0627_Chapter_4.pdf (Accessed: 11 January 2023).

Thornley, A. (2014) *'Indonesia's Social Media Elections'*, April 2. Available at: http://asiafou ndation.org/2014/04/02/indonesias-social-media-elections/ (Accessed: 12 April 2021).

Titley, G., Keen, E. and Foldi, L. (2014) *'Starting Points for Combating Hate Speech Online'*, Council of Europe, Youth Development.

UNODC. (2013) *Comprehensive Study on Cybercrime*, New York: UN.

Vaughan, J. (2020) *'What is data governance and why does it matter?'* *Tech Target.* Available at: https://searchdatamanagement.techtarget.com/defination/datagovernance (Accessed: 05 January 2023).

Vyas, B.M. (2008) 'Sharing of Information with citizens', *All India Reporter* (Journal Section), 2008, pp. 171–176, at 176.

Williams, R. (2019) *'App Annie: WhatsApp overtakes Facebook as social giant's top app'*, January 16. Available at: www.markeingdive.com/news/app-annie-whatsapp-overtakes-facebook-as-social-giants-top-app/546134 (Accessed: 10 March 2020).

World Bank (2016) *'International operability derives from cohesion legal frameworks dedicated to cybercrime issues that are adopted in various countries'*.

World Bank (2017) *'Illicit Financial Flows (IFFs)'*, Brief, 7 July [online]. Available at: www. worldbank.org/en/topic/financialsector/brief/illicit-financial-flows-iff (Accessed: 10 January 2023).

3 Cyber Laws

SUMMARY

Readers of this chapter will learn about the existing laws and rules on hate speech and cyber laws in many nations, including Europe, the United Nations, and some Asian and African nations, which present a significant challenge to the legal system and how the law still needs to adapt to these developing technologies. We will also discuss how well each country regulates laws. In this, we will also cover how the misuse of social media brings about the growth of e-violence and various cybercrimes on social media and their consequences for society, as well as the cyber laws that governments around the world have imposed to restrict crimes and activities on social media. We will also go over several provisions in existing so-called cyber laws that can be used to seek redress in the event of a violation of any rights in cyberspace, the internet, or social media, and about the enormous power that the government has and how the government is working hard when it comes to cyber security. At the end of the chapter, we will also highlight some of the most significant social, ethical, and technological difficulties encountered by users and LGBT (lesbian, gay, bisexual, and transgender) people worldwide.

3.1 INTRODUCTION

In today's digital age, cyber law is also referred to as internet law and digital law. With the freedom of digitization, the internet is vulnerable to misuse today, justifying the state to regulate online content in the public interest. Today's surge in internet traffic contributes to an increase in the legal problems associated with cybercrime, which affects not only a nation but the entire world. Fraud, theft, money laundering, and many other types of cybercrimes are committed via computers or networks. Cybercrime mostly has an impact on items connected to the use of computers, mobile phones, email clients, and data storage devices. The protection of users from undesired activities and the security of information access, communication, and intellectual property are all made possible by cyber law. Every nation has a unique set of cyber laws since, as was already established, cybercrime harms the entire planet. Several cyber-crimes, including defamation, privacy issues, offenses, derogatory remarks on caste, race, and religion, stalking, abuse, hacking, harassment, and many others, can be easily committed via social media, and once such objectionable content is uploaded, it becomes viral on different social media platforms, resulting in huge controversies across the nation.

Therefore, cyber laws in many countries now include provisions for website blocking, monitoring and collecting internet traffic data, intercepting or decrypting such data, unrestricted access to sensitive personal data, holding intermediaries, such

DOI: 10.1201/9781003403784-3

as social media websites, liable for hosting user-generated objectionable content, and so on.

The first step taken by the government to combat cybercrime was the adoption of cyber law. Cyber law encompasses laws governing cybercrime, electronic and digital signatures, intellectual property, data protection, and privacy.

As there is increasing human dependency on digital technology, cyber laws require constant upgrading and improvement in different countries around the world. Most of the workforce has also been pushed into a remote working pattern (work-from-home) by the pandemic, which has increased the need for security for different apps.

There are a few justifications as to why the world needs cyber law in this present digital age. Cybercrime law establishes standards of conduct and behavior for the use of computers, the internet, and other related digital technologies, as well as for the actions of the general public, governments, and private organizations. It also establishes rules of evidence, criminal procedure, and other aspects of criminal justice in cyberspace, and it regulates to lower risk and/or lessen damage to people, organizations, and infrastructure if cybercrime occurs. As a result, substantive, procedural, and preventive laws all apply to cybercrime.

- The majority of transactions take place in an electronic or online form.
- Companies today heavily rely on computer networks to complete their tasks.
- Different forms for the government are filled out electronically or online.
- The payment is made by consumers through online card transactions, i.e., digital payments.
- Mobile phones, email, SMS messages, and other technologies are used for communication.
- Important legal documents are also stored on data storage devices.
- The prevalence of cybercrimes, including fraud, spamming, terrorism, hacking, pornography, etc., is rising more quickly.

3.1.1 Types of Cyber Law

Different types of laws are shown in Figure 3.1.

Online fraud: Consumers are protected by several regulations from internet scams like identity theft, credit card theft, and other sorts of online theft.

Online hate speech: Hate speech has been on the rise on social media sites, particularly Facebook. Online hate speech is governed by cyber law, which has imposed many restrictions to limit it globally.

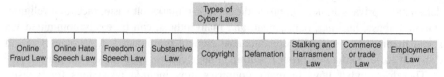

FIGURE 3.1 Types of cyber laws.

Freedom of speech: Cyber law imposes numerous limits, but it also emphasizes the freedom for people to express themselves without hurting the feelings of others.

Substantive law: Crimes like fraud, forgery, organized crime, money laundering, and theft that are committed online are referred to as "cybercrime."

Copyright: Cyber law offers copyright defenses to uphold individual and corporate rights.

Defamation: False claims made online that damage a person's reputation or a business are protected by defamation laws.

Stalking and harassment: Users are protected by cyber law from threatening remarks or stalking when it occurs online or on another platform.

Commerce or trade: When legal action is required to preserve trade secrets, cyber attorneys assist their clients.

Employment law: Contracts and agreements exist to safeguard the interests of both individuals and businesses, but they can be amended if necessary, so lawyers must try to present their clients with the greatest options.

3.1.2 Advantages of Cyber Law

Cybercrime legislation shields users against various forms of cybercrime so they can easily and securely browse the internet. We are all aware that online communication and commerce are growing in popularity, but they require privacy protection, which is something that cyber law offers to everyone. The benefits of cyber legislation are as follows:

- Protection from online fraud.
- Security for software and hardware on computers.
- E-Commerce security for internet firms.
- Blocking undesired internet disturbances.
- Creation of security organizations like Cyber Cell.
- Keeps a watch on every online activity.
- All online and digital transactions are protected.
- Digital signatures are now recognized by law.

3.2 CYBER LAWS IN THE WORLD

In many countries around the world, unlawful content and hateful material on the internet have proliferated over the past few years. Today's social media platforms offer a far wider platform for the dissemination of hate speech and criminal activity online. In recent years, many countries have witnessed communal riots, violent attacks between various religious groups, and caste discrimination due to the rise of online hate speech. As a result of this violence, the country's peace and order have been destroyed.

In today's digital world, hate speech regulations and laws have become challenging to implement for governments and legislators. Despite new and stringent legislation, the number of hate speech cases is on the rise. In addition to the existing provisions, the Law Commission recommended in its 2017 report that new provisions be added to the penal code that specifically punishes incitement to violence (Law Commission of India, 2017).

Hate speech is often presented as a "restriction" on one's right to freedom of expression and speech. The government also has the right to impose necessary restrictions, such as the removal or deletion of various harmful and unsuitable contents and filters on information or data stored on the internet.

Although it is phrased differently in each country, this fundamental idea is mentioned in the majority of constitutions. In India, hate speech or content on the internet is mainly about an individual's caste, religion, language, color, or gender, all of which are very sensitive topics. Many trials are normally carried out by citing a variety of offenses under the statute, some of which may have considerable overlap, without putting anyone in a situation where they're suffering double harm or loss. India specifically mentions that an individual's right to free speech is protected by Article 19, although Indonesia refers to this as their right to freedom of expression (Article 28 [e]). Australia stands out as an outlier, as its constitution only loosely and implicitly protects freedom of "political communication."

2018 was declared "The Year of Online Hate" because many people used social media platforms to spread their hatred on a large scale through their unlawful or illegal content or posts. Hate speech on social media platforms, especially Facebook, has become a big concern. Today, social media is rife with poisonous and hateful debates. Combating or regulating hate speech on social media has become a major challenge for governments all over the world.

As a result, online hate speech has become a major problem all over the world. The availability of information online, which can be accessed for free by everyone in the world, has intensified this problem. Similarly, the use of social media has also given rise to online hate speech.

Therefore, it is very important to reform the existing system's structure to begin combating hate speech using legal frameworks.

3.2.1 United Nations

International Covenant on Civil and Political Rights (CCLA, 2015)
Article 19 states that:

1. Everyone shall have the right to hold beliefs without hindrance;
2. Everyone shall have the right to freedom of expression, which includes the freedom to seek, receive, and impart information and ideas of all kinds without regard to boundaries, whether orally, in writing or print, through art, or any other medium of his choice;
3. The exercise of the rights provided for in paragraph 2 of this article carries with it special obligations. As a result, it might be subject to some limitations, but only those necessary and permitted by law:
   (a) To respect the reputations or rights of others;
   (b) To safeguard public morality, public health, public order, or national security.

Article 4 states that "State Parties condemn all propaganda and all organizations based on ideas or theories of superiority of one race or group of persons of one color or ethnic origin, or which attempt to justify or promote racial hatred and discrimination in any form, and undertake to adopt immediate and positive measures aimed at eradicating all incitement to, or acts of, such discrimination, having due regard for the principles embodied in the Universal Declaration of Human Rights and the rights expressly outlined in Article 5.

(a) All expression of ideas of racial superiority or hatred, incitement to racial discrimination, acts of violence or incitement to violence against any race or group of people of a different color or ethnic origin, as well as any assistance given to racist activities, including their financing, shall be declared offenses punishable by law;

(b) Shall declare unlawful and proscribe groups that encourage and instigate racial discrimination, as well as organized and all other propaganda efforts, and shall recognize that joining such groups or activities is a crime punishable by law.

Article 20(2) states that any provocation of discrimination, animosity, or violence that promotes national, racial, or religious hatred is illegal.

Article 5: Nothing in the present Covenant should be interpreted as giving any state, group, or individual the right to carry out any actions or engage in any activities that have as their goal the destruction of any of the rights and freedoms acknowledged herein or their limitation to a greater extent than what is permitted by the present Covenant.

3.2.2   EUROPE (EUROPEAN CONVENTION ON HUMAN RIGHTS, ROME, 4.XI. (1950))

Article 10: Freedom of Expression

1. Freedom of expression belongs to everyone. This freedom must include the ability to express ideas freely across national boundaries without intervention from the government and to hold opinions. The licensing of broadcasting, television, or movie theater businesses is not prohibited by this article.

2. Since exercising these freedoms entails duties and responsibilities, it may be subject to the formalities, conditions, restrictions, or punishments that are required by law and are essential to a democratic society to protect national security, territorial integrity, or public safety, to prevent disorder or crime; to protect one's health or morals; to protect one's reputation or other people's rights; to stop the spread of dissension; or for other reasons.

Article 17: Prohibition on the Abuse of Rights

Nothing in this Convention should be read to grant any state, group, or individual the right to engage in any action or act that has as its goal the destruction of any of the freedoms and rights outlined here or their limitation to a degree greater than that which is permitted by the Convention.

Regarding the criminalization of crimes of a racist and xenophobic nature performed using computer networks, an additional protocol to the Convention on Cybercrime is given below:

Article 2: Definition

1. In accordance with this protocol, any written material, any image, or any other representation of ideas or theories that encourages hatred, discrimination, or violence against any individual or group of individuals based on race, color, descent, national or ethnic origin, as well as a religion if used as a pretext for any of these factors, is referred to as "racist and xenophobic material."
2. This Protocol's terminology and expressions must be understood in the same way that they are understood by the Convention.

Article 3: Dissemination of Racist and Xenophobic Material Through Computer Systems

1. Each Party shall adopt such legislative and other measures as may be necessary to designate the following conduct, when committed intentionally and without authorization, as criminal offenses under its domestic law: disseminating or otherwise making racist and xenophobic material to the general public via a computer system.
2. If the material, as defined in Article 2, paragraph 1, advocates, promotes, or incites discrimination that is not related to hatred or violence, a party may reserve the right not to criminalize such behavior, provided that other effective remedies are available.
3. Despite paragraph 2 of this article, a party may reserve the right to refuse to apply paragraph 1 to instances of discrimination for which it is not possible to offer effective remedies as described in said paragraph 2 because of established principles in its national legal system regarding freedom of expression.

Article 4: Racist and Xenophobic-Motivated Threat

1. Each party shall adopt the legislative and other measures that may be required to designate the following actions as crimes under its domestic law when done intentionally and unlawfully: by using a computer system to threaten individuals for the reasons that they are:
   i.   a member of a group that is distinguished by race, color, descent, national or ethnic origin, as well as religion,
   ii. a group of individuals that are distinguished by any of these characteristics and have committed a serious crime as defined by their domestic law.

Article 5: Racist and Xenophobic-Motivated Insult

1. Each party shall adopt any legislative and other measures that may be required to define the following conduct as crimes under its domestic law when it is done willfully and without authorization: publicly insulting through a

computer system I individuals because they are members of a group that is distinguished by race, color, descent, national or ethnic origin, as well as a religion if any of these characteristics are used as an excuse; or (ii) a group of individuals.

2. A party may either:
   a. require that the offense mentioned in this article's paragraph 1 have the result of exposing the person or group of people mentioned in that paragraph to hatred, contempt, ridicule; or
   b. reserve the right to not apply, in whole or in part, paragraph 1 of this article.

Article 6: Denial, Gross Minimization, Approval, or Justification of Genocide or Crimes Against Humanity

1. Under this, distributing or otherwise making available, through a computer system, to the public, material that denies, grossly minimizes, approves, or justifies acts constituting genocide or crimes against humanity, as defined by international law and recognized as such by a final and conclusive international judgment, shall be prohibited under each party's domestic law when committed intentionally and without authorization.

3.2.3 COUNCIL OF THE EUROPEAN UNION

Article 1: Offenses Including Racism and Xenophobia

1. Every Member State must take the steps required to make sure that the following intentional acts are criminally punished:
   a. openly inciting hatred or violence against a person or a member of a particular group of people based on their race, color, religion, ancestry, or national or ethnic origin;
   b. committing the act mentioned in point (a) by means of the public dissemination or distribution of pamphlets, images, or other materials;
   c. openly endorsing, downplaying, or grossly trivializing war crimes, crimes against humanity, or genocide, as they are defined in Articles 6, 7, and 8 of the Statute of the International Criminal Court, when they are committed against a group of people or a member of that group based on race, color, religion, descent, or national or ethnic origin;
   d. openly endorsing, downplaying, or grossly trivializing the crimes outlined in Article 6 of the International Military Tribunal's Charter, which is annexed to the London Agreement of August 8, 1945, against a group of people or a member of that group based on race, color, religion, descent, or national or ethnic origin, when the conduct is done in a way that could incite violence or hatred against that group or a member of that group.

European Parliament and Council: Directive 2018/1808 of the European Parliament and of the Council of November 14, 2018, amending Directive 2010/13/

EU on the coordination of certain provisions set forth by law, regulation, or administrative action in the Member States concerning the provision of audiovisual media services. This amendment was made in response to the shifting nature of the market.

(45) There are new difficulties, especially in relation to video-sharing websites where users, especially minors, are increasingly consuming audiovisual information. Concern over offensive language and hazardous content on video-sharing platforms has increased in this setting. Establishing reasonable regulations in these areas is required to safeguard minors and the wider public from such content.

Code of Conduct for the European Commission to combat online hate speech (Brussel, 2016)

The European Commission and IT companies (Facebook, Twitter, YouTube, and Microsoft) together launched a code of conduct that contains several promises to stop the spread of unlawful hate speech online in Europe. It is necessary to make sure that appropriate national legislation fully implementing the Council Framework Decision on countering racism and xenophobia is enforced by Member States in both the online and offline environments to stop the spread of illegal hate speech. IT firms are as dedicated to combating online hate speech as the European Commission and EU member states. A group of people or a member of such a group defined by reference to race, color, religion, descent, or national or ethnic origin is the target of illegal hate speech, combating certain forms and expressions of racism and xenophobia through criminal law and national laws transposing it. By the Code, IT companies agree to assess the majority of legitimate requests for the removal of unlawful hate speech in less than 24 hours and, if necessary, to remove or disable access to such content.

3.2.4 AUSTRALIA (OFFICE OF PARLIAMENTARY COUNSEL, 2017)

Section 80.2A: Urging for Violence against Groups

1. A person (the first person) commits an offense if they:
   a. purposefully urge another person or group to use force or violence against a group (the targeted group);
   b. do so with the intent that force or violence will occur;
   c. The targeted group can be identified by its race, religion, nation, ethnicity, or political views.
   d. The use of force or violence would threaten peace, order, and good order.

   Punishment: 7 years of imprisonment

2. If a person (the first person) intentionally urges another person or a group to use force or violence against a group (the targeted group), and if they do so with the intent that force or violence will be used, and if the targeted group can be identified by race, religion, nationality, national or ethnic origin, or political opinion, then they have committed an offense.

3.2.5 Austria

New Legislation against Online Hate Speech (epicenter.works, 2020)

The Austrian "Hate on the Net Prevention Act" (Netzwerkdurchsetzungsgesetz: NetDG) and the Austrian "Communication Platforms Act, (Kommunikationsplattformen-Gesetz: KoPlG) which operators were required to implement by April 1, 2021, and in some cases have already done to great media impact, came into force on January 1, 2021.

The Austrian government unveiled a legislation package on September 3 to address hate speech online. The package also includes a provision that gives web platforms new responsibility to delete illegal user-generated content in addition to comprehensive justice reform.

NetzDG Act: The Austrian NetzDG covers a list of 15 criminal acts, including incitement to hatred, coercion, stalking, and denigration of religious doctrine. Platforms must have a way for users to report this illegal content and must respond quickly to notifications. Within 24 hours after receiving notice, content that is manifestly prohibited for legal laypeople must be blocked. A maximum of 7 days may pass before the platform responds if the illegality is not immediately apparent. Both the deleted content and the poster's identity must be kept by the platform for a period of ten weeks in case any disputes arise. If required, law enforcement agencies can request this information or have the time frame extended by an additional 10 weeks. There is no requirement to alert law enforcement about prohibited illegal content.

The main advancement of NetzDG is the existence of complaint and redress procedures, which allow for more oversight of the platform's choices and better content control techniques. Both sides have the right to challenge a platform's decision if it removes something that either the poster or the person reporting the content thinks to be legal. The platform itself is being reviewed in the first step, which must be finished in two weeks.

KoPLG Act: Austria implemented the KoPlG on April 1, 2021. The German NetzDG appears to have been the inspiration for the KoPL-provision. This act applies to all platforms worldwide with a relationship with Austria. Similar to the NetzDG, the KoPL-G needs functionalities that are simple to access, always available, and simple to use to report illegal content. If the content is illegal to a layperson familiar with the law, it must be removed within 24 hours. The social network provider must remove the item no later than seven days after the assessment is complete if the content's illegality can only be determined after a thorough investigation. Content that violates Austria's Criminal Code, such as stalking, persistent harassment, unauthorized image recording, or the portrayal of children in pornographic material, is illegal.

3.2.6 Turkey

Law No. 5651 (Official Gazette, 2020)

According to Article 4, No. 5651, The phrase "access blocking" in the first paragraph of the law's Article 8 indicates "removal of content, and/or to the blocking of access," while the phrase "to be fulfilled by decisions to block" appears in the second paragraph's first sentence. Law No. 5651 regulates processes for some internet crimes perpetrated through content, hosting, and access providers to counteract those crimes. According to the law, social network service providers with more than one million daily users must appoint a representative in Turkey. The representative will take the appropriate steps in response to notifications or requests from the relevant authorities and ensure that the law's requirements are met. Social network providers are required to keep data in Turkey and submit a report to the appropriate authority every six months regarding the removal of content and barring of access. The removal of content ordered by a judge, public prosecutor, or the head of the authority must be carried out as soon as possible and, at the latest, four hours after the decision has been made known.

3.2.7 UNITED KINGDOM OF GREAT BRITAIN AND NORTHERN IRELAND (PUBLIC ORDER ACT, 1986)[1]

Section 21: Distributing, showing or playing a recording.

(1) A person who distributes, or shows or plays, a recording of visual images or sounds which are threatening, abusive or insulting is guilty of an offence if—
   (a) he intends thereby to stir up racial hatred, or
   (b) having regard to all the circumstances racial hatred is likely to be stirred up thereby.

(2) In this Part "recording" means any record from which visual images or sounds may, by any means, be reproduced; and references to the distribution, showing or playing of a recording are to its distribution, showing or playing of a recording are to its distribution, showing or playing to the public or a section of the public.

(3) In proceedings for an offence under this section it is a defence for an accused who is not shown to have intended to stir up racial hatred to prove that he was not aware of the content of the recording and did not suspect, and had no reason to suspect, that it was threatening, abusive or insulting.

(4) This section does not apply to the showing or playing of a recording solely for the purpose of enabling the recording to be [included in a programme service].

Section 23: Possession of racially inflammatory material.

(1) A person who has in his possession written material which is threatening, abusive or insulting, or a recording of visual images or sounds which are threatening, abusive or insulting, with a view to—
   (a) in the case of written material, its being displayed, published, distributed, [or included in a cable programme service], whether by himself or another, or
   (b) in the case of a recording, its being distributed, shown, played, [or included in a cable programme service], whether by himself or another,

[1] Contains public sector information licensed under the Open Government Licence v3.0.

is guilty of an offence if he intends racial hatred to be stirred up thereby or, having regard to all the circumstances, racial hatred is likely to be stirred up thereby.

(2) For this purpose regard shall be had to such display, publication, distribution, showing, playing, [or inclusion in a programme service] as he has, or it may reasonably be inferred that he has, in view.

(3) In proceedings for an offence under this section it is a defence for an accused who is not shown to have intended to stir up racial hatred to prove that he was not aware of the content of the written material or recording and did not suspect, and had no reason to suspect, that it was threatening, abusive or insulting.

(4). . . . .

Section 29B: Use of words or behaviour or display of written material

(1) A person who uses threatening words or behaviour, or displays any written material which is threatening, is guilty of an offence if he intends thereby to stir up religious hatred [or hatred on the grounds of sexual orientation].

(2) An offence under this section may be committed in a public or a private place, except that no offence is committed where the words or behaviour are used, or the written material is displayed, by a person inside a dwelling and are not heard or seen except by other persons in that or another dwelling.

(3) . . . .

(4) In proceedings for an offence under this section it is a defence for the accused to prove that he was inside a dwelling and had no reason to believe that the words or behaviour used, or the written material displayed, would be heard or seen by a person outside that or any other dwelling.

(5) This section does not apply to words or behaviour used, or written material displayed, solely for the purpose of being included in a programme service.

Section 29C: Publishing or distributing written material

(1) A person who publishes or distributes written material which is threatening is guilty of an offence if he intends thereby to stir up religious hatred [or hatred on the grounds of sexual orientation].

(2) References in this Part to the publication or distribution of written material are to its publication or distribution to the public or a section of the public.

Section 29D: Public performance of a play

(1) If a public performance of a play is given which involves the use of threatening words or behaviour, any person who presents or directs the performance is guilty of an offence if he intends thereby to stir up religious hatred [or hatred on the grounds of sexual orientation].

(2) This section does not apply to a performance given solely or primarily for one or more of the following purposes—
   (a) rehearsal,
   (b) making a recording of the performance, or
   (c) enabling the performance to be included in a programme service; but if it is proved that the performance was attended by persons other than those directly connected with the giving of the performance or the doing in relation to it of the things mentioned in paragraph (b) or (c), the performance shall, unless the contrary is shown, be taken not to have been given solely or primarily for the purpose mentioned above.

(3) For the purposes of this section—
   (a) a person shall not be treated as presenting a performance of a play by reason only of his taking part in it as a performer,
   (b) a person taking part as a performer in a performance directed by another shall be treated as a person who directed the performance if without reasonable excuse he performs otherwise than in accordance with that person's direction, and
   (c) a person shall be taken to have directed a performance of a play given under his direction notwithstanding that he was not present during the performance;
   and a person shall not be treated as aiding or abetting the commission of an offence under this section by reason only of his taking part in a performance as a performer.

(4) In this section "play" and "public performance" have the same meaning as in the Theatres Act 1968.

(5) The following provisions of the Theatres Act 1968 apply in relation to an offence under this section as they apply to an offence under section 2 of that Act—

   section 9 (script as evidence of what was performed),
   section 10 (power to make copies of script),
   section 15 (powers of entry and inspection).

Section 29E: Distributing, showing or playing a recording

(1) A person who distributes, or shows or plays, a recording of visual images or sounds which are threatening is guilty of an offence if he intends thereby to stir up religious hatred [or hatred on the grounds of sexual orientation].

(2) In this Part "recording" means any record from which visual images or sounds may, by any means, be reproduced; and references to the distribution, showing or playing of a recording are to its distribution, showing or playing to the public or a section of the public.

(3) This section does not apply to the showing or playing of a recording solely for the purpose of enabling the recording to be included in a programme service.

Section 29J: Protection of freedom of expression

Nothing in this Part shall be read or given effect in a way which prohibits or restricts discussion, criticism or expressions of antipathy, dislike, ridicule, insult or abuse of particular religions or the beliefs or practices of their adherents, or of any other belief system or the beliefs or practices of its adherents, or proselytising or urging adherents of a different religion or belief system to cease practising their religion or belief system.

3.2.8 VENEZUELA (NICHOLAS, 2018)

Article 8

In accordance with Article 8, the following actions are taken specifically to avoid xenophobia, harassment, discrimination, and acts of moral or physical violence between people:

- Education and training in education.
- The spread of moral and educational messages via the media.
- The creation of initiatives and programs for legal and social aid.
- Psychotherapy and other medical treatments.
- Any other individuals or groups that the Commission for the Promotion and Guarantee of Peaceful Coexistence determines.

Article 12

Public, private, and community media service providers in charge of radio, television, subscription, and print media must spread messages that encourage harmony, tolerance, equality, respect, and diversity.

Article 13

Under this article, any Propaganda and messages are against the law to advocate for hatred based on one's nationality, race, ethnicity, religion, political or social origin, ideology, gender, sexual orientation, gender identity, gender expression, or any other basis, and it is also against the law to advocate for hatred based on any other basis. The state is required to make sure that this clause is followed to the letter by all radio, television, print, subscription, public, private, and community media outlets, as well as all electronic media service providers.

Article 14: Social Networks' Responsibility

Dissemination of messages encouraging war or inciting hatred based on nationalism, race, ethnicity, religion, political or social origin, ideology, gender, sexual orientation, gender identity, gender expression, or any other grounds that amount to inciting discrimination, intolerance, or violence is prohibited through social networks and electronic media. The governing bodies of social networks and electronic media are obligated to rigorously abide by the terms of this article and will take the necessary steps to stop the spread of these messages.

3.2.9 Vietnam

Cybersecurity Law (Everus, 2018)

The Cybersecurity Law (CSL), which governs operations for the protection of social order and national security in Vietnam's cyberspace, was adopted by the National Assembly of Vietnam on June 12, 2018.

Every Provision in the CSL is intended to safeguard and improve Vietnam's cybersecurity and cyber sovereignty. As a result, CSL is set up so that all of the following illegal activities will be handled and stopped:

- Using information technology, electronic media, and the internet to circumvent laws governing social order, safety, and national security.
- Cyberterrorism, cyberattack, cyberespionage, or cybercrime.
- Preventing or interfering with Vietnam's cyberspace's normal operation.
- Opposing or blocking CA's operations.
- Assaulting, neutralizing, deactivating, or making ineffective any cybersecurity safety measures illegally.
- The misuse or abuse of cybersecurity protection measures to compromise national security, social order, or legitimate agency, organization, or individual rights and interests.

3.2.10 Brazil (Baretto et al.)

The Brazilian "Internet Law" No. 12.965/2014, sets rights and guarantees for all internet users in Brazil, such as the secrecy and integrity of user communications while they are transmitted over the internet and as they are preserved, unless required by a court order.

The fundamental guidelines for protecting personal information are outlined in the Brazilian Federal Constitution ("CF/88"). The CF/88 guarantees the right to compensation for any financial or moral harm caused by a violation of an individual's privacy, private life, honor, or reputation. Data protection was explicitly added as a fundamental right to article 5o of the Brazilian Constitution in February 2022 thanks to Constitutional Amendment No. 115.

Brazil passed the General Data Protection Act (Law No 13,709/2018, or "LGPD") in August 2018. The majority of its provisions took effect in September 2020. Through Law No. 14,010/2020, the provisions that outline the administrative penalties that non-compliance agents are subject to become effective in August 2021.

The LGPD offers a comprehensive set of data protection regulations, covering the gathering, storing, registering, overseeing, processing, and disclosing of personal data processing agents. According to the LGPD (Lei Geral de Protecao de Dados), personal data processing must adhere to many criteria, including non-discrimination, purpose, transparency, security, and free access for the data subject.

The National Data Protection Authority, or "ANPD," is functioning under Brazilian law. The ANPD published its initial regulatory agenda at the end of

January 2021 through Decree No. 11, which prioritized an educational and regulatory agenda with the provision of key issues in the privacy and data protection context, including small and medium-sized enterprises, rights of data subjects, administrative sanctions, and communications on data breaches, among others. To date, the ANPD has released two fascicules, one on data protection and the other on data breaches, intending to increase public knowledge of the key ideas presented by the LGPD.

The ANPD has also released the following guidelines:

- The first one is the Guideline of Definitions of Personal Data Processing Agents and Data Protection Officers, which defines these two roles by the LGPD and provides explanations and examples. The following is a guide on how to protect your data that is meant to inform data subjects about the significance of the issue.
- The second one is the Guideline on Information Security for Small-Sized Processing Agents, which governs the applicability of specific LGPD provisions to small-sized processing agents, including the administrative procedures to be followed and information security precautions to be taken, among other things.

There are further sectorial rules governing data protection and privacy rights, including:

Civil Code (Law No. 10,406/2002): Any person is entitled to general privacy rights under this law, as well as the right to sue any party who attempts to violate those rights.

Consumer Code (Law No. 8,078/1990): The principles of transparency, information, and quality of data on its provisions are protected under this law.

Positive Credit Registry Act (Law No. 12,414/2011): This law allows for databases of "positive" credit information but forbids excessive information for example sensitive information and excessive data collection.

Telecommunications Act (Law No. 9,472/1997): gives users of telecommunications services the right to privacy.

Bank Secrecy Act (Complementary Law No. 105/2001): Under this Act, financial institutions and other similar entities are required to keep financial information about people and entities private, unless a court order is issued to look into potential criminal activity or make a discovery in a criminal case.

Law No. 14,129/2021: outlines data security and privacy as a governmental principle and mentions conformity with LGPD. It also outlines principles, norms, and tools for digital governance and the improvement of public efficiency.

Law No. 13,989/2020. Outlines the use of telemedicine during the COVID-19 situation is allowed. The Federal Council of Medicine is already studying the law for telemedicine use following the pandemic setting to develop an ethical, technical, and secure regulation to offer acceptable telemedicine practice in Brazil while taking into account privacy and data protection for both patients and doctors.

Brazilian Agency for Health Regulation ("ANVISA"): Resolution 68/2022, which addresses the use of software as medical devices, states that patient data shall be processed in compliance with data protection regulations, exclusively for the purposes specified in the resolution, and as required for the assessment of data on the product's safety and efficacy.

3.2.11 CANADA (CALLEGARI, 2022)

Personal Information Protection and Electronic Documents Act ("PIPEDA") is the federal law that governs the protection of employee personal information by federally regulated businesses like banks and telecommunications firms as well as the protection of personal information in the course of commercial activities in all nations without substantially equivalent legislation.

The Digital Privacy Act is responsible for storing and safeguarding personal data. Canadian firms risk severe fines under the Digital Privacy Act restrictions if they fail to protect personal data and appropriately notify individuals when a breach occurs.

Health Information Protection Act: This law protects private health information. Concerning health information, only three provinces have privacy laws that are comparable to PIPEDA (Ontario, New Brunswick, Newfoundland). Data breaches must be reported by these laws.

PCI and E-Commerce: The standards established by the Payment Card Industry Data Security (PCI DSS) These standards are the most prevalent and well-known of these rules. This PCI compliance standard establishes a security baseline for companies and their virtual environment and applies to all merchants that receive, store, or send credit card information.

3.2.12 REAL-WORLD CASES

Challenges (Cybersecurity: Challenges to Democratic Governance) (Benjamin, Fred and Theodor, 2015)

States acting alone are ill-equipped to deal with both conventional and unconventional security concerns. The solution has increasingly been ad-hoc security governance networks and, in particular, public–private partnerships. Such networks enable participants to benefit from geographic, technological, and information resources they would not be able to marshal on their own and entail collaboration between governments, the business sector, non-governmental organizations, and international organizations. The issues posed by the establishment of new governance networks, both theoretical and practical, have received very little attention so far. The difficulties in monitoring posed by cyber security and related public–private cooperation are made worse for several reasons, which are listed below, followed by several instances of state practice from the UK, the US, and Australia.

Network complexity: Network complexity makes oversight tasks more difficult. The involvement of numerous and different state, private, international, and other non-state players in cyber security is demonstrated here. Similar to this, a vast variety of actors take part in what we can generalize as "cyber-attacks." Due to network complexity, it is challenging for oversight authorities, such as legislative committees, to keep track of pertinent actors, learn about their existence and actions, or even obtain a legal mandate to do so. These entities frequently have limited capacity.

Technical complexity: Technical complexity also makes oversight tasks more difficult. Because cyber security issues and solutions are highly technical, oversight authorities frequently lack the necessary knowledge to comprehend and properly supervise them. By creating a gap between the highly paid and sophisticated technical experts involved in putting a directive into action and the (often) less paid and less informed government actors responsible for their oversight, public–private cooperation exacerbates the problem.

Legal complexity: Legal complexity makes oversight challenges more difficult. Cybersecurity raises difficult legal issues, including those involving the right to privacy and freedom of expression. Public–private collaboration and the related legal issues surrounding accountability and control serve to further amplify this complexity.

Engagement of diversity of the actors makes oversight challenges worse. Institutions responsible for monitoring are typically divided into agencies or functional groups. A legislative committee might be in charge of the criminal system, the armed forces, and intelligence operations. However, the public–private partnership in cybersecurity crossed agency borders and, as a result, mandated areas of control. As a result, there are many areas where oversight is absent or insufficient.

Requirement perceptions make supervision issues worse. Government oversight committees are often interested in the government entities they have direct control over. This exempts the private partners of these organizations from monitoring, even when they receive direct funding from or collaborate closely with these organizations.

Breach of principal–agent bonds: this exacerbates monitoring issues. Every government employee has a chain of command that connects their actions from the principal to the agent. For instance, a police officer in Paris is connected to the pre-vote, the senior officer in the force, to the prefect, the force's politically appointed chief, and finally to the interior ministry and the executive, through his or her superiors. Thus, there is a connection between those carrying out government orders and those responsible for overseeing them, such as members of the parliament. The entry of private actors and the development of public–private cooperation mechanisms broke these ties. Although a publicly hired IT company can appear to be the state's (the major) straightforward agent, the relationship is usually far more complicated and tainted by many information asymmetries that diminish openness and make it difficult for oversight systems to function properly.

3.3   CYBER LAWS IN AFRICAN COUNTRIES

3.3.1   SOUTH AFRICA (GOVERNMENT GAZETTE, REPUBLIC OF SOUTH AFRICA)

Illegal access: It is unlawful and intentional conduct for anyone to behave in a way that puts them or another person in a position to commit an offense listed in Sections 3(1), 5(1), or 6(1). This includes acting in a way that involves a computer system or a computer data storage media.

(2) (a) Anyone who gains unauthorized access to a computer system or a computer data storage media with the intent to do so violates the law.

ILLEGAL INTERFERENCE OF DATA OR A COMPUTER PROGRAM

(1) It is unlawful and purposeful interference with data or a computer program that constitutes a crime.
(2) "Interfere with data or a computer program" has the following meanings for this section:
 (a) Delete data or a computer program;
 (b) Alter data or a computer program;
 (c) Make data or a computer program vulnerable, damaged, or deteriorate;
 (d) Make data or a computer program meaningless, useless, or ineffective;
 (e) Obstruct, interrupt, or interfere with the lawful use of data or a computer program;
 (f) Deny providing access to information or a computer program that is stored on a computer data storage medium.

Cyber fraud and uttering

(1) Cyber forgery is the illegal creation of (a) fake data; or (b) false computer programs, to mislead and to the actual or potential detriment of another person.
(2) A person commits a cyber uttering offense if they fraudulently pass off either
 (a) False data or (b) a fake computer program to the actual or potential detriment of another person.

3.3.2   SOUTH SUDAN (WANYAMA, 2021)

Cybercrimes and Computer Misuse Provisional Order 2021: This law was passed by South Sudan to tackle cybercrime. In the Order, terms like "computer abuse," "indecent content," "pornography," and "publish" are given extremely broad definitions that are so imprecise and inclusive that the state might use them to target political opponents, dissidents, and critics. The definitions mainly restrict the use of electronic devices and impose restrictions on the right to free speech and access to information.

Article 22: The right to privacy is protected by Article 22 of the South Sudanese Transitional Constitution of 2011. The nation has ratified both the African Charter on Human and Peoples Rights, whose article 5 guarantees the right to respect one's dignity, which includes the right to privacy, and the International Covenant on Civil and Political Rights (ICCPR), which guarantees the right to privacy under its article 17 as well. The Order appears to violate these documents by endangering people's right to privacy.

3.3.3 ETHIOPIA

Computer Crime Proclamation 2016: In June 2016, Ethiopia's house of people's representatives launched the Computer Crime Proclamation 2016 (the Proclamation). The Proclamation addresses a wide range of topics, including preventing child pornography, unauthorized use of a computer system which is also referred to as "hacking", spamming, etc. The expansion of criminal defamation and the creation of numerous new criminal offenses, along with far-reaching investigative powers, such as law enforcement agency surveillance, however, also result in the creation of many new criminal offenses that are likely to have a significant negative impact on the exercise of the right to freedom of expression and other human rights. This raises severe concerns for the protection of the right to free expression online in Ethiopia in the future in a nation where numerous bloggers, journalists, and human rights activists have recently been imprisoned in apparent violation of international human rights law (Kinfe, 2016).

Criminal Code of 2004: Ethiopia has adopted legislation in response to increased access to information and communication technology, such as the internet. The adoption of cybercrime regulations as a part of the Criminal Code of 2004 is one such legislative measure. These regulations punish three different types of computer crimes: hacking, spreading malware, and denial-of-service assaults. Due to advancements made in the realm of cybercrime since the Code's passage, the cybercrime regulations are, nonetheless, somewhat out of date (Kinfe, 2014).

3.3.4 KENYA (CIVIC SPACE, 2020)

The National Cohesion and Integration (NCI) Act of 2008 in Kenya establishes speech restrictions. A toxic political climate that promotes animosity among the populace forced the government to take action and implement reforms. For instance, the NCI Commission has looked into online hate speech, which resulted in the arrest of six people who were well-known for regularly distributing incendiary views and spreading hate speech online.

From the perspective of "ethnic hatred," the NCI definition of hate speech is overly inclusive and includes written materials, public performances including plays, visual images, and programming. It also includes threatening, abusive, or insulting statements or behavior.

ARTICLE 13: HATE SPEECH

(1) Any person who
   (a) Engages in verbal or physical threats, abuse, or insults, or displays any written material;
   (b) Publishes or disseminates written material;

(c) Presents or oversees the staging of a play for an audience;

(d) Disseminates, exhibits, or plays a recording of moving images; or

(e) If someone intends to incite ethnic hatred by providing, producing or directing a program that is threatening, abusive, or insulting, or that uses threatening, abusive, or insulting language or behavior, they are guilty of an offense (or, given the circumstances, are likely to incite ethnic hatred).

(2) Anyone who violates this section is subject to a fine that does not exceed one million shillings, a term of imprisonment that does not exceed three years, or both.

(3) "Ethnic hatred" in this section refers to animosity toward a group of people who are identified by their color, race, nationality (including citizenship), or ethnic or national origins.

Article 19: The claim made by Kenya's Inspector General, Hillary Mutyambai that the police will keep an eye on political players' local remarks and social media posts worries. In addition to being used to "broadcast harsh comments to a wide audience of innocent people," the IG stated that these social media posts are also used to promote violence.

Article 19 EA points out that this would need the employment of social media surveillance software, which is already in use for data collection, general user monitoring, and, in the case of the Cambridge Analytical data scandal, manipulating users' voting choices.

According to Article 19 EA (Enrolled Agent), the two MPs' thoughts and ideas constitute, at the very least, offensive expression, Given international protections for freedom of expression and the fact that it does not meet the "threshold of severity" that justifies the imposition of criminal sanctions, expression may still be legal under international human rights law even if it is upsetting, provoking, shocking, or has offended an individual or a group.

3.4   CYBER LAWS IN ASIAN COUNTRIES

3.4.1   BANGLADESH

The Digital Security Act of 2018 (Bangladesh, 2018)

The purpose of the Digital Security Act of 2018 was to combat the rise in digital-based crimes against persons and businesses. However, the measure can serve as a barrier to Bangladesh's media and expression rights. The freedom of expression and the freedom of the press are recognized as fundamental rights by the Bangladeshi Constitution (Article 39), yet the current law is neither appropriate nor effective in the digital age to facilitate the free flow of information. The government of the nation is accused of frequently misusing the law for its political gain, according to numerous complaints. This article demonstrates that a variety of broadly defined offenses with harsh penalties are included in the act, which may have dangerously deterring consequences on Bangladesh's freedom of speech.

Section 8: Power to Remove or Block some Data-related Information

(1) The Director General may ask the Bangladesh Telecommunications and Regulatory Authority (BTRC) to remove or block any data-related information regarding a subject that falls under his or her purview that has been published or spread in digital media if it poses a threat to digital security.

(2) If it is clear to the law and order enforcing security force that any information published or spread through digital media jeopardizes the nation or any part of it in terms of national unity, financial activities, security, defense, religious values, public discipline, or incites racism and hatred, the law and order enforcing security force can request BTRC to block or remove the information via the Director General of the agency.

Section 19: Damage of Computer, Computer System, and Punishments

(1) If any person,
   (a). Intentionally inserts or attempts to insert any virus, malware, or other harmful software in any computer, computer system, or computer network;
   (b). Intentionally damages or attempts to damage the data or data storage of any company; or
   (c). Collects any data or data-storage, information, or part of it from any computer, computer network, or collection of transferable information from the said computer, computer system, or collection; or
   (d). Collects any transferable information, or
   (e). without the consent of the sender or recipient, intentionally sends or attempts to create spam or unwanted emails for any product or service marketing, or
   (f). any unreasonable interference with a computer, computer system, or computer network, as well as the enjoyment of a person's service or the charging of or attempting to charge for such service into the account of another, will constitute violations of the Act.

(2) If a person violates any of the provisions of subsection (1), they may be sentenced to a term of imprisonment not to exceed seven years or a fine not to exceed ten lakh taka or both.

(3) If a person violates subsection (1) of this article a second time or repeatedly, they will be penalized with either a term of imprisonment not to exceed ten years, a fine not to exceed twenty-five million takas or both.

Section 22: Electronic or Digital forgery

(1) Any act of forgery committed by a person using digital or electronic media is considered a violation of the Act.

(2) If a person violates any of the provisions of subsection (1), they may be sentenced to imprisonment for a term not to exceed five years, a fine not to exceed five lac aka, or both.

(3) Anyone who repeatedly commits the offense listed in subsection (1) will be punished with either imprisonment for a term not to exceed seven (seven) years, a fine not to exceed ten (ten) lac taka, or both.

Section 27: Punishment for Committing Cyber-terrorism

(1) If anyone,

    (a). with the intent to compromise national security, jeopardize the nation's sovereignty, sow fear among the general public or a segment of it, obstructs authorized access to any computer, computer network, or internet network; or

    (b). produces such pollution in any digital equipment or introduces malware that results in a person dying, suffering a serious injury, or increases the probability of it happening; or

    (c). damages the public's access to daily essentials or negatively impacts any crucial information infrastructure.

    (d). If anyone intentionally or knowingly enters or penetrates any computer, computer network, internet network, any secured data information or computer database, or such a secured data information or computer database that can be used to harm friendly relations with another foreign country; damages or destroys the supply of daily necessities of the public; or adversely affects any critical information infrastructure.

Section 28: Publishing, Broadcasting, etc. of such Information that Undermines Religious Sentiment or Values

(1) If any person or group knowingly or intentionally publishes or broadcasts any information through the use of any website or any electronic format with the intent to undermine religious sentiment or values or to provoke, such activity will be regarded as unlawful;

(2) If a person violates subsection (1), they may be punished with a period of imprisonment not to exceed seven years, a fine not to exceed ten lakhs or both;

(3) Anyone found guilty of the offense listed in subsection (1) a second or subsequent time faces a sentence of up to 10 years in jail, a fine of up to 20 lac taka (20 LAKHS), or both.

Section 31: Act-Order Deterioration and Punishment

(1) Any intentional publication or broadcast of any type of file on a website or other digital platform that degrades or threatens to degrade law and order, fosters animosity, hatred, or adversity among people, destroys communal harmony, or causes unrest or disorder is considered to be unlawful behavior by that person.

(2) Anyone found guilty of committing any of the crimes listed in subsection (1) faces a sentence of up to seven years in jail, a fine of up to five lakh taka, or both.

(3) If a person violates subsection (1) of this article a second time or repeatedly, they will be penalized with either a term of imprisonment not to exceed ten years, a fine not to exceed ten lakh taka (10 lakhs), or both.

3.4.2 China (Creemers, Webster, and Triolo, 2018)

Article 1: Under this law, cybersecurity is ensured, cyberspace sovereignty, national security, and social and public interests are protected, the legal rights and interests of individuals, businesses, and other organizations are safeguarded, and the economic and social benefits of information technology are encouraged.

Article 2: Within the People's Republic of China's continental area, this Law applies to network development, operation, maintenance, and use as well as cybersecurity supervision and management.

Article 3: The State upholds the values of active use, scientific advancement, management in compliance with the law, and maintaining security. The State continues to place equal emphasis on cybersecurity and information technology development. The State promotes the development of network infrastructure and interconnectivity, promotes network technology innovation and application, supports the training of qualified cybersecurity personnel, creates a comprehensive system to protect cybersecurity, and increases capacity to protect cybersecurity.

Article 4: The State develops and continually enhances its cybersecurity strategy, outlines the essential conditions and principal objectives for ensuring cybersecurity, and proposes cybersecurity rules, work tasks, and processes for important industries.

Article 5: The State takes action to monitor, thwart, and address cybersecurity risks and threats that may arise both inside and outside of the People's Republic of China's continental territory. Critical information infrastructure is protected by the state from attacks, incursions, interference, and destruction. Illegal and criminal cyber activity is punished in line with the law, maintaining the security and order of cyberspace.

Article 6: The State promotes sincere, honest, healthy, and polite online behavior; it encourages the spread of core socialist values; adopts measures to increase the general public's awareness of and proficiency in cybersecurity; and creates a favorable environment for the general public to collaborate on the advancement of cybersecurity.

Article 7: The State promotes building a peaceful, secure, open, and cooperative cyberspace as well as establishing a multilateral, democratic, and transparent Internet governance system. It also actively engages in international exchanges and cooperation in the areas of cyberspace governance, research and development of network technologies, formulation of standards, and other similar areas.

Article 8: State cybersecurity and information technology departments are in charge of thoroughly organizing and coordinating cybersecurity initiatives, as well as any associated oversight and management activities. By the provisions of this Law and other pertinent laws and administrative regulations, the State Council departments for telecommunications, public security, and other relevant organs are in charge of cybersecurity protection, supervision, and management efforts within the scope of their responsibilities.

Article 9: Network operators who conduct business and provide services must abide by legal and administrative requirements, uphold social morality and business ethics, be trustworthy and honest, fulfill their obligations to protect cybersecurity, submit to oversight from the government and the general public, and assume social responsibility.

Article 10: The development and operation of networks, or the provision of services through networks, shall be done by the provisions of laws and administrative regulations, as well as the obligatory requirements of national standards; adopting technical measures and other necessary measures to safeguard operational stability and cybersecurity; promptly responding to cybersecurity incidents; preventing cybercrimes and unlawful activity; and maintaining the integrity of networks.

Article 11: In accordance with their articles of association, the relevant Internet industry organizations are required to improve industry self-discipline, develop cybersecurity norms of conduct, assist their members in enhancing cybersecurity protection in accordance with the law, raise the bar for cybersecurity protection, and promote the industry's healthy growth.

Article 12: The State ensures the lawful, orderly, and free flow of network information and protects the rights of individuals, legal entities, and other organizations to use networks in accordance with the law. It also encourages widespread network access, raises the standard of network services, offers secure and practical network services to society, and ensures the availability

Any individual or group using networks must uphold the Constitution and laws, maintain public order, and uphold social morality. They must also refrain from endangering cybersecurity and using the Internet for activities that could jeopardize national security, national honor, or national interests. They must also not promote terrorism or extremism, ethnic or racial extremism, or incite subversion of national sovereignty.

Article 13: The State will legally punish the use of networks to engage in activities that endanger the psychological and physical well-being of minors and will provide a safe and healthy network environment for minors. The State will also encourage research and development of network products and services conducive to the healthy upbringing of minors.

Article 14: Everyone has the right to report behavior that endangers cybersecurity to the departments of cybersecurity and information technology, telecommunications, public security, and other departments. When receiving reports, departments must swiftly process them in conformity with the law and promptly transfer any items that are outside of their purview to the department that has the authority to handle them.

Article 19: All levels of people's governments and their pertinent ministries shall plan and carry out routine cybersecurity publicity and education, and assist and encourage pertinent units in inappropriately trying out such work.

Public awareness campaigns and education about cybersecurity must be conducted by the media.

Article 20: The State supports businesses and educational or training institutions, such as colleges and vocational schools, in providing education and training related to cybersecurity. It also employs a variety of techniques to cultivate qualified cybersecurity personnel and foster professional networking.

3.4.3 INDIA

In today's digital world, hate speech regulations and laws have become challenging to implement for governments and legislators. Because it conflicts with Article 19, the anti-hate speech law is difficult to implement (freedom of speech and expression).

The Indian Constitution, as interpreted by the government, provides for broad regulations and legislation to be imposed to restrict hate speech on the internet. The government imposed this law with the passage of the Information Technology Act, of 2000.

According to this act, "online hate speech" is described as any information or message sent through any computer device or communication network that is considered highly offensive and illegal, or any kind of information that is fake and is sent by a sender intentionally to cause any kind of harm, threat, insult, difference, obstacle, criminal act, hatred, or with the wrong intention. Any individual found guilty and involved in such conduct could face a sentence of up to three years in prison and also be charged with a fine.

Apart from the Constitution, there are a plethora of other laws and self-regulatory frameworks in India to curb hate speech:

The Indian Penal Code, 1860 (The Indian Penal Code, 1860, Act 45 of 1860)

The Indian Penal Code 1860 contains several provisions that restrict freedom of speech and expression on various grounds.

Several cybercrimes are punishable under the Indian Penal Code (as amended by the IT Act). The Indian Penal Code (IPC), 1860, which is invoked with the Information Technology Act of 2000, includes provisions for identity theft and related cyber offenses. The primary relevant section of the IPC covers cyber fraud.

- Forgery (Section 464).
- Forgery pre-planned for cheating (Section 468).
- False documentation (Section 464).
- Presenting a forged document as genuine (Section 471).
- Damage to one's reputation (Section 469).
- Section 124A penalizes sedition.
- Section 153A makes it illegal to "promote animosity between various groups based on religion, race, place of birth, language, or other factors," as well as to engage in acts that are detrimental to maintaining peace.

Under this section, whoever

(a) promotes or attempts to promote, based on religion, race, place of birth, residence, or language, through words, whether spoken or printed, signs, visible representations, or other means; caste or community, or any other ground, disharmony or feelings of enmity, hatred, or ill-will between various religious, racial, language, or regional groups or castes or communities, or;

(b) commits any act which is detrimental to the maintenance of harmony between various religious, racial, or regional groups, castes, or communities and which disturbs or is likely to disturb the public tranquility, shall be punished with imprisonment, which may include fines and/or community service.

Section 153B

1. Punishes imputations and assertions that are harmful to national integration.
2. Assertion, propagation, or publication that any religious, linguistic, regional, caste, or community should be denied their rights as Indian citizens simply because they belong to that group.
3. Any claim or publication regarding a group's obligation "that is likely to provoke discord, feelings of animosity or hatred, or ill will between such a member and other members".
   - Section 295A prohibits "deliberate and malicious activities aimed at insulting any class by disparaging its religion or beliefs".
   - Section 298 makes it a crime to say or do anything with the intent to offend someone's religious feelings.

Section 505 Remarks That Encourage Public Mischief

(1) Anyone who makes, publishes, or spreads any statement, rumor, or report (c) with the intent to incite, or which is likely to incite, any class or community of persons to commit any crime against any class or community of persons shall be punished with imprisonment that may not exceed six years, a fine, or both.

(2) Remarks that incite or encourage animosity, hatred, or malice between classes
    Anyone who makes, publishes, or disseminates any statement or report that contains rumors or alarming information with the intent to sow discord, hatred, or ill-will among various religious, racial, ethnic, linguistic, or regional groups, castes, or communities, or with the knowledge that such discord is likely to sow such discord, shall be subject to imprisonment that may include fines. (3) A violation of section 2 committed in a house of worship, etc.

Anyone who violates subsection (2) while in a house of worship, a gathering where religious ceremonies are being performed, or any other place of worship is subject to a fine along with a prison term of up to five years.

The Companies Act of 2013

The Companies Act of 2013 is cited by corporate stakeholders as the law that must be followed to improve daily operations. This Act's directives bind all required techno-legal compliances, putting less compliant businesses in a legal bind. Under the Companies Act of 2013, the SFIO (Serious Frauds Investigation Office) was given powers to prosecute Indian firms, and their directors' directives bind all required techno-legal compliances, putting less compliant businesses in a legal bind. Under the Companies Act of 2013, the SFIO (Serious Frauds Investigation Office) was given powers to prosecute Indian firms and their directors. Also, since the notification of the Companies Inspection, Investment, and Inquiry Rules, 2014, SFIOs has become even more proactive and stern in this regard. All regulatory compliance is covered by the legislation, including cyber forensics, e-discovery, and cybersecurity due diligence. The Companies (Management and Administration) Rules, 2014 establish severe requirements for corporate directors and leaders in terms of cybersecurity obligations and responsibilities.

Information Technology Act, 2000, and Social Media

Information Technology Act, of 2000 is also known as the Internet Act or IT Act of 2000. Social media platforms in India have become an integral part of the digital world. Every hour, the majority of Indians are active on social media. Social media platforms such as Facebook, Instagram, and WhatsApp, among others, are now widely used and well-known among users in the country. With the freedom of digitalization, access to social media has become easily available to everyone, so many internet users post unsuitable content or data on social media without knowing its implications.

The Information Technology Act, 2000

(a) Under Section XI of the Act, Sections 65, 66, 66A, 6C, 66D, 66E, 66F, 67, 67A, and 67B contain punishments for computer-related offenses that can also be committed through social media, viz. tampering with computer source code, committing computer-related offenses given under Section 43, sending offensive messages through communication services, identity theft, cheating by personation using computer resources, violation of privacy, cyber terrorism, publishing or transmitting obscene material in electronic form, material containing sexually explicit acts in electronic form, and material depicting children in sexually explicit acts in.

(b) Section 69 of the Act grants power to the Central Government or a State Government to issue directions for the interception, monitoring, or decryption of any information through any computer resource in the interest of the sovereignty or integrity of India, the defense of India, the security of the State, friendly relations with foreign states, public order, preventing incitement to the commission of any cognizable offense, or the investigation of any offense.

(c) Section 69A grants power to the Central Government to issue directions to block public access to any information through any computer resource on similar grounds.

(d) Section 69B gives the Central Government the authority to direct any agency to monitor and collect traffic data or information through any computer resource for cyber security.

(e) Section 79 provides for the liability of an intermediary. An intermediary shall not be liable for any third-party information, data, or communication link made available or hosted by him in the following cases:
  • His function is limited to providing access to a communication system over which such information is transmitted, stored, or hosted.
  • He does not initiate, select the receiver, or select or modify the information contained in the transmission.

- He does his job with diligence and adheres to other rules established by the federal government. Reiterating this, an intermediary is liable in the following circumstances:
- He has conspired, abetted, aided, or induced, by threats, promises, or otherwise, the commission of the unlawful act.
- He fails to expeditiously remove or disable access to the material that is being used to commit the unlawful act upon receiving actual knowledge or being notified by the government.

(f) Any intermediary who fails to assist, comply with the direction, or intentionally violates Sections 69, 69A, or 69B is subject to punishment.

(g) Section 43A states that if a body corporate possesses, deals with, or handles any sensitive personal data or information in a computer resource owned, controlled, or if it is owned, controlled, or if it is owned, controlled, or if it is owned, controlled, or if it is owned, controlled, or if it is owned, controlled, or if it is owned, controlled, or if it is owned, controlled, or if it is owned, controlled, or

(h) According to Section 70B, the Indian Computer Emergency Response Team, which will serve as the national agency for carrying out tasks related to cyber security, will be a government agency to be designated by the Central Government. The Central Government of India has also established the following rules to give effect to various parts of this Act:

The Information Technology (Procedure and Safeguards of Interception, Monitoring, and Decryption of Information) Rules, 2009

The Central Government makes these rules by its authority under Section 87(2)(y) concerning the procedure and safeguards for monitoring and collecting traffic data or information under Section 69B (3).

Rule 3 states that an order issued by the competent authority must be followed while intercepting, monitoring, or decrypting information under Section 69.

In the case of the central government, the secretary is the minister of home affairs, and in the event of a state government or union territory, the secretary is in charge of the home department.

Rule 4 establishes a government agency that is authorized by the responsible authority to perform the functions.

Under Rule 10, the name and identification of the official of the authorized agency with whom such information shall be shared are required.

Rule 13 mandates the intermediary to provide all necessary facilities, cooperation, and support for information interception, monitoring, and decryption.

The Information Technology (Procedure and Safeguards for Blocking Access to Information by the Public) Rules, 2009

The Central Government makes these rules in the exercise of its powers under Section 87(2)(z) about the procedure and safeguards for blocking public access under Section 69A. (2)

Rules 3, 4, 5, 6, 7, and 8 outline the standard procedure for submitting a request for blocking to the Nodal Officer of the concerned organization, who shall examine it and forward it to the Designated Officer of the Central Government, who shall further examine it along with a committee and then send their recommendation to the Secretary, Department of IT, for his approval, upon which the Designated Officer shall direct such blocking. However, Rule 9 empowers the Designated Officer to make a blocking decision in cases of emergencies where the delay is unacceptable.

According to Rule 13, each intermediary shall designate a person to receive and handle directions for information blocking, who shall acknowledge receipt of the directions to the Designated Officer within two hours of receipt via acknowledgment letter, fax, or email.

Rule 10 states that upon receipt of a court order directing the blocking of any information, the Designated Officer shall submit it to the Secretary of Information and Technology and initiate action immediately.

The Information Technology (Procedure and Safeguard for Monitoring and Collecting Traffic Data or Information) Rules, 2009

The Central Government makes these rules in the exercise of its authority under Section 87(2) (za) concerning the procedure and safeguards for monitoring and collecting traffic data or information under Section 69B (3).

Rule 3 states that under Section 69B (3), directions for monitoring and collecting traffic data or information must be issued by an order issued by the competent authority.

The competent authority is defined in Rule 2(d) as the Secretary of the Government of India in the Department of Information Technology under the Ministry of Communications and Information Technology.

Rule 3 also states that the competent authority may issue monitoring directions for cyber security purposes.

Rule 4 states that the competent authority may authorize any government agency to monitor and collect traffic or information and that a nodal officer must be designated by the nodal officer to make requests with instructions under Rule 3 to the intermediary's Designated Officer.

The Information Technology (Intermediaries Guidelines) Rules, 2011

The Central Government makes these rules in the exercise of its powers under Section 87(2) (zg) concerning the guidelines to be followed by intermediaries under Section 79(2).

Section 2(w) of the Information Technology Act of 2000 defines "intermediary" concerning any particular electronic record as any person who receives, stores, or transmits that record on behalf of another person or provides any service concerning that record, and includes telecom service, network service, internet service, web-hosting service providers, cyber cafe search engines, online payment sites, online auction sites, and online market places.

Rule 3 requires the intermediary to inform users by clearly stating that they are not to host, display, upload, modify, publish, transmit, update, or share any information that is objectionable under Rule 3(2) in the rules and regulations, privacy policy, and user agreement that are published on the website.

When a violation of Rule 3(2) is observed by or brought to the attention of any intermediary in writing or via e-mail by an affected person, Rule 3(4) requires the intermediary to remove the objectionable content within 36 hours.

The Information Technology (Reasonable Security Practices and Procedures and Sensitive Personal Data or Information) Rules, 2011

The Central Government makes these rules in the exercise of its powers under Section 87(2) (ob) read with Section 43A about reasonable security practices and procedures and sensitive personal data or information.

Rule 6 states that any disclosure of sensitive personal data or information to a third party by a body corporate requires prior permission from the provider of such information. However, without prior consent, the information can be shared with government agencies for identity verification or the prevention, detection, and investigation, including cyber incidents, prosecution, and punishment of offenses.

Section 66A: Information Technology Act, 2000

Section 66A has received the most attention recently, albeit for the wrong reasons.

Before going into the details, it's worth taking a look at Section 66A, the provision itself. Section 66A of the Information Technology Act of 2000, as amended by the Information Technology (Amendment) Act of 2008, provides for punishment for sending offensive messages via communication services, etc., and states:

Any person who sends, using a computer resource or a communication device:

(a) Any information that is grossly offensive or has a menacing character;
(b) Any information that he knows to be false but uses such a computer resource or communication device repeatedly to cause annoyance, inconvenience, danger, obstruction, insult, injury, criminal intimidation, enmity, hatred, or ill will;
(c) Any electronic mail or electronic mail message sent with the intent to annoy or inconvenience the addressee or recipient, or to deceive or mislead them about the origin of such message,

Shall be punished by imprisonment for a term of up to three years and with a fine.

Section 66A was added to the Act by an amendment in 2008. The first two sub-clauses of Section 66A were only included in the Amendment Bill, which was introduced in Parliament in 2006. Section 66A was designed to combat spam, which is defined as unwanted and unwarranted e-mails.

According to the Department of Information Technology, sub clause (b) of Section 66A and clause I of Section 43 of the Act adequately address the issue of spam. However, in its 2007 report, the Standing Committee on Information Technology recommended that the bill be strengthened. As a result, sub-clause (c) was added to the provision, in addition to increasing the penalty for a violation to three years' imprisonment from up to two years.

A cursory examination of the provision reveals an inherent inconsistency between the phraseology of Section 66A and Article 19(1) (a) of the Constitution, which guarantees freedom of speech and expression to all citizens. Restrictions on freedom of speech and expression are reasonable under Article 19(2) if they are related to any of the listed grounds, such as India's sovereignty and integrity, the security of the state, friendly relations with foreign states, public order, decency, or morality, or concerning contempt of court, defamation, or incitement to an offense. However, restrictions on freedom of speech and expression have been imposed under Section 66A for a variety of reasons other than those mentioned in the Constitution.

Various provisions contain several anomalies that are incompatible with free speech requirements. Words such as "grossly offensive," "menacing character," "annoyance," "danger," "obstruction," "insult," and "injury" lack precise definitions. A significant question that has remained unanswered is whether these words should be interpreted in light of the sensibilities of the person to whom they are addressed or in light of the sensibilities of a reasonable man. Based on the sensibilities of specific individuals, it is very likely that even the authors of innocent e-mail communication could be accused of breaking the law.

Section 69A: Blocking Access to Content, (Section 2(1), Information Technology Act, 2000)

Section 69A of the IT Act and the rules notified thereunder grant the government the authority to order intermediaries organizations that store or distribute information on behalf of others, which includes internet service providers and social media sites to block online services. The government has the authority under this section to block, filter, or otherwise restrict access to any website or source on the internet.

Section 69A of the Information Technology Act, 2000 ("IT Act")

Empowers the central government to block public access to any illegal or harmful content that the central government deems necessary in the interest of India's sovereignty and integrity, defense, state security, friendly relations with foreign states, public order, or preventing incitement to the commission of a cognizable offense. The order to prevent public access to such content must be in writing.

In Rules 3, 4, 5, 6, 7, and 8, the standard way of transmitting requests for blocking to the Nodal Officer of the relevant organization is described.

Under Rule 13, every intermediary must designate a person to receive and manage directions for information blocking, and that person must acknowledge receipt of the directions to the Designated Officer within two hours of receipt by letter, fax, or email.

Under Rule 10, on receipt of a court order requiring the blocking of any material, the Designated Officer shall transmit it to the Secretary, Department of Information and Technology, and take appropriate action.

Rules for Blocking Online Content on Social Media

Section 69A notes that the government may only block access to information if it believes it is "necessary or expedient" to do so in the interests of one or more of the six stated reasons. The basis on which hate speech is most likely to be silenced among the enumerated grounds is "public order." This is important because it means that the blocking order can be questioned in principle if it does not meet the Supreme Court's requirements for speech restriction in the public interest.

In case of any emergency, the blocking rules also provide special procedures. In this case, the designated officer can review the request and make recommendations to the Secretary of the Department of Information Technology. If the secretary is pleased, temporary orders restricting access to the information may be released. However, the request for emergency blocking must be made in writing. However, within 48 hours of the secretary's interim directions, the request for emergency blocking must be submitted to the committee.

According to the Blocking Rules, any government agency or intermediary may be ordered to block any online material or content. The Department of Telecommunication has been known to give blocking orders to licensed internet service providers (ISP). There has also been contacting with intermediaries through government agencies, such as CERT, to limit content.

NIST Compliance (Joint Task Force, 2020)

As the most trusted global certifying organization, the National Institute of Standards and Technology (NIST) has approved the Cybersecurity Framework (NCFS), which provides a standardized approach to cybersecurity. The NIST Cybersecurity Framework encompasses all required guidelines, standards, and best practices to manage cyber-related risks responsibly. This system is built on the principles of flexibility and cost-effectiveness. It increases critical infrastructure resilience and protection by:

- Allowing better interpretation, management, and reduction of cybersecurity risks—to mitigate data loss, data misuse, and the subsequent restoration costs.
- Identifying the most crucial activities and operations to concentrate on securing them.
- Demonstrates the trustworthiness of organizations that secure critical assets.
- Addresses regulatory and contractual obligations.
- Supports the wider information security program.

Cybersecurity risk management becomes easier when the NIST CSF framework is combined with ISO/IEC 27001. It also makes communication easier throughout the organization and across the supply chains via a common cybersecurity directive laid out by NIST.

3.4.4 INDONESIA (KUSBIANTO ET AL., 2020)

Amendments to Law Number 11 of 2008: Concerning Electronic Information and Transactions, Law Number 19 of 2016, may offer a foundation for the use of electronic transactions with the adoption of Law Number 19 of 2016 about Electronic Information and Transactions.

Electronic evidence can now be used in court as evidence because of the introduction of the ITE Law, which is an expansion of the Criminal Procedure Code. Article 5 of the Law on Electronic Information and Transactions regulates electronic evidence (ITE). Article 5 deals with the admissibility of electronic materials as evidence in courts. The new ITE Law was enacted in response to a ruling by the Constitutional Court that electronic records received by eavesdropping (interception) without a judge's authority are invalid as evidence.

Law Number 21 of 2007 is for the eradication of the crime of human trafficking. The rule respecting electronic evidence is more explicit in Article 29 of the Law on the Eradication of the Crime of Trafficking in Persons than it was in the prior law. It has not yet caught up to the rapidly evolving variety of electronic evidence, nevertheless.

Money Laundering Law Number 8 of 2010: Electronic evidence is governed by Law Number 8 of 2010 concerning Money Laundering, as seen in Article 73. The law of proof is utilized in this statute in addition to the types of evidence allowed under the Criminal Procedure Code.

Additionally, it is acceptable to employ electronic evidence, allowing for the creation of such evidence. Only the information that was spoken, communicated, received, or stored electronically via an optical device or anything similar is permitted to be used according to the law. Electronic evidence has not yet been allowed to be used by this legislation

3.4.5 Nepal (Nepal's Constitution of 2015)

Article 17: Right to Freedom
Under this, no one's freedom may be taken away from them unless it is permitted by law.

(2) Each citizen is guaranteed the following liberties:

(a) The right to free speech and association;
(b) The right to peaceful assembly;
(c) The right to organize political parties;
(d) The freedom to organize labor unions and associations;
(e) The freedom to move and live anywhere in Nepal;
(f) The right to engage in any occupation or profession; and
(g) The freedom to start and run any industry, trade, or business anywhere in Nepal.

Article 19: Right to Communication
(1) No publication or broadcasting, information distribution, the printing of news articles, editorials, features, or other reading materials, or use of audio-visual content by any method, including electronic publication, broadcasting, or printing, must be subject to prior control.
(2) No radio, television, online publication, any type of digital or electronic equipment, press, or another type of media outlet shall be closed, seized, or have its registration revoked for publishing, transmitting, or broadcasting such material. ((2). If there is any broadcasting, publishing

or printing, or dissemination of news, article, editorial, feature, or other material through the medium of electronic equipment or the use of visuals or audio-visuals.

With the caveat that nothing in this section should be interpreted as precluding the passage of legislation governing the use of radio, television, the internet, other digital or electronic devices, printing presses, or other forms of communication.

(3) No form of communication, including the press, electronic transmission, and telephone, may be hindered unless required by law.

Article 21 Rights of a Victim of Crime

(1) The right to information regarding the investigation and court procedures involving one's victimization belongs to the victim of crime.
(2) The right to social rehabilitation, justice, and compensation as specified by law belongs to the victim of crime.

Article 28: Right to Privacy

The right to privacy regarding a person, their home, their possessions, their records, statistics, correspondence, and their reputation is unalienable unless otherwise specified by law.

Article 29: Right against Exploitation

(1) Every person must be protected against exploitation.
(2) No one shall be the victim of any form of exploitation based on their religion, culture, customs, traditions, practices, or any other basis.

The Electronic Transaction Act, 2063 (2008)

In this Act, "Asymmetric Crypto System" means, unless the topic or context otherwise requires, a system that generates a secured key-pair made up of a private key for producing a digital signature and a public key for verifying the digital signature.

(b) "Licence" refers to a licence obtained by Section 18's subsection (3).
(c) A person who generates, saves, or transmits electronic records is referred to as an "originator," and this term also includes a person who directs another person to perform such tasks, as long as there is no middleman involved.
(d) "Computer" refers to an electromagnetic, optical, or other high-speed data processing device or system that manipulates electromagnetic or optical impulses to perform logical arithmetic, and memory functions. It also includes all input, output, processing, storage, and computer software operations, as well as any communication facilities that are linked to the computer as part of any computer system or computer network.

(e) "Computer Database" refers to any information, knowledge, concept, or presentation of instructions that is being prepared, has already been prepared, or has been produced by a computer, computer system, or computer network for use in a computer, computer system, or computer network in word, image, voice, or audio-visual form.

(f) "Computer network" refers to a grouping of two or more computers that are connected or in communication with one another.

(g) A device or group of devices that contain all computer programs, including input and output support devices, electronic instructions, input and output data, and input and output data that performs logical, arithmetic, data storage and retrieval, communication, and control functions, is referred to as a "computer system."

3.4.6 PAKISTAN (DETAILS OF IPC SECTIONS 153A, 295 & 295A)

Article 153(A) consists of the following concerns:

- The act of inciting hostility between groups of people based on their shared religion, race, place of birth, place of residence, language, caste, community, or any other group.
- Acts that undermine public peace and are harmful to the maintenance of harmony between various groups, castes, or communities.
- Acts that use criminal force or violence against members of any caste, community, racial, or ethnic group to instill dread, alarm, or a sense of insecurity in them.
- This Section 153 A, punishes those who engage in the willful denigration of or attacks on any particular group or class, as well as its founders and prophets, or on grounds of race, religion, nationality, place of birth, domicile, or language. The scope of this Section is expanded to include the propagation of hostility, animosity, hatred, or other negative emotions toward other castes, communities, racial groups, or ethnicities. In this section, the offense of moral turpitude is also covered.

The offense is recognizable, and the maximum sentence is three years in prison, a fine, or a combination of the two. But the penalty for an offense committed in a house of worship is increased up to five years with a fine.

3.4.7 REAL-WORLD CASE

INDIA (TAKE DOWN OR REMOVE ANY INAPPROPRIATE CONTENT OR MATERIALS FROM SOCIAL NETWORKING SITES)

In the year 2020, India accelerated to another milestone, becoming the world's second-largest internet user. But, on the other side, these unquestionable figures forced the need for the country's strong cybersecurity framework.

According to Indian law, cybercrime must be voluntary and willful, involving an act or omission that harms a person or property. On October 17, 2000, the

Indian parliament passed the first "Information Technology Act, 2000" to address cybercrime in the fields of e-commerce, e-governance, and e-banking, as well as penalties and punishments. The Information Technology (IT) Act of 2000 defines the punishable acts.

The fundamental right under the Indian Constitution to freedom of speech and expression for Indian citizens can be practiced only against the state. The right shall be subject to fair restrictions laid down in Article 19(2) of the Constitution of India. These restrictions are also applicable to the press.

There are various reasons to take down or remove any inappropriate content or materials from social media websites. When we receive a request to delete material, whether through our formal web form or informally through other channels, by court order, or by a government agency, we choose a justification from a list of reasons, similar to how an individual reporting chooses a justification from a list of reasons. Posting content that depicts live terror attacks or includes hate speech, child pornography, cyberbullying content, fake news, or misinformation on the internet, particularly on today's social media platforms, are a few examples.

The Supreme Court of India held in *Shreya Singhal v. Union of India* that the intermediary is only required to remove or take down online content or posts upon receipt of actual information from a court order or the relevant government or its agency, however, not based on consumer complaints (*Shreya Singhal v. Union of India*, 2012).

The constitution of India strictly prohibits online hate speech based on religion, ethnicity, culture, or race. In the year 2020, India was among the five countries that accounted for 95% of global legal requests to remove or delete illegal or unlawful online content, with Japan, Turkey, South Korea, and Russia being among the other countries (White, 2022).

By adding Section 66A to the Information Technology Act of 2000 in 2008, a significant step was made toward criminalizing online hate speech. To prevent annoyance, inconvenience, danger, obstruction, insult, injury, criminal intimidation, enmity, hatred, or ill will, the provision was made applicable to "any information sent utilizing a computer resource or communication device that is grossly offensive or menacing in character, or any information that the sender knows to be false but sends anyway" (Section 66A).

According to a recent survey, the government has issued certain draft rules to control social media, streaming platforms, and online news material, including a code of ethics and a system to report and request the removal of unsuitable or inappropriate content on the internet.

The IT (Intermediary Guidelines and Digital Media Ethics Code) Rules 2021, which impose takedown and complaint restrictions on important social media intermediaries with more than five million users, were recently introduced by the Indian government, and Facebook responded favorably to them (Mendiratta, 2021). This new law requires Facebook and other major platform companies to remove illegal content at the request of the government or its agency within 36 hours, and non-consensual sharing of intimate images within 24 hours. It also requires them to appoint Grievance Officers who are required to acknowledge complaints about content and resolve them within 15 days, as well as to publish a monthly compliance report on complaints actions.

3.5   NON-LEGAL MEASURES

Government regulations alone are insufficient to stop online hate speech and other forms of cybercrime. Along with the rules established by sovereign states, social media platforms like Twitter, Facebook, and YouTube have also established some rules and community standards. Therefore, it is crucial to use non-legal measures to bridge the gap between the legal environments. Social media is the primary tool used nowadays for both online crime and social communication. This social media, which comprises tweets, blogs, chat messages, SMS, and phone conversations, for instance, can be utilized offline to look into crimes or in real-time to prevent them. Social media serves as a platform for both community dialogue and criminal activity because of its quick response times. Social media is currently being used by law enforcement to prevent crime. Increased accountability from internet intermediaries like search engines, social media platforms, and internet service providers helps stop online crimes.

Internet service providers might dramatically lessen harassment online if they voluntarily increased their involvement in cyber-racism censorship and complaint handling through their terms of service (ToS). Facebook and YouTube have already incorporated anti-racism policies into their terms of service as community standards for users to follow to keep users of all backgrounds safe. According to the specific community standards of Facebook and YouTube, hateful content is not allowed. These guidelines describe hate speech as "a direct attack on people based on what we term protected characteristics—race, ethnicity, national origin, religion, sexual orientation, caste, sex, gender, and significant disease or disability," the use of "violent or demeaning remarks, declarations of inferiority, or appeals for exclusion or segregation." According to this policy, they can censor, remove, block, or take down illegal information from their websites. Additionally, the reporting rules urge users to report any illegal content that violates the ToS and promote transparency. Additionally, users have the option to self-report content that they believe violates YouTube's community guidelines by flagging it. The categories "hateful content," "violent and graphic content," "harmful or dangerous content," "nudity or sexual content," and copyright infringement all include references to these rules. Therefore, social media intermediaries have been advised to assume greater responsibility for governing and managing complaints to combat cybercrime.

3.6   CHALLENGES IN CYBER LAWS: INDIAN SCENARIO

Cyberstalking, cyberbullying, identity theft, and other crimes are on the rise as a result of improper social media use. Despite the efforts of key stakeholders, social media privacy is going to be severely compromised. It would be difficult for cyber legislators to control social media abuse and offer compensation to victims of social media crimes. Concerning the association or nexus with the output of social media, social media litigation is also projected to rise.

- Ignorance about cyber security and its culture, both at the individual and departmental levels.
- A lack of skilled workers to carry out the recommended actions.
- Along with the widespread usage of pirated software, a basic problem that has persisted for a while is the lack of e-forensic knowledge and ability. Controlling cybercrimes becomes increasingly difficult due to the widespread usage of pirated software, which is more vulnerable to attacks from viruses, malware, and Trojan horses. Developing nations like India, Brazil, China, Malaysia, and Pakistan have been major factors in the rise in piracy rates.
- The absence of an email account policy, particularly for members of the armed forces, police, and security agencies.
- Cyberattacks are being launched against our national interests not only by terrorists but also by neighbors.
- The government sector is unable to pinpoint the source of these cybercrimes because of the speed at which cyber technology is evolving.
- Promotion of R&D (research and development) in the IT sectors are not up to par.
- Law enforcement and security personnel lack the necessary training and tools to manage or respond to high-tech crimes.
- The cost of gathering evidence by using a forensic and scientific crime-solving approach is very expensive compared to gathering evidence in terrestrial crimes because of the high-tech tools, materials, and expertise required to conduct such investigations.
- Budgets set aside by the government for security objectives, specifically for educating law enforcement, crime security officers, and investigators in ICT, are insufficient.

3.7 TECHNOLOGICAL, ETHICAL, AND SOCIAL CHALLENGES

3.7.1 TECHNOLOGICAL CHALLENGES

With the rising use of digital technology, numerous new issues are anticipated to affect cyber law. Among the many new trends are:

Problems with mobile laws: There are many activities taking place in the mobile ecosystem nowadays. New mobile phones and personal digital assistant (PDA) devices, tablets, smartphones, and other communication devices are constantly released in the international market.

The mobile ecosystem has expanded due to the widespread usage of mobile devices, and the content produced will probably create new difficulties for global cyber legal jurisprudence. In many jurisdictions throughout the world, where the use of mobile devices for input and output activities is growing daily, there are no specific regulations governing the use of these new communication devices and mobile platforms.

The need to address the legal issues arising from the usage of mobile devices and assure mobile privacy and protection is growing as a result of the rise in mobile crimes.

Cloud computing and legal issues: With the advancement of digital technology, the world is moving towards cloud computing as it is cost-effective, but it also presents new difficulties for legislators. Data security, data privacy, jurisdiction, and other legal concerns are among the specific difficulties. Legal issues arise as a result of the storing, processing, and sharing of cloud-based data across multiple jurisdictions. Today, with the help of information, communication, and technology (ICT), many micro, small, and medium-sized enterprises (MSMEs) around the world are progressively implementing cloud-based solutions. But due to a lack of knowledge about the legal difficulties, the cloud service provider (CSP) may face legal or jurisdictional concerns. In particular, when cloud computing is used by small and medium enterprises ("SMEs"), licensing agreements, contracts, sharing agreements, and other documents may not offer the legal repercussions and remedies typically associated with these levels of protection for corporations. Additionally, this new trend raises many risk issues related to intellectual property, trade secrets, foreign direct investment (FDI), and company governance that have not yet been extensively investigated, put into practice, or contested in domestic and international markets and courts. From the perspective of the cloud community, there is also a foresighted concern about privacy and data protection, as well as regarding the capacity of the service providers to guarantee that privacy is not violated and data is not lost or improperly used.

Also, because of the dispersed geographical locations of the service providers, cloud-based storage becomes problematic. Therefore, in terms of legal concern, many stakeholder roles and duties inside the cloud computing infrastructure can be complicated. For example, a mobile phone made in South Korea can include the data of a user from India. A US-based corporation with data servers located in Europe may provide cloud services to a mobile phone manufacturer as well. Thus, it is clear from this example that the data of a single Indian user is stored across four different sites.

Another one of the worst types of legal sanctions levied by regulatory bodies around the world is copyright infringement. An individual or business owns the intellectual property rights to the data. Data leaks and theft could make a cloud-based service provider ineffective.

Legal Issues in Social Media

National security concern: National security is the first and most important challenge. This means the military's contribution to the development of the internet and cyberspace. One example of the social media platforms that worry security services is encrypted messages. Social media is shown to have a dual nature in this context, highlighting both its positive and negative traits. In addition to serving as a casual allusion to other instances of domestic or international criminal conduct, it serves as a reminder of the destructive threat that terrorism poses.

Confidential information disclosure: On social media, people frequently unintentionally reveal private information. The strength of your security should then be continually reviewed through precautions like software updates, virus protection, firewalls, passwords, and data backups. Make sure to frequently check your privacy settings because the website may occasionally change them.

Copyright infringement: Internet technology makes it simple to copy and paste information, images, and videos from one website to another, infringing on the rights of third parties. They transfer the burden of copyright to the users and make this clear in our copyright agreement because it is nearly impossible to monitor all the messages before posting, especially in high traffic. Additionally, social media platforms offer a function that enables other users to spot copyright violations and report them to us.

Data protection: The protection of users' rights to their privacy and the applicability of data protection to providers raise serious issues. This issue is crucial because it involves the user's data and establishes high standards for the protection of individuals in the processing of their data.

By the ease with which users disclosed personal information on various social media platforms without a lack of awareness and understanding regarding the threats and dangers of revealing personal information. As a result, there is a higher chance that personal information may be exposed and tracked down, which will violate that person's privacy and data protection.

Privacy and security issues: Social media is an important platform for connecting people, user interaction, and information sharing. But because they can be used by attackers to reveal a variety of sensitive or personal information, the main problems with social media revolve around user security and privacy as well as their data. These problems frequently arise due to social media service providers, unauthorized users, or other parties that utilize social media platform data for commercial purposes. Online social networks have provided built-in control mechanisms to limit access to this personal information and enforce its protection. However, users of social networks generally fall short of completely protecting their identities and personal information from unwanted kinds of access, which increases the risk to privacy.

Social networking platforms can also mine, copy, or preserve user data whenever they want and frequently without the users' awareness. Personal information can be mined and utilized to uncover details about users' private lives, their social connections, or other details that they would prefer to remain secret. Therefore, due to the abundance of information sources that are easily accessible online, it becomes very challenging to preserve users' privacy and security on social media.

Defamation: When someone's reputation is harmed by a defamatory statement or piece of writing, that person has been defamed. Here, there may be legal repercussions because a defamatory comment can spread quickly online to multiple jurisdictions. Legal problems resulting from defamation on social media sites may have broad repercussions. This is because the publication of a defamatory comment online spreads to many jurisdictions in a matter of seconds. A person's reputation may suffer severe harm as a result of this.

However, written communication is thought to have a larger potential for harm, and defamation law has long made a distinction between spoken and written communication. Social media, when considered as an online dialogue, acts as a transcript and puts the "speakers" in a stronger position to be held accountable legally. Additionally, it could be argued that the permanent nature of social media comments place the person at home in a position similar to that of a publisher defendant in common defamation cases because this form of communication must be viewed as going beyond what was previously considered.

Employment law: Online abuse and harassment are made possible by social media platforms. Employers are vicariously accountable for the actions of one employee against another throughout the course of their employment, which might result in allegations of discrimination or constructive unfair dismissal. Having adequate social media rules in place for its employees is crucial for a business.

3.7.2 ETHICAL CHALLENGES

The ethical issues associated with online social media are increasing with the freedom of digitization. Below are a few ethical issues that today's various users of social media face:

Privacy invasion: The term "privacy" is described as the ability to live without interference with private data collection or unauthorized revelation of personal information. Social media is completely private; it is like an open book to the public, and therefore material uploaded on social media cannot be deleted forever. However, social media in particular has changed the idea of where privacy is expected and what obligations its makers and users have legally.

If a social media user violates the law or the conditions of their privacy, it should be regarded as unethical if it damages their reputation on a personal or professional level. Any non-permissive method used to obtain personal information or any other type of information about a person that could endanger him or have any negative effects on him would be considered an invasion of privacy.

Behavioral targeting raises ethical concerns when talking about social media ethics. To leverage this information in retargeting ads, advertisers track our online shopping habits and click-through tendencies. The viewers may recognize the relevance of the information being offered to them, which is a plus, but this is still a form of privacy invasion. Thus, it is everyone's responsibility to educate themselves on how to protect it, as social media-related ethical challenges are growing quickly in this digital age.

Software piracy: Software piracy is the act of making an unauthorized copy of software. Whether or not users are allowed to make backup copies of their software is entirely up to the software's owner. Legislation to prevent the unauthorized reproduction of software is being considered as copyright protection laws change. The software sector is ready to fight back against software theft. A growing number of cases involving the protection of software are being heard in court.

Trust issues: Investigations into the use of online social networks have also focused heavily on trust. The definition of trust given by Mayer et al. is: "Regardless of the ability to watch over or control the other party, trust is defined as "the preparedness of a party to be vulnerable to the acts of another party based on the anticipation that the other will execute a certain action significant to the trustor."

A social media user will always struggle with trust issues to some degree because social media platforms are unpredictable as people from all over the world connect and share information. Therefore, trust is a crucial element in coping with future or uncertain consequences. However, in today's digital age, many users on social media platforms commit fraud, cheat, deceive numerous people globally, and violate trust.

For instance, a third party may often create a fake account when purchasing online to defraud other customers by lying and applying various fraudulent methods.

Public criticism: People who use social media may believe that their online identities are private and that they are free to express whatever they want, but this is not the case, and it raises ethical issues. Because of the wide spectrum of unfavorable effects, disparaging your rivals on SNS (social networking sites) is regarded as immoral. Once something is uploaded, it is no longer private property and has the potential to spread like wildfire without your consent. As a result, it can negatively impact not just your reputation but also that of the person or business you insulted. Such situations may also increase the likelihood of legal action.

Spamming: Spam, or unauthorized e-mails, is a problem that is getting worse as the world becomes more digital. Sending excessively unwanted promotional messages for misleading and unethical advertising is also regarded as unethical behavior. In today's digital world, approximately 40% of all internet emails are spam, with very little cost, and this has become a global challenge. These advertising emails cover a wide range of topics, including employment schemes, work-from-home schemes, real estate investments, health and diet scams, gambling, domestic and international mail-order brides, pornography, and so on. These actions highlight the general absence of ethical and moral character in societies around the world and how widespread this issue is. Therefore, one can send thousands of unauthorized messages, resulting in the leakage of private data and the transmission of viruses through email attachments, in less than an hour for very little money and effort. Along with reducing internet traffic, the result burdens the recipient in an unfair, costly, pointless, and time-consuming way.

Numerous initiatives in several countries have been taken to lessen spamming and its negative effects. These initiatives include controlling and regulating email traffic, using anti-spam filters, avoiding "junk" email lists, and being more aware of the tricks senders use to get email addresses. In spamming, people are frequently loaded with fake and unauthorized information that either does not interest them or, even if it does, is too vast to be digested. Because of that meaningless pile of spam, which is immoral from the user's perspective, the user's related information that he may be wanting becomes buried and may get disregarded in this case.

In addition to violating customer privacy, spam eats up stolen bandwidth and frequently forces ISPs to shut down completely. Numerous people view spammers as thieves, liars, and cyber terrorists who will go to considerable measures to forcefully market their goods or interests to any unwilling victim.

Falsehood and deception: There is currently no mechanism that is applied to assess the activities related to the sincerity and authenticity of users on social media. Today, in this digital age, transparency is the most effective tool for communications and other actions posted on social media. Even on social media, lying about anything is considered unethical. Therefore, if you continue making false statements about yourself or others or commenting on offensive material, it will eventually harm your personality or your business. You put your reputation as an individual and the name of your business in danger by engaging in such unethical behavior. As a result, it is an individual's responsibility to keep ethics and morals in mind whenever they use social media.

Improper anonymity and false endorsements: It is immoral or unethical to become anonymous while presenting yourself as someone other than who you are if you portray yourself with false affiliations, credentials, or knowledge. There are fraudsters on social media who give businesses anonymous feedback that is untrue and has done a lot of harm to said businesses by fabricating consumer stories about their products. It is also immoral to hire people to write complimentary stories about your business or your products. Some employees have also been found guilty of exaggerating their weaknesses in the marketplace.

Furthermore, many cybercriminals create fake accounts on different social media platforms, which leads to a variety of crimes. One of the most frequent offenses is having someone else open credit card accounts in your name; this is known as identity theft. Your name, birth date, contact number, social security number, and address are all that cybercriminals need to commit this type of crime.

Misuse of free advice and contests: As Facebook contests and other forms of crowdsourcing are more frequently used to gather design ideas, participants run the risk of disclosing their secrets for no compensation. The majority of the time, design suggestions go to the social network sponsor's most lucrative partners, leaving many others with unpaid work. This misuse is especially immoral if the sponsor purposefully solicits better design ideas from competitors they don't intend to pay.

Business Ethics-Related Issues

Risk of integrity: Risk is the main ethical issue relating to social media. The company's commitment to ethical behavior can be weakened and its integrity put at risk when an employee uses social media carelessly, whether on behalf of the business or through their personal social media account. Controlling this is harder for businesses. As an alternative, staff members could criticize the business on their personal social media pages.

Duty of care: As mentioned, social media makes it difficult to distinguish between personal and professional life. An ethical problem arises when comments made by individuals on social media sites such as personal profiles or online forums are made about a business. What control, if any, the corporation has over remarks shared in this fashion is unknown, as is the appropriate course of action. It may be challenging for businesses to uphold their duty of care to employees if personal and professional lives become increasingly entwined.

Marketing and advertising techniques: Social networking sites are widely used by businesses to market their goods and services. As compared with traditional media, social media is an efficient tool for businesses to sell their brands and products because of its reach and speed. Several businesses, including Facebook, Instagram, and Google, use the data they gather via online behavioral advertising to either sell a certain product or advertise their own. Companies have a responsibility to promote properly while using any kind of marketing technique. Social media's interactive features allow businesses to interact with their clients more directly than they can with other traditional media. This raises new ethical issues.

3.7.3 SOCIAL CHALLENGES

Social problems like homophiles are also caused by social media. Homophile is known as the "Tendency to form intimate social bonds with people who have similar characteristics to oneself, such as age, gender, ethnicity, socioeconomic status, personal values, etc., is known as homophile."

Homophile is "a core organizing element" in society and is influenced by things like geography, links to one's family, academics, employment, and volunteer activities. While homophile promotes inter-group rivalry and segregation, it also strengthens intra-group solidarity. Age, religion, education, occupation, and gender come in nearly that order after homophobia in race and ethnicity as the biggest dividers in our private surroundings."

According to research (Tullo, 2017), users with more friends on social media tend to be happier. When the person's new friends comment on and like their posts, their confidence rises. Accordingly, homophile can be advantageous for users in terms of assisting them in making more connections and friends who will support their postings by liking and commenting on them.

While homophile may result in positive emotions, it can also develop terrorism and has been linked to bullying and extremism. When someone feels secure and is surrounded by people who share their views, it is simple for them to feel strong enough to bully or terrify. For instance, someone might criticize a friend's political opinions on Facebook, confident that their other friends will support them and engage in debate. It's interesting to note that while terrorists utilize social media to legitimize violence, most recruits are not found there. However, social media does aid terrorists in maintaining their message and establishing legitimacy (Tullo, 2017).

3.7.4 SOCIAL CHALLENGES WITHIN THE LBGT COMMUNITY

The LGBT (lesbian, gay, bisexual, and transgender) community continues to face numerous significant LGBT legal and social concerns despite various advancements made in the last decade in the battle for equality and human rights. The propagation of harmful and hateful content on social media platforms has a negative influence on social media users, particularly LGBT people. In this digital age, there is a rise in the amount of hate speech directed at lesbians, gay men, bisexuals, and transgender people on social media sites. LGBT persons experience a variety of socioeconomic and cultural discrimination since they are a social minority group. They are more likely to encounter discrimination, hatred, harassment, bullying, and the threat of violence because of their sexual orientation. Therefore, social media platforms have become toxic places that the LGBT community finds offensive since they lead to major societal problems. LGBT people are prevented from participating fully in society due to fear and intimidation caused by hate crimes and hate speech.

Effects of exclusion and discrimination: As LGBT people are constantly misunderstood and even hated by society as a whole, they are more likely to face discrimination in many ways at work and almost every aspect of their social lives, such as:

- isolated and neglected by society;
- rejection from family and friends;
- leaving home and family;
- leaving or quitting school early;
- moving to new locations such as the city and urban areas;

- attempting suicide;
- unable to obtain regular employment; fewer possibilities than others;
- unable to access services and unaware of their rights;
- migration to other nations in search of a better way of life and acceptance;
- rejection from certain religious groups, particularly those belonging to the fundamentalist branches of Islam and Christianity.

Marriage-related issues: To the LGBT community, legal equality does not always apply. The fights for equal adoption rights and same-sex marriage are still going on. Marriage between men and women is the norm for marriage partners and a legal requirement in many countries. Even though same-sex marriage is now permitted in several nations, including the United States, Germany, France, and India, it is still prohibited in others. Few nations, including Indonesia, Afghanistan, Pakistan, Saudi Arabia, etc., forbid marriage between people of the same gender since it goes against social, cultural, and religious standards. Society views LGBT individuals as odd because they deviate from social and religious norms, and they are therefore seen negatively.

Impact on their mental health and wellness: Social media platforms have been found to have a significant impact on LGBT people's experiences of connection, support, understanding, and identity exploration. Contrarily, social media had a negative influence on the mental health and wellness of LGBT teens as well as the experiences of harassment, bullying, isolation, and mental health issues among bisexuals and pansexuals (those who are attracted to all genders).

In terms of mental health issues and behaviors, LGBT people are more likely to have suicidal thoughts, self-harm, depression, stress, anxiety, and post-traumatic stress disorder. Today, in this digital age, social networking platforms are a modern necessity for a variety of reasons. Using social media for work depends on our profession or kind of work. However, it's not always a good method of communication because the majority of users are negative in their posts, content, and tweets, which could harm their physical and emotional health. As LGBT populations are neglected by society in every aspect of their lives, they are more likely to experience assault, prejudice, and adversity. Due to their heightened exposure to prejudice and violence at school, LGBT teenagers in particular experience victimization at a higher rate than non-LGBT youths.

This risk of mental health issues is considerably raised by unsupportive family, friends, and society. LGBT youth who experienced family rejection due to their identity had substantially lower self-esteem and few resources available to them. In comparison to individuals who were accepted by their families, they are also less supported and more alone. When they are young adults, LGBT youth who experience severe rejection from their parents and other caregivers are at a very high risk of developing physical and mental health issues.

The risk and well-being of LGBT children are significantly influenced by families and caregivers. Recent findings from the Family Acceptance Project (FAP) support this. In response to their LGBT children's identities, families and caregivers exhibit more than 100 behaviors, according to FAP researchers. These actions fall into two categories: 50% accepting and 50% rejecting. Each of these behaviors was measured by FAP researchers to demonstrate how families' responses impact the risk and well-being of LGBT young people. According to FAP research, the health and mental well-being of LGBT young people are negatively impacted. Conflict in families is caused by parental miscommunication and misunderstanding of their LGBT children. Communication issues and a lack of understanding of sexual orientation and gender identity can cause arguments and family strife, which may result in the removal or forcible eviction of an LGBT youth from the home.

Compared to young LGBT people who are accepted by their families, they are in worse health. They experience more issues with drug use. They are far less likely to protect themselves from HIV or other sexually transmitted infections (STDs) because they feel more hopeless. Additionally, their risk for HIV and AIDS is increased by this conduct.

Psychology-related stress: Numerous LGBT people also experienced additional stress as a result of incidents like the extremely high rates of homophobic bullying in schools and physical and verbal assaults. Their mental health suffered as a result, and they developed severe degrees of psychological distress, self-harm, and suicidality. These people are more likely to suffer from sadness and anxiety. These feelings could include extreme melancholy, worry, loneliness, and discomfort in social conditions.

These symptoms of psychology-related stress mainly arise due to the following reasons:

- family conflicts and rejection by parents;
- hatred or rejection from religious organizations;
- childhood sexual abuse;
- verbal harassment;
- poor economic conditions;
- drug addiction;
- increased fear of physical violence, and discrimination;
- bullying at school/workplace;
- bullying by neighbors;
- hate comments daily;
- prejudice/embarrassed response from professionals;
- no protection against discrimination at work, housing, education, etc.

3.8   CHAPTER CONCLUSION

Controlling hate speech has proven to be a very challenging issue, especially in this present digital age. The ineffectiveness of social media legislation and law enforcement often encourages hate speech for those who provoke hate in a country. Although judicial intervention has allowed the law to advance consistently over time, the emergence of social media platforms has raised unique legal and governance concerns. Given the rapidity and scope of its dissemination across numerous interconnected channels and formats, online hate speech presents unique issues. Therefore, there is an urgent need for a strong legal framework to address emerging types of hate speech. Additionally, the law that now protects social media companies from being held accountable for the actions of their users, known as "intermediary liability," has to be reviewed. In addition to constitutions, Asia-Pacific countries must address the region's cultural, religious, and ethnic diversity. As a result, they may try to stifle hate speech using a variety of legal strategies that take this diversity into account. These are laws and measures that could be used to stop hateful acts against religions and religious institutions, racial minorities, diverse cultures and individuals, and a person's gender and/or sexual orientation. Therefore, it is necessary to educate and inform the users about the adverse effects of social media usage and what is and is not suitable for these widely used networks.

EXERCISES

1. What is cyber law and why do we need cyber law around the world?
2. Which country has adopted the international convention on cybercrime?
3. How many types of cyber law are there?
4. What is the significance of cyber law?
5. What are the different types of cyber law?
6. Explain Austria's NetDG and KoPLG Acts.
7. Explain the Cybersecurity Law (CSL) of Vietnam.
8. What are the cybersecurity challenges to democratic governance?
9. Explain Ethiopia's Computer Crime Proclamation of 2016.
10. Explain the Digital Security Act of 2018 in Bangladesh.
11. What kinds of cybercrimes are prohibited by the Indian Penal Code (IPC)?
12. What do India's Section 69A guidelines for social media content blocking entail?
13. According to Nepal's Electronic Transaction Act of 2063, what does 'asymmetric crypto system' mean?
14. What steps have social media companies taken to prevent hate speech and online crime?
15. What are the legal problems with social media?
16. What challenges exist with employment law?
17. What is piracy in software?
18. What ethical problems are raised by online social media?
19. What effects do social media platforms have on the mental health and wellness of the LGBTQ community?

REFERENCES

Bangladesh, (2018) *'Digital security act 2018'*. Available at: www.article19.org/wp-cont ent/uploads/2019/11/Bangladesh-Cyber-Security-act-2018-analysis-FINAL.pdf (Accessed: 12 January 2023).

Baretto R. et al. (n.d) *'Brazil: Data Protection & Cyber Security'*. Available at: www.legal 500.com/guides/chapter/brazil-data-protection-cyber-security-law/ (Accessed: 02 January 2023).

Benjamin S., Fred, S. and Theodor, H. (2015) *'Democratic Governance Challenges to Cyber Security'*. Available at: www.dcaf.ch/sites/default/files/publications/documents/Cbyer Paper_3.6.pdf (Accessed: 04 January 2021).

Brussel (2016) *'European Commission and IT Companies announce Code of Conduct on illegal online hate speech'*, May 31, Available at: http://ec.europe.ec/comission/presscor ner/detail/en/IP_16_1937 (Accessed: 12 January 2021).

Callegari, C. (2022) *'Cybersecurity Laws and Regulations in Canada'*, June 13. Available at: www.softwaresecured.com/cybersecurity-laws-and-regulations-in-canada/ (Accessed: 12 January 2023).

CCLA (2015) *'Summary: International Covenant on Civil and Political Rights (ICCPR)'*, October 27, Available at: HTTP://ccla.org/privacy/surveillance-and-privacy/summary-international-covenant-on-civil-andpolitical-rights.iccpr/ (Accessed: 23 January 2020).

CIVIC SPACE. (2020) *'Kenya's: use of hate speech laws and monitoring of politicians on social media platforms'*, September 14. Available at: http//www.article19.org/resources/ kenyas-use-of-hate-speech (Accessed: 04 January 2023).

Creemers, R., Webster, G. and Triolo, P. (2018) *'Translation: Cybersecurity Laws of the Peoples Republic of China'* (Effective June 1, 2017). June 29. Available at: www.digich ina.stanford.edu/work/translation/cybersecurity-laws-of-the-peoples-republic-of-china-effective-june-1-2017/ (Accessed: 12 January 2023).

Details of IPC Sections 153A, 295 & 295A. Available at: https://adrindia.org/sites/default/files/ Details%20of%20IPC%20Sections%20153A,%20295%20&20296A.pdf (Accessed: 16 March 2020).

Epicenter. Works. (2020) *'First analysis of the Austrian anti-hate speech law'* (NetDG/KoPlG), September 10. Available at: https://edri.org/our-work/first-analysis-of -the-austrian-anti-hate-speech-law-netdg-koplg/ (Accessed: 12 January 2023).

Everus, S. (2018) *'Vietnam-Law on cybersecurity'*, November 9. Available at: www.roedl.com/ insights/veitnam-law;cybersecurity-csl-cyberspace/ (Accessed: 12 January 2023).

FAP (2002) *'Family acceptance and rejection affect the health, mental health, and wellbeing of lesbian, gay, bisexual, and transgender (LGBT) youth'*, FAP is affiliated with San Francisco State University.

Government Gazette (2021) *'Republic of South Africa'*, vol. 672, June 1, Cape Town. Available at: www.cogta.gov.za/cgta_2016/wp-content/uploads/2022/02/01062021_L_G_Munici pal-Structures-Amendment-Act-3-of-2021_English.pdf (Accessed: 02 January 2023).

Indonesian Cyber Law Verdict No. 1152/Pid.Sus/2020/PN.Tjk: *'Review of Indonesian Cyber Law'*. Available at: http://repository.dharmawangasa.ac.id/638/2/Indonesia%20cy ber%20law.pdf (Accessed: 02 January 2023).

Joint Task Force (2020) *'Security and Privacy Controls for Information Systems and Organizations'*. NIST Special Publication 800-53 Rev. 5. Available at: https://doi.org/ 10.6028/NIST.SP.800-53r5

Kinfe, M. (2016) *'Comment: Some Remark on Ethiopia's New Cybercrime Legislation'*. doi: http://dx.doi.org./10.4314/mlr.v10i2.7

Kinfe, M. (2014) 'Developments of cybercrime law and practice in Ethiopia', November 19. Available at: www.sciencedirect.com/sicence/articles/abs/pii/S02673364914001605 (Accessed: 02 January 2023).

Kusbianto, et.al (2020) *'Indonesian Cyber Law Verdict No. 1152/Pid.Sus/2020/PN.Tjk: Review of Indonesian Cyber Law'*. Available at: http://repository.dharmawangasa.ac.id/638/2/ Indonesia%20cyber%20cyberlaw.pdf (Accessed: 02 January 2023).

Law Commission of India, 267th Report on Hate Speech (March 2017).

Mendiratta, R. (2021) *'Information Technology (Intermediary Guidelines and Digital Media Ethics Code) Rules'*, 2021. March 26. Available at: https://wilmap.law.stanford.edu/entries/information-technology-intermediary-guidelines-and-digital-media-ethics-code-rules-2021/ (Accessed: 01 July 2021).

Nepal's Constitution (2015), Available at: www.constituteproject.org/constituition/Neapl_2015.pdf (Accessed: 03 January 2023).

Nicholas, E. (2018) *'Understanding the State Party Referral of the Situation in Venezuela'* November 1, Available at: www.ejitalk.org/understanding-the-state-party-referral-of-the-situation-in-venezuela/ (Accessed: 03 January 2023).

Office of Parliamentary Counsel (2017) Canberra. *'Australia AU463'*, July 17. Available at: www.wipo.int/wipolex/es/text/449006 (Accessed: 02 January 2023).

Official gazette (2020) Available at: www.resmigazette.gov.tr/eskiler/2020/07/20200731.htm (Accessed: 02 January 2023).

Public order act (1986) Available at: www.ligislation.gov.uk/ukpga/1986/64 (Accessed: 12 April 2020).

Rome, 4.XI. (1950) *'European Convention on Human Rights'*, Convention for the Protection of Human Rights and Fundamental Freedom.

Section 2(1), Information Technology Act, 2000.

The Electronic Transaction Act, 2063 (2008) Available at: www.tepc.gov.np/uploads/files/12the-eclectronic-transaction-act55.pdf (Accessed: 02 January 2023).

Tullo, A. (2017) *'Dangers of Homophily in Social Media'*, May 5. Available at: https://medium.com/@alisabethtullo/dangers-of-homophily-insocial-media-1e7d13ebe138 (Accessed: 02 March 2021).

The Indian Penal Code, 1860 (Act 45 of 1860).

Wanyama, E. (2021) *'South Sudan's Cybercrimes and Computer Misuse Order 2021 Stifles Citizens Rights'*, December 14. Available at: www.cipesa.org/2021/12/south-sudans-cybercrimes-and-computer-misuse-order-2021-stifles-citizens-rights/ (Accessed: 04 January 2023).

White, T (2022) *'Twitter receives record number of gov't requests to remove posts'*, January 26. Available at: www.aljazeera.com/news/2022/1/26/twitter-sees-record-number-of-govt-demands-to remove-content/ (Accessed: 11 March 2022).

Writ Petition (Criminal) No. 167 of 2012. Shreya Singhal v Union of India Section 66A, Information Technology Act, 2000.

4 Pros and Cons of Digitalization

SUMMARY

In this chapter, we will discuss how the freedom of digitalization in this digital world has given the world a chance to make use of emerging digital technologies and digital media and how these technologies are adopted in different organizations such as business, education, banking, media, healthcare, transportation, communication, and many more. We will discuss digital platforms such as smartphones, tablets, desktops, laptops, and other devices that are now replacing traditional media such as newspapers, books, and radio broadcasts. Further, the chapter also focuses on how our lifestyles have completely changed with the emergence of advanced digital tools and technologies and also both about positive and negative aspects of using this technology in a digital society.

4.1 INTRODUCTION

Digital freedom has transformed the world we live in. Almost everything in our environment is rapidly changing from analog to digital. The freedom of digitalization has had a positive impact on every industry around the world. Every business has benefited from digital transformation. Today, almost every part of modern life has been changed by digital technology. Every year, new developments in emerging technology have aided the world in making significant progress. There are many advantages of using digital technology and digital media.

Digitalization has played a significant role in our everyday lives because of its latest innovations and advancements. It has become a very important part of our lives. The evolution of digital technology has resulted in a variety of shifts in emerging technology trends and patterns. It has made our lives easier and simpler, and it has greatly helped the consumer save both time and money. Education, healthcare, entertainment, and various other fields have all benefited from technological advances. In today's digital world, we've learned that our lives would be slower if we didn't have technology. Therefore, every person today must be technologically savvy because this is where our future lies.

Some examples of digital tools and technology:

- Social media
- Blogs
- Smartphones
- eBooks
- Websites

DOI: 10.1201/9781003403784-4

- Video streaming
- Digital cameras
- Computers, laptops, iPads, etc.
- Printers
- Digital clocks
- Geolocation
- ATMs
- Self-scan machines
- Digital vehicles

4.2   ADVANTAGES OF DIGITALIZATION

We'll go through some of the advantages of digital technology in brief, which will help us grasp the idea more clearly.

- Social connectivity
- Communication speed
- Versatile working
- E-Learning opportunities
- Automation
- Information storage
- Editing
- Exact duplication
- GPS and mapping
- Transportation
- Low cost
- Entertainment industry
- News
- Warfare
- Online banking
- Portable devices
- Digitization of restaurants/digital kitchen
- The dark web

SOCIAL CONNECTIVITY

Digital freedom has enabled us to keep in touch with our friends, families, and colleagues and work remotely, from any corner of the world. Communication and socializing with family and friends have become simpler and easier. Everyone can now communicate via messages, videos, and audio, and exchange other forms of media, thanks to digital freedom (Poudal, 2019).

Various websites, apps, and software have all been developed to help in the socialization of users. Nobody needs to feel isolated in the digital world, thanks to the most popular social media platforms such as Facebook, Twitter, and Instagram, as well as messaging, texting, laptops, tablets, and smartphones. Users can regularly update their local events and social events.

COMMUNICATION SPEEDS

Since dial-up methods have been used for internet access, the data transfer rate or internet speed has rapidly increased. Faster broadband allows huge volumes of data to be sent across the internet instantly, allowing users to stream video and audio in real-time, send large data files, and access data from almost any part of the world. Our lifestyles and how we interact have been transformed by digital technology. Mobile phones, laptops, and web-enabled computers have revolutionized our everyday lives and the way we communicate.

Before, communication through traditional media would take a long time. But now, broadband technology has boosted the internet's pace even further. Because of broadband technology, internet speeds have improved, so you'll be able to work in real-time from anywhere in the world. Many online and freelance jobs can be completed without difficulty from anywhere. Particularly during the COVID-19 pandemic, the internet enabled many employees to work effectively from home.

DIGITAL DEVICES ARE PORTABLE

The advancement in digital technology has made it to the point that digital devices are usually smaller, lighter, quicker, smarter, more compact, and more flexible, so they are now much more portable for humans to use than they were previously.

Storage capacity has improved a lot with the advancement of digital technology. The storage medium can now store a huge amount of data on a small chip. The invention of transistors resulted in a significant reduction in the size and weight of digital devices. Huge quantities of data may also be processed locally or internationally and transferred from one place to another with a single click or tap.

DIGITAL LEARNING OPPORTUNITIES

Digital freedom has accelerated e-learning not only in India but around the world. In the conventional classroom, only teachers used to teach. Students were entirely reliant on teachers for knowledge acquisition and other materials. However, with the advancement of digital technology, many schools and universities around the world have embraced and valued e-learning courses.

Many developed countries have always been a center for education, and technology has grown quickly in recent years to revolutionize the way students in developed countries consume educational materials. In addition, the invention of smartphones is fueling the expansion of the digital learning system. During the COVID-19 pandemic, educational systems all across the world were forced towards digital learning.

AUTOMATION

With the advancement of digital technology today, machines are becoming increasingly intelligent and quicker. Automation means the use or introduction of automatic equipment in various technologies. In certain cases, humans are no longer needed to run the machines, allowing workers to focus on more interesting tasks. In this digital world, smarter computers imply higher safety levels or a better user experience. As digital technology advances and becomes more popular, the cost of products and services has decreased globally.

INFORMATION STORAGE

The advancement in digital technology has reached the point where digital devices are usually smaller, lighter, quicker, smarter, more compact, and more flexible, so they are now much more portable for humans to use than they were previously.

Storage capacity has improved a lot with the advancement of digital technology. The storage medium can now store a huge amount of data on a small chip. The invention of transistors resulted in a significant reduction in the size and weight of digital devices. Today, in this digital world, large quantities of media, such as images, music, videos, contact information, and other documents, can be stored on small devices like mobile phones, tablets, etc. Huge quantities of data may also be processed locally or internationally and transferred from one place to another with a single click or tap.

EDITING

As a result of digital freedom, the most significant benefit of digital technologies over conventional media is that data can be edited or manipulated far more easily.

Text editing has undergone a revolution as a result of word processing. Before conventional media, video editing used to require costly studios and equipment, but now, with technological advancement, it can be performed from the comfort of one's own home on a laptop or computer. All kinds of photographic effects, as well as the ability to crop, resize, and creatively change images, are easily available.

Digital video editing has also become very easy with the advent of new digital technology. Digital video editing provides the opportunity to enhance and improve problems with light and sound. Color correction can also be made by a digital video camera's automatic settings, which look more realistic. And the sound that has a lot of background noise can be enhanced. It also makes it easier to edit the videos to make them more attractive.

EXACT DUPLICATION

The advancement in digital technology has greatly allowed the user to accurately duplicate the media. You may, for example, write a work report and send it to multiple people through email, or send multiple copies of images to family and friends. Digital advancement in the field of 3D printing has drastically transformed the world.

GPS AND MAPPING

Today, the GPS (Global Positioning System) signal is available everywhere around the world. There is no cost to use the GPS service since the GPS is funded by the US Defense Department. GPS-enabled smartphone applications, such as Google Maps, are usually free. GPS is most commonly used in navigation systems.

When compared to conventional methods and technologies, such as map reading, GPS navigation is usually very simple to use. GPS services can track our locations, give real-time updates on traffic and weather alerts, and are also used to identify structural issues in roads and houses as well as predict natural disasters such as earthquakes. In addition, GPS can be used to provide information about the surrounding area even when using smartphones. For example, determining the location of the nearest hotel, restaurant, or gas pump is especially important when you are on a trip.

TRANSPORTATION AND LOGISTICS

Digital freedom in the transportation and logistics industries has rapidly reshaped and transformed the world. Several government initiatives around the world have brought new opportunities and revolutionized this industry. The transportation industry is positively affected by digital advancement and technological development. As transportation technologies progress, the efficiency of transporting people and goods has increased, making it safer, less polluting, and requiring less fuel.

It's never been easier or faster to move from one place to another. But the latest advancements in technology have completely transformed the essence of travel. Digital technology is being significantly used in transportation industries such as aircraft, trains, and ships to reliably navigate routes on the sea and land. Even land transportation such as trains, buses, and cars today has become fully automated. In many metropolises, automated trains and buses have helped to save time and manpower and have also helped to manage the issue of a growing population (Poudal, 2019).

The introduction of digital technology in transportation has made it more environmentally friendly. Online access to timetables, as well as online booking of tickets for planes, buses, and trains, has now become very common and convenient. Due to digital advancements, passports that contain digital chips that store all the information of the passengers have allowed self-service machines to expedite the check-in and customs processes. Overall, advancement in digital technology has increased transportation quality, people's protection on the highways, traffic congestion control, and environmental sustainability.

ENTERTAINMENT INDUSTRY

The media and entertainment industries have undergone a rapid digital transformation in recent years. Many years before, people used to watch analog films. But with the latest innovation in digital technology, the movies we see in theaters are now "digitalized." The introduction of 3D, 4D, and 5D (fifth dimension) film technology has greatly improved picture and sound quality. Because of the advanced editing features now available, many independent filmmakers are shooting digital videos. Many big-budget filmmakers move their films to computers so they can be edited using digital video editing tools. The film industry has been influenced by developments in the latest digital technology.

Because of innovation and development, everything has become digital, which has helped film editors not only edit content easily but also make it more afford-able. There are now numerous online games that you can play on your smartphone. Listeners can now search for and download songs or watch music videos online for free from a variety of websites. If you missed watching your favorite shows on televi-sion, you can easily watch them online on your smartphone or laptop.

WARFARE

Because of technological advancements and the freedom of digitalization, wars can now be fought remotely, removing the risks associated with having troops present on or above the battlefield, where there was a higher risk of deaths and danger. Advancements in digital technologies have made wars particularly hor-rific. Advanced technology has always been used to create better weapons. The latest technologies and developments have been introduced for military and civilian applications.

Advancements in communications technology, computers, information systems, monitoring, and target acquisition systems have all enhanced the commander's ability to command and control. Drones and missile technology are especially dependent on digital technology to operate properly, but most military equipment is increas-ingly becoming more automated. Many military-developed technologies, such as the internet, GPS, and mapping, are now widespread in civilian use.

Fly-by-wire technology had replaced manual flight controls in favor of an elec-tronic interface that moves control mechanisms using signals produced by a computer and transmitted through wires.

DIGITAL BANKING

With the adoption of digitalization, today's banks can provide improved customer support services. Freedom from digitalization is a very important factor for the banking industry.

The advancements of digital technology in the banking and finance sectors have also transformed the face of the world. Previously, customers had to physically visit the bank and wait in long lines for different bank services. But today, in this digital world, online banking is done through smartphones, laptops, or mobile apps very quickly and easily.

As a result of digital freedom, there have been many innovations and developments in the banking and finance industries in recent years. Managing huge amounts of cash has also become easier in recent years. Bank customers can now monitor their incoming and outgoing payments, as well as make money transfers and bill payments, from anywhere in the world. Apart from banking, other financial issues, such as the buying and selling of currencies and shares, can be handled online. You can quickly transfer money between accounts, both nationally and internationally.

Customers have benefited from digitalization because it has made cashless transactions easier. Customers no longer need to keep cash in their hands, and they can make their purchases at any time and from any place around the world. Customers would appreciate the ease and time savings. Customer satisfaction has increased as a result of digitalization, which has also helped to eliminate human error.

DIGITIZATION OF RESTAURANTS/DIGITAL KITCHEN

Today, digitization is present in every aspect of our lives. Indian restaurants have therefore welcomed the newest era of transition, i.e., digitization. With the arrival of advanced digital technologies like AI, robotics, IoT, 3D printers, etc., an entire task in a digital kitchen or restaurant has been digitalized, from digital menus to digital food serving to their customer's digital food orders to digital payment methods, and so on. Digital menus become more dynamic and appealing to customers with meaningful product placements, high-quality visual pictures, customer feedback, and so on. By removing consumer reliance on employee help, restaurants have seen a large increase in average order value. This dynamic feature not only benefits customers in terms of convenience and security, but it also benefits eateries. All of these technologies contribute to the advancement of the restaurant business. "In addition, the COVID-19 pandemic has changed the way people eat and order food; the pandemic is also responsible for bringing the entire world to a new level."

CRYPTOCURRENCY

A cryptocurrency is a form of digital or virtual money that is secured by encryption. Cryptocurrencies such as bitcoin, monero, Ethereum, and others exist in this digital age and are used for a variety of financial transactions. The primary advantages of using cryptocurrencies are that they simplify the process of transferring money between two parties involved in a financial transaction. These transactions are made possible by the use of public and private keys, which are used for security. Due to the low processing costs involved in these financial transfers, consumers can avoid paying the high fees that banks impose on internet-based transactions. It is transparent and anonymous at the same time. In this regard, the advent of cryptocurrencies has transformed the system of global payments in many ways.

THE DARK WEB

Websites on the "dark web" are those that cannot be accessed using standard browsers or search engines like Google. People can keep their privacy and express themselves freely on the dark web. Especially for many innocent people who are tormented by stalkers and other criminals, privacy becomes important. The dark web is frequently used by journalists, law enforcement, the military, political dissidents, and activists because it has encryption characteristics including protection and anonymity.

The dark web is also used for corporate and government surveillance for comparable reasons. The dark web is used by journalists, whistleblowers, and other professionals who are vulnerable to targeted surveillance to exchange sensitive information. And groups like Human Rights Watch and the Electronic Frontier Foundation encourage access to and usage of the dark web.

4.3   DISADVANTAGES AND CHALLENGES OF DIGITALIZATION

Whatever we come across in our lives has both benefits and disadvantages. Everything in the world has both its good and bad sides. No doubt, freedom, and advancement in digital technology have played a very significant role in the development of every country. But on the contrary, there are various disadvantages to using these technologies as well. Therefore, the use of digital technology requires rules and laws. We will study each disadvantage of digital technology in more detail below.

- Data security
- Privacy concerns
- Poor students' academic performance
- Crime and terrorism
- Complexity
- Social disconnect
- Work overload
- Digital media manipulation
- Job insecurity
- Plagiarism and copyright
- Anonymity and fake identity
- Overreliance on gadgets
- Addiction
- Artificial living
- Organization and storage
- Longevity
- Social alienation
- Psychological effects
- Physical health issues
- Cryptocurrency
- The dark web

Data Security

With the freedom of digitalization, data, and information security have become big matters of concern. In today's digital world, a large amount of data or information is collected, processed, and stored. This information or data that is stored can be an individual's or any organization's personal information or data. So it is very difficult for this data to be safeguarded. Since in this digital world, all electronic equipment is linked to the internet from all over the world, this personal information or data can be attacked by theft, hackers, terrorists, business competitors, international adversaries, or other bad cyber criminals.

PROTECTING PRIVACY

In today's digital world, privacy should be considered a critical right for us as a culture and as a community. With the freedom of digitalization, today a large number of pieces of information or data are available on the internet. So it has become very difficult to protect every individual's or organization's privacy from various threats and harms.

For example, anyone with a smartphone can take photographs and video footage and upload it to the internet. In public places, there are digital cameras that track and record our every step and movement. Therefore, it has become very tough, if not impossible, to protect and have control over our details.

Digital privacy can be split into three categories: information privacy, communication privacy, and individual privacy.

Information privacy deals with how individual private information and documents are used, collected, and stored by their respective companies.

Communication privacy deals with communication to avoid obstacles related to directional microphones, telephone or wireless contact interception or recording, and access to email messages.

Individual privacy deals with the individual's rights and freedom of thoughts, feelings, opinions, etc.

POOR STUDENTS' ACADEMIC PERFORMANCE

Digital tools and technologies have fundamentally altered how we perceive the learning process today. Numerous studies have also revealed that digital tools, digital media, and the internet can affect students' academic performance in both favorable and unfavorable ways. Recent research has proven that digital tools and technology harm the student's fundamental three skills of being able to read, write, and do arithmetic calculations (Wentworth and Middleton, 2014). Texting also harmed students' abilities to construct complete sentences, use correct punctuation, and maintain grammatical accuracy by utilizing social media platforms and digital devices such as smartphones, tablets, and PCs. Digital tools and technologies in classrooms also hurt students' writing skills, particularly in the areas of spelling, punctuation, grammar, and critical thinking (Alhusban, 2016). Also, frequent usage of short forms in texting hinders students' capacity to exert effort in their writing and makes it difficult for them to discriminate between formal and informal writing standards.

Another impact is that in many places around the world, with the increase in smartphones and internet users, smartphones with internet connections are now commonly used. Smartphones are also viewed as a promising method of teaching, especially at the higher educational level, and are supported by a huge variety of educational apps. As a result, smartphones are currently viewed as facilitators of messaging-based content sharing and communication. According to a study of students who use smartphones in primary schools, their texting habits (e.g. b4 instead of before) have led to the use of grammar being negatively affected (Van Dijk et al, 2016). Studies have also shown that the widespread use of smartphones in the educational process results in student distraction, knowledge fragmentation, and teachers' failure to control classes. An additional problem is that students' creativity has been negatively impacted by the abundance of materials available on the internet and Google. They simply copy and paste any materials they desire without making an effort.

CRIME AND TERRORISM

As a result of digital freedom, the number of cybercrimes and acts of terrorism has been rapidly increasing all around the world.

There are different forms of cybercrime:

- Phishing: using fake email messages to get personal information from internet users;
- Identity theft: misusing personal information;
- Hacking: shutting down or misusing websites or computer networks;
- Spreading hate speech and inciting terrorism;
- Distributing child pornography;
- Grooming: making sexual advances to minors.

SOCIAL DISCONNECT

With the freedom of digitalization, today we are digitally connected with our families and friends through our smartphones, laptops, tablets, etc., messaging apps, and social media. People are increasingly preferring to socialize and interact through digital devices rather than face-to-face communication. But it has led to physical disconnection and social isolation among people at various social events.

This way of communicating and socializing can lead to misunderstanding. According to studies, many people suffer from depression, loneliness, and other mental illnesses as a result of a lack of real-life communication.

Several psychological studies have suggested that the digital world is increasing the likelihood of mental illness (Jarai, 2020). The study has suggested that social interaction, rather than digital interaction, with our families and friends, has a much more positive effect on our mental happiness and well-being.

WORK OVERLOAD

Innovation and advancement in digital technologies has no doubt increased work speed and improved performance, but it also have its disadvantages. Today, in this digital world, many employees spend their days attempting to keep up with the hundreds or thousands of emails they receive each week, all of which must be read and some of which require quick or immediate responses or actions. Employees all over the world are required to process and handle vast amounts of emails, which can be stressful, and because of this, they may feel more exhausted. Many employees, along with their hectic schedules, have to handle huge amounts of data such as meeting minutes, training videos, photos, and reports, which can be a nightmare.

Digital Media Manipulation

With the advancements in digital technology, we can edit, alter, change, and even manipulate digital media, like photographs, audio, and videos, very easily. Today, in this digital world, there are different methods and editing tools available, such as Photoshop, that can be used to change, edit, and manipulate digital media. The size and quality of the image can be changed and edited, and the voice of any person can be changed. So it has become very difficult to differentiate between the original and fake documents.

The disadvantage of using various digital editing tools is that it is very time-consuming. Running the video onto the screen, splitting it into clips, editing, adding effects, rendering it, creating digital versatile disk (DVD) menus, and eventually burning it to DVD consumes a lot of your free time.

Another issue is the cost of purchasing the requisite video editing equipment. All the equipment, like digital cameras, computers or laptops, DVD video tapes, batteries, etc., requires a good amount of capital.

Complexity

The advancements in digital technology have steadily increased the complexity of the digital environment. Since the world is becoming increasingly digital every single minute, digital activities ranging from simple consumer goods to industrial sensors are becoming increasingly "smart" and internet-connected, resulting in a huge complexity of data.

Therefore, to reduce complexity, it is very important to have deep knowledge and understanding of how to make appropriate and accurate use of the devices and machines with which we communicate regularly.

Job Insecurity

Digitalization is changing the nature of the workplace. With the freedom of digit-alization, new types of organizational structures are now possible worldwide. The internet's widespread use, Big Data, Artificial Intelligence (AI), the Internet of Things, and online platforms are a few recent advancements. Although the "platform economy" may make it easier to match employees with jobs and tasks, it also raises concerns about workers' salaries, labor rights, and access to social safety. As a result, job insecurity has rapidly increased because many jobs are being lost as a result of digital transformation activities around the enterprise. "No job is truly secure" when it comes to employment that may be replaced by digital transformation. Economic History says that advances in the steam engine, electricity, and the assembly line have proved mass unemployment in the long term (Mokyr, Vickers, and Ziebarth, 2015).

As computers have increasingly replaced humans, humans are no longer needed to perform various tasks. Artificial intelligence (AI) or machine learning could evaluate a large number of legal cases much more quickly than a person could. Jobs that generally require lengthy, monotonous manual actions are expected to be replaced by AI or other automated processes. With the advancements in digital technology, more and more automated technology is being used in the workplace, which is decreasing your chances of securing a job. As a result, an increasing disparity in access to jobs, quality, and career potential is a concern associated with digitalization, which will open up new chances for some while creating obstacles for others.

Plagiarism and Intellectual Property

"Copyright" is described as a legal right that protects one's work in a printed or published form that can be seen or accessed by other people. With the freedom of digitalization, copyright and trademark infringements have also steadily increased around the world. It's very natural that as digital technology advances, every individual will be able to access ever-increasing amounts of material online. Copyright laws are becoming increasingly difficult to implement for any internet user or organization. Any data and information available online may appear to be free for the user. There are many consequences that any internet user can experience if any data or information available online is used inappropriately or unlawfully.

Plagiarism is described as the act of modifying others' work and then passing it off as their work, whether online, in a class, or at work. Anyone around the world can copy and paste information or data from the internet without any effort. Unfortunately, this method is most popular in the academic field because students today have become very lethargic due to easily and freely available data or content online, so they mainly modify works they find online or read in books and send them to their teachers as their own.

Furthermore, the material or information available on the internet may appear two-faced and very ambiguous. Because, first of all, you are violating copyright laws if you use it without the author's permission. Second, if the original material is not correctly updated, there is a possibility that the content produced with that knowledge will be declared as plagiarism.

Anonymity and Fake Personas

With the freedom of digitalization, digital platforms are being used for several illegal activities and crimes now and then around the world. The free and convenient availability of internet access has resulted in a variety of crimes and activities, including the hiding of real identities and the spreading of fake news on the internet. Anonymity promotes antisocial activities on the internet.

On the internet, especially on social media platforms, false identifications (ID), pseudonyms, and unverified or unauthorized user accounts have been growing increasingly over the past few years, which has given many internet users plenty of opportunities to conceal their true identities when posting messages.

Overreliance on Gadgets

With the freedom of digitalization, too much reliance on mobile phones, computers, and other digital devices has become very common among users. As technology has made our lives simpler and more convenient, many people today are too dependent on gadgets.

In today's digital world, many people's phones contain all of their contact details, photos, emails, and other personal information. People today can't even think, live or breathe without gadgets like smartphones, laptops, etc. Digital technology, no doubt, has a plethora of advantages. However, overreliance on phones and machines has hurt humans as well. This has become so popular that it has its own term: "Nomophobia," which means "no-mobile-phone-phobia," which is described as a fear of losing or being separated from one's phone.

ADDICTION

At the beginning of the twentieth century, people could entertain themselves in many ways, most of which included communicating with others without the use of computers or any digital devices. But with the freedom of digitalization and the advancement of technology, today's people are too addicted to their digital devices like smartphones, laptops, tablets, etc.

With the introduction of phones, computers, and other related technology into our daily lives, the way we entertain ourselves has changed drastically. Addiction to social media, video games, messaging apps, and a variety of popular websites has been discovered.

Many children nowadays play video games on smartphones, computers, and other devices. This has increased their reliance on technology, which has resulted in them being distracted. With the freedom of digitalization, many internet users with fake accounts have behaved in a much more uncivilized manner which has resulted in many anonymous activities like bullying, trolling, fraud, scamming, harassment, intimidation, and insulting activities that have all increased drastically. Therefore, social media platforms would have to work hard to build strategies that are genuinely comprehensive when it comes to user authentication. People who use pseudonyms as their true identities are checked, and they are held responsible for any wrongdoing.

ARTIFICIAL LIVING STYLE

With the freedom of digitalization and the advancement of technology, today's people are living their lives artificially and not in the real world. Digital devices like smartphones, laptops, tablets, etc. have made our lives almost entirely digital. Many people no longer have direct access to real-life activities. Music concerts, award shows, or live shows are recorded on smartphones, events are captured, and audio is recorded rather than attending them in person.

Many people prefer to attend weddings and other social events virtually rather than in person. Life is now presented through the lens of digital media rather than real-time experience. Furthermore, many interviews, exams, and seminars are held virtually worldwide, which has deprived every individual of physical activities and led to the adoption of artificial lifestyles.

ORGANIZATION AND STORAGE OF DATA

With the vast amount of information and content available on various digital devices, it has become extremely difficult to organize and store digital media properly. For example, photographs, images, music videos, audio, etc. can be found on many devices, including smartphones, tablets, laptops, and portable hard drives.

Individual objects may be difficult to identify but easy to delete or lose, and the computer on which they are stored may be misplaced, stolen, or even suffer catastrophic failure. Therefore, long-term storage and maintenance of digital media can be very difficult. So it is a big challenge that needs a well-thought-out strategy, good picture management software, and a lot of patience.

LONGEVITY

Digital devices normally have a very short lifetime and become obsolete easily. Many digital devices undergo upgrades and innovations every year. Many devices and computers quickly become outdated as technology progresses, either because they are too slow or incompatible with other devices, or because they have been superseded by newer, improved models or versions. As older digital devices are discarded when they are no longer usable, this results in a great deal of waste and inefficiency. It may also become prohibitively costly for consumers to move to a new system every few years.

SOCIAL ALIENATION

With the freedom of digitalization and the advancement of technology, digital computers have taken the place of humans, and society is becoming increasingly impersonal. Today, people are increasingly shopping, banking, paying bills, booking tickets, and working online.

Transportation is also expected to become more automated, with taxis and delivery vehicles becoming driverless in the future. Loneliness and a lack of human interaction with a living person are becoming more prevalent.

PSYCHOLOGICAL EFFECTS

In many cases, the freedom of digitalization has also had many psychological effects. Many researchers have found that overuse or dependence on technology may have adverse psychological effects. Various studies have also found that overdependence on technology can lead to depression and anxiety (Jarai, 2020).

Children who use digital technology excessively are more likely to have problems like:

- lack of attention
- poor academic result
- low creativity
- delays in language development
- delays in social and emotional development
- physical inactivity and obesity
- poor sleep
- social issues, such as nervousness and anxiety
- aggressive behaviors
- addiction to these technologies
- higher BMI (body mass index)

Furthermore, a recent study of 15–16-year-olds showed that those who used a lot of digital media had a higher risk of showing symptoms of attention deficit hyperactivity disorder (ADHD).

PHYSICAL HEALTH ISSUES

Excessive use of digital technology may increase the risk of physical issues as well, including:

Eye stress: Advanced digital technologies such as smartphones, tablets, and computers keep a person's attention for long periods. This may cause eyestrain. Common symptoms of digital eye stress are blurred vision and dry eyes. Eye stress can cause pain in other parts of the body, including the head, neck, and shoulders.

Various technological factors may lead to eye stress, such as:

- screen time
- screen glare
- screen brightness
- too close or too far away viewing
- poor sitting posture
- underlying vision issues

Poor Body Posture

The way many people use their phones, computers, and other devices can also lead to poor posture. As a result of this, the neck and spine can be subjected to unnecessary stress.

Reduced Physical Activity

The majority of common digital technologies are sedentary. More intensive use of these technologies facilitates a more sedentary lifestyle, which has been related to several health issues, including:

- obesity
- cardiovascular disease
- type 2 diabetes
- premature death

Thus, the average Indian's lifestyle has changed due to recent technological growth. While there are numerous benefits to digital technology, there are also some drawbacks.

CRYPTOCURRENCIES

Because cryptocurrency transactions are essentially anonymous, it is easy for them to become the target of illegal activities like money laundering, contract murder, buying and selling illegal drugs and medicines, the transfer of illegal weapons, tax evasion, online identity theft, hacking, and maybe even financing for terrorism. Many financial experts have found that cryptocurrencies are volatile in nature and that their payments are not non-refundable. Due to inexperience and low-risk tolerance, those who are less fortunate than others in understanding market trends and volatility may suffer serious consequences. Furthermore, some Muslim countries do not accept cryptocurrencies as legitimate money or currency. Unacceptance by regulatory organizations is a major drawback that comes along with that. The Middle East may be a very dangerous place for bitcoin. This risk results from the governments' Sharia (Islamic religious laws and rules) rejection of it. While some ethnic groups may utilize cryptocurrencies, the majority of individuals in these nations are more worried about the potential political penalties of not using official money.

Cryptocurrency Frauds

Fake websites: Scam sites with bogus reviews and cryptocurrency jargon that promise enormous, guaranteed profits as long as you keep investing.

Virtual Ponzi schemes: Cybercriminals that deal in digital currencies advertise fictitious investment possibilities and give the impression of big profits by paying off previous investors with funds from new investors.

Scams involving romance: The federal bureau investigation (FBI) issues a warning on a surge in online dating scams in which con artists convince victims they meet on dating apps or social media to make investments or transact in virtual currencies. In the first seven months of 2021, the FBI's Internet Crime Complaint Center received more than 1,800 reports of romance scams with a cryptocurrency theme, with losses totaling $133 million (Kaspersky, no date).

THE DARK WEB

Along with its positive side, the dark web also has a negative side because some of the worst crimes have been committed more easily on it. Although the dark web claims to protect users' privacy, it can equally be used to attack the privacy of others. There are many criminal activities such as the purchase and sale of illegal drugs such as marijuana, cocaine, methamphetamine, heroin, etc., the theft and distribution of credit card information, hacking, the dissemination of child pornographic materials, the transfer of illegal weapons, falsifying documents to create fake identities or fake accounts, illegally violent content, contract murders, money laundering, and so on that are committed globally. As the dark web is fully hidden or untraceable, criminals take advantage of it, and this dark web has developed into a marketplace for crimes and activities worldwide. This dark web market frequently accepts cryptocurrencies like Bitcoin and Monero as payment, giving criminals more power to thrive there (Kaur and Randhawa, 2020).

4.4 CHAPTER CONCLUSION

Digital technology and digital media are tools that can be employed both construct-ively and destructively. How the user uses this tool for his or her own needs entirely depends on the user. We all know that technology is improving to help us or give us a better future, but some people utilize it in very risky ways to commit crimes. Therefore, it should be the duty of the users, parents, and teachers to enact tough regulations against them and to educate the users in the positive and negative sides of these advanced technologies.

EXERCISES

1. What are the benefits of using digital tools and technology in your studies?
2. How does the negative impact of digital tools and digital media affect students' academic performance?
3. How can digital tools and media cause social connection and disconnection?
4. What are the top three advantages that digital technology has shown digital banking?
5. Explain how innovative digital technologies facilitated life in kitchens and restaurants?
6. Explain the impact of digitization on employment?
7. Explain how digitization violates copyrights and Intellectual Property rights?
8. Define the term "cryptocurrency"? Is a country adopting it a blessing or a curse?
9. What privacy and data security issues arise when using digital technology?
10. What are the advantages of adopting innovative technologies in logistics and transportation?
11. How do criminal actions and activities benefit from the use of current digital technology?
12. Explain the causes and effects of too much reliance on digital media and technology on our overall health?
13. What is the dark web? What advantages does it offer a nation?
14. What are two negative things about the dark web?

REFERENCES

Alhusban, A.M. (2016) 'The Impact of Modern Technological Tools on Students' Writing Skills in English as a Second Language', *U.S-China Education Review*, 6(7), 438–443.

Jarai, M. (2020) *'Negative effects of technology: Psychological, social, and health'*, February 25. Available at: www.medicalnewstoday.com/articles/social-media-and-relationships (Accessed: 12 May 2020).

Kaspersky (no date) *'What is Cryptocurrency and how does it works?'* Available at: www.kaspersky.com/resource-center/definations/what-is-cryptocurrency (Accessed: 07 January, 2023).

Kaur, S. and Randhawa, S. (2020) *'Dark Web: A Web of Crimes'*, Wireless Personal Communications, https://doi.org/10.1007/s11277-020-07143-2

Mokyr, J.C., Vickers and Ziebarth N. (2015) 'The History of Technological Anxiety and the Future of Economic Growth: Is this Time Different?' *Journal of Economic Perspectives*, vol. 29, no. 3, pp. 31–50.

Poudal, D. (2019) *'14 Pros and Cons of Digital Technology'*. September 23, Available at: https://honestproscons.com/pros-and-cons-of-digital-technology/ (Accessed: 12 May 2020).

Van Dijk *et al.* (2016) *'The influence of texting language on grammar and executive functions in primary school children'*, *Plos One*, 11(3), e0152409.

Wentworth, D. and Middleton, J. (2014) 'Technology use and academic performance', *Computers & Education*, 78, 306–311.

5 Digital Education and Digital Library

SUMMARY

In this chapter, we will study today's fast-paced digital era and examine how crucial digital learning is. We will also look at how emerging and advanced digital technologies have changed the education system worldwide and the impact of the COVID-19 pandemic on the education system. In recent years, the education sector has experienced rapid growth assisting in the country's transformation into an information hub. The chapter also highlights how, with the help of digital learning, we may learn about any part of the world and also about how recent technological trends are pushing digital education forward in India and around the globe, which is undoubtedly increasing education levels and expanding the nation's ability to compete in the global market. In addition to this, the chapter also discusses the digital library's role in changing to fulfill the needs of teaching and learning methods, its benefits, and as well as challenges that need to be addressed in the future. The government has also taken major initiatives for the improvement of the digital education system in India. Thus there are some technical issues that the government has to deal with in the digital education system. But as a result of digital freedom, digital teaching, and learning methods have earned the highest appreciation and reward around the world. By overcoming the limitations of traditional learning techniques, the convergence of digital technology and education has made education open to everyone all over the world.

Also in this chapter and the rest of the chapters, we will discuss how the numerous technological trends and various initiatives and investments made by the government of India, pushing India forward not only in education but also in other sectors such as health, agriculture banking, and so on, have aided in the growth of the country's economy.

5.1 DIGITAL EDUCATION

Teaching that can be facilitated with the help of computing devices like mobile devices, computers, and other digital resources from a distance is called "digital education." With the advent of digital technology, digital freedom has become increasingly relevant in all areas of digital organizations, including those in the fields of education, health care, banking, finance, business, etc. There are several digital organizations all over the world where digital freedom is actively involved in the country's growth. The key aim of digital freedom is to move the world to the next level. The teaching that can be facilitated with the help of computing devices like mobile devices, computers,

DOI: 10.1201/9781003403784-5

and other digital resources from a distance is called "digital education." With the advent of digital technology, digital freedom has become increasingly relevant in all areas of digital organizations, including those in the fields of education, health care, banking, finance, business, etc. There are several digital organizations all over the world where digital freedom is actively involved in the country's growth. The key aim of digital freedom is to move the world to the next level.

As a result, in today's digital world, digital freedom has become very crucial for achieving numerous social and economic goals for every country worldwide. In fact, for users all over the world, digital platforms have proven to be the most reliable source of knowledge and information in all areas.

5.1.1 Digital Freedom in Education

Education plays a very significant role in the overall development of students as well as the overall development of a country. Education itself is one of the most significant sectors in the world that has experienced transformative changes in recent years.

The process or method of learning that uses digital technology and digital devices is known as "digital education." The term "digital education" actually means digital learning.

In this highly competitive digital world, if the education industry had to succeed in the long term, digital would certainly be an important element of the solution. With the advancement of the latest digital technologies, there is a need for technology to be integrated into the education field. Now, thanks to digital freedom in education, both students and educators achieve a better quality of education and life.

As a result of digital freedom, digital learning has proven to be a very satisfying experience all over the world. Digital education, also known as Technology Enhanced Learning (TEL) or digital learning, is the creative use of modern digital technologies and resources in teaching and learning.

Digital learning is learning that is enabled by modern digital technology and allows students some influence over where they study, when they learn, and how they learn. With the advent of digital freedom, digital learning is increasingly replacing the conventional educational system.

There is no single definition to define digital or online learning. A digital learning strategy may consist of any one or a combination of any of the following:

- adaptive learning
- badging and gamification
- blended learning
- classroom technologies
- e-textbooks
- mobile learning, e.g. smart phones, laptops, computers, and iPods.
- personalized learning
- online learning (or e-learning) or web-based learning
- open educational resources (OERs)
- technology-enhanced teaching and learning

- virtual reality
- augmented reality

5.1.2 DIGITAL EDUCATION SYSTEM

Over the past few years, digital technology has rapidly developed, transforming the way students learn from manual to computing device sources. In digital freedom, many schools, colleges, and universities are gradually implementing digital technologies to keep up with technological advancements. Since today's students are familiar with computers, iPads, and smartphones, these creative instructional approaches ensure greater student involvement.

During the Covid-19 pandemic, digital schooling increased in popularity, emphasizing the importance of a digital learning system. The solution to educational problems is adopting digital technology. Therefore, to improve the quality of education, the majority of schools and universities, and the governments worldwide are attempting to keep up with technology trends by introducing them to boost the standard of education with the most up-to-date digital technology. The main aim of introducing the digital education system:

- To develop quality e-content in all local languages.
- To integrate education systems and technology to build digital classrooms.
- To develop a system for evaluations in the world of digital education.
- To introduce skills learning courses, virtual classrooms, and virtual vocational training.
- To provide multi-mode access to education through mobile apps, web portals, TV channels, radio, and podcasts to ensure a consistent user experience.
- To allow increasing mobile phone use to allow "anytime, anywhere" access and penetration.
- To take advantage of e-learning opportunities, Teachers receive special training to teach digital teaching.

Advantages of Digital Education System

Digital freedom has given a great opportunity to all schools, colleges, and other institutions to create interactive digital courseware and other instructional materials. The entire learning environment is becoming more personalized and interactive. As a result of digital freedom, education services are becoming more available to even remote learners through various mobile apps. It has provided the students with new possibilities for their future.

In the year 2019–2020, when the world was battling with the ongoing COVID-19 pandemic, digital education was the only source for students to learn. As a result of digital freedom, many schools and universities all around the world have encouraged all students to use digital resources and devices for learning. The pandemic also had a major impact on teaching and learning outside of the classroom. It forced countries all over the world to introduce digital learning systems and make use of the latest digital tools and devices in schools and universities to continue the academic session. The following are some benefits of the digital education system:

Interactive Learning

The use of digital tools and devices makes the learning process more interactive and enjoyable, allowing all learners to come together and create a learning environment across the world. Also, the use of multimedia and new methods like gamification makes learning more fun and interesting.

Learn from Home

Digital learning has no physical boundaries as it has no location and time limits. You can save transportation costs and traveling time as there is no need to visit anywhere. Today in this digital age, we refer to the internet for solutions if we are stuck in a situation, before consulting our mentors. This helps to save us time and money. As it has no physical boundaries and time restrictions, digital learning allows you to learn from the comfort of your own home on your own time.

Cost-Effective

Digital learning is a very cost-effective method of education as compared with traditional learning techniques. You do not have to pay huge prices for textbooks in schools or colleges if you use digital sources of learning. Since textbooks often become outdated after a certain period, e-learning is therefore a cost-effective method of learning.

Smarter Students

Digital learning makes students smarter and sharper by increasing the quality of their work and their productivity. Creativity and thinking skills, which are the foundation for the development of systematic reasoning, are sharpened by interactive digital learning resources and technology.

Recorded Lectures

One of the most important benefits of digital learning is that some of your classes will be recorded. In case you miss any lecture or class or if you forget some concepts or later realize you don't understand something, you can download the recorded lectures and watch the class to clear your doubts. Therefore in digital learning, you can go back and revise whenever you want.

24-Hour Resources Available

With digital learning, all the study materials or contents are always available. You can easily access your learning materials online at any time and from any place in the world.

Makes Students Self-Motivated

Those students who make use of learning through digital tools and devices become more interested in expanding their knowledge and skills and more involved in the process of learning.

Awareness of the Latest Technology

When you use digital technology or devices more often, you get more and more familiar with those technologies, and also you will gain a lot of software and technological experience. Learners also improve their knowledge of using the internet confidently. Especially with the use of smartphones, laptops, 4G, and 5G latest technologies, users become more aware of using these technologies skillfully. Digital learning has helped learners to become more technology-based learners and rely more on modern digital technologies and networks for a better learning experience.

It's Fun to Learn Online

Learning online while making use of digital tools and devices is very effective and enjoyable not only for students but for everyone. It is very interesting to learn online rather than to study with traditional resources. Online learning can also involve interesting activities like puzzles and quizzes. Therefore this form of learning is more effective and successful for the students because it helps them to easily grasp and understand various complex concepts.

5.1.3 COMPONENT OF DIGITAL EDUCATION

Figure 5.1 illustrates various significant components of digital education. These components' specifics are as follows:

Digital materials are maintained in the modern education system in educational organizations. It avails the repositories of the digitized library of books, audio,

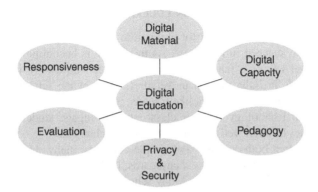

FIGURE 5.1 Components of digital education.

videos, CDs, DVDs, research materials, and other teaching-learning resources. It provides smooth delivery and learning with freedom in the digital age.

Digital capacity is the main source to facilitate the digitized form of education. It includes the infrastructure of high bandwidth, high-speed machines, smart classrooms, eligible students, teachers, technical staff, servers, and ICT centers.

Pedagogy is the focus and objective for learning by stating and explaining targets at the beginning of the sessions and lessons. Sharing digital resources for learning and setting agendas are at the root of education. Simplifying technology with synchronous and asynchronous assistants and checking the progress frequently. It can become overloaded due to many on-screen distractions, apps, and programs. It states to target and focus on the pertinent information.

Privacy and security is the key components to keeping the teaching-learning community on the right track and providing safety. It protects the privacy and security of students' data, including the collection, use, handling, and governance of personal information. It mitigates the personalized dashboards; accessibility, and authenticity are important. Technology can disrupt, distract, marginalize, and oppress the need to empower and affirm the student and their families. Students' data can be secured from misuse and abuse. It guides to save students from meaningless streaming, images, videos, and Apps and includes a privacy agreement in procurement contracts.

Evaluation helps to assure the alignment between digital technology, and students and staff. It assists to promote and improve the educational system. The parents and students get strength against anti-resist, anti-oppressive, equity-informed, sustaining, and revitalizing policy. It empowers the organization and tracks the execution in every section of teaching-learning.

Responsiveness is the art of designing the course and content that performs smoothly on a variety of devices and screen sizes. The technology used is multi-functional for multiusers. It empowers the students to achieve necessary work easily and efficiently within the course through accessibility. The navigation and interaction needs to be simple and sound.

5.1.4 IMPACT OF DIGITAL TOOLS ON EDUCATION

Schools are very important places for children to learn the skills and competencies they will need to succeed in the future. As this world is becoming more and more "digital," Digital adoption tends to be more advanced especially in primary and secondary schools in India than in universities. Most of the schools in developed countries in India, including others like Canada, Scotland, etc. are seamlessly using advanced digital technology in their classrooms to engage students and achieve desired outcomes through well-structured learning techniques.

To teach children both complex and simple concepts, many schools are making use of multimedia resources such as smartboards, LCDs, audio-visual images, digital records of older lectures, and so on. Many schools all over the country are running smart classes and all the teachers have been trained well with the latest digital technology for different subjects.

According to many studies, the use of digital tools can also improve learning and teaching in technology-related topics, including math (Gunbas, 2015), biology (Buckley et al., 2004), and chemistry (Frailich et al., 2009).

The use of digital tools can help abilities and methods that are very important in the study of science and math, such as solving practical problems (Hertleif, Greefrath and Sillar, 2018).

Digital tools can also give students the chance to put their prior understanding of a subject into practice, which is crucial, for instance, to develop mathematical principles at a more fundamental level (Soliman & Hilal, 2016).

Digital technologies are influencing student writing in a variety of ways and have evolved into useful instructional tools for middle and high school students, according to a study of 2,462 Advanced Placement (AP) and National Writing Project (NWP) teachers. According to these educators, the internet and other digital tools like social networking sites, mobile devices, and texting generally encourage the youth to express themselves creatively and personally, increase the audience for their writing, and write more frequently than in previous generations (Purcell, Buchanan, and Friedrich, 2013).

The AP and NWP teachers surveyed believe that the use of modern digital technologies has positive, concrete effects on students' writing (Purcell, Buchanan, and Friedrich, 2013).

These teachers believe that digital technology helps students write better in a variety of ways:

- Digital tools "enable students to share their work with a wider and more varied audience," according to 96% of respondents (including 52% who strongly agree).
- 79% of respondents agree (with 23% strongly agreeing) that these technologies "promote increased student collaboration."
- Digital tools "promote student creativity and personal expression," according to 78% of respondents (26% strongly).

But on the contrary, they are concerned that students' use of digital tools is harming their writing, such as the "creep" of casual language and style into professional writing.

Some challenges among them include:

- The distinction between "formal" and "informal" writing is becoming less clear, and some students have a tendency to utilize informal vocabulary and writing styles when completing formal writing projects.
- Students' varying levels of access to and proficiency with digital tools.
- Contesting the "digital tool as toy" mindset that many kids adopt when they first start using digital tools as children.

The growing requirement to instruct students in writing in many "voices" and "registers" for various audiences.

Benefits of Digital Tools to Universities

- A really solid analytical framework is what drives digital transformation. To make good decisions, the advanced analysis it offers is quite helpful. It can significantly enhance course delivery, boost institutional brand promotion, and better plan and carry out admission marketing campaigns.
- The digitalization process makes it easier for teachers and students to participate deeply. It enables the faculty to create a curriculum that is designed to each student's needs.
- Better teaching and learning results can result from improved teacher–student interactions using digital technologies. With digitalization, institutions can handle their data more effectively. The adoption of digital technology can also increase professor and staff productivity and overall efficiency.
- It's interesting to note that by easing faculty workloads, digital integration in higher education might enhance the research output of academic institutions. Institutions and universities can free up faculty time to conduct high-caliber research by automating crucial institutional operations.
- By creating a more impartial assessment system, these innovative technologies support the evaluation process' efficiency. Teachers can adapt their pedagogy to students' development and aptitudes thanks to digital performance tracking for every single student.

Thus, digital tools and technologies can improve the teaching and learning process, provide our students with useful digital skills, and most importantly, it can result in better academic results if used properly and effectively. Also, freedom of the Internet and digital devices like smartphones has ushered in a huge growth in information and communication technologies (ICT) during the last several decades. Hence, schools across many countries including India are already noticing the benefits of digital technology.

5.1.5 REAL-WORLD CASE

The Indian government has developed many networks for the widespread use of educational resources and methods for students all over the country.

- Many initiatives are launched by the Government of India such as SWAYAM Prapha, eBasta, e-VIDYA and so on which are intended to improve the infrastructure that students will need to pursue online education. India's Online Education Market (2020–2024)

During the projection period, the online education market in India is expected to increase by $14.33 billion, representing a CAGR of 21% (BusinessWire, 2020).

- A KPMG analysis titled "Online Education India 2021" discusses the various types of online content consumers, their motivations for using the online medium, their preferences for content consumption and payment methods, and the elements that influence customer acquisition and retention (KPMG, 2017).

5.2 TECHNOLOGICAL TRENDS IN DIGITAL EDUCATION

With the advancement of digital technologies and freedom of digitization, there is a rapid change in the online education system. Older conventional methods of teaching, where teaching was only confined to four walls of a classroom, are now upgraded or discontinued as today modern digital tools and methods for knowledge transfer have become more available. With the advancement of digital technology, new ways of disseminating knowledge also appear in the education sector. Knowledge transfer and technology are becoming more and more intertwined with the introduction of online spaces like virtual learning environments (VLEs) with integrated discussion forums, video hosting websites like YouTube, and the widespread sharing of electronic educational content via emails and Dropbox.

5.2.1 AI in Digital Education

New technologies and technological components are developing day by day. Their capacity and efficiency are also taking the devices and uses towards the next step of life. AI is supporting the new era of students to learn in any shape of content like text, audio, video, etc. Several patterns of AI are integrated into digital education that will be discussed here.

Digital Classroom/Flipped Classrooms

With the advances in digital technology everything is shifting towards digital and in this digital world even classrooms have now changed to smart or digital classrooms to improve students' learning experience. And with the freedom of digitization, from chalk and board teaching methods, teachers have now shifted to digital screens over traditional textbooks. Students are more engaged in this classroom as it makes use of digital tools and modern learning methods. With modern digital technology used in these classrooms, students find learning in this environment more enjoyable. As today students are more addicted to laptops, computers, mobiles, etc. bringing the same technology into the classrooms makes them more comfortable.

Video-based learning is more interesting, enjoyable, and exploratory. Through the fantastic Apps, podcasts, movies, interactive software, e-books, and online interactive electronic boards, the interactive preamble of this segment ignites learning with a pedigree of learning out of leisure with creativity, enjoyment, and entertainment. The classes now cater to students, are run by students, and are information-rich.

Game-based learning is becoming more popular in digital learning. Gamification is currently the most effective e-learning method in the digital age. Gamification is very different from playing a game. It is the process of using game-design concepts in their applications that are not games. The environment that is created by game-based learning allows the learners to relate to it and participate.

The learning process is made more interesting, much like it is when playing a game. In today's digital world, where students are more aware of their environment and their strengths and capabilities, gamification helps them to grasp knowledge and information more easily. This type of learning method is especially beneficial for children since it sparks their attention and motivates them to utilize it repeatedly over an extended period. Gamification not only improves the effectiveness of knowledge and skill acquisition for online learners, but it also helps them remember the material and commit it to long-term memory for later usage. Game-based learning will surely revolutionize the education system and will produce a better generation of self-taught learners.

Mobile-based learning: With the freedom of digitization and fast internet penetration, today's learning has shifted to the digital environment. In today's world of digitization, everybody has smartphones in their hands. As it is a portable device, you can carry it from one place to another at any time and can have access to the internet whenever you need it. Many mobile learning apps are huge sources of information that can be easily installed on your mobile phones. Mobile learning tools including tablets, portable audio players, mobile phones, laptops, etc. are helpful in the classroom. The ability to use mobile learning technologies properly and efficiently is advantageous to both learners and apps. Additionally, it also supports distance education.

The portability and information accessibility of mobile technologies play a significant role in improving English language teaching and learning (El Hussein and Cronje, 2010).

Hidayat and Utomo (2014) claim that we can learn electronic information through mobile learning. Mobile learning is a platform that gives students the freedom to learn whenever and wherever they want.

Adaptive e-learning: In adaptive e-learning, computers are used as active learning tools. According to each learner's particular learning needs, learning style, and knowledge level, these methodologies allocate human and technological resources. This also goes by the name of "intelligent tutoring," and it was first introduced in the last few decades. Its roots are in AI. Adaptive learning has been used in a variety of educational systems, including computerized adaptive testing, intelligent tutoring systems, adaptive hypermedia, and computer-based pedagogical agents.

Adaptivity is a critical component of modern e-learning systems. Adaptive learning has become a basic idea and paradigm for contemporary e-learning systems (Rodrigues et al., 2019), and it is becoming more common in studies on educational technology (Xie et al., 2019).

The "one size fits all" approach to the design and development of e-learning systems is thought to be improved by AESs. AESs have advanced in fields such as adaptive hypermedia, intelligent tutoring systems (ITSs), and web-based educational systems (Park and Lee, 2003).

Beacon e-learning: Another advantageous technology trend for e-learning is "Beacon e-learning." Beacon technology, also known as beacon e-learning, uses wireless devices to send messages to other adjacent devices over low-energy

Bluetooth connections. As an indoor positioning system, this is employed (IPS). This technology trend has several outstanding advantages, including:

- Simpler campus navigation
- Improved accessibility
- Stronger communications
- More intellectual exploration
- Knowledgeable data
- Better in-class experiences

Cloud-based learning: Cloud computing infrastructure is a perfect area to offer a positive learning environment for e-learners. Cloud computing refers to the act of remotely accessing, replicating, and altering physical and software resources. In Cloud-based learning, there is no restriction to accessing a huge amount of learning materials. The development of technology has made it simpler to share and disseminate information. Without consulting the cloud service provider, the service can be used easily (Radulescu, 2014).

AI-supported e-learning (AIeL): To transform the Indian educational system, artificial intelligence (AI) is used to create innovative learning and teaching methods. AI approaches, such as fuzzy logic, decision trees, Bayesian networks, neural networks, evolutionary algorithms, and hidden Markova models, are used in e-learning, which is known as AI-supported e-learning (AIeL) (i.e. using a computer and network technologies for learning or training) (Colchester et al., 2017).

Different AI technologies have been widely used in many educational subfields, including personalized e-learning environments, intelligent learning styles identification, and adaptive item-based learning (Wauters et al., 2020).

Data mining has a significant impact across several industries. Numerous modeling methods are applied in the e-learning processes including neural networks, genetic algorithms, clustering and visualization methods, fuzzy logic, intelligent agents, and inductive reasoning.

The main sources of data mining techniques and approaches, AI and Machine Learning (ML), and educational processes are closely related, according to some researchers (Margo, 2004; Fasuga and Sarmanova, 2005).

Studies on the successful integration of data mining techniques into e-learning environments and how they could enhance learning tasks were conducted. It was recommended that data clustering be used to support group-based collaborative learning and offer incremental student diagnosis (Tang and McCalla, 2005).

The study provided an overview of the potential uses of web mining (web usage mining and clustering) approaches to address some of the existing issues in distance education (Ha, Bae, and Park, 2000).

The study provided the use of ML approaches to the creation and induction of student models, as well as the background information required for student modeling (Resende and Pires, 2002).

Machine learning and deep learning are regarded as game-changer in a variety of fields, including education (Langer, 2020).

In terms of enhancing teaching and facilitating future digital education, ML can create new opportunities for the field of digital education. Teaching and learning activities that integrate digital technology as part of an in-person, blended, and fully online learning environment is supported by ML and DL techniques.

The ability to automatically learn from experiences and data is provided by ML, a subset of AI, whereas the ability to analyze various factors and structures in a manner resembling human brain thinking, is provided by deep learning (DL), a subset of ML methods (Rajendran and Kalidasan, 2021).

ICT-based learning: Information and Communication Technologies (ICT) are changing the concept of the traditional learning process. Due to the daily, increased usage of ICT tools, education quality has increased dramatically. Online and digital learning approaches have replaced prior conventional methods. The educational system in our nation has undergone significant changes as a result of the integration of ICT. In the educational process, it has improved not only the traditional classroom teaching and learning process but also the students' knowledge of ICT tools and the online learning environment.

The application of ICTs in the teaching and learning process has proven to be innovative and successful. ICT has also developed distance education programs across the world. The education system is being greatly transformed by devices like smartphones, portable laptops, digital cameras, and MP3 players. Colleges and universities are putting a wide range of student services, from snack delivery to laundry monitoring, online as the need for technology keeps increasing.

The **Internet of Things (IoT)** is a network of intelligently connected objects with built-in sensors and actuators that can be used to collect data and even share it with other objects. IoT in the simplest term is the interconnection of "things" that are connected to the internet. IoT is a ground-breaking idea that has applications in nearly every industry, including banking, logistics, agriculture, management, and the education system as well. IoT can be used in digital learning to make learning systems more smart, engaging, and interesting.

IoT "could serve as a backbone for the ubiquitous learning environment, and enable smart environments to recognize and identify items, and retrieve information from the internet to enhance their adaptive functionality (Xue, Wang, and Chen, 2011).

Zhu et al. (2016) have presented a research framework on smart education. In this, three important components of smart education are smart learning environments, smart pedagogies, and smart learners.

Smart learning environments: Unlike conventional learning environments, smart learning environments offer learners ubiquitous access to materials and learning systems, allowing for learning to take place at any time and in any location. Even technologies are available in these contexts to determine where and when a student should study. More efficient and "engaging" is the smart learning environment.

Such learning environments can be implemented using a variety of hardware and software techniques. Examples of hardware include an interactive whiteboard, a tablet, a smartphone, smart classroom furniture like a smart table, an e-bag, etc.

Learning systems and tools, online resources, messaging, social network and blog resources, and analytical and virtualization tools are all examples of software components.

Smart pedagogies: The traditional pedagogical approaches are no longer effective in today's digital age. Pedagogical difficulties are undoubtedly going to become more prevalent as IoT is integrated into education. This motivates researchers and educators to create innovative pedagogical approaches that will aid students in learning more quickly and effectively.

The knowledge-pull approach to learning "is based on providing learners with access to a wealth of tacit/explicit knowledge nodes and handing over control to them to select and aggregate the nodes in the way they deem fit, to enrich their knowledge networks" (Chatti, Agustiawan, and Jarke, 2010).

Smart learners: The students would be the final user of the system. They would be "smart" because they would select an advanced digital educational approach that is very different from the traditional learning methods. Smart gadgets will be used by the students to engage with the system.

Hence the Internet of Things will advance e-learning in the realm of education. With the application of the IoT in the education system, we can create intelligent learning environments that promote improved retention and learning. This improvement in education will result in people who are more capable and knowledgeable.

Augmented reality in education: Technology has certainly been a huge help to students and learners in general. Students can obtain all the information about an object whenever they want to learn more about what they are seeing in the real world by using their smartphones on which the augmented reality software is been installed.

In the field of education, augmented reality (AR) has frequently been hailed as a game-changing invention (Fernandez, 2016). Students will soon be able to view 3D animals on their mobile devices, which will help them better grasp their features, motions, and habitat (Dong and Si, 2018).

Micro-learning is a brief, digital media environment, such as the internet, in which an individual or end user engages in learning. It can be defined as the learning that took place in easily palatable bite-sized pieces. Since the learning takes place in a small format, it is known as microlearning. That is said to be a learning of the next generation that makes it quick, simple, and fully customized to the learners. It is easily accessible via smartphones, tablets, computers, etc., as well as the variety of available videos, games, quizzes, simulations, podcasts, or slideshow forms. Microlearning focuses on short-term learning activities and relatively small learning units. The main purpose of microlearning is to increase user knowledge and significance in the Stage of Knowledge production.

Massive open online courses (MOOCs) are the freedom of digitization and advances in digital technologies, there is a transition in every sector including education. MOOCs are becoming more popular, and this trend is an illustration of how technology is transforming how education and training are delivered. The MOOC model is gaining attention as a means of enhancing developing economies' urgently required access to higher education and workforce skill development.

As a method of delivering educational content, MOOCs are an improved platform for online distant learning. The courses can reach an exponentially larger number of people in a single course cohort by eliminating course fees, prerequisites, and admissions procedures.

5.2.2   REAL-WORLD CASE

e-Pathshala is a web portal and mobile App (Android, iOS, Windows) established by the central Institute of Educational Technology (CIET), and National Council of Educational Research and Training (NCERT). In November 2015, it was jointly introduced by the Ministry of Human Resource Development, CEIT, and NCERT (Kennedy and Thangiah, 2020).

BENEFITS AND FEATURES
- It is accessible as an Android, iOS, and Windows app
- It can be accessed by students, teachers, researchers, and parents.
- It is very helpful to access e-textbooks across the country.
- Its content is available in different languages such as English, Sanskrit, Urdu, and Hindi.
- This portal also includes a large number of resources like textbooks, audio, video, magazines, and a variety of other print and non-print materials to learn.
- It consists of instructions for creating e-content.
- It provides access to flipbook-style e-comic cum activity book with linked ISL (Indian Sign Language) movies.

FOR THE DIFFERENTLY-ABLED
- One DTH channel with sign language is accessible for pupils who have hearing impairments.
- For those who are blind or deaf (hearing and visually impaired.), study materials have been created in the Digitally Accessible Information System (DAISY) (Chaisanit, 2012).

5.3   INFORMATION AND COMMUNICATION TECHNOLOGY (ICT) IN EDUCATION

The collection of different technology tools and software is the core part of information communication technology (ICT). It helps to exchange, transmit, and store information from one end to the other using technology. It includes the internet, database, networking, computers, and server to establish an ICT center.

5.3.1   DATABASE IN DIGITAL EDUCATION

Database Management

It would be difficult to access information without the database if the data is organized and stored systematically. Every information system needs to structure and organize the data that can be accessed easily. Organized data take less time to process and are retrieved quickly. Normal to complex data structures are accessed efficiently by any information system. For students and teachers to have access to vast volumes of data for both academic and administrative purposes in this digital age, databases are used extensively in higher educational institutions (Ayebi-Arthur et al., 2018).

Today, every piece of data is stored in some form of a database. A database is related to another database in a distributed system. Each set of data is recognized by each database. Figure 5.2 shows database and relation.

The database designer should understand the concept of structuring the data that would help the organization and people for their strategic value.

Concept of Database

The mechanism of grouping the element and arranging the data in tabular forms. The collection of the organized table is called a database.

Datatype

There are most common types of data that technically shows the category of arrangements of data in character or string, numeric, date and time, and miscellaneous. Each datatype has a different size in terms of bit and byte and limits to storage.

Table

A table is a form of organizing the data into rows, also known as records and columns, also known as fields, as shown in Figure 5.3.

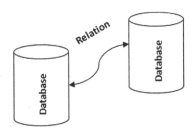

FIGURE 5.2   Database and relation.

	Field_1	Field_2	...	Field_n
Record|_1				
Record|_2				
...				
Record|_n				

FIGURE 5.3   Fields and record.

Field

The heading of a column or data item is called a field that consists of similar types of data. For example, the personal details of the students can have detail fields FirstName, LastName, Address, Course, ID, etc. The fields can be structured for any place, person, or thing.

Record

One row of information of tabular data with multiple fields also called attributes can be said to be a record of a table in the database. The group or attributes represent the record. For example, payroll, bank account detail, purchase detail, sales detail, etc.

File

The group of the record is a file. In the case of a database, the complete information of rows and columns is also referred to as a file. Generally, the file refers to the bold relation like student registration file, grade record file, employee record file, etc., that is stored for a long time in the repository.

Database

A consolidated record is stored in a separate file in a common pool of data displayed in Figure 5.2 for related elements from another database. It allows you to connect and access the data whenever required. A separate database language is used to store the data which is not integrated by front-end languages. Therefore, the database can relate to each other which we study in the relational database. YouTube, Facebook, and Cloud are giant databases of the modern age.

Database Structure

The model of arranging data into a group of attributes in a specified datatype is database structure. It helps end-users to retrieve quickly and easily. It relates one structure of the data to the other so that relation can be engineered in one-to-one, one-to-many, and many-to-many. There are five ways to structure the database, namely relational, network, object-oriented, multidimensional, and hierarchical.

5.3.2 Networking and Telecommunication in Digital Education

The technology of networking and telecommunication revolutionized the world and digital education. All the types of networking processes and interdepartmental connections between students and society are connected with each-other.

Networking

Interrelated chains, group, or system is a network. The connectivity of networks is found in every area in today's digital society like networks of students, networks of teachers, networks of politicians, and networks of celebrities. Majorly, all connections are established using social media of Facebook, WhatsApp, Telegram, and many more.

Mathematically, networking can be analyzed and seen as the number of people connected. The N^2-N shows the total number of nodes (N) connected in a network.

The network of 10 nodes may have a maximum of 90 connections and 100 would have 9.900. It calculates the attached nodes exponentially. Likewise, the connected city, people, and network of a friend of a friend can be analyzed.

Telecommunication

Telecommunication plays a major role in networking to exchange text, audio, video, and image as information between users. Telecommunication supports our day-to-day activities widely which become more capable than before. Several services are provided by telecommunication like the internet, broadcasting, catalogs, networking transaction, banking, billing, marketing, and wireless cellular. Nowadays, services are provided by the government and private parties competitively. Web hosting, YouTube, and Facebook are strong domains of service in the modern era. It supports faster accessibility of the library, privacy, security, and all the related structure of communication medium.

Trends of Technology

Technologies are being applied in all forms of networks and the internet with electronic collaboration. For example, HTML, XML web page editors, servers, Browsers, networking software, and products, etc.

Digitalization in education provides the movement of a high amount of information, high speed in communication, probability of fast growth, ease to approach the students and parents, transparency within the system, and confidence with low errors. The detail of networking and the internet with functionality are discussed in Chapter 1.

Software in DE

A variety of educational and communicative software and application packages are available to support digital education; freeware software like canvas, Blackboard Learn, Google Classroom, Wisenet, Leading Cloud, Workday Student, Aqion, GCompris, and many more. The developers are thinking in a way of subject and area specification that can be found by search engines. Software is available according to the fields: computer science needs several compilers, and integrated development environment (IDE), Chemistry needs structural software, mathematics requires calculative software, statistics needs Statistical Package for Social science (SPSS), Software as a Service (SAAS), and basic sciences like biology and physics have another category. Open communication software used for discussions is Zoom, meet now, and Skype provides vital services worldwide. Storage of data in the database is important using structure.

These structures are supported by database software like MS Access, Structured query language (SQL), Oracle, DB2, etc.

5.3.3 CHANGES IN DIGITAL EDUCATION DURING COVID-19

The world is becoming more digital, and the education industry cannot escape this trend. In many ways, technology has served as a source of hope and a lifeline during the COVID-19 Pandemic period to support the learning process globally. Various ICT tools, such as Google Classrooms, Microsoft Teams, Zoom, and others, have been used by educational groups to continue students learning during the pandemic. ICT tools have helped to transform the education industry for the better, with digital instruction being the most popular way.

The Indian educational system also underwent a significant shift to online learning beginning in April 2020 as a result of the COVID-19 pandemic, which increased the demand for online education. Major private colleges and universities transitioned to an online classroom approach as a result of the lockdown, with professors conducting lectures using the Google Meet and Zoom apps, mobile apps, and many more to continue their education. Also, beginning in March during the lockdown itself, the higher education sector underwent a massive transition by switching to online classroom teaching in colleges and institutions.

5.3.4 REAL-WORLD CASES (1–2)

REAL-WORLD CASE 1: DIGITAL EDUCATION INDUSTRY'S GROWTH

The Ministry of Human Resource Development (MHRD) has launched the "Bharat Padhe Online" (India Study Online) initiative to solicit suggestions for strengthening India's online education system. In April 2020, the campaign lasted for a week and received suggestions via Twitter and email (drishti, no date).

The Ministry of Human Resources and Development (MHRD) has officially established the YUKTI (Young India Combating COVID-19 with Knowledge, Technology and Innovation) portal, which will assist institutions in recording and monitoring academic, scientific, and social activities relating to the COVID-19 problem and students' well-being (PIB, 2020).

Many sectors have been rendered impotent by the COVID-19 pandemic, which has harmed the economy, while EdTech businesses are booming in the markets. The second-largest industry in the world, the Indian EdTech market is a broad and expanding sector with 327 EdTech start-ups, or 10% of all EdTech businesses worldwide. This industry is aiming to provide effective online learning and development solutions, and private EdTech firms are benefiting from the rapid acceptance of online learning (Sikandar, no date). The EdTech sector helped governments, educational institutions, and students in these difficult times with disruptive technological advancements in education.

REAL-WORLD CASE 2: STATES-LEVEL INITIATIVES IN INDIA

To meet the issues of learning continuity among the students in public and private schools during the lockdown, the state governments established creative educational initiatives and programs. The state has implemented many best practices in many states in India.

Various ICT-led initiatives have been adopted by all states in India to offer essential resources for the transition to online education. Due to the COVID-19 pandemic, state governments experimented with new means of delivering syllabus-based e-content. States have recognized the difficulties of digital education and have made numerous efforts to reach out to everyone utilizing technological tools.

KERALA–KITE

KITE (Kerala Infrastructure and Technology for Education) is a government of Kerala enterprise established to encourage, promote, and implement the modernization of educational institutions owned by the state or administered with government assistance in Kerala. KITE was a significant benefit and a solid foundation for the state's transition to a digital education model (Sharma, 2021).

CHHATTISGARH–EDUCATION AT YOUR DOORSTEP

To combat the impact of the COVID-19 crisis in the education sector, the state government launched the "Padhai Tuhar Duar" (Education at Doorstep' Portal). The mission of this platform is to bring teachers and students together by allowing them to access high-quality educational information from the comfort of their own homes. This portal consists of live classes, offline video lectures, simulations, animations, workbooks, podcasts, and other resources are also available (Staff Reporter, 2020).

MADHYA PRADESH'S DIGILEP PROGRAM

Madhya Pradesh's government launched a new initiative called DigiLEP (Digital Learning Enhancement Program) in April 2020. Under this program, textbook-based videos are available for Classes 1 and 2. The DigiLEP program goal was to help students who lack adequate access to high-speed internet access online resources. This Program uses WhatsApp as a platform to offer educational possibilities. Three main components make up the program: selection of very high-quality digital content; development of a well-defined WhatsApp architecture with 50,000+ groups covering all clusters and secondary schools in the state. One of the most popular apps for smartphone users, WhatsApp, has proven to be an essential tool for continuing education during the COVID-19 pandemic (Sharma, 2021).

MAHARASHTRA–THE LEARNING FROM HOME PACKAGE

The Maharashtra State Education Department has started a program to have lectures broadcast on television and the radio for students. To broadcast lectures for classes I to IX, the Department has reserved two slots every day on Doordarshan (TV Channel). Under this program, classes from VIII, IX, and X received audio lectures via radio.

Maharashtra also made history as the first state in India to work with Google India on the state-wide rollout of its Google for Education program. The partnership's goal is to simplify distant learning and aid in teachers' ability to maintain contact with their pupils (Sharma, 2021).

"TEACH AT HOME"

As part of a program to assist educators in finding the most recent and pertinent material on technology-enhanced learning, Google has created an information center that is also available in the Marathi language. One of the states that has consistently prioritized the use of technology in the classroom as a means of improving learning results for children all around the state of Maharashtra. For a variety of learning environments inside the state that may be scaled up, the state has been keen on identifying the most efficient ICT tools and methodologies to reach every student (Sharma, 2021).

Other than the above-mentioned initiatives, there have been independent initiatives by numerous corporate and non-profit organizations and people. Numerous EdTech companies have taken advantage of the chance to scale up their interventions, which need high-end ICT resources and equipment like high-speed internet, desktops or laptops, etc. While other programs have taken advantage of the crisis's potential to use technology to get services to everyone.

5.4   DIGITALIZATION OF HIGHER EDUCATION

Higher education institutions are now starting to transform to accommodate the digital age. In India, some Tier-one universities provide excellent higher education. But the same level of education is not seen in tier-3 schools and universities in both rural and urban areas of the country.

As a result, some of the universities have introduced a government-funded program that aimed to help students all over the world to learn different concepts by providing free access to YouTube videos. Therefore for the advantage of students in rural and urban areas, professors record their lectures and post them online. Students now can also get free access to high-quality educational videos.

5.4.1   DIGITAL LIBRARIES

A Digital library is an electronic collection of documents and information that is accessible via the internet. The documents or information available can be in the form of texts, pictures, audio videos, electronic books, etc.

Through the recent advancements in digital technology, especially Information and communication technology (ICT), the internet of things (IoT), printed materials are being translated into electronic format and made accessible for users with the use of computer networks. The situation is rapidly shifting, however, as a result of the introduction of ICT. Enabling access to scholarly literature via the World Wide Web led to the development of digital libraries at the publisher, institutional, and individual levels (WWW). Today, both industrialized and developing nations are accelerating the establishment of digital libraries using both proprietary and open-source technologies. Due to this transformation, libraries are now providing information to users in a different way.

Definition of a Digital Library

The term "digital library" has many different meanings. Many definitions of digital libraries are available in the literature.

"A digital library is an assemblage of digital computing, storage, and communications machinery together with the content and software needed to reproduce, emulate and extend the services provided by conventional libraries based on paper and other material means of collecting, cataloging, finding, and disseminating information" (Gladney et al., 1994).

There are two major classes of digital libraries; those coming from digital library researchers (in the US context they are mostly computer scientists and engineers), and those coming from library and information professionals (Borgman, 2000).

The American Digital Library Federation has defined the digital library as "Digital libraries are organizations that provide the resources, including the specialized staff, to select, structure, offer intellectual access to, interpret, distribute, preserve the integrity of, and ensure the persistence over time of collection of digital works so that they are readily and economically available for use by a defined community or set of communities" (Waters, 1998).

The term digital library can be described in several ways as follows:

- An online library or an internet library
- A digital collection of data or information
- Helping users with information objects
- Organization and presentation of those objects
- Available directly or indirectly
- Electronic/digital availability

Types of Digital Libraries (Chowdhury and Chowdhury, 2003)

The following categories can be used to classify digital libraries.

- Digital libraries created in the United States as part of The DLI1 and DLI2 (Digital library initiatives).
- Online libraries created as part of the UK's eLib (electronic libraries) Program.
- Individual institutions have created their digital library.
- The National Libraries' digital collections.
- Digital libraries affiliated with universities, organized chronologically or geographically.

E-Books

An e-textbook is a digital version of printed textbooks that is carried out in a school bag. It can be downloaded on a computer, laptop, smartphone, PDA, or any other kind of computer, and is read on the screen. E-textbooks are more advanced in their trans-formation than the printed textbook because they contain multimedia and different interactive features. E-textbooks contain text, images, and even audio and videos packaged into a single electronic file.

As a result of digital freedom, electronic books are becoming more popular and widely used all over the world. E-textbooks have gained more popularity in previous years. Around 20 countries including India, Singapore, the UK, the US, South Korea, Japan, France, and Malaysia have introduced e-Textbooks in their educational systems.

Advantages of E-Books

No purchasing cost: Since e-textbooks are electronic files, they can be easily downloaded from websites free of cost. Of course, buying an old-fashioned textbook is always an option, but considering the price, convenience, and technological future, e-textbooks appear to have the advantage (Young, 2010).

Multimedia format: E-textbooks contain not only text and images, but also audio and videos. If your e-textbooks are in pdf format and you want to read in text format, you can convert them from pdf to text.

Easily searchable: E-textbooks contain a "search button" which allows you to jump to whatever page you are interested in very easily.

Updated regularly: E-textbooks also have the benefit of being easier to update than traditional paper textbooks, which require new printing, making them more environmentally friendly. E-readers and e-textbooks continue to advance thanks to innovative digital technology, and now there are websites available with interactive features that encourage student participation and cooperation.

Easy to use: Students have found e-textbooks easier to use since the majority of students have been brought up in the digital age and use some form of technology every day in their lives. The majority of students have smartphones with internet access. Additionally, students are used to connecting to the internet via social networks like Facebook, Twitter, etc.

Benefit for faculty: Using e-textbooks proves beneficial for faculties since they might be able to adapt the textbook to their course and include lecture notes, prac-tice exams, and links to relevant websites to improve the course material. Since the majority of professors who teach online courses are technologically savvy, the add-ition of e-textbooks could make it simple to replace the traditional printed textbook.

5.4.2 KEY DRIVERS FOR ONLINE EDUCATION

The motive of online education is to provide easy, convenient, smart, and flexible learning to e-learners. It is the platform where students can start unrealistically. It helps the students to learn better and faster. The instructor's role is an essential one in the process of online learning because it is up to them to inspire, encourage, and ensure that students are not feeling as though they are taking their educational journey alone.

Persistence: Persistence is perhaps the biggest key to success in online learning. Students who succeed are those who are willing to tolerate technical problems, seek help when needed, work daily in every class, and persist through challenges.

- When you run into a challenge, keep trying and ask for help.
- Set up a manageable study schedule for yourself and stick to it. Students who succeed are those who log in and make progress every day. This is especially important after the novelty of going to school online starts to wear off!

Effective time management skills: You must be able to manage your time well. Most courses are not taught in real time. There are no set times for classes.

This flexibility is one of the great benefits of online learning. It can also be a drawback for a student who procrastinates, is unable to stick to a routine study schedule, or is not able to complete assignments without daily reminders from a teacher.

Effective time management skills don't just happen. They have to be learned. Once you learn them, they will benefit you throughout your life. Follow the tips below to develop yours:

- Review the syllabus for each of your courses. Develop a long-term plan for completing your major assignments.
- Make a daily "to do" list. Have fun checking things off the list as you complete them.
- It takes time to develop good habits, but you'll gain satisfaction from being well-organized and accomplishing your tasks.

Effective tools: Many online programs provide several ways for students and/or parents to communicate with trainers. These might include e-mail, discussion groups, chat room office hours, cell phones, and even text messaging. If a trainer has a chat room or cell phone, it can be used as a tool to communicate with the trainer. Because of the distance, it's tempting for some students to say things out of anger or frustration that they would never say to a teacher in person. Online teachers are professionals. Treat them with respect and courtesy.

Generation change: This younger demographic is an ideal target market for online education because online forms are more acceptable to this age group than older age groups, and the reduced cost appeals to a budget-conscious consumer.

Affordability: Online UG and PG courses are far more economical than traditional programs; students save money on tuition, lodging, and travel because they may complete the course from the comfort of their own homes and, in many circumstances, at their speed. Many certificate courses are available free of cost.

Technical skills: Online learners need basic technical skills to succeed. These include the ability to create new documents, use a word processing program, navigate the internet, and download software.

Most online schools have new student orientation programs. These teach students how to use the school's learning management system and other online tools, but they typically don't cover the basics.

5.4.3 BENEFITS AND CHALLENGES OF DIGITAL LIBRARIES

Over time, digital education has increased in popularity worldwide. The future of education will soon include digital schools. There are, however, many challenges that must be overcome before digital schools may be widely employed to guarantee that digital education will reach every student worldwide. Therefore the government will have to make several technological adaptations and has to make serious considerations.

Benefits of Digital Libraries in Higher Education

Today many libraries and institutions are digitizing their collections to make them more accessible to everyone. Let's look at some of the most important advantages of digital libraries.

No physical barriers: A user of a digital library does not need to physically visit the library; instead, they just need an internet connection and can access all the information from all over the world at anytime from anywhere. Students can benefit from the convenience of learning at their own pace thanks to digital libraries.

Easy access to resources: The user can easily search for any word or phrase in the full collection using any search keyword. The digital library has very user-friendly interfaces that allow users to access its materials with a single click.

24/7 resources available: Resources in the digital libraries are available at all times. Every day of the year, 24 hours a day, 365 days a year. Users can access information from anywhere at any time with a strong internet connection.

Conservation of resources: Traditional libraries require more investment for the significant resources for the preservation of their collections. But in digital libraries, the content is digitized and the digital resources are regularly accessible to a large number of readers without a focus on the preservation of physical materials. There is no limit to how many times an exact copy of the original can be manufactured without losing quality.

Multiple access to resources: In a traditional library, multiple readers cannot read the same book at the same time. They have to wait for the book to be returned by the other readers. While in digital libraries, multiple users can easily access the same resources at the same time. With the freedom of digitization, many colleges and universities now have digital libraries so that a big number of students can access the same book at the same time from different locations.

Allows real-time interactions: One of the key advantages of adopting a digital library is that students can get answers to their questions right away using cutting-edge management software that allows readers and administrators to connect. Students can also interact by creating online communities and getting real-time answers to their questions. This interactive and innovative element, which is dynamic and real-time can shift readers from traditional libraries to digital libraries.

Limited space: As digital information requires limited physical space to store information, a large amount of information or data can be easily stored in digital libraries, whereas traditional libraries require huge physical spaces.

Updated information or resources available in the digital libraries in higher education institutions or organizations are updated regularly. However, in traditional libraries, it lags in purchasing the latest editions of books, journals, magazines, and other content resources, but digital libraries enable you to access updated resources with the latest technology available.

Lower cost: Maintaining a digital library is comparatively less expensive than maintaining a traditional library. A traditional library needs to spend a significant amount of money on employees, book maintenance, rent, etc. All these costs are eliminated with the use of digital libraries.

Fun and interesting: Today's users prefer digital learning methods over traditional learning methods because they find digital learning to be more fun and interesting as digital learning provides access to knowledge in a variety of media such as texts, animation, graphics, audio, and video.

Challenges of Digital Libraries

Digital libraries face many challenges, including:

- To create more advanced analog material digitization technology.
- To create search and retrieval tools that make up for omitted or insufficient cataloging or descriptive information.
- To create tools that make it easier to improve cataloging or descriptive data by incorporating user input.
- Establishing standards and protocols to make the construction of distributed digital libraries easier is the fourth challenge.
- To address the legal issues surrounding the use, distribution, and copying of printed and digital materials.
- To integrate access to both tangible and digital materials.
- To create methods for presenting disparate resources.
- To make the National Digital Library suitable for various user communities.
- To offer more effective and adaptable tools for modifying digital information to meet end-user requirements.
- To create financial plans to support the National Digital Library.

5.4.4   DISTANCE EDUCATION SYSTEM

As a result of freedom in digitization, digital libraries play a vital role as it helps in the growth of the distance education system and distance learning. Open and distance learning is one of the fastest-growing fields of education, and its potential impact on all education systems has been greatly appreciated. Digital libraries serve an important part in facilitating an effective e-learning process. Therefore, digital libraries are the only way to develop the remote education system.

The freedom of the internet and its networks, such as the World Wide Web (WWW), have had and will continue to have a profound impact on the transformation of the education system across all developing countries. The internet provides a global platform for teaching courses that can be dynamically updated in ways never before feasible. Every student can access a vast number of resources, which are unrestricted by time or space.

As freedom in digitalization has taken over most of the components in classroom learning and higher education systems, students nowadays prefer to obtain information and study content without visiting a physical library in the which has resulted in a drop in visits to traditional libraries.

E-Learning Process

Digital libraries have always played a significant role in the e-learning process. E-learning is defined as the ability for students to access electronic resources from any location without having to know where they are physically located. Over the past few years, traditional libraries had printed and handwritten documents, but with the freedom of digitization, new forms of storing information have emerged over time, and traditional libraries have shifted to digital libraries. The students' learning habits have evolved in this digital era. Currently, the majority of students prefer digital learning methods over traditional learning methods because they find digital learning to be more engaging.

With this transition from traditional to digital, higher education institutions such as colleges, universities, and academic and research institutes, thus rely heavily on digital libraries for their educational and research development. The digital library's key goal is to enable rapid access to digitized information, and it includes a wide range of information sources, from paper to paperless, as well as multimedia such as images, graphics, audio, and videos.

5.4.5 REAL-WORLD CASES (1–3 OF INDIA)

REAL-WORLD CASE 1: DIGITAL CHALLENGES IN INDIA
(*SHARMA AND CHAUHAN, 2019*)

Lack of proper resources and poor internet connections: One of the most important criteria for digital education is that everybody has access to a computer and the internet. But there is very poor internet connectivity and a lack of certain resources in rural areas and some part of urban areas. Slow internet connections also make learners frustrated and make them give up. Therefore without these criteria, it is very difficult for students to proceed with digital learning.

Unskilled teachers: Training teachers is also the biggest challenge for digital learning. One of the major barriers to the use of digital technology in rural areas is the lack of expertise and trained teachers. Most of the teachers are not computer literate in remote areas. Technological literacy is also one of the major concerns in digital learning systems. Teachers should have proper knowledge of computer skills, and internet browsers and also manage all computer files and software properly. As technology is becoming more and more advanced day by day teachers should upgrade their technological skills constantly. Teachers can only conduct digital classes if they are technically proficient to use such software.

Lack of proper facilities and equipment: There must be proper maintenance and upgradation of digital equipment in schools and other institutions to conduct digital classrooms. Lack of proper equipment like old and outdated or poorly configured computers makes accessing course materials very difficult for the learners. Limitations of modern technology and poor infrastructure is also a major barrier to the digital learning system.

The language barrier and content-related challenges: Given the number of various languages that are spoken in India's states and throughout the nation, it can be challenging for organizations to provide digital material in all of these regional languages.

Inadequate funds: In developing countries like India, digital technology implementation into education systems is a challenging task because it requires a huge amount of funds and financial investment for better infrastructure. Therefore the government's main goal should be to make digital more cost-effective.

REAL-WORLD CASE 2: INDIAN GOVERNMENT INITIATED PROGRAM (DAS, 2021)

DIKSHA (DIGITAL INFRASTRUCTURE FOR KNOWLEDGE SHARING)

- It is a part of eVidya, and was announced under the Atma Nirbhar Bharat (self-dependence) program. DIKSHA is the "one nation; one digital platform" for school education in India.
- It is a national digital platform available for school students in grades 1 up to 12 in all states with high infrastructure. With English language and multiple Indian languages (Hindi, Tamil, Telugu, Marathi, Kannada, Assamese, Bengali, Gujarati, and Urdu) are supported by this app. It contains Scan QR codes in your textbook for quick access to related lessons.

NATIONAL PROGRAM ON TECHNOLOGY ENHANCED LEARNING (NPTEL)

- The peak traffic and downloads of educational content videos due to the disruption caused by the COVID-19 pandemic and the suspension of classroom programs were recorded by the National Program on Technology Enhanced Learning (NPTEL), a project of the Ministry of Human Resource and Development (MHRD), which provides higher education courses in science and technology. Seven Indian Institutes of Technology (IIT) and the Indian Institute of Science Bangalore also participated in this project.

REAL-WORLD CASE 3: DIGITAL LIBRARY INITIATIVES
(WANI, 2021)

Today there are many digital libraries worldwide. From the international scenario, there are many popular digital libraries, there as the California Digital

Library, Alexandria Digital Library, Digital Library of Georgia, Digital South Asia Library, and so on. In India too, the idea of organizing digital libraries is gaining momentum. Advances in digital technology have fueled the growth of digital libraries across the world. Some of the important digital library initiatives and programs that are undertaken by the government of India and by various organizations are explained below.

DIGITAL LIBRARY OF INDIA

Digital Library of India become officially released by the then president of India Dr. A.P.J. Abdul Kalam on 8th September 2023 to maintain the understanding and cultural history of India. The Venture is to create a portal for the Digital Library of India to foster creativity and free access to all human knowledge. This scheme is supported by the Ministry of Communication and Information Technology, Government of India, and coordinated by the Indian Institute of Science, Bangalore. It Digitizes and Preserves all huge libraries, and creative and medical works in its 3 local mega scanning centers and 21 scanning facilities and makes it free to the world of education and research.

NCERT ONLINE TEXTBOOKS

NCERT stands for "National Council of Educational Research and Training" and it was launched by the Government of India in 1961 as an autonomous organization to assist and advise the state and central governments in the implementation of their rules and regulations for education, particularly to bring about qualitative changes in school education. The NCERT has initiated a national portal where school textbooks, supported by the National Curriculum Framework 2005, are available freely on the internet for students as well as teachers.

NATIONAL DIGITAL LIBRARY OF INDIA

The Ministry of Human Resource Development (MHRD) launched the National Digital Library of India (NDLI) as a national mission project to engage, facilitate, and inspire all Indian students, regardless of age, demographics, or ability. It is a platform that was made to make digital educational resources available to all citizens of the nation to inspire, motivate, empower, and promote learning.

To gain access to books on a wide range of topics, NDL India has worked with public libraries, educational libraries in India, and large international libraries.

BENEFITS

- The NDL India portal was designed with a variety of users in mind, for all academic levels including primary and postgraduate students, researchers, librarians, professionals, learners with disabilities, and all other lifelong learners. For primary through graduate students, all kinds of learning materials are available here.

- It contains a huge variety of educational resources, including e-books, articles, films, audio, and video lectures, question papers, and online courses, which are accessible through the NDL India, in numerous configurations like PDF, HTM/ HTML, DOC, PPT, XLS, TXT, ZIP, XML, SGML, JPG, JPEG, GIF, PNG, MP3, MP4, MPG4, FLV, F4V, etc. It has a single-window search engine feature that makes it easy for users to find the right materials with a very minimum amount of effort and in the shortest amount of time.

- The National Digital Library of India contains all information about a variety of subjects from different branches like natural sciences, health science, life sciences, physical sciences, computer science, information science, health & medicine, agriculture, engineering, chemistry, biology mathematics, information science, social sciences, legal studies, religion, philosophy, psychology, education, history, geography, languages, literature, arts, and fine arts. The resources are offered in more than 70 languages.

5.5 DIGITAL EVALUATION

Monitoring and evaluation are more important in a digitized education system than manual efforts. It was easy to observe, assess, evaluate, and monitor staff and students while they are around the organization. It loses faith and trust in the effectiveness of delivery to far-sitting students and staff.

5.5.1 MONITORING

Monitoring, evaluating, and tracking the strategy is part of quality management. Administering the technicality, allocated resources, delivery of the services, and defined objective as described by Valadez and Bamberger (1994). It seems against freedom but it provides the digitized freedom to produce quality and disruption in the organized digitized system. Another reason is that it links strongly between information and users.

It is important to remember what has not been completed in a prescribed task within a time frame. It not only checks the completion of the job but also checks whether any problem was encountered by the users and the way the problem was tackled.

Eventually, the software development life cycle requires the events of design, testing, implementation, maintenance, and monitoring which is the verdict of digitalized education also.

The key questions for digital education are important because the students use technology that can diversify. The question forms are: what is done in what manner? Is the problem encountered and handled during implementation?

The answer to track the above question will finalize the goal of improvement in the digitized version of education.

5.5.2 EVALUATION

Common goals of the program are achieved through internal or external evaluation. It helps to assess the evaluation of using factors (Valadez and Bamberger, 1994).

Evaluation is one of the important activities of an educational organization, whether in the digitized or non-digitized pattern of execution. It helps to look at the status of the organization, funding, staff, and student performance and modify better practices.

The evaluating committee should know the parameters of evaluation and can ask the following questions: What to evaluate? For whom should evaluation be done? What is the proper time for evaluation?

Role of Evaluation

Reviews are made yearly or half-yearly that are taken for analysis and utilized in the future. The instrument of review is data collection automatically using a format and certain parameters. Evaluation is done in the time frame for funding, ranking, and reputation among the students.

5.6 PRIVACY AND SECURITY

Privacy refers to not being disturbed or watched by outside boundaries and other people. Connecting alone with the internet, web, Mobile App, or social media might get tracked by other people who are not known to you and are near to you. You get interrupted through the streaming of videos, Ads, and promotions during web content retrieval. Thus, an unwanted invocation in personnel activity needs to be protected and should not be tracked by any other trackers.

5.6.1 PERSONAL DATA AND ITS IMPORTANCE

Personal data is the identity that is related to anyone's livelihood and which leads to the identification of that person. Safety is most privileged and fundamental in online surfing and the digital world. It helps in snatching and looting secured information through hackers and crackers. Personal data includes your name, date of birth, family status, contact number, email address, location address, workplace, and detail of school, college, or any institution. It applies and is essential to all usable applications and technology.

The Importance of Privacy

Privacy and security provide safety from online extortion, looting, torture, harassment, and abuse. No one likes to publicize scheduled activities if living alone in a remote location. Similarly, personal pieces of information are important that cannot be shared with hackers and crackers.

They snatch information by installing cookies, malware, promotional games, malicious emails, and Ads. It becomes severe when they record the operating data of your screen and may take a password, OTP, bank details, etc. without your knowledge and permission. We need privacy and security to avoid cyber attackers and keep our data safe.

Sharing images, text, and videos on social media are tracked by cyber attackers to get important notes or images that may fulfill their goal.

There are common agreements between users and digital service providers to provide the security and safety given by the digital right that is discussed in Chapter 3. You can think about thieves and dacoits present instead of the police administration system. The same way digital users threatens by the hackers and crackers despite of presence of security components.

5.6.2 THREAT TO PRIVACY

Free available applications are riskier for the users which reduces safety during online services. There are several errors made by users discussed here.

Weak and Repeated Passwords

This is one of the biggest threats to digital users. Password-breaking tools like CeWL, Hashcat, THC-Hydra, Burp Suite, Pack, John the Ripper, and many more are becoming stronger every day due to the high speed and high configuration of the machines. Similar passwords should not be used for different logins that help cyber attackers to break multiple accounts. A strong password is made up of twelve to sixteen alphanumeric characters with a combination of special characters, numbers, and small letters.

Oversharing

People want to stay connected with family and friends who insist they share each activity of daily life. Your post speaks clearly about relationships, the background of your life and habits, traveling details, etc. It becomes easy in the technological era which gives digital freedom and also becomes a fruit for hackers and trackers.

IoT Devices

These smart devices are collecting data on all events happening through recording and finding out about you. Every piece of information is outsourced through our own connected smart devices of home utilities which harms your privacy.

We are using various insecure sources like unsecured browsers, free anti-viruses, and computer games, in the digital age providing us freedom, comfort, and luxury but we need to be careful and safe.

5.7   CHAPTER CONCLUSION

Digital libraries have emerged as important tools for developing knowledge abilities among learners in this era of digitization. While digital libraries serve as a center for knowledge and offer services through several information technology methods, they also provide services to students by utilizing cutting-edge digital technologies. Many digital library initiatives contribute to the growth of knowledge in learners. Hence, digital libraries without a doubt, play a significant role in the education and learning sector. And as a result of digital freedom, both of these sectors have revolutionized the delivery of the right content to the right person at the right moment all across the world.

EXERCISES

I. Describe the Terms

1. Digit
2. Digitalization
3. AI
4. AR
5. VR
6. Digital Library
7. Monitoring
8. Digital Literacy
9. ICT
10. Database
11. Table
12. Field
13. Rows
14. Record

II. Answer the Questions

1. Do you think extreme digital freedom is important? Describe your reasons.
2. What are the factors stopping students from freely using digital sources?
3. Describe all the parameters of the digital evaluation of any organization.
4. How do you keep your identity safe from theft?
5. There is various way that data is stolen, discuss a few areas.
6. What is a weak area that your country is failing to apply digitization?
7. Discuss five modern tools that help the government to assist society in digitalization.
8. Is there any role of AI in digitalization? Describe the tools that support AI.
9. Create a database of students that store their personal identity and a separate table that holds the detail of the home.
10. Do you think digital education is helping society? Give your reason.
11. Differentiate between digitization and digitalization?
12. What is the role of augmented reality in society?
13. Do you think that you are secure in the digital world? Give your reason.

REFERENCES

Ayebi-Arthur et al., (2018) 'Catching the Technology Wave- Educational Benefits of Database', *International Journal of Advancements in Research and Technology*, vol. 7, no. 11, November, ISSN: 2278–7763.

Borgman, C. (2000) *From Gutenberg to the global Information infrastructure: access to information in the networked world*. ACM press, New York.

Buckley et al. (2004) 'Model-Based teaching and learning with BioLogical TM: What do they learn? How do they learn? How do we know?' *Journal of Science Education and Technology*, 13 (1) (2004), pp. 23–41.

businesswire (2020) '*Online Education Market in India 2019–2024, 2020 Report on the $14.33 Billion Industry; ResearchAndMarket.com*', September 15. Available at: www.businesswire.com/news/home/20200915005828/en/Online-Education-Market-in-India-2019-2024-2020-Report-on-the-14.33-Billion-Industry--ResearchAndMarket.com (Accessed: 04 December 2020).

BYJUs (no date) '*Shiksha Vani- The All New CBSE podcast App'*. Available at: https://wwwbyjus.com/cbse/shiksha-vani-cbse-podcast-app (Accessed: 10 December 2020).

Chaisanit, S. (2012) 'DAISY Technology and Print Disabled', *International Journal of Soft Computing*, vol. 7, no. 2, pp. 63–70, ISSN: 1816-9503.

Chatti, M.A., Agustiawan, M and Jarke, M. (2010) 'Speech, Toward a Personal Learning Environment Framework.' *International Journal on Virtual Perspective Learning Environment*, 1(4), 66–85.

Chowdhury, G.G. and Chowdhury, S. (2003) Introduction to digital libraries, Facet Publishing, London.

Kennedy, R.V. and Thangiah R. (2020) 'Digital India Initiatives: An Overview', Conference Paper, December, DOI: 10.6084/m9.figshare.14398727

Colchester, et al. (2017) 'A survey of artificial intelligence techniques employed for adaptive educational systems within e-learning platforms.' *Journal of Artificial Intelligence and Soft Computing Research*, 7(1), 47–64. Available at: https://doi.org/10.1515/jaicr-2017-0004

Das, D. (2021) 'Government of India Initiatives Towards Education During Covid-19', *Illkogretim Online- Elementary Education Online*, vol. 20, no. 6, pp. 2859–2866, doi.10.17051/illkonline.2021.06.265

Dong, C. and Si, Z. (2018) 'The research and Application of Augmented Reality in in 3D Interactive Books for Children', In Zhao, P., Yun, O., Min, X., Li, Y., Ren, Y., (Eds) *Applied Sciences in Graphics Communication and Packaging* (pp. 293–299), Springer, Singapore.

drishti, (no date) '*BHARAT PADHE ONLINE AND YUKTI PORTAL: MHRD'*, Available at: www.drishtiiias.com/printpdf/bharat-padhe-online-and-yukti-portal-mhrd (Accessed: 11 December 2020).

El-Hussein and Cronje (2010) '*Defining Mobile Learning in the Higher Education Landscape'*, *Education Technology and Society*, 13 (3), pp.12–21.

Fasuga, R. and Sarmanova, J. (2005) 'Usage of Artificial Intelligence in Education Process', In: *International Conference for Engineering Education & Research*, ICEER2005. Tainan, Taiwan.

Fernandez, C.J.O. (2016) 'Virtual and augmented reality in education', Are we ready for a disruptive innovation in education? ICERI, *9th International Conference in Education, Research and Innovation*, pp: 2013–2022, ISBN: 979-84-617-5895, ISSN: 2340-1095.

Frailich, M., Kesner, A., and Hofstein (2009) Enhancing students' understanding of the concept of chemical bonding by using activities provide on an interactive website, *Journal of Research in Science Teaching*, 46 (3) (2009), pp. 289–310, DOI:/10.1002/tea.20278

Gladney et al., (1994) *'Gross Structure and Requirements'*, IBM Research Report RJ 9840, May, IEEE Computer Society Press.

Greefrath, C., Hertleif, H., and St. Siller (2018) Mathematical Modelling with digital tools- a quantitative study on mathematising with dynamic geometry software ZDM Mathematics Education, 50 (1), pp. 233–244, DOI:/10.1007/s11858-018-0924-6

Gunbas (2015) Students' mathematics word problem-solving achievement in a computer-based story. *Journal of Computer Assisted Learning*, 31 (1), pp.78–95, DOI:/10.1111/jcal.12067

Hidayat and Utomo (2014), 2018 'A review of Current Studies of Mobile Learning', *Journal of Educational technology & Online Learning*, vol. 1, no. 1, pp. 14–27.

Ha, S.H., Bae, S.M., and Park, S.C. (2000) 'Web Mining for Distance Education', In: IEEE *International Conference on Management of Innovation and Technology*, ICMIT'00. pp. 715–719.

KMPG (2017) *'Online Education in India: 2021'*, May 31. Available at: www.kpmg.com/in/en/home/insights/2017/05/internet-online-education-india.html   (Accessed: 05 September 2020).

Langer, A. (2020) *'Analysis and Design of Next-Generation Software Architectures: 5G,IoT, Blockchain, and Quantum Computing'* Springer International Publication, New York NY, USA.

Margo, H. (2004) 'Data Mining in the e-Learning Domain', *Computers & Education*, 42(3), pp. 267–287.

Park, O. and Lee, J. (2003) 'Adaptive instructional systems', *Educational Technology Research and Development*, 25, 651–684.

PIB, (2020) *'YUKTI 2.0'* Union HRD Minister, Delhi. Available at: https://pib.gov.in/Press ReleasePage.aspx?PRID=163370, (Accessed: 14 March 2021).

Purchell, K., Buchanan, J., and Friedrich, L. (2013) *'How Teachers Are Using Technology at Home and in their Classrooms'*, February 28, Available at: www.pewresearch.com/inter net/2013/02/28/how-teachers-are-using-technology-at-home-and-in-thier-classrooms (Accessed: 03 August 2020).

Radulescu, S.A. (2014) 'A perspective on e-learning and cloud computing', *Procedia- Social and Behavioral Science*, 141, 1084–1088.

Rajendran, R. and Kalidasan, A. (2021) *'Convergence of AI, ML and DL for Enabling Smart Intelligence: Artificial Intelligence, Machine Learning, Deep Learning, Internet of Things'*, In Challenges and Opportunities for the Convergence of IoT, Big Data, and Cloud Computing: IGI Global: Hershey, PA, USA, pp. 180–195.

Resende, S.D., Pires, V.M.T. (2002) 'Using Data Warehouse and Data Mining Resources for Ongoing Assessment of Distance Learning', *In IEEE Conference on Advanced Learning Technologies,* ICALT 2002.

Rodrigues, H. et al. (2019) 'Tracking e-learning through published papers: A Systematic review', *Computers* & Education, 136, 87–98. https://doi.org/https:doi.org/10.1016/j.compedu.2019.03.007

Sharma, A. (2021) *'Education through ICT Initiatives during the Pandemic in India'*, ICT India Working Paper, No. 42, Columbia University, Earth Institute, Centre for Sustainable Development (CSD), New York, NY.

Sharma, V.P. and Chauhan, S.K. (2019) *'Digital Libraries Challenges and Opportunities: An Overview'*, Library Philosophy and Practice (e-journal), 3725.

Sikandar, M.A. (no date) *'THE RISE OF EDTECH START-UPS IN INDIA'*, *Recent Trends in Management and Social Science*, vol. 2.

Soliman and Hilal (2016) 'Investigating the effects of computer assisted instruction on achievement and attitudes towards mathematics among seventh-grade students in Kuwait', *International Journal for Technology in Mathematics Education*, 23 (4). (2016), pp. 145–159.

Staff Reporter (2020) 'Education for Doorstep' for students in Chattisgarh, Available at: www.dailypioneer.com/2020/state-editions--education -at-doorstep---for- students-in-chattisgarh.html (Accessed: 10 January 2021).

Tang, T.Y., and McCalla, G. (2005) 'Smart Recommendation for an Evolving e-learning System: Architecture and Experiment', *International Journal on e-learning* 4(1), 105–129.

Valadez, J. and Bamberger, M. (1994) *'Monitoring and Evaluation Social Programs in Developing Countries'*, *A Handbook for Policy-makers, Mangers and Researchers, EDI Development Studies*, The World Bank, Washington D.C.

Waters, D.J. (1998) *'What are digital libraries?'*, CLIR Issues, Enabling Access Digit Libraries, 2 (99):36.

Wani, G.A. (2021) 'Digital Libraries Initiatives: An overview of national and international scenario', *IP Indian National Journal of Library Science and Information and Technology*, vol. 6, no. 2, pp. 66–72, https://doi.org/10.18231/j.ijlsit.2021.015

Wauters, et al., (2020) 'Adaptive item-based learning environments based on the item response theory: Possibilities and challenges', *Journal of Assisted Learning*, 26(6), 549–562. Available at: https://doi.org/10.1111/j.1365-2729.2010.00368.x.

Xie, H. et al., (2019) 'Trends and development in technology-enhanced adaptive/ personalized learning: *A Systematic review of journal publications from 2007 to 2017'*, *Computers & Education*, 140, 103599. https://doi.org/https://doi.org/10.1016j.compu edu.2019.103599

Xue, R. Wang, L., and Chen, J. (2011) 'Using the IoT to construct ubiquitous learning environment', Mechanic Automation and Control Engineering (MACE), *Second International Conference on IEEE*.

Young, J.R. (2010) 'To save students money, colleges may force a switch to E-textbooks', *Chronicle of Higher Education*, 57(1), 1–8.

Zhu, et al. (2016) 'A research framework of smart education', *Smart Learning Environment* 3.1 (2016): 1.

6 Digital Healthcare

SUMMARY

In this chapter, we will study how innovative and advanced emerging digital technologies like AI, machine learning, blockchain, the IoT, the Internet of Medical Things (IoMT), and big data analytics have all contributed to the development of the digital healthcare industry globally. We will also study how the freedom of digitization in this healthcare industry has made it easier for patients to access their treatments without having to go to the doctor every time they need treatment. The chapter also highlights the importance of digital healthcare and government efforts to provide value-based services across the healthcare spectrum. This chapter also discusses how digital literacy and emerging technology have helped to progress the healthcare sector worldwide.

6.1 INTRODUCTION

Healthcare has grown to be one of the largest industries in terms of revenue and employment. In many developing countries, hospitals, medical supplies, clinical trials, outsourcing, telemedicine, medical tourism, health insurance, and medical equipment are all part of the healthcare industry. Due to expanding development, good facilities, better infrastructure, and increased investment by both public and private sources, the industry is rising at a breakneck rate.

As a result of digital freedom in the healthcare industry, advancements in digital technology have transformed the way doctors and patients communicate with each other. In recent years, the healthcare industry has experienced rapid development and growth with the advancement of digital technology and improved quality of services. The experience of patients has completely changed due to the freedom of technology and improved medical processes.

With the freedom of digitization, the IoT, virtual care, remote monitoring, artificial intelligence, big data analytics, blockchain, smart wearables, platforms, various digital tools enabling data exchange and storage, tools enabling remote data capture, the exchange of data and sharing of relevant information across the health ecosystem, and other technologies have demonstrated potential to improve healthcare.

If digital health supports equitable and universal access to high-quality healthcare, improves the sustainability and efficiency of health systems in providing high-quality, affordable, and equitable care, and strengthens and scales up health promotion, disease prevention, diagnosis, management, rehabilitation, and palliative care, including before, during, and after an epidemic or pandemic, in a system that upholds privacy, it is valued and adopted.

DOI: 10.1201/9781003403784-6

There are two types of healthcare industries: public and private. The government, or public healthcare system, has a small number of secondary and tertiary care institutions in major cities and focuses on delivering basic healthcare in rural areas through primary healthcare centers (PHCs). The majority of secondary, tertiary, and quaternary care facilities are operated by the private sector, with a concentration in metros and tier I and tier II cities. A country's competitive advantages depend on its latest and most advanced medical equipment, infrastructure, and well-trained medical professionals.

6.2 WHAT IS DIGITAL HEALTH?

In today's digital world, digital well-being has become an important factor. The biggest transition in the healthcare industry today that the doctors and patients are witnessing is freedom of digitization. Patients who connect with their doctors via digital media are taking advantage of an improved healthcare experience. The digital health industry is rapidly increasing around the world.

Therefore ethical, secure, reliable, safe, equitable, and sustainable use of digital health should be a top priority for the health sector. Transparency, accessibility, scalability, replication, interoperability, privacy, security, and secrecy should all be considered when developing it.

If health systems and services become more digitized, digital health has the potential to significantly alter health outcomes if it is supported by adequate investments in governance, institutional capacity, and workforce capacity to support the necessary changes in digital systems and data use training, planning, and management.

6.2.1 A FEW DEFINITIONS OF DIGITAL HEALTH

The phrases "mHealth" (mobile health), "eHealth" (electronic health) (i.e., technology and digital applications to support people in their health), "virtual care," and "telehealth" (telephonic health) to name just a few, are frequently used interchangeably when discussing digital health. To thoroughly evaluate current definitions of digital health and pinpoint themes and concepts, a search of the definitions in both empirical literature and gray literature (such as online sources) was conducted.

The term **"digital health"** refers to the use of digital tools and technology, as well as electronic communication tools, services, and processes, to provide health care or to improve one's health, which is used for the prevention, diagnosis, treatment, monitoring, and management of various diseases.

The term "digital health" broadens the definition of "eHealth" to encompass digital consumers and a larger array of smart and connected devices. Additionally, it covers additional applications of digital technology for health, including robotics, the Internet of Things, high-end computing, big data analytics, and artificial intelligence, including machine learning.

The Australian Digital Health Agency's (ADHA) governing legislation's explanatory statement defines digital health as "any application of information and communication technology to improve healthcare and health outcomes" (Cormann, 2016).

The World Health Organization (WHO) defines the term "digital health" in a broader concept as "combining e-health ('the cost-effective and secure use of ICTs for health and health-related fields'), m-health ('the provision of health services and information via mobile technologies'), and emerging fields like the use of advanced computing sciences in big data, genomics, and AI" (WHO, 2019, p. ix).

"The application of electronic communication and information technology to deliver healthcare services and promote better health" is defined by Canada Health Infoway (Canada Health Infoway, 2019).

All these definitions concentrate on the use of digital technologies to enhance the provision of healthcare, such as enhancing the holistic view of patients, achieving improved health objectives, improving the practice of medicine, and delivering evidence-based therapeutic treatments to prevent, manage, or treat a disease or disorder, monitoring and enhancing patient health and wellness, measuring and intervening to support human health, and enhancing the progress and performance of the healthcare system. The transition of health systems toward a strong focus on and prioritization of health and wellness is also a key component of each of these definitions.

6.2.2 Components of Digital Health

Different components of digital health, viz. big data, Cloud computing, Gamification, Connected Health ePatients and eHealth are shown in Figure 6.1.

Big data is a huge volume of information that is extremely useful. Hospital records, patient medical records, medical test findings, and the internet of things-enabled gadgets are just a few examples of the big data sources used in the healthcare sector. Modern healthcare may take advantage of new opportunities made possible by effective big data administration, analysis, and interpretation. In order to gain financial advantages, the healthcare business is widely adopting big data.

Cloud computing: Cloud computing in healthcare is the practice of using remote servers that may be accessed online to manage patient data. When it comes to gathering, analyzing, displaying, storing, and protecting data, cloud computing offers

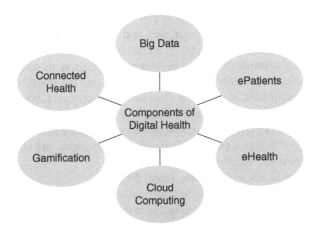

FIGURE 6.1 Different components of digital health.

a cutting-edge answer. This is crucial for sectors where data is used in virtually every step of the process.

Connected health: In its simplest form, connected health is a global framework that keeps telehealth and telemedicine programs running through connected health tools and technologies. It offers countless advantages to the patient as well as the healthcare system. However, connected care health services are also advantageous for the entire community and the nation. Telehealth tools, remote health monitoring tools, and integrated healthcare tools are all part of connected health.

Benefits of connected health:

- support clinical decisions
- improves patient and healthcare professional coordination
- improve patient health
- enhance the effectiveness and quality of healthcare
- lower healthcare costs

eHealth refers to the use of information and communications technology (ICT) for any activities that provide large benefits to the healthcare industry. In addition to patient-centered health systems for individuals and communities, eHealth systems include tools for national and international health authorities and professionals, including nurses, medical experts, administrators, doctors, hospital managers, and patients. eHealth aims to save expenses and improve healthcare quality. There are many eHealth applications available. These applications are made to assist users in developing healthy habits or a healthy way of life. Applications for eHealth can help doctors in every area, from disease prevention to informational support and therapeutic adherence. eHealth applications are created to successfully communicate in a world where digital communication has taken over as the norm, resulting in behavioral changes that support a healthier lifestyle.

ePatient is a person who makes an effort to completely engage in their medical care by learning more about their illness, consulting experts, and finding support online. An electronic patient may be defined more broadly to include those who act on behalf of friends or family members.

Gamification in the healthcare industry is the process of incorporating gaming aspects, gaming principles, game mechanics, and game design techniques into non-gaming apps, such as healthcare apps. Gamification's main goals are to add enjoyable and engaging features to tedious tasks, encourage users to adhere to wellness regimens, and enhance patients' emotional, cognitive, and behavioral health.

Healthcare gamification is a growing trend in this digital world. While gamification won't totally treat patients, it can encourage individuals to maintain healthy living habits and successfully perform difficult health chores, which will lead to better patient outcomes. Users of health apps, including patients, providers, and practitioners, can greatly benefit from gamification.

Benefits of Gamification: (Emerline Team, 2021)

Effective physical therapy: The best method to reduce the risk of cardiovascular disease, especially if you use a wheelchair, is to exercise.

Boost educational initiatives: Researchers from Brigham and Women's Hospital (BWH) and the Veterans Affairs Boston Healthcare System found that doctors who used online video games as their main learning tool outperformed their conventionally educated counterparts. Interns who were competing with one another produced superior learning and practical application outcomes. For businesses, this translates into improved patient outcomes, more staff accuracy and productivity, and lower expenses for professional training.

Increase surgical accuracy: Additionally, gamification in healthcare can help ensure greater precision during laparoscopic surgery. A Beth Israel Hospital in New York study found that playing video games helps professionals better control the movements of laparoscopic tools.

Improves employee health: Implementing a corporate wellness program can boost employee productivity and well-being. It can be difficult for workers who aren't already active to establish healthy habits. A standard wellness program can benefit from the addition of gamification, which can boost participation and long-term engagement. Employees who are not in good health use more sick days, which lowers their productivity and can be expensive for the business.

More useful patient information: A gamified healthcare app encourages users to provide more feedback, making it an excellent source of patient data that businesses can utilize to spot patterns, develop better products, and enhance service offers and delivery.

More people using the app: Gamification makes it possible for consumers to efficiently follow their path, from making an appointment to playing a game. Self-services also free up medical staff from tedious paperwork, allowing them to concentrate on treating more people by moving certain offline appointments online. Gamification is a challenging area, even if it is a great tool.

Gamification in healthcare apps:

- Children's health apps
- Mental health apps
- Health apps for managing medication and chronic conditions
- Physical therapy/rehabilitation apps
- Nutrition and fitness apps
- Cancer treatment

6.3   GROWING DEMAND FOR THE DIGITAL HEALTHCARE MARKET

The integration of cutting-edge digital technologies and tools and digital communications into various healthcare processes for improving people's overall health and welfare is referred to as "digital health." The digital healthcare market is growing globally due to the following factors:

The increasing adoption of innovative technologies, including telehealth and telemedicine services, wearable devices, IoT, mHealth apps, sensors, and AI, has contributed to the revolutionary changes in the healthcare sector that have accelerated market expansion. The world has experienced how the growth of mobile apps, especially during the COVID-19 pandemic, has helped the healthcare industry expand globally.

The expanding elderly population, childhood illnesses and deaths, high costs and poverty-related problems, as well as racial prejudice connected to access to health care, had made technological improvements in healthcare industries necessary. Additionally, the COVID-19 pandemic has increased the importance of digital health, which is still developing and driving the market's growth.

Using digital health tools may help identify emerging diseases or the worsening of pre-existing ones. Digital health tools may enable health professionals to treat patients earlier in the course of a disease, shortening the illness's length or easing symptoms before they get worse. Digital health may not only enhance people's quality of life, but it may also reduce the lifetime cost of healthcare, saving money for both patients and healthcare professionals.

The rising need for mobile health apps, the rising demand for remote patient monitoring services, the increase in smartphone and internet penetration, and tablets have all contributed to the growth of the worldwide digital health industry. With the evolution of healthcare using online symptom checks, patient-facing tools, remote patient monitoring tools, telehealth, and patient portals, among others, the COVID-19 pandemic has proven to be a game changer for ongoing innovations in digital health. As a result, these innovative innovations in the field of digital health are expected to open up attractive business opportunities.

Due to the establishment of numerous beneficial government initiatives world-wide, there is also a growing demand in the healthcare industry to enhance healthcare quality in order to have a long-term impact, particularly in the country's rural areas.

The market has also experienced tremendous growth, mostly as a result of rising demand for healthcare software, fitness apps, and different healthcare analytics platforms. As a result, an increasing number of companies are creating digital health and wellness software to enhance productivity and give contractors and their clients the best possible user experience. In addition to this, it is estimated that advancements in wellness-living software, health-tracking technology, wellness coaching software, and other fields would enhance current healthcare services and strengthen the immune system.

Although some technologies are still in the development stage, digital healthcare holds the promise of some truly remarkable and exciting advancements in recent years. A significant number of developers and researchers are working on innovative technologies in the area of digital healthcare.

Countries around the world are trying to bridge the gap between patients and doctors by implementing modern digital health technologies and initiatives. It is also making efforts to transform how people engage with national health services. All of this digital freedom will boost the quality of life while also providing peace of mind.

6.3.1 Global Digital Healthcare Market

The global healthcare market is expanding as a result of improvements in internet connectivity with the launch of 4G and 5G, rising smartphone usage, rising healthcare IT costs, improving IT infrastructure, technology readiness, a growing dearth of healthcare providers, overcrowded healthcare facilities, and rising medical costs.

The COVID-19 pandemic dramatically increased the need for digital health solutions in the healthcare sector and unveiled a number of business opportunities.

Key players were encouraged by the surge in demand to continually concentrate on cutting-edge product development techniques in order to increase their market share. The pandemic caused a rise in mHealth platforms, telemedicine, wearables, virtual care, and healthcare IT systems, among other digital health applications. The growing use of digital communication and information technology for virtual home health care is another factor contributing to the segment's expansion. Many non-healthcare corporations and private equity firms are investing capital and non-capital resources in the healthcare industry, contributing to its growth. The global healthcare market had grown to become one of the largest in terms of income and employment, and the industry was rapidly expanding.

Asia-Pacific Region: Because of the following factors, the Asia Pacific region dominates and is the fastest-growing digital health market:

- Due to the number of government initiatives to create digital healthcare platforms, the market is expected to grow over the next few years.
- Furthermore, the market growth is being supported by the increasing use of smartphones and internet penetration in these regions.
- A rise in the manufacturers' creation of health and fitness apps in response to increasing consumer demand supported the market's expansion. (Research and Markets, 2022)

China: By embracing new digital technology, tools, and apps, China is currently dominating the digital market. The new digital ecosystem's major trends in health care include digital health sites, virtual communities, patient engagement platforms, telehealth, digital communication platforms, virtual conferences, electronic medical databases, and artificial intelligence (AI).

According to a survey, Chinese patients are far more accepting of using digital health services in the coming five years. In China, patients and healthcare professionals are investigating different, more effective care delivery models, like virtual medical consultation. As in many Western economies, these digital health solutions have increased the capacity of the healthcare system and allowed patients and clinicians to communicate more affordably.

In order to ensure that internet-based medical services are covered by the nation's medical insurance system, the National Healthcare Security Administration (NHSA) launched the electronic medical insurance system in 2019. This system regulates insurance premiums and policies. Under this system, patients are allowed to use digital channels like WeChat and Alipay to access hospital diagnosis and prescription services without presenting any medical insurance identity cards, which will encourage the wider adoption of telemedicine.

India: In the COVID-19 pandemic, due to national lockdowns, and certain restrictions, it had a beneficial effect on the market as many patients chose telemedicine and telehealth solutions. As a result, in 2020–2022, telehealthcare dominated the market. The healthcare sector and governmental organizations are currently recognizing telehealth and telemedicine services. New programs are being launched by governments all around the world to promote digital health. For instance, the Ayushman Bharat Digital Health Mission (ABDM) was launched by the Indian government during the 2022 budget session. The government contributed more than $3.5 million to this effort to enhance the infrastructure for digital healthcare (Research and Marketers, 2022).

Australia has one of the best healthcare systems in the world; it offers affordable and safe medical care to all citizens. It is jointly managed by the federal, state, territorial, and local tiers of the Australian government. The Australian Government is contributing funds to the modernization of the healthcare system in order to implement Australia's Long-Term National Health Plan (Shah, 2023).

With rising smartphone penetration, better internet connectivity, improved healthcare IT infrastructure, rising healthcare costs, an increase in demand for remote patient monitoring services, and increased accessibility of virtual care, these are some of the factors driving current and future trends in the digital health market. Businesses in the digital health space are improving deep learning (DL) to forecast a person's risk of developing dementia and Parkinson's disease. Some businesses are becoming more accurate at detecting potential illness tendencies in people by using AI. eHealth technologies that boost productivity in healthcare institutions, like telemedicine, laboratory management systems, and clinical decision support systems, are being adopted more widely by IT corporations, utilizing a variety of implementation methodologies.

North America: North America was one of the first regions to adopt digital healthcare solutions, which use a number of innovative digital technologies, including mobile apps, smart wearables, and eHealth services such as EHR and telemedicine, to provide remote access to information on serious and chronic medical issues. The expansion of digital health services in this area is due to the fast penetration of smartphones, improvements in coverage networks, an increase in the prevalence of chronic diseases, an increase in the number of elderly people, rising health care costs, a severe shortage of primary caregivers, and a rise in the demand for better prevention and management of chronic conditions.

Europe is already a hub for digital health pioneers. Some of the world's top digital healthcare systems are found in Europe. There are prestigious research institutes and businesses that generate a goldmine of digital health data. Europe's approach to healthcare is already concentrated on providing the best value for patients. And digital solutions have assisted in meeting people's needs fairly, ethically, and securely. Some nations like Estonia, the Netherlands, Denmark, and Sweden are relatively advanced in terms of having implemented numerous digital health tools and having suitable financial, legal, and institutional frameworks for digital health in place. All of Europe's nations still have great potential for digital health services.

6.4   MEDICAL EXPERT SYSTEMS

The phrase "expert system," an area of artificial intelligence, was first used by Professor Edward Feigenbaum, who is considered a pioneer in the medical sector. He defined the term "expert system" as "an intelligent computer program that uses knowledge and inference techniques to tackle problems that are difficult enough to necessitate a substantial amount of human talent for the solution" (Busruk et al., 2016).

An expert system (ES) is a type of computer system that transfers human knowledge to the computer so that it can tackle problems that are typically handled by experts. Expert systems are a subset of artificial intelligence (AI) that imitate human experts' capacity for decision-making. The main purpose of a medical expert system is to assist doctors in making diagnoses. To provide a diagnosis, it takes into account both facts and symptoms. There are numerous expert systems for detecting diseases; however, they are either standalone or web-based.

A medical expert system is well-designed computer software that provides decision assistance by providing precise diagnostic information and making recommendations for a course of treatment or a prognosis. The program provides recommendations after receiving data or inputs about the patient from the doctor. These recommendations can be diagnostic, therapeutic, or prognostic. Expert systems may now be accessible to any doctor with a microcomputer, thanks to the development of more potent microcomputers and effective microcomputer languages.

Medical expert systems are classified into five types.

- MYCIN is an expert system.
- CADUCEUS is an expert system.
- Clinical decision support system.
- Computer-aided diagnosis (CAD) expert system.
- Computer-aided simple triage (CAST) expert system.

The list of different medical expert systems in healthcare is illustrated in Table 6.1.

6.5 IMPACT OF INFORMATION SYSTEMS IN DIGITAL HEALTHCARE

A health information system (HIS) is any type of structured data, information, or knowledge repository that may be utilized to support the delivery of healthcare or to advance health development. One of the three primary axes along which they are arranged is the concept of the health information system, which originates from the field of health information and communication technologies. Health information systems are commonly defined as the interplay of people, processes, and technology to support basic information operations, management, and availability to enhance healthcare services. Health information systems' major objective is to provide effective and high-quality healthcare (Panerai, no date). Electronic medical records, computerized patient records, and the more recent electronic health records are now frequently used phrases with a health information system that are almost interchangeable.

In this digital age, the terms "health information system," "electronic medical records," "computerized patient records," and the more modern "electronic health records" are often used interchangeably.

One type of IS is represented by a HIS. It consists of the management information system, which considers the administrative component of the health sector, and the medical information system, which addresses the medical, medico-economic, and environmental elements (Verdier and Flora, 1994).

TABLE 6.1
Medical Expert Systems

Name of the Medical Expert Systems	Developed by/in:	Description	Benefits
MYCIN	1970s, at Stanford University.	An early expert system is MYCIN. It recommended medications with dosages suited for the patient's body weight after utilizing artificial intelligence to identify germs that cause serious infections including bacteremia and meningitis. Since many antibiotics end in "mycin," the name is derived from the drug itself (Rai, Sahu and Sawant, 2018).	MYCIN provides great level of accuracy.
CADUCEUS expert system	Harry Pople in the middle of 1980 at Pittsburg University.	On the INTERNIST-1 algorithm, CADUCEUS was constructed. The phrase "most knowledge-intensive expert system in existence" was used to describe CADUCEUS at the time (Donald, Lindberg and Mary, 2010).	CADUCEUS was able to identify up to 1000 distinct diseases.
Clinical Decision Support expert System(CDSS)	1980s	CDSS aims to enhance medical judgments with focused clinical knowledge, patient information, and other health data, so improving healthcare delivery. Its main goal is to help medical professionals by allowing them to analyze patient data and use that knowledge to help make diagnoses.	CDSS helps to improve efficiency and reduce costs.
Computer-aided diagnosis(CAD) expert system	Fred Winsberg in 1970s	CAD helps medical professionals diagnosing disease and measurement of illness progression (Sharma et al., 2013).	CAST minimizes hospital visits and saves time in the administrative process.
Computer-aided simple triage(CAST) expert system		CAST is a sub-set of CAD system. CAST is designed for diagnostic imaging in urgent situations. CAST deals with urgent, life-threatening illnesses when timing is crucial for an early diagnosis (Goldenberg and Peled, 2011).	It intends to improve diagnostic precision.

Source: Table developed by the authors.

The World Health Organization defines health information systems (HIS) as coordinated efforts to "collect, process, report, and use health information and knowledge to influence policy making, program action, and research." HISs are critical to the efficient operation of global health systems (WHO, 2016).

The health information system has a very important role in the world of digitalization and globalization. In healthcare, as in many other industries, the adoption of advanced digital tools and technologies is very important for sustaining businesses and overcoming current obstacles around the world. Advanced medical technology, pharmaceuticals, biotechnology, and, more recently, medical tourism are significant actors in a country's vast and diverse healthcare industry. Over the years, the HIS has achieved a great deal of respect in the healthcare industry globally. The usage of HIS has given value to a variety of healthcare applications, improving population health, resource allocation accuracy, and management capabilities, among others. The use of digital health information systems aids in gathering the data and information required for training and recording by healthcare professionals and is efficient for health systems.

6.5.1 STRUCTURE OF HEALTH INFORMATION SYSTEMS

It can be seen from Figure 6.2 that the input phase is simple to understand. Copies of the questionnaires may be added to the patient records and stored in a file cabinet. A review of questionnaires and simple statistics of the key pieces of information, such as the number of children in the family, the distribution of ages, the proportion of couples using each method of contraception, and so on, may be included in the processing process. A summary report that is given to the team in charge of the program is a common output.

Health information systems can be used by anybody involved in digital healthcare, including patients, professionals, and public health officials. They compile data and arrange it so that it may be used to make healthcare decisions. Health information systems also comprise systems that handle data important to the operations of healthcare organizations and providers. Combining these could influence research, improve patient outcomes, and enhance policy and decision-making. Since health information systems often access, handle, or store substantial volumes of sensitive data, security is of the utmost importance.

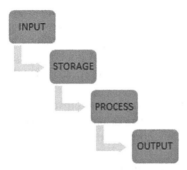

FIGURE 6.2   Phases of a health information system.

Thus HIS is used to perform the following tasks:

Electronic Medical Record (EMR) and Electronic Health Record (EHR): The phrases "Electronic Medical Record" (EMR) and "Electronic Health Record" (EHR) are sometimes used synonymously. The paper version of a patient's medical history is replaced by an electronic medical record. More health information, test reports, and treatments are included in the electronic health record. For other healthcare practitioners to access a patient's medical information, it is also made to share data with other electronic health records.

Portals for patients: A patient can see their own recent visits' information by creating a secure account on the patient portal. Patients can communicate with their doctors securely and privately through patient portals to ask follow-up questions. Patients can access their personal health information, including appointment details, medication information, and lab results online with the help of patient portals.

Practice management software: Healthcare professionals can manage daily tasks like scheduling and billing with the use of practice management software. Healthcare providers, including practitioners and hospitals, employ practice management systems to automate many administrative tasks.

Master patient index: A master patient index (MPI) links various patient records from various databases. Hence, MPIs are used to lessen the number of duplicate patient records and unreliable patient data that could result in claim denials.

Remote patient monitoring (RPM) or telehealth: Although they are sometimes used interchangeably, telehealth and remote patient monitoring are not nearly the same thing. Medical sensors can send patient data to healthcare professionals through remote patient monitoring, commonly known as telehealth. RPM entails using connected electronic instruments to record patient health and medical information in one area, which is then examined by a practitioner in another location. For patients with long-term illnesses such as asthma, hypertension, and most recently patients with COVID-19 symptoms, it frequently checks blood pressure and blood glucose levels.

6.5.2 CATEGORIES OF HEALTH INFORMATION SYSTEMS

Patient-facing health information systems: Patient portals are now provided to patients by many healthcare organizations. Patients can access safe information regarding their medical histories, such as past doctor visit records, by logging into their accounts. The patient can take part in their care by having a care plan, including any prescribed medications or follow-up appointments, written down by doctors or nurses. Patient portals can also be used to book non-urgent appointments, monitor the status of payments or insurance benefits, and view the results of blood tests or another testing.

Provider-facing health information systems: This is another type of system that is designed for healthcare providers or professionals. These systems provide details on the general state of health, hospital-specific trends, or other information that can help with treatment planning.

Cloud-based health information systems: Many healthcare organizations work with a health IT infrastructure made up of various digital tools and technologies used by staff members with various demands. In collaborative care, cloud-based systems are crucial. The patient's journey is not always straightforward, and a thorough treatment plan can require the patient to consult with a variety of doctors, therapists, and other professionals. It ensures a clear image of the patient's treatment history, reduces duplicative therapies, and keeps providers all on the same page when each member of this chain can quickly access the same information. Cloud-based health information management systems work as SaaS applications and can be accessed through a desktop app or web browser. Cloud-based software-as-a-service (SaaS) apps are frequently used in healthcare organizations to manage information and record patient interactions. Cloud-based health information management systems provide cloud computing with some of the advantages of high availability, decreased hardware maintenance, and decreased operating costs (Articles, 2020).

Clinical decision support (CDS): To assist healthcare professionals in making clinical decisions, clinical decision support systems evaluate data from multiple clinical and administrative systems. To assist doctors in providing individualized patient care, these tools filter data and information.

6.5.3   Data and Information in Digital Healthcare

Data and information are very important elements for the effective development of a healthcare system. With this information, access to patient and population health data allows administrators, physicians, and nurses to make critical decisions about patient care that could have a profound impact on their patients. For instance, instant access to a patient's medical history may reveal past therapies. The foundation of the entire health system is health information, which may be utilized for global epidemics, quality assurance and improvement, clinical diagnosis and management, strategic planning and priority-setting, and global planning. Health information helps organize services, enforces accountability, and promotes excellence in care. It also offers useful data on the community's health state and characterizes the people who use a service and the types of service they receive.

Information will consequently facilitate better decision-making, which will result in improved health. A lack of information, for instance, prevents decision-makers from identifying issues and needs, monitoring progress, assessing the effectiveness of treatments, or making evidence-based decisions. Additionally, the use of digital tools and technology aids in achieving the appropriate scale and level of integration. Integration of systems and services is acknowledged as being necessary for both primary health care and digital health (WHO, 2016). Moreover, various governments rely on the data from HIS to produce high-quality, comprehensible statistical data on the state of the community's health.

Data are becoming an ever more important factor to measure performance, monitor progress, and assessing the efficacy, efficiency, and impact of health services (Pacific Health Dialog, 2012). More healthcare decisions are now being influenced by data. Healthcare data is continuing to grow quickly because more healthcare professionals are moving their practices and data administration to online platforms or portals. Medical professionals and administrators can find areas that need improvement or are at risk by using data from the health industry. Therefore, once the data is collected, healthcare administrators and experts need to know how to best use it when making critical decisions and changes. As a result, a growing number of programs have been formed to leverage data in monitoring performance improvement efforts, enhancing outcomes, and serving as comparable benchmarks. The rise in organizations and publications devoted to the subject of health data is evidence of its increased significance. Healthcare data analytics have greatly benefited from the recent COVID-19 pandemic. Thus, big data tools have played a more significant role in healthcare decision-making.

Some organizations have acknowledged the importance of data and information in healthcare services. Various organizations, such as the Fundamental Principles of Official Statistics of the United Nations, World Health Organization publications on improving data quality, and more recently, the establishment of the Health Metrics Network in 2005, with its focus on enhancing global health and strengthening the systems that produce health information, Further, better information for better results was named as the top suggestion for enhancing the health of women and children by the WHO's Commission on Information and Accountability for Women's and Children's Health (World Health Organization, 2003).

Big Data in Health Information Systems

Big data is currently one of the most popular issues in data analytics and healthcare information systems. The management of the healthcare sector's rapid data development is made possible by the application of big data architectures and approaches. Therefore, the role of big data in the health information system is very significant. Big data has been used extensively in the healthcare field. Big data can be managed by utilizing modern security mechanisms and machine learning techniques.

A big data analytics-based paradigm for HIS was presented by Ahmed E. Youssef in 2014 (Youssef, 2014), shown in Figure 6.3. Huge amounts of data were managed and analyzed using this framework for the benefit of both patients and medical professionals.

The HIS framework is made up of five elements. The first element is the cloud environment, which is utilized to offer different services and permit data sharing with authorized users. The electronic health record, which is the second element, is used to combine patient data from various sources. The third component is the security layer, where numerous security challenges like authentication, authorization, and patient data confidentiality are efficiently controlled. Advanced Encryption Standard (AES) and RC4 are only two of the encryption techniques used in this layer to secure data. In order to prevent unwanted users, various authentication methods, including OTP and two-factor authentication (2FA), were also implemented. OTP

FIGURE 6.3   Health information system framework.

is a technique for periodically creating a unique password to secure network data. Additionally, the privileges of authorized users were granted or revoked using this layer. Big data analytics methods were employed to deploy the fourth layer of HIS and gain insight from the raw data. Care delivery organizations finally disseminate healthcare information in many areas. To increase the safety and caliber of medical services, this framework ensures the privacy and confidentiality of patient information.

6.5.4 INTEGRATION OF ELECTRONIC HEALTH RECORDS (EHR) IN HEALTHCARE

An EHRS is a computerized health information system in which healthcare professionals keep thorough records of patient demographics, encounter summaries, medical histories, allergies, intolerances, and lab test histories. Order entry, outcomes management, and decision support may be supported by some (Ludwick and Doucette, 2009).

Therefore, Electronic Health Records can be viewed as a Health Information System from the perspective of digitalization since it improves interoperability between various systems and because one of its key aspects is the integration of various information sources. These systems have many benefits, but we want to emphasize the quick access to information that is necessary for making decisions at the point of care, the promotion of safety and data confidentiality, the centralization and constant updating of information, the information structuring by medical standards, and the promotion of statistical control and performance optimization.

An EHR is filled out with data from all healthcare providers (hospitals, clinics, emergency departments, small offices, multispecialty groups, etc.). Then, through electronic communication, this information is networked to regional and national databases. Then, guidelines for prevention and treatment are used to channel data flows from EHRs and local registries, which may then be further processed to produce data for decision-making and decision-support (Ngafeeson, 2014).

Many healthcare sectors in developed countries around the world adopted these cutting-edge, quick, and efficient systems right away due to their speed and accuracy. As a result, both developed and developing nations now place a high focus on implementing EHRSs.

6.5.5 APPLICATIONS OF HEALTH INFORMATION SYSTEMS

A digital healthcare sector can benefit from health information systems in many ways. However, the company needs to set up the appropriate technology infrastructure before it can enjoy these advantages. Utilizing information systems in healthcare organizations has several advantages. They can cut health expenses by coordinating services and enhancing the quality of care, in addition to reducing errors, speeding up care, and increasing accuracy (Articles, 2020)

Population health management: In developing nations, the population's health needs to be improved immediately. HIS can be a tool for bringing about changes in resource allocation, priority setting, and service management of resources for health care and prevention limited. Information systems are important tools to spot patterns in community health issues. For instance, simple statistical analysis might show whether a particular region has a particularly high prevalence of diabetes. With the ability to track cases and keep an eye on local outbreaks, public health workers have the resources they need to support population health, as demonstrated by the COVID-19 pandemic in recent years. Greater community participation in systems that not only gather data but also provide feedback and promote health education at the PHC level could be expected to have positive effects. Factors in the environment, behavior, genetics, demographics, society, and economy all affect population health. By avoiding or reducing the occurrence of disease and restoring health through the use of curative services, health policy seeks to maximize the use of a society's resources to promote health.

Maintains data security and privacy: Hospitals secure all the personal information, records, and data of their patients. Thus, it guarantees data security and privacy as it can only be accessed by authorized users. On the server or in the cloud, all the data is safely stored. Since HIS relies on portals, data privacy, and security are completely safe and secure because it allows access to data based on the user's role, such as receptionist, doctor, nurse, or an administrator.

Aids in patient care processes: All treatments administered to patients by nursing personnel are considered patient care processes. Nursing interventions are the actions and demeanors used to carry out nursing care. Nurse observations, their examinations, and observations that form nursing diagnoses, the scheduling of treatments and medication administration, medical record charting, dietary registration, workload assessment, and the discharge or transfer of the patient are all examples of data gathered for documenting nursing work. Clinical documentation, according to some experts, also includes interactions between members of the healthcare team. An integrated health information system can be used to manage orders, appointments, family and work-related communication, medical outcomes, and information transfer to other specialists.

Greater efficiency: When procedures are automated using software, they are handled mechanically without human interaction, which immediately ensures increased efficiency. The software won't experience human issues like exhaustion, misunderstandings, or lack of concentration, but it will consistently complete any task given to it with greater accuracy.

Better patient care: Better and quicker healthcare judgments are made possible by increased patient data access and increased job efficiency. The more quickly the doctor receives the diagnostic reports and her prescriptions are carried out in the era of evidence-based medicine, the faster the patient recovers and the higher the patient care index. All hospital departments are connected through automation, and the quicker information is available, the better the patient care quality.

Reduces the scope of error: Because procedures are automated and a lot of duties are delegated to software to complete with the highest level of accuracy and the least amount of human involvement, the scope of error is drastically reduced.

Cost-effective: When HIS is properly implemented, it eliminates a lot of the manual labor that is typically undertaken in hospitals, especially for those that need to maintain records and documentation. Because a lot of work is automated and doesn't need human intervention to store or interpret the data, it helps reduce the need for labor. Additionally, it reduces storage costs significantly.

6.6 DIGITAL HEALTH TECHNOLOGIES

The digital health industry globally is rapidly expanding in the past few years and undergoing numerous technological advancements. The government of countries around the world's main goal is to ensure that everyone has fair access to high-quality services, and digital health is a key enabler for the health system's overall transformation. The emergence of digital technologies such as AI, ML, and robotics are the major driving forces in the healthcare industry worldwide.

Some of the most important emerging technologies used in the digital healthcare industry are:

- Telemedicine
- RAS
- Mobile health
- AI
- HER
- IoMT
- Cloud computing
- Telehealth
- Point-of-care tests (POCD)
- Medical virtual assistance
- E-Pharmacies
- Self-monitoring healthcare devices
- Health service aggregation

6.6.1 TELEMEDICINE AND TELEHEALTH

Telemedicine is a combination of medical research and information and communication technology. Telemedicine is described as the diagnosis and treatment of patients from a distance using telecommunications technology and its purpose is to achieve high-quality healthcare services in rural areas of the country. Digital health policy promotes the use of digital technologies to improve the quality and development of the healthcare system, with telemedicine facilities.

Telemedicine has made it easy for the patients to connect with their doctors to provide timely and best possible treatment. It has increased the use of telemedicine to fight the coronavirus pandemic (COVID-19). During the global crisis of the COVID-19 pandemic, telemedicine and telehealth has proved to be the most cost-effective and time-efficient options. Also Telemedicine is proved to be a lifeline in a healthcare system. Doctors may use teleconferencing to check patients' symptoms, prescribe them some medication, precautions, and necessary tests, and refer them to a healthcare facility if their symptoms worsen.

As a result of digital freedom in the healthcare industry, Telemedicine is now migrating healthcare services from hospitals and clinics into homes. It provides 24-hour housing monitoring. In some cases, patients who are chronically ill or elderly patients may receive treatment in certain procedures while remaining at home.

Telehealth

Telehealth is the provision of healthcare services remotely via technology without physically visiting a doctor. Everything from conducting doctor visits online to remotely checking on patients' vital signs can be included. Its definition is broader than telemedicine's, which solely encompasses the provision of healthcare remotely. Telehealth also includes the training and continuing education of medical specialists. Telehealth is frequently offered through safe websites and applications, and it makes use of several technologies, including email, messages, phone calls, and video chats.

There are three ways to deliver telehealth:

- **Synchronous:** When a doctor and patient speak on the phone or computer simultaneously
- **Asynchronous:** When information is recorded to be shared with the physician at a later time.
- **Remote patient monitoring:** When measurements like weight or blood pressure are forwarded to a healthcare professional, this is known as "remote patient monitoring."

Benefits of Telehealth:

Increased availability of services: Due to increased accessibility, patients are generally more willing to seek out medical care. They can now visit providers from the convenience of their homes.

Greater flexibility and ease in scheduling appointments: Telehealth is a desirable alternative because appointments can be scheduled during business hours. Patients no longer need to request leave from work or obtain additional child or elder care because they are not required to attend in-office appointments.

Cost-effective: Patients can save on additional costs like transportation, tolls, and parking when they have to attend in-office medical appointments.

Protects your data: Many people are concerned about the online disclosure of their personal medical information. But telehealth clinics and providers are required to safeguard all of your data, even if it is stored electronically.

Mobile Health

A mHealth application is a mobile application for iOS or Android that allows patients to access health-related information. mHealth is a rapidly growing field in the digital health sector that provides healthcare support and delivery via mobile devices like smartphones, tablets, etc. As maintaining social distancing became the new norm, doctor–patient interactions were a big matter of concern, especially due to the ongoing COVID-19 pandemic. In this situation, the Mobile Health app played a significant role in bridging the gap between doctors and their patients.

mHealth technologies can become effective medical devices or tools that can help with healthcare delivery at all levels. For example, it can provide Skype GP appointments via mobile phones, as well as wireless blood pressure and glucose monitors that bind to your phone and send data to your doctor automatically. Many of the conventional obstacles that healthcare practitioners have to face, such as time and cost constraints, have been overcome by this technology.

In the age of digitalization, Smartphones are widely used technology around the world. Today, even the majority of people who are not educated or have poor incomes use mobile phones or other mobile devices. Thus, they are one of the most widely used, affordable, and accessible instruments for gathering data, including healthcare data. As a result, their use in healthcare has taken on strategic importance for the growth of healthcare in low- and/or middle-income nations, where they are employed for a variety of functions including patient monitoring, health surveys, epidemiological surveillance, and public health awareness.

6.6.2 ARTIFICIAL INTELLIGENCE (AI) IN HEALTH

In the healthcare system, AI is becoming more commonly used. AI in the healthcare industry is used for treatment design, virtual nurses, drug creation, health monitoring, etc. AI has equipped healthcare organizations with tools to help them handle their workloads and rethink their processes. Significant evidence of the potential usefulness of Artificial Intelligence methods based on Deep Learning for use in medical diagnostics has been provided. AI includes machine learning as a subset.

Accurate diagnosing of a disease: In the healthcare industry, diagnosis accuracy is crucial since erroneous diagnoses can have serious implications. The likelihood of a fatal outcome rises if an operation is performed when none was required or if a misdiagnosis results in incorrect amounts of prescribed medication. AI also helps in diagnosing many diseases like cancer. To help with screening tests for numerous types of cancer, including breast cancer, scientists have created AI tools. Artificial intelligence allows access to a large amount of information and data collected from hundreds of thousands of patient cases. Advanced AI algorithms are also assisting doctors in analyzing and predicting a much broader range of medical data. AI algorithms have also been widely used to analyze chest x-rays and other radiological images, and read ECGs, CT scans, and MRIs, for other reasons. Medical practitioners may use the AI-powered diagnostic device to diagnose early signs of chronic illnesses like cancer. Thus, it enables medical professionals to more accurately diagnose illnesses, gather disease information quicker, and treat illnesses more promptly (Wang and Preininger, 2019).

Disease prevention and the fight against sickness have benefited greatly from artificial intelligence. Social media and artificial intelligence analysis algorithms can be used to combine human behavioral data to spot mental disease risk factors. Artificial intelligence analysis has been used to determine the suicide risk among psychiatric patients or a particular demographic, such as soldiers and inmates (Wang and Preininger, 2019).

Decision-making: Artificial intelligence also helps in improving nursing decision-making, technology aids nurses in collecting and recording patient data more precisely and quickly. A nursing diagnosis guideline can be derived using an artificial intelligence-based nursing data system to help nurses decide on a clinical course of action. The time required for artificial intelligence-assisted nursing decision-making was practically halved when compared to manual nursing diagnosis. In addition, nurse work satisfaction and the standard of patient care have also increased (Wang and Preininger, 2019).

Integration of health data: A key objective of the healthcare system is the structured unification of health data since it should promote hospital efficiency and provide better patient health outcomes. The historical physical documentation that is still in existence, however, is a serious issue. If employees were recruited to manually enter this data into an electronic system, it would be challenging, time-consuming, and expensive to convert these existing papers into an electronic format. Natural language processing (NLP) is a machine learning application that could help with this issue. These systems aim to extract legible data from the free text by quickly scanning these papers and integrating the resulting images into a database. They also integrate image processing to recognize keywords and concepts.

Virtual nurse: A smart robot can act as a potent nursing assistant in a clinical setting. A carrier robot has been suggested and developed in the United States for individuals with mobility issues, such as a patient with back problems. When given the order by the nurse through a smart touchpad, an intelligent carrier robot helps patients change positions or move from the bed to a wheelchair. It substantially lessens the physical strain on nurses and helps to solve the problem of moving a sick patient.

Medical imaging: Medical imaging for risk assessment, precision medicine, and screenings can be improved by artificial intelligence. A patient may require medical imaging in many different situations. AI can make a prompt diagnosis and recommend a course of action for any ailment, including cardiac events, fractures, neurological disorders, and thoracic difficulties. Since the invention of digital photography, retinal pictures can now be routinely digitally recorded using Picture Archiving and Communication Systems (PACS) (Snowdon, 2015). Through non-invasive imaging of the retina through the pupil, several eye illnesses can be detected. Early detection of diabetic retinopathy is crucial because, with the constantly expanding number of individuals with diabetes, prompt treatment can avert vision loss and even blindness. A test like this offers the chance to spot more eye conditions as well as heart disease warning signs (Pesapane, Codari, and Sardanelli, 2018).

The objective of low-cost, quantitative retinal image analysis is motivated by the growing need for such screening and the need for professional analysis that it creates. Additionally, researchers are creating AI tools for cancer imaging.

Robotics and Robot-assisted Surgery

In this digital age, robots are revolutionizing the healthcare sector. The newest innovative technology, robots, is anticipated to improve patient quality and safety. Healthcare robots are anticipated to be used because of their lower cost and expanding capabilities, which include aiding clinical practice, biological research, and interventional procedures. Robotics technology advancements have demonstrated a strong potential to encourage the development of novel medical therapies for a wide range of diseases and disorders to improve patient health outcomes.

Robotics technology has a remarkable opportunity to assist healthcare personnel in physical and cognitive rehabilitation, surgery, telemedicine, drug delivery, and patient management. This has been demonstrated through an examination of the previous and current performance of robotics within the field of healthcare (Riek, 2017).

There are three main types of robots in healthcare:

- Surgical robots
- Assistive robots
- Healthcare service robots

Surgical Robots

Robotic surgery has gained popularity in hospitals around the world as a minimally invasive surgery (MIS) since the Food and Drug Administration in the United States of America (USA) approved the da Vinci surgical system (Intuitive Surgical Inc., Sunnyvale, California, USA) (Buabbas et al., 2020).

As a result of digital freedom, robotic-assisted surgery (RAS) in the healthcare industry has been used for quite some time. Robotics technology is increasingly being used in many countries around the world for the treatment of various surgeries such as laparoscopic surgery, automated pharma, and so on. The introduction of robotics into the healthcare industry is one of the biggest advances toward the development of the industry, especially in many developing countries. There are robotic surgeries now that are performed without the presence of a surgeon.

In many countries around the world, there is a higher demand for Robotic-assisted surgeries because they help to improve the quality of life. The use of robots in surgical procedures has helped surgeons perform their complicated tasks more easily. It also makes the procedures more reliable, quicker and more cost-effective in the long run. In developing countries, many healthcare professionals are using robotic-assisted surgery to improve patient outcomes. One of the most important benefits of robotically assisted surgeries over open and laparoscopic surgeries is that they have a relatively shorter recovery time, less pain, and less blood loss.

While RAS benefits doctors, it also poses several difficulties. According to a review of 14 years' worth of FDA data, if a robot surgeon suddenly powers down in the middle of an operation owing to a system malfunction or imaging issues, the patient could sustain harm or even die. Robot parts that have broken or burned could fall onto the patient, an electric spark could burn human flesh, and an instrument could work accidentally, all of which could result in injury, including death (Alemzadeh et al., 2016). There are further privacy and cybersecurity concerns.

How It Works

- The da Vinci surgical system, which consists of equipment, a computer, and electronics that give doctors an easy-to-use tool for directing surgical tools, is used to perform robotic surgery or robot-assisted surgery.
- Through a very small hole, a doctor or surgeon uses a robotic arm to insert the instruments and camera into the patient's body, giving the surgeon a far better image and greater tool mobility.
- This technology allows the surgeon to view a 10x magnified, high-definition 3D representation of the complex anatomy of the body.
- Using controls on the console, the surgeon controls unique surgical instruments that are more flexible, agile, and smaller than the human hand.

- The robot mimics the surgeon's hand movements, which lessens hand tremors. As a result, the surgeon can work with more accuracy, dexterity, and control during even the most difficult procedures.

Socially Assistive Robots

A socially assistive robot has been designed to interact with people and offers a user, such as an elderly person, functional, emotional, and cognitive support (Hegel et al., 2019). The user enjoys interacting with the socially helpful robots because they are simple to grasp and have a pleasant user interface. Service robots and companion robots are the two main categories of socially assistive robots. The task-performing service robots assist the user with daily duties. A service robot's duties include, among others, assisting the user with eating, using the restroom, and dressing; performing home chores; and keeping an eye on the user's health and safety.

People who are paralyzed have trouble working or doing activities of daily living (ADLs). Helping people complete ADLs is where assistive robots are mostly focused. Tasks that include drinking and eating are given top priority. A wheelchair-mounted robotic arm (WARM) has served as the foundation for several assistive robotic devices. The FRIEND system, which is an intelligent wheelchair-mounted manipulator, is an illustration of an assistive robotic system. The FRIEND has gone through four generations; the first three generations focused on assisting quadriplegics with ADLs such as eating and drinking, while the fourth generation focused on assisting these individuals in everyday situations. The FRIEND IV is made up of a wheelchair platform, a robotic arm with seven degrees of freedom that has a two-finger gripper and a hand camera, a head control interface with a chin joystick, a stereo camera, and a laser scanner (Martens, Prenzel, and Graser, 2007).

Healthcare Service Robots

The International Federation of Robotics (2014) emphasizes the element of autonomy in its definition: "A service robot is a robot that operates semi- or fully autonomously to perform services useful to the well-being of humans and equipment, excluding industrial automation applications." More specifically, the International Standardization Organization (2014) defines the term "service robot" as "a robot that performs useful tasks for humans or equipment, excluding industrial automation applications."

Furthermore, the COVID-19 pandemic has sparked the development of service robots in the healthcare industry as a means of avoiding the challenges and suffering caused by this virus. The employment of service robots is useful because it not only stops the spread of disease and lowers human error, but also frees up front-line employees to concentrate on more important jobs and avoid direct contact with patients and other infected people. Many hospitals all across the world deployed humanoid robots in their COVID-19 wards throughout the outbreak. Moreover, an interactive robot was used at the entry to screen visitors and medical personnel. Additionally, several hospitals shifted to using robots as a means of maintaining social distance as a result of the danger posed by the COVID-19 pandemic.

Advantages of Robotics in Healthcare

Excellent patient care: When robots reduce workloads, nurses and other healthcare providers can contact patients more personally and show more compassion, both of which can improve patients' long-term well-being.

Effortless clinical workflows: The use of robots streamlines regular tasks, eases the physical burden on human workers, and promotes more reliable operations. Cleaning and sanitizing robots make it possible for hospital rooms to be promptly cleaned and prepared for new patients, freeing up staff members to concentrate on patient-centered, value-driven work.

In a secure workplace: In hospitals where there is a possibility of disease exposure, robots are used to convey supplies and linens to help keep healthcare staff safe. Hospital-acquired infections (HAIs) can be decreased by deploying cleaning and disinfection robots, which are already being used by hundreds of healthcare facilities.

The Internet of Medical Things

The term Internet of Things is defined as "a network of everyday devices, technology, and other tools or devices fitted with computer chips and sensors that can capture and distribute data over the Internet." As a result of digital freedom in the healthcare industry of India, the IoT has the potential to improve the efficiency of healthcare systems. IoT also allows healthcare technology to be more user-friendly, with interfaces that make it simple for consumers to understand what an application can do for them in their daily lives.

The benefits of IoT in the healthcare industry are given below:

Low medical costs: By using IoT in Healthcare facilities, it can easily track patients in real-time using IoT solutions and connected medical devices. As a result, there will be fewer unnecessary hospital visits, hospital stays, and re-admissions, resulting in lower medical costs.

Better patient experience: The ability of healthcare providers to deliver evidence-based treatments for patients will be enhanced by easy access to patients' healthcare data via simultaneous reporting and tracking through connected devices. This would result in a shorter care time and more patients being covered.

Reduce medical errors: Through interconnected devices, diagnostic devices, and mobile health apps that can be used to track health parameters, with real-time reporting to doctors. Health professionals may use this reliable health data to make informed decisions, reducing the risk of medical errors.

Healthcare access in rural areas: Interconnected devices have helped in the health monitoring of patients and have allowed patients in remote villages to consult with doctors in urban specialty hospitals from their homes. Thus this system of IoT will extend the scope of quality healthcare to rural areas in the future.

Medical Virtual Assistants

MVAs or Medical Virtual Assistants are a new trend in the m-health industry. Virtual health assistants and Chabot fill in the gap between patients and doctors and tend to patients' needs in between physical appointments by reminding patients to fill their prescriptions, giving them information on their conditions, scheduling appointments, keeping track of their health records, and performing other administrative duties. MVAs typically use AI-based software to evaluate enormous data sets, offer individualized advice, and carry out individual-specific tasks. MVAs are used in hospitals and other healthcare facilities for carrying out administrative chores.

6.6.3 ELECTRONIC HEALTH RECORDS (HER)

An electronic health record (EHR) is a digital version of a patient's paper chart which is also widely used in the healthcare industry. EHRs are patient-centered, live records that give authorized users instantaneous, secure access to information. EHR contains medical history, diagnosis, prescriptions, care plans, immunization dates, allergies, radiology photos, and laboratory and test results of a patient all stored in this register. Information can be accessed at any time and from any place when it is required with EHRs.

The hospital record is a dynamic informational entity that permits ongoing monitoring of a patient's health status. It integrates all relevant data, including clinical history, therapies, considerations, and findings from various diagnostic tests that have been run. The electronic health record (EHR) of a patient is regarded as a chronological collection of clinical data arising from the treatment he has received, cataloged by the location of performance and the individuals who performed the provided acts.

These systems have the significant advantage of providing instant access to relevant information required for decision-making at the point of care, in addition to superior information management and flexibility when compared to paper records.

The benefits of HER in the healthcare industry are:

- It improves patient care
- It improves *many* patient outcomes
- It improves care coordination
- It has proven to be very effective and pocket friendly
- It improves the privacy and security of personal information
- It continually updates the information

Point-of-care Tests (POCD)

Point-of-care Tests are a developing trend in the health sector and include a wide range of technologies that allow patients to perform precise diagnostics in settings with limited resources or medical professionals. It makes disease management, monitoring, and real-time condition diagnosis easier. Recent years have seen the development of numerous applications, including biosensors, portable x-rays, handheld ultrasounds, and smartphone-based POCD.

Traditional clinical diagnostic methods, which typically call for pricey and large instruments, have been streamlined into software or portable POCD devices that may be utilized at the patient's location rather than a hospital or a lab. POCD devices are often automated technologies that utilize machine learning and artificial intelligence algorithms to simplify complex diagnostic procedures and deliver instant test/diagnosis findings. The patient might utilize these findings to get in touch with a medical expert for a more precise diagnosis and treatment options. Additionally, implantable bio-sensors provide ongoing surveillance of a specific medical condition. They are helpful for point-of-care analysis because they have the potential to deliver timely and precise results. This makes it possible to track, monitor, and control the disease, which can directly help patients with medical decisions and doctors with prognoses because it provides huge data sets of minute health changes.

E-Pharmacy

E-pharmacy is a kind of online medical store where you can order drugs and other pharmacy items from your own home. You can conveniently order medicines from your smartphone. E-pharmacies provide convenience and comfort in many ways.

The electronic prescribing technology known as "e-prescription" enables medical providers to send digital prescriptions instead of handwritten ones, thus eliminating the need for paper prescriptions. Doctors are progressively favoring electronic prescriptions to give their patients quick access to medication. The introduction of e-prescription is receiving more attention from nations like the United Kingdom. By 2020, all NHS hospitals in England are expected to be paperless. The future demand for e-prescription technology may rise dramatically as a result of this. The main benefit of an electronic prescription is that it is simple to upload it to the website of an online pharmacy and place an order for medication there. As a result of the growing use of e-prescriptions, posting prescriptions online has become simpler and quicker.

The market for online pharmacies is booming in industrialized nations like the US and Europe and is a component of the more organized market for medical services. Doctors write prescriptions for medications, which are then barcoded and tracked to assure a regular supply. E-pharmacies aid in tracking the occurrence and transmission of diseases in India. Every e-pharmacy keeps a thorough record of all online drug sales, including the transactions and payment methods used. COVID-19 undoubtedly increased e-pharmacies' sales. Online pharmacies provide good discounts and cash back on all services provided, just like other E-Commerce portals. The majority of these individuals, who would have a high need for easy access to their treatments without visiting their doctor each time they need a refill for their meds, are certain to play a significant role in e-pharmacies in the future.

Benefits of E-Pharmacies

Growing internet penetration, various government e-healthcare initiatives, growing health insurance penetration, accessibility in remote areas, cost savings on bills, and doorstep delivery within a short period all these factors have led to customer preference for online pharmacies over offline retail pharmacies.

Pocket friendly: With the growth of digital freedom, e-pharmacy is becoming more prevalent. E-pharmacies provide consumers with increased access, lower transaction product costs, and convenience. Customers can also purchase pocket-friendly full-body checkup packages from online pharmacies. Companies send professional lab executives to collect blood samples at home, making pathology lab tests at home easy and possible. They send the test reports to you online through email.

Ease of accessibility: People living in rural areas with limited mobility can easily use them. These provide several discounts, quick home delivery, and prescription validation by licensed pharmacists.

Privacy: Customer data or information is fully protected by online portals. This ensures that the customer is not bombarded with intrusive communication that could harm the customer's relationship with the online portal.

Self-monitoring Healthcare Devices

Rural areas across the globe have limited access to doctors and medical facilities, relying instead on community health workers. Wearable health devices have made it easier to track health conditions and connect doctors and patients in urban settings. Self-monitoring healthcare devices are intended to manage villagers' overall health through real-time patient monitoring, preventive care advice, increased health awareness, and self-monitoring at a low cost.

Benefits of self-monitoring devices:

- It helps you save money and time.
- It increases awareness, curiosity, and consciousness within the user.
- It is very cost-effective.

Health Service Aggregation

Data that is tracked across time, across institutions, across patient populations or some other variable is referred to as "aggregate data." Patient data is created in the healthcare industry when a patient interacts with a healthcare facility. An individual patient's data contains name, medical history, age, diagnosis, treatment outcome, and family medical history. So this type of information is necessary to provide the best treatment to the patients. Doctors can make more accurate and intelligent decisions about a patient's future treatment if they have a thorough understanding of their medical history, previous diagnoses and treatments, and family medical history.

Benefits of data aggregation in the healthcare industry:

- It helps to maintain reliability and transparency.
- It helps in the effective monitoring of healthcare trends.
- It also helps to build and maintain trust in data reliability and quality.

As a result of the freedom of digitalization, advanced digital devices and technology played an important role in boosting the performance and growth of India's healthcare industry. When there is efficient utilization of technology, it can save the lives of thousands of people. Therefore, digital freedom plays a very active role in the healthcare industry of any country in resolving a variety of medical issues.

6.6.4   REAL-WORLD CASE: INDIA

GROWING DEMAND FOR E-PHARMACY

With the freedom of digitalization, more than 200 e-pharmacies exist in India, with more on the way. The most common is 1 mg, Medlife, Netmeds, Pharmeasy, and Myra. With around 30% of the Indian e-pharmacy market, Medlife is now the market leader. The most important thing about e-pharmacy is that it also stocks some of the most obscure drugs, so you won't have to waste time searching for them. Also, governments are requiring the use of e-prescriptions and e-health records, which are automatically fed into e-pharmacies for fulfillment (Dhote, 2021).

In terms of volume and value, the Indian pharmaceuticals market is the third largest in the world. In India, the trend of ordering prescription drugs online is growing. The penetration of the organized pharmacy industry will further expand with the entry of online pharmacy retailers into the Indian market. Over the next ten years, it is anticipated that the e-pharmacy model will contribute growth in India, partly as a result of improving medication availability and adherence for the vast majority of the underserved population (Dhote, 2021).

With an impressively increasing market penetration rate, these online pharmacies are steadily gaining attention in the e-commerce industry, both from the government and from customers.

6.7   TRANSFORMING FACTORS OF THE DIGITAL HEALTH INDUSTRY

The healthcare industry is one of the biggest industries in the world in terms of employment and revenue. Digital freedom in the healthcare industry is transforming the health sector rapidly all over the world. Modern digital technology is gradually revolutionizing the healthcare industry in better, longer, and more prosperous ways. Globally, the healthcare system has been completely transformed with the use of advanced digital technologies.

In the era of digitization, nowadays not only do doctors choose to provide medical help online, but patients as well prefer to use various health apps to get their work done. In addition, there are several advanced technologies and health-related apps that will continue to transform the health industry. The healthcare industry would benefit from the integration of technological solutions such as data analytics, artificial intelligence (AI), robot-assisted surgery, cloud computing, telecommunications, and wireless technology to increase accessibility and better handle labor shortages.

6.7.1 FOREIGN INVESTMENTS IN DIGITAL HEALTH

Healthcare is one of the fastest-growing service sectors in the world. Therefore, the growth of the hospital industry has been significantly influenced by foreign investors. Foreign direct investment (FDI) in the healthcare industry has accelerated recently due to the sector's expanding importance and the enormous growth of trade in healthcare sectors.

FDI can help with fundamental requirements for humans like access to healthcare, balanced nutrition, a decrease in infant mortality rate, and availability of additional doctors. Thus, FDI has a positive impact on healthcare sectors across the world. FDI has a favorable impact on health mostly by increasing the availability of goods and services in the healthcare industry (Burner et al., 2017).

Due to this, there is an increasing interest among foreign businesses to enter the healthcare sector through financial investments, technology partnerships, and joint ventures across a variety of categories, including diagnostics, medical equipment, hospitals, and education and training. Thus, foreign investments assist in boosting the standard and quality of healthcare by modernizing hospital beds, and the latest diagnostics equipment, and by providing super-specialty centers.

6.7.2 GLOBAL DIGITAL HEALTH INITIATIVES AND STRATEGIES

Global health organizations are developing and putting into practice digital health initiatives, and business strategies from start-ups to established players are promoting digital health. Governments around the world have been experimenting with many health programs in the area of digital healthcare. A nation should employ cutting-edge digital technologies to make sustainable health systems and universal health care possible. To reach their full potential, digital health initiatives have been integrated into the ecosystem for digital health and a broader set of health needs. They must also be driven by a solid strategy that unifies leadership, funding, organizational, human, and technological resources. This strategy serves as the foundation for a cost-effective action plan that facilitates coordination among various stakeholders. The governance of these efforts is well established. The approach is supported by standards and an architecture that allows for this integration across many health priorities. Recently, many digital initiatives have been launched by governments across the world, like in Australia, India, and the U.S. The main goal of this initiative is to reshape healthcare systems and boost the market growth. These initiatives have provided many benefits to the country's healthcare sector. The main objective of this program is to improve the accessibility, transparency, and equity of health services in an assured manner around the country. The government's push for digitization will allow patients to access accurate information about the qualifications and costs of services provided by various healthcare facilities, providers, and diagnostic laboratories, in addition to sharing their health profiles with providers for treatment and monitoring. Thus, as a result of digital freedom, these initiatives are "completely technology-based," which would revolutionize the healthcare industry and provide many benefits in the country's healthcare sector globally.

Globally, many digital initiatives have been launched by the governments of different developed and developing countries. The main goal of this initiative is to reshape healthcare systems and boost the market growth. These initiatives have provided many benefits to the country's healthcare sector.

6.7.3 REAL-WORLD CASES (1–2)

REAL-WORLD CASE 1: AUSTRALIA NATIONAL HEALTH STRATEGY

The Australian government established the Australian Digital Health Agency with the mission of advancing digital health competence through innovation, collaboration, and leadership to enable digital health integration in the healthcare system. Through broad community outreach in Australia and a thorough review of the available data, the agency established the National Digital Health Strategy. The strategy suggests achieving seven key priorities:

*   My Health Record offers a platform for the development of digital tools and apps assist Australians and their healthcare professionals in enhancing health and wellness. The patient health information from My Health Records, giving access to reports of their medications, allergies, lab results, and chronic conditions that could save their lives. Patients and customers will have 24/7 online and mobile app access to their health information.
*   Every healthcare practitioner has access to secure digital channels for communication with other healthcare professionals and their patients. This will eliminate the need for paper-based correspondence, faxes, and the postal system, as well as enhance continuity and coordination of care, promoting the development of innovative techniques for diagnosis and specialist referral, and deliver considerable advantages to the safety, quality, and costs of Australian healthcare.
*   Through the My Health Record system, all patients and their healthcare professionals have access to detailed views of their prescribed and delivered medications. This lessens patient damage and result in significant cost savings by decreasing the frequency of medication errors and adverse drug events. (Australia's National Digital Health Strategy, 2020)

REAL-WORLD CASE 2: INDIA

National Digital Health Mission (NDHM)
The National Digital Health Mission is an Indian government initiative to provide medical identification documents to Indian citizens. The Prime Minister of India launched the **National Digital Health Mission (NDHM)** on the 74th anniversary of Independence Day in 2020 (National Digital Health Mission, no date).

The four main features of the digital platform of the National Digital Health Mission:

- **The national health ID:** Every Indian's health-related information is stored in the national health ID. This ID is created using basic details and an Aadhar number or mobile number, and it is unique for every person.
- **Personal health records:** A personal health record (PHR) is an electronic record of an individual's health-related information that can be accessed from multiple platforms and maintained, exchanged, and monitored by the individual.
- **Digi Doctor:** The Digi Doctor option makes it possible for doctors to link to India's digital health ecosystem. Doctors from all over the world are able to enroll in the Digi Doctor program, and add their information, including their contact numbers if they want to include them. These doctors also get free digital signatures, which they will use to write prescriptions.
- **Health Facility Registry (HFR):** All the health facilities, such as hospitals, must be registered in the system with all information, such as services provided, specialties, etc.

NATIONAL DIGITAL HEALTH BLUEPRINT (NDHB)

This National Digital Health Blueprint is an extension of the National Health Policy of 2017 (NHP 2017), which aimed to provide universal healthcare to all Indians through the use of digital technology to improve quality and effectiveness. It also intends to use artificial intelligence (AI) in conjunction with medical records (National Digital Health Mission, no date).

The key goals of the NDHB:

- Creating and maintaining the core digital health data as well as the infrastructure needed to share it seamlessly
- Developing a system of personal health records that is readily available to citizens and service providers and assuring the quality of health care services
- Increasing the quality and efficacy of health data analytics at all levels and making use of the healthcare information system that already exists.

6.8 CHAPTER CONCLUSION

Every country recognizes the importance of healthcare. Our health and well-being are heavily dependent on the infrastructure and technology in our country. Thus, with digital freedom, the landscape of the healthcare industry is being reshaped with the advancement and innovations of digital technologies. Healthcare is the industry where digitalization will have the greatest and most positive effects. Medical personnel are benefiting from the digitalization of medical systems by being able to quickly and accurately diagnose patients and choose the best course of therapy for them based on those findings. And therefore, in the healthcare sector, advanced digital technology not only allows hospitals to deliver quality patient care, but it has also developed rapidly as an information technology industry.

EXERCISES

1. What do we mean by digital health?
2. How does WHO define the term digital health?
3. What is eHealth and mHealth?
4. What are benefits of gamification in healthcare?
5. What are different types of medical expert systems?
6. What is a Health Information System? What are its benefits to healthcare?
7. What is the role of EHR and Big Data in a Health Information System?
8. What are digital health technologies?
9. What is the role of AI in healthcare?
10. What is RAS? Give its types?
11. What are benefits of IoT in healthcare?
12. What is main goal of Digital Health Initiatives?
13. What are the major goals of National Digital Health Strategy?
14. What is National Digital Health Blueprint?
15. What are the major goals of National Digital Health Mission?

REFERENCES

Alemzadeh, H., Raman, J., Leveson, N., Kalbarczyk, Z., and Iyer, R.K. (2016). 'Adverse Events in Robotic Surgery: A Retrospective Study of 14 years of FDA Data'. *PLOS ONE* 11(4): e0151470. https://doi.org/10.1371/jounal.pone.0151470

Articles, (2020) 'Health Information Systems: Health Care for the Present and Future', July 31. Available at: www.onlinemasters.ohoi.edu/blog/health-information-systems/ (Accessed: 04 September 2020).

Australia's National Digital Health Strategy (2020). Available at: www.digitalhealth.gov.au/sites/default/files/202011/Australia%27s%20National%20Digital%20Health%20Strategy%20-%20Safe%2C%seamless%20and520secure.pdf (Accessed: 19 March 2021).

Buabbas, et al. (2020) *'BMC Medical Informatics and Decision Making 20:140'* https://doi.org/10.1186/s12911-020-01167-1

Burns, et al. (2017) 'Is foreign direct investment good her health in low and middle income countries?' An instrumental variable approach. *Social Science and Medicine*, 181, pp. 78–82. https://doi.org/10.1016/j.socscimed.2017.03.054

Busruk, et al. (2016) *'Medical Science and Discovery'*, 3(11): 342–9, ISSN: 2148–6832, doi: 10.17546/msd.64430

Canada Health Infoway. (2019) *'What Is Digital Health?'* Available at: www.infoway-inforoute.ca/en/what-we-do/benefits-of-digital-health/what-is-digital-health on 12 July 2019 (Accessed: 11 April 2020).

Cormann, M. (2016) *'Explanatory Statement, Public Governance, Performance and Accountability Act 2013, Public Governance, Performance and Accountability'* (Establishing the Australian Digital Health Agency Rule (2016) *'Australian Government'*. Available at: www.legislation.gov.au/Details/F2016L00070/Explanatory%20Statement/Text (Accessed: 9 April 2021).

Dhote, R. (2021) *'Growth of E-pharmacies in India'*, March 14. Available at: www.linkedin.com/pulse/growth-e-pharmacies-india-rhea-dhote/ (Accesses: 07 April 2021).

Donald, A.B., Lindberg, and Mary, M. (2010) *'A History of INTERNIST-1 and Quick Medical Reference (QMR) Computer-Assisted Diagnosis Projects, with lessons learned'*, Department of Biomedical Informatics, Vanderbilt University Medical Center, Tennessee, USA.

Emerline Team, (2021) *'Gamification in Healthcare: Increase loyalty and Motivation Among your Patients and Medical Professionals'*, August 18. Available at: https://emerline.com/blog/gamification-in-healthcare (Accessed: 08 April 2022).

Goldenberg, R. and Peled N. (2011) 'International Journal of Computer Assisted Radiology and Surgery', vol. 5, pp. 705-11, DOI: 10.1007/S11548-011-0552-x

Hegel, et al. (2019) *'Understanding Social Robots [Internet]'* February 19. Available at: https://aiweb.techfak.uni-bielefeld.de/files/2009hegelACHI.pdf (Accessed: 11 April 2020).

International Federation of Robotics. (2014) 'Definition of service robots.' August 7. Available at: www.ifr.org/service-robots/ (Accesses: 01 April 2020).

International Standardization Organization. (2014) *'Robots and robotics devices- Vocabulary.'* August 7. Available at: www.iso.org/obp/ui/#iso:8373:ed-2:v1:en:term:2.10 (Accessed: 12 April 2020).

Ludwick, D. and Doucette, J. (2009) 'Primary Care Physician experience with Electronic Medical Records: barriers to implementation in a fee-for-service environment.' *International Journal of Telemedicine Application* 2009:853524.

Martens, C., Prenzel, O., and Graser, A. (2007) *'Rehabilitation robots FRIEND-I & II: Daily life independency through semi-autonomous task-execution'*, *Rehabilitation Robot.* 1, 137–162.

National Digital Health Mission, (n.d), Available at: www.drishtiias.com/printpdf/national-digital-health-mission (Accessed: 03 February 2021).

Ngafeeson, M. (2014) *'Health Information Systems: Opportunities and Challenges'*, Book Sections/Chapters. Paper 14. Available at: http://commons.nmu.edu/facwork_boohchapters/14 (Accessed: 10 August 2022).

Pacific Health Dialog, (2012) *'Health Information System in the Pacific'*, April, vol. 18, no. 1.

Panerai, R.B. (no date) *'GLOBAL PERSPECTIVE IN HEALTH-'* Health Information System vol-1. Available at: www.eolss.net/sample-chapters/c03/e1-14-02-01.pdf (Accessed: 07 February 2023).

Pesapane, F., Codari, M., and Sardanelli, F. (2018) *'European Radiology Experimental'*. Available at: https://doi.org/10.1186/s41747-018-0061-6

Rai, R.B, Sahu, S., and Sawant, S. (2018) 'An Analysis of MYCIN Expert System', *International Journal of Research in Engineering, Science and Management*, vol. 1, no. 9, September, ISSN: 2581-5782.

Research and Marketers, (2022) *'Asia Pacific Digital Health Market Report 2022–2030: Market Size is Expected to Reach $326.7 Billion-Rise in Artificial Intelligence, IoT, and Big Data'*, March 28, Available at: www.globalnewswire.com/en/news-release/2022/03/2410962/en/Asia-Pacific-Digital-Health-Market-Report-2022-2030/Market-size-is-expected-to-reach-326.7/Billion-rise-in-artificial-intelligence-IoT-and-BigData.html/ (Accessed: 12 July 2022).

Riek, L. D. (2017) 'Healthcare Robotics'. *Communications of the ACM*, 60(11), 68–78. Available at: https://doi.org/10.1145/3127874

Shah, N. (2023) *'Digital Health Market Analysis'* Last updated on: January 19 Australia. Available at: www.insights10.com/report/australia-Digital-Health-Market-Analysis/ (Accessed: 02 February 2023).

Sharma, P. et al. (2013) 'Computer Aided Diagnosis Based on Medical Image Processing and Artificial Intelligence Methods', *International Journal of Information and Computation Technology*, ISSN 0974-2239, vol. 3, no. 4, pp. 887–892.

Snowdon, C. (2015) 'Implementing Computer Aided Diagnosis with PACS', *International Journal of Engineering, Research and Technology*, ISSN: 2278-0181.

Verdier, C. and Flora, A. (1994) *'An information system for epidemiology based on a computer-based medical record'*, *Journal of Information in Medicine*, vol. 33, 5/94, December, pp. 496–501.

Wang, F. and Preininger, A. (2019) 'AI in health: Stage of art, challenges, and future directions'. *Yearbook of Medical Informatics*. 28(1): 16–26. Available at: www.ncbi.nlm.nih.gov/pmc/articles/PMC6697503 (Accessed: 09 August 2020).

World Health Organization (WHO). (2019) *'Recommendations on digital interventions for health system strengthening. Geneva'*. Available at: https://apps.who.int/iris/bitstream/handle/10665/311941/9789241550505-eng.pdf (Accessed: 11 April 2020).

World Health Organization (WHO). (2016) *'Framework on Integrated-People Centered Health Services'*, Available at: www.who.int/gb/ebwha/pdf_files/WHA69/A69_39_en.pdf?ua=1&ua=1 (Accessed: 11 April 2020).

World Health Organization (2003) 'Data quality of statistical reports. ' In *Improving Data Quality: A guide for developing countries'*, Chapter 5, pp 54–67, Geneva.

Youssef, A. E. (2014) 'A framework for secure healthcare systems based on big data analytics in mobile cloud computing environments'. *International Journal of Ambient Systems and Applications*, 2(2): 1–11.

7 Digital Agriculture and Digitalization in Food Industries

SUMMARY

In this chapter, we will study how, in different ways, advanced and innovative digital tools and technologies like AI, robotics, smart sensors, drones, etc. have the potential to change the agricultural sector across the world. Also, we will study how digital adoption has provided farmers with better answers and lessons in the evolution of the agriculture sector. This chapter also discusses the need for digitalization in the agriculture industry for better outcomes. At the end of this chapter, we will also highlight how digital transformation in the food industry is growing rapidly worldwide.

7.1 INTRODUCTION

Agriculture is at the backbone of every economy. It is considered one of the most important sectors of the country. Almost 60% of the population depend on agriculture for their livelihood. Freedom of digital technology, such as sensors, computers, robots, and information technology, have changed modern farms, and agriculture operations have evolved in the past few years.

The agricultural and farming industries are transforming as a result of information and technology. Farming items such as fertilizers, seeds, machines, and equipment are available through personalized E-Commerce stores and marketplaces and assist farmers in growing high-quality crops. Educational portals, on the other hand, provide farmers with access to cutting-edge farming knowledge, enabling agriculture to contribute more to the economy.

While digitization has significant potential to benefit both producers and consumers, implementing technological solutions is very important to overcome various challenges in the agricultural industry. Emerging digital technologies can completely transform the agricultural industry.

7.1.1 CONCEPT OF DIGITAL AGRICULTURE

Agriculture has been impacted by these technological advancements, much like other industries, and has started a process of transformation and development. Under the umbrella of "smart agriculture," numerous institutions, companies, and universities worldwide carry out numerous studies using emerging technology. These studies have led to the emergence of numerous new terminologies and definitions. The notions of "digital agriculture," "precision agriculture," "precision farming," "smart agriculture," and "smart farming" have emerged as a result of various forms of digitalization

DOI: 10.1201/9781003403784-7

in agriculture. These terms related to agricultural digitization were occasionally used singly in studies and literature, and at other times two or three different terms were combined.

The phrase "digital agriculture" was first used in the early 2000s, when it started to rise exponentially, the number of articles, journals, and conferences on digital agriculture with "digital agriculture" in the title, keywords, or abstracts remained constant.

The term "digital agriculture" describes a type of farming and, more broadly, a food system that "utilizes ICT technologies, sensors, connected objects, smartphones, etc., 3G/4G coverage, and remote processing at every level of agricultural production" (Bellon-Maurel and Huyghe, 2016).

According to Shen et al. (2010), precision agriculture, which stresses agricultural production processes, and digital agriculture are both implementations of the 1990s-proposed concepts of "digital world" and "precision agriculture." "Digital agriculture" is the practice of using computer and communication technology to boost agricultural productivity and sustainability.

The information-based agriculture concept commonly referred to as "digital agriculture," bases its processing and interpretation of digital data on agricultural production and management systems (Zhang, 2011).

The Ministry of Agriculture and Forestry (2021) defines "smart agriculture" as a contemporary agricultural production technology based on the use of cutting-edge information technologies and control systems in an agricultural enterprise that is based on the needs that differ spatially and temporally in the production area.

The term "digital agriculture," also known as "e-agriculture," refers to the use of modern and advanced digital technologies to integrate agricultural production. These innovations will give farmers the resources and knowledge they need to make better decisions and increase food productivity.

E-agriculture is an emerging field that focuses on improving agricultural and rural development through better information and communication systems. The costs of replicating, transporting, recording, verifying, and searching for data are all reduced by implementing digital technologies in the agriculture industry. Digital technologies help increase productivity in the agricultural value chain as costs decline. By using digital technology, it will improve the traceability of agricultural products, giving customers peace of mind and increasing the value of the farmers.

7.2   NEED FOR DIGITIZATION IN THE AGRICULTURE INDUSTRY

The worldwide population is increasing rapidly, day by day. The demand for food around the world has significantly increased as a result of population expansion. Thus, to satisfy this ever-increasing demand for food, it has become very important to upscale, upgrade, and modify the agriculture sector. This problem could be solved by introducing digital technologies to the agricultural sector. The IoT, AI, and nanotechnology, among other things, are gaining momentum in this industry.

To improve production quality, the agriculture industry is implementing genome editing and smart breeding technologies, as well as incorporating digital AI-based technologies with microbial soil mapping. In developing countries like India, digital freedom in the farming industry is generally accepted and recognized. The use of digital tools is not limited to the farming process; it also assists farmers with post-harvest pricing, storage, transportation, and logistics. These tools, in addition, aid in increasing the value of products and ensuring the effective and long-term usage of resources.

As a result of digital freedom in the digital world and the advancements in emerging technologies like artificial intelligence, and machine learning, there are many opportunities to capitalize on its role as an IT powerhouse and revolutionize the agriculture industry.

A "zero hunger world," one of the sustainable development objectives that the United Nations promotes, will require more productive, efficient, sustainable, inclusive, transparent, and long-lasting food systems to be achieved by 2030. The current agriculture-food system needs to adapt and evolve urgently to address this.

Today, digital transformation is becoming more and more common in various regions of the world. The main driver of sustained and long-term economic growth is this developing digital transformation. The term for this is the "digital revolution," which has affected every sector of society and industry. One of those sectors is the agricultural one (Victorovich et al., 2020).

The agriculture-food value chain transformed by digitization, which will also improve and personalize resource management throughout the entire system. These new digital innovations will open up new possibilities for incorporating farmers into the digitally controlled agriculture-food chain.

A major factor that has both implicit and explicit effects on agriculture on a broad scale is climate change. Consequently, changes in the climate have an impact on agriculture and its linked industries. Therefore, climate change may result in many issues, including challenges with food access and availability as well as poorer food quality. Additionally, changes in temperature, precipitation patterns, unexpected changes in weather, and large reductions in the water supply can all result in a decline in agricultural productivity (Singh, Vaidya, and Pathania, 2021).

Today's digital world is experiencing drastic changes, transformations, and developments in every sphere of endeavor due to factors like economic expansion, developing technologies, technical advancements, population growth, urbanization, globalization, and many other factors of a similar nature. The global ecological system is impacted by these developments as well as the environmental repercussions and variables brought about by industrialization.

According to recent studies and research, the aforementioned conditions will accelerate and have a greater impact on the alterations. The rate of consumption, particularly of food, will increase due to the growing global population in the not-too-distant future. The correct utilization of those resources will therefore become more of a problem as a result of the substantial changes that a lack of resources would bring about in every profession.

This transition and transformation may be solved by digital technology and advances. Under the umbrella of the fourth industrial revolution, these technologies including blockchain, AI, the IoT, and virtual reality (VR) are drastically altering all fields of endeavor (Industry 4.0) (Trendov, Varas, and Zeng, 2019). It has been noted that the advancement of mobile technologies, the creation of remote sensing systems, and distributed computer systems have started to improve the accessibility of many areas, including information, data, markets, finance, and education, for small businesses operating in the agriculture and food sector.

7.3   MARKET POTENTIAL FOR DIGITAL AGRICULTURE

With the help of the digital agriculture market, it is hoped that farmers who have difficulty influencing market prices will be able to sell their goods at a price that benefits them and profit from this opportunity. This effective agricultural marketing system is used to collect data more frequently and precisely to manage output effectively and maximize resource use for income generation.

The lifecycle of market products could be improved via digital agriculture. High expenditures and uncertain long-term results are two obstacles, though. To overcome these obstacles, the value chain's various actors must work together to adapt to digitalization.

Stakeholders in the agricultural industry, as shown in Figure 7.1 below, including farmers, industrialists, exporters, transporters, banks, and wholesale dealers, join together and communicate in the digital farming market. All players have profited from one another as a result of this extensive network, which also makes it possible for them to satisfy their supply and demand demands with practical and effective solutions.

Private companies from the agricultural industry, as well as input firms, software firms, and startups, are driving the development of digital agriculture. The market for digital agriculture has enormous potential since it has multiple impacts on the Sustainable Development Goals (SDGs), which not only boost food security but also increase production and revenue. Additionally, the OECD Global Forum on Agriculture 2021: Policies for a more resilient agro-food industry recently explored how the digital transition in agriculture offers new potential to improve policy. A technology called "Uber for Tractors" is offered by one of the creative start-up businesses, allowing traditional small-scale farmers to use tractor rental services. The technology has the potential to lower transaction costs by enabling the monitoring of tractors and operators through GPS devices (Duam et al., 2020).

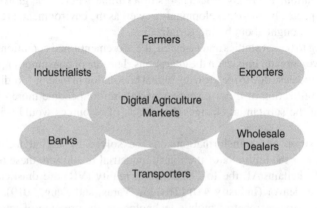

FIGURE 7.1   Stakeholders in digital agriculture markets.

According to numerous criteria, including those listed below, the size of the digital agriculture market depends on farmer demand:

- Level of mechanization and scale economies.
- Input expenses, such as labor costs, and output costs.
- Environmental laws and public pressure.
- The ability to transfer digital technologies across geographical boundaries and farming practices.

The technologies of agriculture 4.0, which were created under the influence of Industry 4.0, also known as the digital industrial revolution, go beyond the manufacturing process and are not just restricted to it. These technologies also significantly influence, transform, and develop several stages after the production process (Duman and Ozsoy, 2019).

The promotion and sale of agriculture and food goods must now include the use of E-Commerce, which is being employed by more and more industries. Business-to-government (B2G), business-to-consumer (B2C), and business-to-business (B2B) E-Commerce (B2G) An enormous network of object-to-object communication opportunities emerges with the aid of E-Commerce, government-to-consumer (G2C), human-to-human, and human-to-object communication alternatives. Such a network would be created, providing a market to almost everyone by reducing the impact of borders between countries, cities, businesses, and people (Alpaslan and Delibalta, 2018).

Some producers are prosperous enough to conduct their E-Commerce business on their own. Many producers use social media, websites, and online marketplaces to offer their goods. The number of businesses utilizing social media platforms like Facebook, Instagram, and WhatsApp as well as marketplace programs like Amazon is increasing daily. Examples of agricultural E-Commerce applications include:

using one's E-Commerce website:

- Utilizing social network services
- Utilizing online stores
- Utilizing ad networks
- Utilizing internet advertisements

The following are some of the advantages of E-Commerce for the agricultural sector:

- Producers benefit from market and price advantages
- The ability to trade without regard to time or space constraints
- Access to a large number of customers and buyers
- Access to new markets

Benefits of digital agriculture markets:

- integration of industry and agriculture
- the development of product design
- supply-demand-price

- to prevent food waste
- close the gap between areas of production and consumption
- increase productivity by using proper inputs
- produce the quality and quantity that the market demands
- it protects demand from price volatility
- make access to international markets
- making bank financing easier

7.4   DIGITAL AGRICULTURE TECHNOLOGIES

Many advanced digital technologies with numerous applications in the agriculture industry for its development are shown in Figure 7.2 below:

- Big Data
- AI
- IoT
- Agricultural drones
- Digital communications technologies (for e.g. mobile phones, social media, etc.)

7.4.1   ARTIFICIAL INTELLIGENCE IN AGRICULTURE

Artificial intelligence plays an important role in improving agricultural activities and achieving the target of doubling farmer income with every passing year. There is worldwide demand for artificial intelligence in agriculture. The core concepts of AI in agriculture are adaptability, quick performance, precision, and economic viability. In addition to assisting farmers in using their farming expertise, artificial intelligence in agriculture also changes direct farming to produce larger yields and better quality with reduced resources.

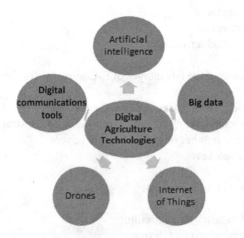

FIGURE 7.2   Digital agriculture technologies.

The issues faced by the agricultural sector, such as crop harvesting, irrigation, soil content sensitivity, crop monitoring, weeding, and harvest, are all managed by AI technology, which also helps to increase efficiency across all sectors. On farms, AI technology aids in the diagnosis of pests, illnesses, and malnutrition. AI sensors can also detect and identify weeds. AI technology can reduce the overuse of water, pesticides, and herbicides; preserve soil fertility; assist in the effective use of labor; increase output; and enhance product quality.

Application of AI in Agriculture

Improving crop productivity: Traditional agricultural knowledge has become obsolete as a result of climate change, especially in terms of forecasting weather patterns that determine farming practices for the season. As a result, farmers could greatly benefit from the use of AI-assisted predictive analysis. It helps the farmers determine the best crops to grow in a favorable climate as well as the best sowing methods to increase productivity and lower costs.

Sowing is the first step in crop management, which also includes crop harvesting, crop storage, and crop distribution. It can be summed up as actions that increase the yield and growth of agricultural products. Crop production will undoubtedly increase with a thorough understanding of crop classes based on their timing and thriving soil types. An agricultural management technique called precision crop management (PCM) targets crop and soil inputs based on field needs to maximize profitability and safeguard the environment. The lack of timely, widely disseminated information on crop and soil conditions has hindered PCM. To deal with a water deficit brought on by the soil, the weather, or insufficient irrigation, farmers must combine a variety of crop management techniques (Moran, Inoue, and Barnes, 1997).

The decision-making process that leads to a high-quality agricultural output can be aided by a proper understanding of weather patterns (Aubry, Papy, and Capillon, 1998).

For assessing the operational behavior of a farm system, PROLOG makes use of meteorological information, machinery capacity, labor availability, and data on authorized and prioritized operators, tractors, and implements. Additionally, it calculates crop yield, gross income, and net profit for both the entire farm and each field.

By detecting numerous soil factors and parameters connected to the atmosphere, crop prediction methodology is utilized to anticipate the appropriate crop. Soil type, PH, nitrogen, phosphate, potassium, organic carbon, calcium, magnesium, sulfur, manganese, copper, and iron, as well as depth, temperature, precipitation, and humidity (Snehal and Sandeep, 2014).

Demeter is a speed-rowing machine that is computer-controlled and fitted with two cameras as well as a GPS for navigation. It can plan out harvesting activities for a full field and then carry out those plans by cutting crop rows, rotating to cut subsequent rows, moving around the field, and spotting unforeseen obstructions (Pilarski et al., 2002).

AI helps in soil management: Agriculture activities include soil management as a key component. Crop production will be improved and soil resources will be conserved with a solid understanding of diverse soil types and conditions. It is the application of actions, procedures, and treatments to enhance soil functionality.

Historical monsoon data, local snapshots of the farm, crop output data, the history of soil health, and other data are used as inputs for AI models. These models provide important information about farmland, allowing farmers to plan activities such as soil regeneration, crop development, and farm irrigation.

Management-oriented modeling (MOM) is the best soil management technique. Because it consists of a set of plausible management options, a simulator that assesses each alternative, and an evaluator that chooses which alternative fulfills the user-weighted multiple criteria, MOM decreases nitrate leaching. To determine the shortest path between start nodes and goals, MOM employs "hill climbing" as a strategic search technique and "best-first" as a tactical search technique (Li and Yost, 2000).

Based on characteristics from existing coarse-resolution soil maps and hydrographic parameters generated from a digital elevation model, an ANN model predicts the composition of the soil (including the amounts of sand, clay, and silt) from the DEM (Zhao et al., 2009). ANN also forecasts soil moisture and predicts soil texture. It is cost-effective, time-saving, and 92% accurate.

AI helps in disease detection and control: Disease detection and disease control is essential for agricultural harvests to produce their best yield. Diseases in plants and animals are a significant barrier to increased output. These diseases, which affect both plants and animals, are caused by a variety of factors, including genetics, soil type, rain, dry weather, wind, temperature, and others. Managing the impacts is a huge difficulty as a result of these elements and the unstable character of some diseases' causal influences, especially in large-scale farming. The system for making intelligent inferences for agricultural disease, management employs a novel approach of rule based on fuzzy logic.

Image Processing

Image processing is a method for disease diagnosis in agriculture. The steps of image processing are shown in Figure 7.3 (Kamble and Pise, 2019).

Image acquisition: In this method, pictures of the diseased leaves are captured. The photos of the many plant diseases in this collection are kept in JPEG format. The read command in MATLAB is then used to read these images.

Image pre-processing: Using various pre-processing techniques, image pre-processing is used to remove noise from the image or exclude other objects. The reason why image scaling is utilized to turn the original image into thumbnails is that the original image's pixels are huge and the process overall takes longer. After the image is scaled, the pixel size will drop, and the process take less time.

Image segmentation: This method is one of the most popular for clearly differentiating image pixels in a targeted app. It divides an image into a variety of discrete

FIGURE 7.3   Steps for disease diagnosis in agriculture.

states so that the pixels are highly similar within each area and highly dissimilar to other areas.

Feature extraction is a crucial component of illness detection. It is crucial for correctly identifying an object. In many image processing applications, feature extraction is used. The features that are used in illness identification include color, texture edges, and morphology.

Disease detection and classification in plants: This is the final step in which the detection of diseases and the classification of the plants with diseases match the provided dataset.

Convolutional Neural Network

Convolutional Neural Network (CNN) models were developed through deep learning approaches for disease identification and diagnosis utilizing straightforward leaf images of healthy and diseased plants. The user first takes a screenshot of a plant leaf using the app. This photograph will be sent by the app to our AI system. The image is processed through several steps, including preprocessing, feature extraction, feature selection, etc. CNN, a deep neural network with 97.8% accuracy in identifying four species of insects, was trained using an innovative approach to building a visual database. Convolutional neural networks may process data in any format, including speech, pictures, video, audio, and natural language. CNN is a deep, feed-forward ANN class that has been effectively used in computer vision applications. Its prediction rate is 90% (Kamilaris and Prenafeta-Boldu, 2018).

AI helps in Pest and Weed Management

Artificial intelligence can be used to predict pest behavior, which can help with pest control planning. Pest management that is effective results in less crop and environmental harm. To discern the weed from the seed, a combination of remotely sensed data, effective image recognition software, weather data, and other related data points can be used. A weed-control system developed by a US company named "See & Spray" uses AI to reduce weedicide costs by 90%.

An ongoing demand for the growth of agricultural activities is the continuous improvement of weed control procedures. The differential management of these weeds is crucial in the context of the search for sustainability and efficiency due to the loss in productive potential and quality that they cause in the crops. Current developments in this area are based on the integration of advanced technologies like deep learning, computer vision, UAV robots, multisensor systems, etc. with remote sensing.

Artificial intelligence methods for weed detection and classification are becoming more prevalent. The potential of these inexpensive technologies that use various photos has expanded the field of weed management. Tiny, inexpensive UAVs or UAS with digital systems can map the distribution of weeds for further operations using GIS software and internal algorithms.

Ground-based systems enable the acquisition of high-quality details on crops and weeds, and the employment of UAVs for weed and crop monitoring in tandem with AI is demonstrating its potential in weed research. To get precise weed pressure levels, presence, or pre-emergence models for targeted control, terrestrial platforms can use a wide range of sensors, including image reflectance sensors, depth cameras, or optical distance sensors.

Precision weed management is evolving and becoming more widely used thanks to improvements in spectral image processing methods and the usage of AI-based systems. Artificial neural networks and digital cameras are both capable of achieving high levels of accuracy quickly. Online treatments could result from this, avoiding the time lag between mapping and therapy, which would lower costs and effort while enhancing efficacy.

AI improves water management

Agriculture can have a significant effect on the issue of water shortages if water management is handled properly. Thermal imaging cameras can be used to continuously track whether crops are getting enough water on agricultural land, allowing water used to be optimized. When AI image classification models are applied to agriculture, they can increase yield efficiency, reduce manual intervention, and reduce crop disease incidence.

The main AI technique employed in the wastewater treatment process is ANN. The ANN technique focuses on the identification of repeatable, recognizable, and predictable patterns in process input and output. The ANN modeling approach simply needs to be aware of significant process-controllable factors. It is not required to explain how processes occur in micro or macro contexts. The ANN modeling approach makes good use of this function as a process option. The ANN modeling approach is a significant alternative for process modeling in the production of drinking water.

7.4.2   BIG DATA IN AGRICULTURE

Big data has now emerged as a vital component in the application of technology to agricultural production. Big data technologies offer a chance for the agriculture sector to go digital. Agriculture's usage of digital technologies generates enormous amounts of very diverse data that are referred to as "big data." It is particularly difficult because observations are made of complex things and settings of various kinds that function at very diverse spatial and temporal levels, have robust intra- and inter-level interactions and involve a wide range of players. The deployment of a technical solution at all levels must be guided by data collection, which raises problems concerning its type, frequency, objective, etc. Thus, big data is a possible technology for assessing decisions made at the farm level, governmental decisions, and market-distorting measures for properly enhancing agricultural productivity. Agribusiness will benefit from big data by increasing harvest yield, reducing risk, and increasing performance. Farmers will use the data generated to help them make timely decisions that result in impressive results. Big data technologies are essential to the transformation of digital agriculture. Deep learning algorithms and machine behaviors can be produced as a result of the analysis of these data in the era of digital agriculture when machines are outfitted with a variety of sensors to measure data in their vicinity. Hashem et al. (2015) found that big data is a complement to strategies that call for integration forms to separate unrecognized values from massive, varied, and complex data sets. Farmers can monitor all production parameters of current activities using big data, which enhances decision-making. When combined with data from external big data sources, such as market data or competitor data, internal data has a leveraging effect. Soil sampling data can help farmers predict their farm's expected to yield as well as how to make the most effective use of chemical fertilizers and pesticides, lowering their input costs.

Application of Big Data in Agriculture

Weather forecasting: Due to crop plant needs, farmers must understand useful temperature and humidity, which can be easily discovered using big data analytics. By examining several aspects of crop cultivation, such as cropping pattern, planting time, intercultural operation, fertilization, pesticide management, harvesting, and crop intensity, big data technology offers farmers the chance to implement improved crop management practices (Pham and Stack, 2018).

Forecasting crop yield: Farmers can use big data strategies to gain insight into the likely crop production and harvesting time by evaluating algorithms. Farmers can simply manage post-harvest activities and avoid harvest losses. Using the data that is useful by monitoring planting, cross-cultural operations, and harvesting times, as well as avoiding unfavorable weather conditions, the farmer can increase yield (Rumpf et al., 2010).

Choosing a crop: By applying algorithmic analysis of the input and outcome factors of a crop, the big data approach aids the farmer in choosing the right crop. K-nearest neighbor, decision trees, and artificial neural networks are a few well-known big data techniques that are commonly utilized for crop selection. Big data technology typically examines natural disasters, climate, famine, soil, and other factors to determine the best crop for a given region (Rao, 2018).

Crop disease and pest control: Although crop disease and insect infestation are common occurrences in crop production, they lower crop quality and yield. A farmer's yield will increase if they can keep disease and pest infestations under control (Alves and Cruvinel, 2016).

By allowing them to detect any disease infestation on the crop, big data gives farmers the chance to easily take action to prevent the disease and keep the crop safe. Big data technology can foresee insect attacks.

Marketing for agriculture: For agricultural products to be profitable, market knowledge is required. A farmer who is unaware of market information may suffer a loss on their goods. For the market analysis, a variety of market data can be employed, including input costs, wages, price trends, cultivation costs, demand and supply, marketing, and transportation costs (Henry, 2015). Farmers may simply make decisions based on the results of big data analytics on this market data. Big data technologies can be used by both public and private organizations to analyze markets and conduct effective market monitoring.

7.4.3 Agricultural Drones

Agriculture drone technology has gained the most attention in the industry due to its versatility and is seen as the way of the future for the agricultural industry. Through their supervision work, they contribute to an increase in agricultural production by lowering costs and reducing losses for the agricultural producer. Drone technology allows for advanced sensors, digital imaging capabilities, soil monitoring, crop spraying, crop tracking, and crop health analysis, including fungus infection. Drones equipped with sophisticated sensors and image systems specifically designed for agricultural applications can detect pests and plant diseases quickly.

Recently, during the COVID-19 pandemic, drones have proven to be successful in protecting agricultural produce from locust attacks in various countries including India. Drones have been deployed in Rajasthan to ensure that the spraying is done efficiently.

Drones use multispectral sensors to explore vast areas hundreds of hectares at once and collect digital imagery. We can map the distribution of different weed species and their varying intensities using the imagery. This information could be shared with farmers. Drones might quickly capture images across large areas while concentrating on certain fields. For a very long time, satellites and aircraft have been utilized to deliver information on agricultural areas. As a result of advancements in drone technology, their use for agricultural purposes has increased, and farmers may now instantaneously get the photographs they need or remotely control activities like applying pesticides at a low cost (Trippicchio et al., 2015).

Drones for water management and irrigation: Agricultural drones are the most practical technology for gathering information on water supplies, soil moisture, the requirement for in-season irrigation, and the effects of droughts and floods. To attend to crop field irrigation, drones equipped with sensors that function at visual bandwidth, infrared, and near-infrared bands have been studied, experimented with, and used (Turner et al., 2011).

Due to their cost-effectiveness, drones are used to inspect irrigation equipment. Monitoring irrigation systems like center-pivot sprinklers is advantageous economically. Farm scouts may struggle to move quickly enough to spot clogged nozzles or erratically moving sprinklers. Observations of water resources like dams, lakes, and small ponds are also made using drones. Water storage and level changes are detected using drones. Drones are also utilized to inform farmers of trends in the use of water from dams.

Drones have also been used by researchers in some areas to track crop genotypes and their tolerance to water shortages, droughts, and floods. Drone technology is being used to screen, identify, and choose genotypes that are resistant to drought. Crop researchers may check a lot of genotypes using drones, capture relevant data, store it digitally, and use it in computerized decision-support systems. In comparison to professional farm technicians, drones are significantly more efficient. As a result, drone use is likely to increase during experimental assessments of crop genotypes' resistance to drought stress.

Using drones to safeguard crops: In the monitoring and maintenance of agriculture fields, drone technology is very important. Drones provide spectral imagery that aids in the suppression and elimination of weeds. Aerial data collection is used to gather specific spectral signatures of crop and plant species. Herbicides are used after proper weed mapping. Drones are destined to play a significant role in the fight against illness and pests. They might lessen the use of dangerous chemicals such as herbicides, insecticides, fungicides, and bactericides. Also, they lower the expense of hiring farm personnel to spray the crops. Profits are increased by the efficiency, speed, and ease with which drones spray pesticides for plant protection.

For mapping weeds in agriculture fields and gathering digital data, drones are quick, precise, and cost-effective. There is still a need for computerized decision-support systems and software that can recognize and recommend the best herbicidal sprays, their timing, and their quantity. According to recent reports, weeds infesting wheat fields might be easily found and controlled by pesticides using drones and computer software at ground stations (Lopez-Granados, 2011). They offer precise imaging and quickly locate wild oats and canary grass. In a field of sunflowers, several broad-leaved weeds could be distinguished with accuracy.

7.4.4 INTERNET OF THINGS IN AGRICULTURE

In this world of digitization, we need to move towards digital technologies known as the "Internet of Things" to increase production, productivity, the global market, and minimize human errors, time, and expense.

The IoT applications in agriculture can help the industry improve operational efficiency, reduce costs, reduce waste, and improve yield quality. In comparison to traditional farming methods, IoT-based smart farming has proven to be extremely effective and efficient.

By connecting sensor networks to the Internet of Things, agriculture can be formed regardless of the distance between scientists, farmers, and crops. IoT technology makes it possible for producers to use resources effectively by enabling them to make timely decisions based on reliable data that is available in real-time

Through the use of cutting-edge networked inventive systems, IoT in agriculture will increase the functionality of already available equipment by integrating the physical world with the information system. The IoT offers countless potential application areas, including monitoring of greenhouses, animals, and agricultural machinery, by combining data from various sensors and RFID tags (Kaloxylos et al., 2012).

The ATMEGA 328P is a more sophisticated microcontroller that serves as the system's brain. We use various sensors, such as temperature and humidity sensors, to calculate various climate parameters. The rain detection sensor and the humidity detection sensor are used to detect rain and humidity in the atmosphere, respectively.

With the use of the internet of things, agricultural businesses can determine how much wheat can be grown in a particular area with a given amount of seed, fertilizer, water, soil chemistry, and weather. Using networked intelligent machinery and cloud computing-based big data analysis tools, agricultural firms can create delicate production mixtures to boost harvest yields (O'Halloran & Kvochko 2015).

IoT-based smart farming is a device that uses sensors to track agricultural land (soil moisture, humidity, light, temperature, and so on) and automate irrigation practices. IoT-enabled irrigation systems not only save water but also ensure that crops receive the adequate amount of water they need for optimal development. Instead of predetermined interval-dependent irrigation, this method of irrigation is based on the soil moisture level.

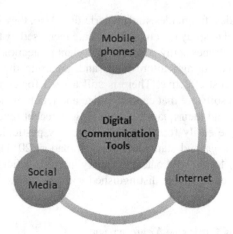

FIGURE 7.4   Digital communication tools in agriculture.

7.4.5   Impact of Digital Communication Tools on Agriculture

The ability to communicate between two or more people at once is enabled through a variety of digital and communication technologies in the twenty-first century, including email, SMS, phone calls, social media, and MMS.

These forms of communication can be written, verbal, visual, or aural. They include, as some examples, communicating with someone via text message on a mobile device or utilizing Twitter or Facebook to communicate with relatives or friends. The examples of digital communication tools used in the agriculture industry are shown in Figure 7.4.

Information on agriculture is disseminated via digital and communication technology (DCT). DCT are defined as electronic and digital tools for communication, information processing, and data storage. Applications for DCT are designed to provide extension services for the right information to the right person at the right time. It can bring together extension functionaries, and store, retrieve, and transmit a variety of information that the farming community needs.

The latest DCT tools, such as mobile apps for agriculture, mobile SMS services, e-learning, video conferencing, e-mail, Facebook, WhatsApp, YouTube, Twitter, blogs, Wikipedia, and web portals, are wireless communication technologies that work with potent software that can process and integrate sound, text, and video into electronic media. In addition to these additional DCT tools, the ones mentioned above are the ones that farmers all over the world use the most frequently and widely to increase their agricultural profits.

Agriculture Development and Social Media

Social media platforms include websites, blogs, microblogs, sites, and groups. It is an emerging field in agricultural marketing. In agricultural marketing, social media is a very powerful tool. It saves both time and money for the farmers. Traditional mass media, such as newspapers, television, radio, and magazines, have historically dominated agricultural knowledge distribution.

Social media has become a very common medium of interaction around the world as a result of digital freedom. Social media, according to some farmers and tech-savvy scientists, is an important communication tool for farmers to communicate with one another and inform or educate others about their industry. The use of popular social media platforms such as Facebook, Twitter, and Instagram as a medium for communication and networking has many benefits in the farming industry. Many of them have realized this and have begun to implement it. Farmers are getting the right information at the right time. Social media platforms such as Twitter, Facebook, LinkedIn, and others make it easy to exchange information and articles of interest. The most popular social media among farmers is Facebook, Twitter, YouTube, LinkedIn, WhatsApp, etc.

Users of social media can also create their groups, pages, communities, and blogs to share information. In this group, they are also selling and buying agricultural products. This can be accomplished by sharing photographs, photos, links, videos, and other media. This knowledge sharing makes it easier for farmers to sell their products and form networks. There are a plethora of blogs devoted to agricultural marketing.

One of the most attractive aspects of social media as a farming tool is the opportunity to communicate with farmers and agribusiness professionals from all over the world over long distances. Depending on how much time we want to spend on it, the advantages can be as big or as minimal as we want. Collecting ideas and soliciting feedback on different farming techniques around the world through social media become easy and fast.

As the number of internet users and smartphone users is increasing with every passing year in developing countries, it is obvious that this is where technology and social networks will spread. Therefore young farmers are more likely to assume that social media will help them sell their products. On YouTube and Facebook, they look for more information. Farmers are more likely to use WhatsApp. The best part is that most farmers are connected to Facebook using their smartphones.

Rural people may use social media as a medium to air their grievances. They can get information easily through social media, and information can reach the masses in seconds. Therefore, as a result of digital freedom in the agriculture industry, most farmers are using social media to exchange knowledge and participate in creative activities.

Development of Agriculture with Mobile Phones and the Internet

Today, in this digital world with the freedom of digitization, emerging technologies such as digital literacy and smartphone and internet use have all increased in recent years, which has revolutionized the agriculture industry worldwide. Mobile phones and the internet are important digital communication tools in digital agriculture for empowering underprivileged farmers to make decisions about their operations, particularly in rural parts of developing nations. The knowledge and information gap can be closed, fair markets and rural companies can be created, and agricultural growth can be supported via effective cell penetration and internet usage based on farmers' demands and with consideration for their rural and socio-economic constraints. Although digital agriculture is advanced in industrialized nations like the US, smallholder farmers worldwide can also use it. Moreover, the internet and mobile devices have brought about several advancements in the past few years (Evans, 2018a). For instance, safer transactions, access to investments, the capacity to save, and eventual expansion of agribusinesses are all advantages of digital payments like mobile money for farmers, agricultural value chain participants, and rural communities.

It has been discovered that using mobile devices and the internet reduces information asymmetries, allowing users to take advantage of marketing, trade, and arbitrage opportunities (Anand and Kumaran, 2017). With the rise in the number of mobile phones and the ease with which they can be used, social media has become a mainstream means of communication around the world. Not only are mobile phones used to deliver information, but they are now being used to deliver a variety of financial services such as payments, credit, insurance, and savings. A farmer in a rural village can access current information about specific farming innovations via mobile phones and the internet; an agricultural extension worker can access updates on new technologies, commodity prices, and rainfall forecasts and use that information to counsel farmers in rural villages. Delivering agricultural information to farmers through low-cost information and communications technologies (ICTs) such as mobile phones is one possible alternative to costly individual extension agents going from village to village.

There are an increasing number of examples of mobile-enabled solutions for food and agriculture designed to overcome literacy barriers. Users also received weekly information and tips via automated voice messages, including weather forecasts and pest management strategies. Other studies show that mobile phones have a positive economic impact on agricultural extension because they provide fast, mobile, timely, and convenient access to personalized content (Mittal, Surabhi, and Tripathi, 2009).

Many fishermen in India (Tamil Nadu) are using SMS to a great extent. They had a mailing list where they would receive information about fish-rich catchment areas, daily rates, and which market was offering the best deals. They added services like storm warnings to this SMS group after the tsunami (Babu, 2012).

WhatsApp Applications in Agriculture

Farmers are becoming increasingly dependent on WhatsApp. There are many WhatsApp groups where they can obtain immediate advice from progressive farmers and agricultural experts. WhatsApp is quickly developing into a big support system for the farming industry. WhatsApp groups are not only linking farmers to their virtual market customers but they're also building a network of tools and support for the country's most vulnerable farmers. It is assisting members in amplifying their voices to gain the attention of the highest levels of government, stressing the importance of issues such as crop insurance, land protection, and farmer education.

Farmers are also using WhatsApp groups to communicate with customers and sell vegetables. In developing countries like India, WhatsApp is transforming the way people grow and purchase food. Some agribusinesses have converted WhatsApp groups into a classified marketplace where farmers exchange grains, vegetables, seeds, irrigation equipment, and tractors, among other things.

7.4.6 OTHER DIGITAL TOOLS AND TECHNOLOGIES IN AGRICULTURE

Machine Learning (ML) in Agriculture

In agriculture, machine learning is used to increase crop productivity and quality. We need to apply machine learning to agriculture data to produce more. Agricultural farmers are now using machine learning models and technologies to their benefit.

Digital agriculture is on the rise, which employs a safe approach to optimize agricultural output while mitigating environmental effects. The data produced in modern agriculture is focused on a variety of sensors that will aid in a better understanding of the climate, including crop, soil, and weather conditions, as well as agricultural machinery.

Nanoscience and Technology

This is a technique that uses a smart delivery system and nanosensors to provide information to farmers on whether or not plants are receiving enough water and other required inputs.

Nanotechnology research and development is likely to help in the stage of development of genetically modified crops, animal production inputs, chemical pesticides, and precision farming techniques in the agricultural sector.

Geospatial Farming

Today, spatial data is increasingly important in agriculture. Geospatial technology is a versatile technology that can help boost productivity and performance in many industries. A large-scale increase in agricultural production can be achieved by introducing geospatial farming. Weeds, soil quality and moisture content, land fertility, seed intensity, fertilizer need, and other factors can all contribute to higher yields.

By lowering prices, expanding access to services, providing more customer value, and reducing inefficiencies, geospatial technology has the potential to have a massive economic and social impact.

Global Positioning System and Geographic Information Systems

The combination of the Global Positioning System (GPS) and geographic information systems have enabled the production and implementation of precision agriculture or site-specific farming GPS. Farm planning, field mapping, soil sampling, tractor guidance, crop scouting, variable rate applications, and yield mapping all use GPS-based precision farming applications. Farmers may use GPS to operate in low-visibility conditions, including mud, dust, fog, and even darkness. Farmers may use GPS to navigate to specific locations in the field to collect soil samples or track crop conditions year after year.

7.5 DIGITALIZATION IN THE FOOD INDUSTRY

Every industry in today's digital world, including the food industry, has benefited from digital innovations. Digital innovation for any business is essentially about investing in emerging technologies that produce long-term rewards in the future. Manufacturers of food and beverages are implementing automation and cutting-edge production technologies to optimize their production, packaging, and delivery processes. Therefore, the adoption and implementation of innovative digital technologies are essential for keeping the food industry's businesses on the cutting edge and up to date with the latest advances. This is especially important given the surge in demand for packaged foods and beverages following the COVID-19 pandemic's lengthy lockdown around the world.

Digital kitchens are relatively new concepts in today's digital age, and they are ruling the globe. Digital kitchens are simply those that use innovative technology to work smarter, such as mobile order-ahead applications and websites, third-party delivery, or kiosks.

7.5.1 DIGITAL TRANSFORMATION IN THE FOOD INDUSTRY

Today, digitization is important in every aspect of the business. It is very important for long-term growth. As a result of the freedom of digitalization, the food industry business is experiencing a surge in demand. As compared with other sectors, this transformation offers opportunities to grow businesses, reduce risk, and provide better service to their customers. As a result, food and beverage companies in India are investing in digital technology.

With the freedom of digitization, today's modern digital technologies such as robotics, blockchain technology, AI, IoT, and processing techniques have revolutionized how we create and find food over time. Digital tools and technologies help food manufacturers produce more effectively to meet the demands of a growing global population. It is possible to improve the safety of food by employing advanced digital technologies to improve processing and packaging.

In terms of adopting innovative digital technologies, the food industry worldwide has seen a massive transition. New-age businesses aren't afraid to use cutting-edge technology like robotics, AI, Digital sensors, and IoT to create and improve solutions.

7.5.2 DIGITAL SENSORS IN THE FOOD INDUSTRY

Digital sensors, due to their capacity to monitor the accuracy of automated operations and increase general transparency, have experienced tremendous growth in the food industry. They keep an eye on the entire food production chain, from manufacturing to distribution, increasing supply chain visibility. Digital sensors aid in ensuring that raw materials and food are continually maintained in the best conditions and do not spoil before being delivered to the client.

Both by enhancing the precision of automated processes and by tracking and storing a range of production data, digital sensors can support traceability. The IoT enables the factory to continuously measure and synchronize time-temperature history, physical shocks, and other crucial credentials.

Systems for food labeling that track product freshness are being widely implemented. These intelligent labels have intelligent sensors that display each item's current temperature and whether it complies with storage regulations. This enables producers, distributors, and customers to assess an item's freshness in real time and learn how long it has left on its shelf life. Smart containers may soon be able to self-evaluate and adjust their temperature to stay within established food safety standards, ensuring food safety and lowering food waste (Choudhury, 2022).

7.5.3   USE OF ARTIFICIAL INTELLIGENCE AND ROBOTICS IN THE FOOD INDUSTRY

Artificial Intelligence, along with Robotics, has brought significant advancements in every sector, and several revolutions to the food processing business too. In the food industry, AI is well-known for its simplicity, precision, and cost-saving capabilities. For years, AI has been used in the food sector for a variety of reasons, including food sorting, food drying, solving complicated problems, and detection, classification, prediction, quality control, and food safety. In the food industry, various techniques and algorithms are implemented, including fuzzy logic, ANN, adaptive neuro-fuzzy inference systems (ANFIS), and machine learning. As a result, AI is widely used in the industry because it provides numerous benefits to the industry's growth.

Robotics are also now widely used in food processing industries. From agriculture to food processing and transportation, smart robots are used in every part of the food supply chain. Robotics is extensively used in the food processing industry, particularly in mixing, defect removal, and sorting applications, as well as in various stages of food packaging. Hospitality robots are also used by the food industry in hotels and restaurants to improve customer satisfaction and safety. Robotics helps with lower demands for intensive human labor, higher final product quality, increased productivity, increased flexibility, improved safety, increased order fulfillment speed and accuracy, increased uptime, and cost savings.

Robot grippers are one of the most notable technological advancements in robotics. The handling, packaging, and risk of contamination of food and beverages have all been made easier by the introduction of gripper technology. Large grippers are being introduced by top robotics companies to bring more effective automation to the food industry. These current grippers are typically formed out of a single piece and are straightforward and strong. Materials that have been approved for direct food contact are used to make their contact surfaces. Fresh, unwrapped, and fragile meals can be handled by vacuum-type robot grippers without running the danger of product contamination.

In the processing of food, too, robots are becoming more common. Robotic applications for automated baking and frying are employed in various industries. For instance, without human assistance, robots can bake pizza. A robotic, touchless, automated pizza oven that can produce a completely baked pizza in five minutes is being developed by pizzeria companies. These robotic devices work in tandem with the "food truck" idea to transport big quantities of freshly made gourmet pizza more quickly than their brick-and-mortar counterparts (Choudhury, 2022).

Impact of Robotics on Food Industries

Robotics in food production: Robotics plays a very major role in food production. Autonomous food production could be the solution to handling rising food demand. In the next five years, the worldwide food automation industry is predicted to quadruple in size, due to the popularity of ready-to-eat foods in various regions of the world.

Robotics in food packaging: For a long time, food packaging robots have been used in various sectors of the food supply chain. However, the efforts to digitize the entire packaging process are the most recent breakthrough.

Robotics in food delivery: Aside from E-Commerce, healthcare, and logistics, the food business is using delivery robots to deliver meals to customers. Snapdeal has successfully tested autonomous robot delivery in a few locations. And therefore, many businesses have begun to use robots, particularly in the delivery of food, as delivery robots provide contactless delivery.

Systems for Measuring Temperature

The preservation of product temperature from farm to fork to ensure that the product is safe for consumption and that its quality is maintained is one of the top concerns among food and beverage businesses. Manufacturers are using digital temperature monitoring systems that automatically capture and manage data throughout the product lifecycle to assure safe temperatures. Low-energy Bluetooth devices are used by food technology firms as part of their safe and sophisticated cold-chain and building solutions.

Without having to open the cargo package, these verified Bluetooth temperature-monitoring solutions can scan data and give delivery drivers and recipients verification that the package has arrived at its destination. By offering simple mobile apps for hands-free monitoring and control, audible alarms, and seamless synchronization with the recording system, new data loggers expedite product release. The courier and the recipient can avoid managing several cloud logins thanks to seamless, one-touch data synchronization with the recording system. The apps make it simple to transmit secure reports.

7.5.4 BLOCKCHAIN TECHNOLOGY

Blockchain technology has also emerged as one of the most promising and leading technologies for the food industry worldwide. It is used in various processes, like preventing food fraud and improving food safety, and thus provides many benefits to the food industry.

Applications of Blockchain in the Food Industry

Quality and consistency of data: Any recorded data has numerous properties such as quality, conformance, and incorrect data recording, all of which are concerns in both types of systems, but willful fraud is less likely with blockchain.

To protect privacy the identities of parties to a transaction are disguised behind advanced cryptography and are only represented by their public addresses (code). While the identity is protected, all transactions made using the public address remain visible. This amount of transparency boosts system confidence while maintaining privacy.

Reduced cost: Another significant benefit of blockchain is that the time it takes to obtain any information about the supply chain and its components is significantly decreased.

Decentralized: One of the most important characteristics of blockchain is that it is decentralized. Due to the distributed (rather than centralized) nature of blockchain technology, each participant has access to the same records. Everyone's information is updated at the same time. This allows the entire supply chain to respond more quickly to any fraud threats or food safety incidents.

7.5.5 INTERNET OF THINGS (IoT) IN THE FOOD INDUSTRY

In today's digital age, the food industry has benefited largely from the Internet of Things in terms of profit, marketing, export, quality, and, most importantly, food safety. With its innovative and modern digital technologies, the Internet of Things has brought meaningful change to the food industry in many ways. These technologies have not only improved the quality of the products but also helped lower the cost of manufacturing food products.

Applications of IoT in the Food Industry

In the food industry, the Internet of Things has a significant impact. The following are examples of IoT applications in the food industry.

Equipment management in the industry: The most useful feature of IoT devices is the ability to resolve problems with kitchen equipment before they become more serious. This feature of the IoT saves time and money in terms of capital expenditures on equipment that needs to be maintained regularly. If a gadget is going to fail, the IoT's signaling and repair functions will alert the owner.

Smart refrigerators: IoT technology improves the refrigeration and storage conditions of foods, which is very important in the food industry because refrigerators hold a large amount of food. The Internet of Things improves the temperature.

The storage of various types of food materials necessitates a specific temperature. The smell and flavors of the food items should be preserved and not lost over time, so the refrigerator is utilized for this purpose. The Internet of Things not only improves the condition of food but also helps preserve its nutrients.

The Internet of Things manages the temperature of the oven, which aids in oven design: The IoT in the oven minimizes overcooking and food harm. Sensors are installed in the oven to alert the person in charge of the condition of the food being prepared in the oven as well as the temperature, which is either ideal or not. The oven will automatically turn off if the response is zero.

Reduce your energy usage: The Internet of Things also helps save money and time by reducing energy use. When a food item is removed from an oven that has been mistakenly left on or in operating mode, the oven's sensors turn it off. This is mostly to keep track of costs and inform the owner.

Lower logistics charges: Transportation and logistics costs are also reduced due to advanced IoT technologies and equipment. The IoT connects a variety of web-enabled devices and can be utilized by organizations to optimize operations and cut expenses. The technologies provide the owner with real-time supply chain insights. Thus, the IoT is revolutionizing the logistics industry and providing significant value to day-to-day operations.

Governing food safety refers to the assurance that food is fit for human consumption. Therefore, the safety of food is a major concern. To avoid food waste, food safety, and hygiene are top priorities. Food quality must be monitored, and it must be kept from deteriorating due to environmental conditions such as temperature, humidity, and darkness. The IoT is a technology vision that allows anything to be connected at any time and from any location. IoT in the food supply chain (FSC) improves food quality of life by tracing and tracking food conditions and sharing collected data in real-time with consumers or FSC supervisors.

As a result, quality monitoring equipment at grocery stores is beneficial. These quality-control devices keep an eye on the environmental conditions that cause food degradation. Later, environmental conditions like refrigeration and vacuum storage can be controlled. Food companies can provide end-to-end traceability using IoT devices.

Report on data analytics: The restaurant's data and records are tracked through the Internet of Things. This gives the person in charge of the information and feedback priority. This, in turn, informs businesses on how to improve their performance and overall growth.

Provide customers with an update: IoT technology provides users with information about customer behavior, feedback, and expectations.

7.5.6 ROLE OF 3D FOOD PRINTERS

The versatility of 3D printers today has made them popular in countries such as the United States, Europe, and India. With the emergence of 3D printing, the food industry has seen a huge advance, with companies all over the world attempting to adopt the technology.

3D printing is a method of producing three-dimensional things with great precision and quality finishing in their dimensions. 3D printing, in its most basic form, is an additive manufacturing method in which 3D deposition printers progressively deposit layers of material, one on top of the other, until a product is formed. A 3D food printer contains a food-grade syringe that holds food material. It also contains nozzles, lasers, and robotic arms.

Impact of 3D food printing: In the food industry, 3D printing is being studied in a variety of areas, including customized food designs, personalized and digitalized nutrition, a streamlined supply chain, and a wider range of food materials. The following are some of the most significant advantages of 3D food printing:

Sustainable food production: 3D Food Printing Technology will be around for a long time. In comparison to traditional food manufacturing techniques, 3D food printing can serve an ever-growing global population. At the same time, food printers might reduce waste by using hydrocolloid cartridges, which, when coupled with water, generate gels.

Saves both time and energy: 3D printing saves both time and energy when experimenting with new types of food dishes. It also helps in the attainment of perfection with minimal work and time.

7.6   CHAPTER CONCLUSION

With the freedom of digitalization, the adoption of digital technology has greatly revolutionized the farming industry worldwide and benefited all farmers, including small landholders, marginalized and poor farmers, and so on. The application of modern digital technologies in agriculture, such as AI, agriculture drones, and ICT, has accelerated the dissemination of information such as best agricultural practices, weather forecasts, flood warnings, market prices, and soil- and region-specific agricultural awareness. In today's digital world, science and digital technology are at the core of society. Over time, we must also improve agriculture by using these innovative technologies in such a way that they are beneficial to us. We can achieve our desired goal of inclusive agricultural growth by using this technology.

EXERCISES

1. Define the term "digital agriculture"?
2. Give two reasons for the need for digitalization in the agriculture industry?
3. Who are the stakeholders in the agricultural industry?
4. What are the benefits of digital agricultural markets?
5. What are the different techniques used in AI for disease control?
6. What are the three most popular applications of AI in agriculture?
7. What is the importance of agricultural drones?
8. What are the applications of digital communication tools in agriculture?
9. What role does digital technology play in the transformation of the food industry?
10. How does the food industry profit from digital sensors and 3D printing?

REFERENCES

Alpaslan, B. A. and Delibalta, E. (2018) *'Global Media Journal TR* Edition', S9 (17), Fall Edition.

Alves, G.M. and Cruvinel, P.E. (2016) 'Big Data Environment for Agricultural Soil Analysis from CT Digital Images', in IEEE *Tenth International Conference on Semantic Computing (ICSC),* pp. 429–431.

Ananad, P.R. and Kumararn, M. (2017) 'Information Seeking Behaviour of Shrimp Farmers and their Perception towards Technology Dissemination through Mobile Phones', *Journal of Extension Education*, 29(1).

Aubry, C. Papy, F. and Capillon A. (1998) *'Modelling decision-making process for annual crop management',* Agricultural Systems, vol. 56, no. 1, pp. 45–66.

Babu, et al. (2012) *'Farmer Information Needs and Search Behaviour',* Case Study in Tamil Nadu, India, IFPRI.

Bellon-maurel, V. and Huyghe, C. (2016) *'Innovation technologies in agriculture'*, 08 May/ June Geoeconomic, pp. 159–180.

Choudhury, N.R. (2022) *'Advances in Digital Technologies for Food Safety'*, 08 August. Available at: www.food-safety.com/articles/7927/adavances-in-digital-technologies-for-food-safety/ (Accessed: 10 December 2022).

Duman, B. and Ozsoy, K. (2019) *'Conference: 4th international Congress on 3D Printing (Additive Manufacturing)'*, Technologies and Digital Industry, April, pp. 11–14.

Duam, et al. (2020) 'Uber for Tractors? Opportunities and Challenges of Digital Tools for Tractor Hire in India and Nigeria', *Hohenheim working Papers on Social and Institutional Change in Agricultural Development,'* WP 001-2020, Stuttgart: University of Hohenheim.

Evans, O. (2018a) *'Connecting the poor: the internet, mobile phones and financial inclusion in Africa'*, Digital Policy, Regulation and Governance, https//doi.org/10.1108/ DPRG-04-2018-0018

Hashem et al. (2015) 'The Rise of Big Data on Cloud Computing: Review and Research Issues', *Information Systems*, 47, 98–115.

Henry, M. (2015) 'Big data and the future of farming', *Australia Farm Institute Q. Newsletter*, vol. 12, no. 4, pp. 1–12.

Kaloxylos, et al. (2012) *'Farm Management Systems and the Future Internet Era, Computers and Electronics in Agriculture'*, 89, 130–144.

Kamble, P. and Pise, A.C. (2019) 'Review on Agricultural Plant Disease Detection by using Image Processing', *International Journal of Latest Trends in Engineering and Technology* (IJLTET), ISSN: 2278-621X.

Kamilaris, A. and Prenafeta-Boldu, F.X. (2018) 'A review of the use of convolutional neural networks in agriculture', *The Journal of Agriculture Science,* June.

Li, M. and Yost, R. (2000) 'Management-oriented modelling: Optimizing nitrogen management with artificial intelligence', *Agricultural Systems*, vol. 65, no. 1, pp. 1–27.

Lopez-Granados, R. (2011) 'Weed Detection for Site-Specific Weed Management Mapping and Real Time Approaches', *Weed Res.* 51, 1–11.

Mittal, Surabhi and Tripathi, G. (2009) 'Role of Mobile Phone Technology in Improving Small Farm Productivity', *Agricultural Economics Research Review*, vol. 22.

Moran, M.S., Inoue, E. M. and Barnes (1997) 'Opportunities and limitations for image-based remote sensing in precision crop management', *Remote Sensing of Environment*, vol. 61, no. 3, pp. 319–346.

O'Halloran, D. and Kvochko, E. (2015) *'Industrial Internet of Things: Unleashing the Potentials of connected Products and Services'*, In World Economic Forum (p. 40).

Pham, X. and Stack, M. (2018*)* 'How data analytics is transforming agriculture', *Business Horizon*, vol. 61, no. 1, pp. 125–133.

Pilarski, T. et al. (2002) The Demeter System for Automated Harvesting, Springer.

Rao, N. (2018) 'Big Data and Climate Smart Agriculture-Status and Implications for Agricultural Research and Innovation in India', *Proc. Natl. Acad. Sci.*, vol. 84, no. 3, pp. 640.

Rumpf et al. (2010) 'Early detection and classification of plant diseases with support Vector Machines based on hyperspectral reflectance', *Computer Electronics Agriculture*, vol. 74, no. 1, pp. 91–99.

Shen, S., Basist, A., and Howard, A. (2010) 'Structure of a Digital Agriculture System and Agricultural Risks Due to Climate Changes', *Agriculture and Agricultural Science Procedia*, 1, pp. 42–51.

Singh, P., Vaidya, M.K., and Pathania, K. (2021) 'Economic impact of climate change on agriculture: Present, past and future', *Journal of Pharmacognosy and Phytochemistry*. S10 (1), pp. 19–27.

Snehal, S.S. and Sandeep, S.V. (2014) 'Agricultural crop yield prediction using artificial neural network approach', *International Journal of Innovative Research in Electrical, Electronics, Instrumentation and Control Engineering*, vol. 2, no. 1, pp. 683–686.

Trendov, N.M, Varas, S. and Zeng, M. (2019) 'Digital Technologies in Agriculture and Rural Areas', Food and Agriculture Organization of the United States Rome, 2019.

Tripicchio et al. (2015) 'Towards Smart Farming and Sustainable Agriculture with Drones', In 2015 *International Conference on Intelligent Environments*, 140–143, IEEE.

Turner, D., Lucieer, A. and Watson, C. (2011) 'Development of an Unmanned Aerial Vehicle (UAV) for Hyper-resolution Vineyard Mapping Based on Visible, Multispectral, and Thermal Imagery,' *Proceedings of 34th International Symposium on Remote Sensing of Environment*, pp. 342–347.

Victorovich, P.A. et al. (2020) '*The Impact of Digital Transformation on the Economy*', DOI 10.24411/2413-04DX-2020-10518

Zhang, Y. (2011) 'Design of the Node System of Wireless Sensor Network and its Application in Digital Agriculture', Computer Distributed Control and Intelligent Environment Monitoring (CDCIEM), *International Conference on* (pp. 20–35), IEEE.

Zhao, Z. et al. (2009) 'Predict soil texture distribution using an artificial neural network model', *Computers and Electronics in Agriculture*, vol. 65, no. 1, pp. 36–48.

8 Digital Banking and Finance

SUMMARY

In this chapter, we will study the innovations of digital technology in the banking sector and the impact of digital banking economies across the world. This chapter also focuses on the government in this industry and its role in pushing the banking industry into digital operations. In this chapter, we'll also look at how the banking industry has used emerging digital technology and various digital payment systems around the world to deliver specific benefits to their consumers, particularly during the COVID-19 pandemic. We will also discuss how the use of cryptocurrency has affected the financial system as well as the technological revolution in the banking industries. Lastly, we will give a brief overview of financial sectors.

8.1 INTRODUCTION

The banking sector has evolved significantly over time. Previously, in traditional banking, consumers would walk into a branch to withdraw money, move cash, or get product details. As of a few years ago, the majority of customers now prefer to perform simple financial transactions electronically, which has given rise to digital banking.

Today in the world of digitalization, most of the customers prefer convenient alternatives, and therefore with digital freedom in the banking industry, digital banking will continue to be a common alternative. Many banks with physical branches also provide online banking or internet banking, which allows customers to access account details, make transfers, and set up automatic payments from their homes online.

8.1.1 WHAT IS DIGITAL BANKING?

Internet banking or online banking are other names for digital banking. Digital banking is a bank that offers its services online, allowing customers to execute transactions, send requests, and perform other banking operations. The majority of banks now provide this online banking service.

A digital bank, like a conventional bank, provides banking services such as deposits, loans, debit, and credit cards, but transactions are completed online and the bank does not have a physical branch. A customer's relationship with a digital bank begins and continues completely online, with no need to visit a physical branch.

Banks provide the following digital banking products and services to their customers:

- Internet banking
- Mobile banking
- Automatic Teller Machine
- Smart Cards
- Electronic fund transfer
- Door step banking

Digital banking is playing an increasingly important role in the economy, as advances in technology have increased the connectivity and transactions for its customers, and performance is improving day by day. The economy is growing and developing as a result of digital freedom in the banking industry.

8.1.2 COMPONENTS OF DIGITAL BANKING

Digitalization is most frequently done for increased sales and decreased costs. Instead of entering new markets, growth is anticipated to come from offering clients more digital products, running operations more effectively, and improving product differentiation and market penetration.

The most important digital challenge for banks is pressure from the public, according to all banks surveyed, which also stressed the importance of the internet and mobile platforms for banking services. Therefore, throughout the world, banks are working to create the digital bank of the future. Banks should change all aspect of their business, including their strategy, to be completely focused on providing services to clients in the future if they want to be truly future-proof. Thus, seven key elements have been identified by a banking analyst as necessary to build the powerful digital bank of the future (Consultancy.eu, 2022). The important components of digital banking are shown in Figure 8.1 below.

Data Analytics

Data offers banks a wealth of chances to evaluate client demands and create goods and services that meet those needs. Despite the enormous amount of data accessible, most banks have not yet fully realized its potential and are unable to derive insightful conclusions and take appropriate action. This is caused, among other things, by complicated and obsolete legacy infrastructure that slows down data processing and makes it difficult to get insights. Also, due to worries about data privacy, cybersecurity, and potential abuse, banks may unduly err on the side of caution.

A data mesh method avoids bottlenecks and delays caused by centralized data teams by making each business domain or function a data owner for specific data segments and responsible for providing its own data. Any bank employee has access to data at any time because it is decentralized. For instance, the responsible business domain will make consumer card transaction data instantly available via a single connection point to which all other business processes can connect and access the data. Using this strategy, business divisions produce and consume pertinent data for and from one another.

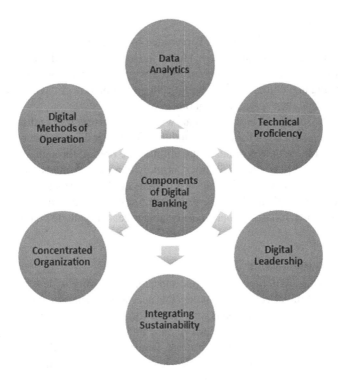

FIGURE 8.1 Different components of digital banking.

Technical Proficiency

The foundation of tomorrow's bank will be standardized, cloud-based banking services, including the basic banking systems. Differentiated offerings and increased cost-effectiveness are made possible by a modern, clean technological stack.

But banks now struggle with the difficulty of migrating their frequently outmoded, compartmentalized, and monolithic technological solutions. Due to historical and cultural barriers, these initiatives frequently lead to massive, complex transformation programs that could take many years to complete without a guarantee of success, ultimately preventing banks from implementing new, standardized technology across the entire organization and from retiring their legacy systems.

Applying a middleware layer, also known as an integration layer, on top of legacy systems in order to establish a bridge across the company is a "fast fix" and a method that is frequently utilized. This enables the integration of third-party services and the unification of access to diverse back-end systems via publicly accessible APIs, which in turn decouples the front-end from the core banking system while maintaining the stability and security of the latter. In this manner, new services can be independently created and made accessible from any location at any time.

Digital Leadership

The basis for the bank of the future is provided by organizational structures and technology, but in the end, people are what make the bank change and function. The difference between those who succeed and those who are lagging behind is leadership. Understanding and embracing the digital economy should begin at the board level of the company and then spread throughout.

The key to success is having a clear, widely held vision that outlines the desired outcome, the justification for change, and the path to get there. Leadership must also guarantee that the required mindset and abilities are present throughout the organization, regardless of jobs, responsibilities, or individual backgrounds.

The potential of new transformation programs might be seriously hampered by the traditional leadership's tendency to be resistant to change. Because there are always new digital efforts, today's leaders must be able to react rapidly to changing situations and settings.

Integrating Sustainability

An important hazard to life, ecosystems, and economies worldwide is climate change. Banks have a crucial role in financing the necessary social change and attracting customers' attention. Hence, banks must transform these aims into business-specific strategies, action plans, and key performance indicators (KPIs), such as specialized policies for the risk department, corporate lending, etc. While defining the existing situation, its goals, establishing strategies, and monitoring their success, banks should take a scientifically based approach. To comprehend such data requires new abilities, knowledge, and experience.

To be effective, the bank must start implementing green practices across the entire organization with defined targets and KPIs in place. As a starting point, banks must run their operations sustainably, for instance, by obtaining renewable energy for building needs or minimizing paper usage. However, financing initiatives that, in conjunction with initiatives to make gray industries more sustainable, decarbonize loan portfolios by investing in businesses such as reforestation and wind energy can have the greatest impact. Incentives for a low-carbon lifestyle can be offered as loyalty points; loans can be tailored for sustainable products (such as hybrid automobiles, low-carbon farms, or green mortgages); and green bonds can even be issued. These are further ways to incorporate sustainability into products.

Concentrated Organization

Customers now have a wider and better selection of goods and services because of increased competition. To do this, one must utilize their core strengths and concentrate on their main business. They can only do this if they want to create truly unique offerings, maintain competition, and adapt to constantly shifting market conditions.

To achieve this, one needs to first assess their current portfolio in order to identify their core markets that are profitable and to identify market segments to exit that are less profitable or that carry higher risks. As a result, one may elect to completely concentrate on a particular niche market segment with propositions designed especially for that segment, such as those oriented around particular products, topics, clients, or geographic areas.

In addition, banks could utilize specialized third-party solutions for non-core skills while concentrating on their core competencies. The upkeep of the technological infrastructure, the creation of apps, or even the execution of certain business operations like customer assistance could fall under this category.

This calls for banks to abandon their preconceived notions and be receptive to new operating models, such as outsourcing mortgage processing, customer assistance, or sales to outside parties. If done correctly, this can lower operating costs, shorten time to market, and help them quickly grow the bank should new possibilities present themselves.

Digital Methods of Operation

The COVID-19 outbreak has demonstrated how quickly and unpredictably change may occur, making it essential for the banking and financial sectors to adopt digitization. Banking organizations may offer better customer service by utilizing technology. The convenience and time savings are to the advantage of the customers. Examples of digital banking operations that have been digitized include electronic signatures, mobile apps, faster transactions, and many more. Hence, one might say that increased efficiency in banking procedures has been brought about by digitalization. Both banks and customers seem to benefit from this.

In order to assist banks in improving their decision-making based on the precise needs of their customer base, several digital applications have arisen. Without digitization, such a grassroots change wouldn't have been easily achievable. Another way that digitalization has stepped in to save the banking industry is by assisting decision-makers in making the best choices based on accurate, direct customer data that is pure, transparent, and effective.

8.2 INCREASING RELEVANCE OF DIGITAL BANKING

The banking industry has undergone a digital change since the widespread adoption of ATMs. Following that, advancements in the banking sector include Telebanking, Electronic Compensation Service, Electronic Funds Transfer System, MICR, RTGS (Real-Time Gross Settlement), Point of Sale Terminal, and so on. The world has advanced toward being a cashless and digital economy. The government have taken various incentives and steps to digitize the economy, and people's digital transactions have seen a remarkable increase.

Digital banking is characterized by high levels of process automation and web-based services. It provides users with financial data via Personal Computers, mobile, and ATM services. Today, thanks to digital freedom, banks have been able to introduce several channels of engagement for their customers as a result of the internet and increased mobile device penetration.

Banks have adopted a variety of technical advances as a result of the rise of digital freedom. Automation, biometrics, Chabot, machine learning, and blockchain technology are only a few of the various digitization methods used by the banking industry. All traditional banking operations and methods that were previously only accessible to customers while physically within a bank branch have been digitized (or transferred online) by digital banking. This can involve things like:

- Money Deposits, Withdrawals, and Transfers
- Checking/Saving Account Management
- Applying for Financial Products
- Loan Management
- Bill Pay
- Account Services

Both the banks and their customers profit from digital banking. Customers save time and money by conducting on-the-go banking transactions, while banks save money on physical infrastructure and hiring costs by bringing a portion of their transactions online. Although banks are turning to digital for protection and cost-cutting, the true benefit of digitalization is what benefits it can bring to their customers. Digital payments provide a massive opportunity for the country's numerous digitalization initiatives.

8.2.1   Digital Transformation of Banking

Digitization refers to the transition from analog to digital technology. The process of integrating different aspects of digital such as digital roles, digital processes, and other digitally enabled operations. It forms online links partially or completely in cross-enterprise which is referred as digital transformation.

The banking industry is the backbone of the world's finance system. Digital banking is playing a significant role in enhancing service quality and strengthening the banking sector because online payments result in higher levels of customer loyalty, improved efficiency, lower costs of banking operations, and quicker services.

Many developing countries around the world are undergoing a huge transformation in the banking industry. To keep up with leading global rivals that deliver a wide variety of sophisticated services, they are heavily investing in digital technology. The process of digitalization picked up speed of the banking and transactional process. Banks have challenged the global leaders to be among the biggest and most dynamic in the world by developing advanced technologies such as artificial intelligence (AI) and cognitive computing.

AI and cognitive computing are changing the face of business in a variety of ways, including banking. AI-enabled, digitally disruptive innovations are also being heavily invested in by many banks. Most of the banks globally have used AI-enabled technology to automate business processes in retail banking, agribusiness, trade, foreign exchange, treasury, and human resource management. Banks are also using AI-enabled technologies, such as facial and voice recognition, natural language processing, and machine learning.

Further, electronic payment systems like NEFT (National Electronic Fund Transfer), ECS (Electronic Clearing Service), RTGS (Real Time Gross Settlement), Cheque Transaction System, Mobile Banking, Debit Cards, Credit Cards, and Prepaid

Cards have all gained widespread acceptance in banks worldwide. These are all significant milestones in the banking industry's digital transformation.

8.2.2 TECHNOLOGICAL REVOLUTION OF BANKING

The banking industry has undergone a significant transformation over the years, and it will continue to do so. The emergence of advanced digital technology has resulted in a drastic revolution in banking operations and processes. Today, as a result of digital freedom, the entire banking process is fully digitized.

In the absence of advanced and innovative technology, modern banking and financial services will fail to remain stable. Banking and finance companies have been using technology for more than half a century. Advanced digital technology began to play a greater role both in the banking and financial sector.

As a result of digital freedom, adoption of advanced digital technologies has benefited banks in a number of ways. Digital banking has resulted in substantial cost savings and has aided in the production of revenue across a variety of platforms. Further, as a result of digital freedom, the banking industry is experiencing a great revolution with every passing year. From the paper/document-based transactions or payments, banking in 1980s to the internet banking in 1990s and from the mobile banking in 2000s to the digital banking, every year has proven to be a game changer for the banking industry across the world.

Online banking has also transformed the face of banking and resulted in significant changes in banking operations. The rising success of mobile banking is also motivating banks across the world. During the COVID-19 pandemic, norms of maintaining social distancing mobile banking payments and transactions have also risen to a great extent. Today's banks strive to provide their customers with a fast, reliable, and high-quality banking experience. Digitization is currently the highest priority for all banks around the world.

We can observe form Table 8.1 that with the rise in the digital era from 2018 to the current year, the digital transactions and payments has dramatically brought

TABLE 8.1
Technological Developments in Banks

Year	Technology used	Mode of Transactions/Payments
1980s	Paper	Standard Cheques, Encoders
1990s	Automation	Electronic Fund Transfer, Branch Connectivity
2000–2010	Internet	Online Banking, ATM, eBanking Tele banking.
2011–2017	Mobile (24x7 Services)	Mobile banking transactions, Mobile payments.
2018–till date	Digital (24x7 Services)	Digital payments, digital transactions, Biometrics. Credit Card, Debit Card, E-Wallet

Source: Table developed by the authors.

changes in the banking and finance industry. Banks are rapidly moving towards digital transactions. During the COVID-19 pandemic full lockdown, digital payments also increased; it has also helped in the growth and integration of technology into banking operations worldwide.

In addition to this, FinTech has grown from a buzzword among tech-savvy business executives to an integrated sector marked by hyper growth over the last few years. As a result of the use of big data analytics and AI, Banks will be able to conduct cross-selling and upselling at considerably lower costs thanks to digital and mobile banking, as well as analytics.

8.2.3 EMERGING TECHNOLOGIES IN DIGITAL BANKING

The world has entered into the world of digitization. The digital five powers—Social media, Mobile, Analytics, Cloud, and Internet of Things (IoT)—are spawning new and useful sources of business data, as well as new and cost-effective ways to view data. The banking sector has recognized the value of emerging technology in recent years and is increasingly adopting digital banking services. They are investing heavily in digital technology in order to provide a variety of services such as mobile banking, e-wallets, and virtual cards, among others. Digital/Virtual Banking, Biometric Technology, Artificial Intelligence, Blockchain Technology, Bitcoin, and Robotics are just a few of the biggest developments in digital banking.

Artificial Intelligence (AI) in Digital Banking

AI is a key emerging technology in a number of sectors, including banking. AI can provide fast and personalized services to their customers. Many financial companies are implementing AI technology into banking operations in order to meet rising consumer demands and have a better customer experience. AI has the ability to detect fraud, minimize unknown threats, and aid regulatory enforcement management.

Applications of AI in Banks

Fraud Detection: Anomaly identification can be used to improve the accuracy of credit card fraud and anti-money laundering detection.

Customer Support and Helpdesk: Humanoid Chabot interfaces can be used to improve customer interaction performance and lower costs.

Security: Suspicious behavior, log review, and forged emails can all be followed to avoid and probably predict security breaches.

Risk Management: By looking at historical records, conducting risk analysis, and removing human errors from hand-crafted models, tailored products can be delivered to clients.

ATMs: At ATMs, advanced AI techniques such as deep learning and image/face recognition using real-time camera images can be used to identify and prevent frauds/crimes.

The Role of Robotics in Digital Banking

Robotics is a technology that replicates human behavior in basic rule-based processes. The use of robotics in the banking industry is expected to grow in the coming years. It requires less human judgement. Banks around the world are using Robotic Process Automation (RPA) to help them become more efficient, flexible, and profitable.

Currently, some banks are using robots to address customer questions about banking transactions, Demat accounts, locker facilities, fixed deposits, and loans, among other things. Retail banking, agribusiness, trading and currency, treasury, and human resource management are just a few of the functions where software robots are used.

Applications of RPA in Banks

Customer Service: Every day, banks deal with a large number of inquiries, ranging from general inquiries to account inquiries to grievances, and so on. RPA assists in the resolution of low-priority questions, allowing personnel to concentrate on higher-priority queries requiring human intelligence. RPA shortens the time it takes to validate customer information through several systems, which speeds up the customer onboarding process. This cuts down on wait times, and fast resolution of complaints aids banks in improving customer ties.

Daily operations: Each and every day the banking industry handles a large amount of data. Processing this large amount of data manually is a time-consuming and error-prone operation. RPA allows for smooth data transfer and connectivity between legacy and newer applications. It reduces the time it takes to process a request by automating manual and repetitive activities. Banks have been able to reduce their turnaround time from days to hours and even minutes, according to reports.

Risk and Compliance Management: The banking industry is subjected to a slew of complicated and wide regulations, as well as shorter deadlines, covering KYC, financial reports, risk assessment reports, periodic disclosures, and so on. Therefore banks are looking at RPA solutions to improve production and lower enforcement costs as a result of the stringent regulatory guidelines.

Loan processing: By automating processes including data entry, paper routing, job assignments, and email alerts, RPA helps to reduce loan processing time. Customers will be able to submit requests using electronic forms through online portals. Customers can check the status of their applications from anywhere, at any time, using a computer or a mobile device on their online portals.

Blockchain Technology (BCT)

Blockchain technology (BCT) is being implemented by banks around the world for operations such as money transfer, record keeping, and other back-end functions. BCT can benefit the banking industry because it helps in fraud prevention, enhances the durability of the bank's IT infrastructure, and improves process transparency. BCT is also very cost effective and offers auditability and provenance.

Augmented Reality (AR)

Augmented Reality (AR) app is integration of digital information with the user's environment in the real world. Emerging technologies, such as AR, have been a blessing and a major contributor to the future of banking by allowing banks to develop immersive consumer interfaces, platforms, and applications that result in higher user engagement, seamless banking solutions, and positive brand communication. AR bank has introduced an AR mobile app that lists property, shopping centers, bank ATMs, branches, and other locations with real-life images, distances, and directions.

Application Programming Interface (APIs)

In many developing countries, open Banking has stepped into a new era of digitalization. The primary building block of this innovative effort is the Application Programming Interface (API).

One of the most significant advantages of API banking is the simplicity and clarity with which end-users can access and use financial services and goods. This simplicity will help India become a truly digital economy in the future. Several major banks have already launched API services. This is an excellent time for companies to start reaping the advantages of banking APIs, gain a competitive advantage, and better meet the needs of their customers.

8.3 IMPACT OF DIGITALIZATION IN BANKING

Banking is an important part of today's financial activity, and as a result of digital freedom, digital banking system is very advanced. Many aspects of almost every industry, especially the financial industry, have changed as a result of digital freedom. With the digital freedom in banking and the finance industry, banking solutions have changed dramatically. Without going to the bank, there are number of options for withdrawing money, depositing checks, and transferring funds, all of which have been revolutionized by technological advances.

With the freedom of digitization, today the banking system is no longer limited to the metropolises, but has expanded to include even the most remote parts of the country. Customers' expectations have risen as a result of the influence of globalization and advancements in digital technology. The banking services sector in developing countries has changed dramatically as a result of Liberalization, Privatization, and Globalization (LPG).

With the introduction of technological advances, banks have been able to maintain a high degree of protection, prevent fraud, violence, or pilferage, and reduce the risk and cost of handling cash. Non-cash payment modules such as RTGS, NEFT, NECS, UPI, and digital wallets have also been introduced and this has helped to completely transform the banking system.

As the entire industry has shifted to more digital banking choices, cybersecurity and data protection have improved dramatically. Online banking, ATM machines, proliferation of mobile phones, the growth of the internet and telecommunication technology and 24-hour access—all these factors have proved that digital banking is becoming essential in today's digital world.

As a result of the banking sector's digitization freedom, banks are using digital means to reach out to their customers' services and their satisfaction in the midst of the COVID-19 pandemic. The COVID-19 crisis has generated new demands for digital banking services as well as increased demand for existing ones. Therefore, many banks globally have been enlisted to create new applications and services to aid in the battle against COVID-19.

8.3.1 BENEFITS OF DIGITAL BANKING SYSTEM

In a world where crime and corruption are rampant, digital banking is a convenient way to do business. When it comes to the benefits of digital banking, there are many more advantages than disadvantages. From improved business performance to increased precision, agility, and stability. The future of digital banking will continue to expand and shows no signs of slowing down.

Customer service: Since banking has become more digitalized, there has been a strong emphasis on providing consumers with a more efficient service, resulting in more developments in a more user-friendly front-end service. As the internet is now widely accessible, all a customer needs to access his account is a laptop and internet access. It saves his both time and money because he no longer has to go to the bank to conduct transactions.

24×7 accessibility: The customer has 24×7 access to his bank accounts at any time and from any place of the world and can also use a variety of banking facilities. Money transfer has now become simpler, faster, and safer.

Saves time: Previously, in a traditional banking system, number banking services necessitated extended wait times. But with the digitalization in the banking sector all the banking operations are instantaneous and free of time restrictions.

Easy and convenient: As a result of digital freedom in the banking sectors, all the banking payments, transactions, money transfers etc. have become easier and more convenient.

Online bill payments: Online bill payment is one of the most important benefits of digital banking. Customers can save a lot of time and money by using digital payments features. Customers do not need to bring cash or wait in line for hours to pay their bills. Customers can do their payments at just one click of the button.

Low operational cost: Banks' operating costs have been greatly reduced thanks to digital banking. Banks have been able to charge lower service fees and deliver higher interest rates on deposits as a result of this. Bank earnings have increased as operating costs have decreased.

Written record: It has allowed us to keep track of our expenses and payments. Any transaction we make is recorded when we use online applications. The transactions are automatically recorded in the passbook or the E-Wallet App.

Discounts from taxes and other incentives: The government and the central bank have announced a slew of discounts to enable people to use digital wallets. Today, many mobile application providers now give discounts to users such as cashback and other promotional deals, which have benefited customers.

Other benefits: The simplicity of banking anytime, anywhere has increased the number of customers for banks. Human error is minimized. Since electronic records of any transaction are kept, it is possible to produce reports and evaluate data at any time and for a variety of purposes.

8.4   WHAT IS DIGITAL PAYMENT?

A digital payment is an online or digital transaction that does not include the exchange of physical currency. This indicates that both the payer and the payee exchange money through digital means. No hard cash is needed in digital payments.

There is a wave of new digital payment services from huge tech companies, established companies, and FinTech startups. Many advances in payment systems are the result of years-long efforts to improve the underlying systems. For instance, over the past few decades, real-time gross settlement (RTGS) systems have been implemented by central banks all over the world, taking advantage of technological advancement. In the meantime, these systems' running hours have increased globally, and in certain places, they now run nearly nonstop. On the retail side, innovation is rife as well. According to our most recent count, 51 economies have rapid retail payment systems that enable quick 24/7 settlement of payments between families and enterprises. They include programs like the FedNow proposal in the US, the CoDi system in Mexico, the Unified Payment Interface (UPI) in India, and the PIX system in Brazil (Bech and Hancock, 2020).

8.4.1   THE NEW FRONTIERS IN DIGITAL PAYMENTS

As payments have become cashless worldwide, there are now different digital payment options. Some approaches have been in use for more than a decade, while others have only recently gained attention. Figure 8.2 shows Digital Payment Technologies viz. Bank Card Payments, E-Payments, Mobile Payments and Cryptocurrencies.

The majority of modern transactions are now conducted electronically as opposed to using cash. The pervasive connectivity of ICT has greatly aided the transformation of the financial industry market and its operations. The use of the internet and the trend toward digitization have had a significant impact on how the global economy operates. Consumers are now able to use a variety of financial technology (FinTech) applications in place of the traditional cash-based payment system. In daily life, digital payments are increasingly the standard. Due to the financial industry's quick technological advancements, it is now possible for both payers and payees to send and receive money through digital apps.

Adopting digital payment systems has several advantages. Digital payments increase the number of potential customers for businesses, lower the cost of processing

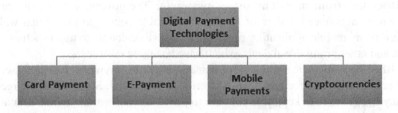

FIGURE 8.2   Digital payment technologies.

currency, and bring numerous unofficial shadow economies to the surface, raising tax collections for governments.

Economic friction can be reduced by all of these elements as well as other benefits of employing digital payment systems. Digital payment also includes electronic transactions made via the internet, such as paying with a credit or debit card online or in person at a store (Adeoti and Osotimehin, 2012). Payments done using cryptocurrencies like bitcoin, which enable encrypted peer-to-peer digital bartering, are also included. Many technologies, including debit cards, credit cards, ATMs, online transactions, and mobile phones, are used to make digital payments. Digital payment technologies make digital payment service possible in many ways.

E-Payment technologies, such as eChecks and BNPL solutions (Buy Now, Pay Later), which start transactions between parties digitally, are among the technologies used for digital payment transactions. E-Payment technologies are the most widely utilized payment technology as online purchasing grows in popularity. Similar to online payment methods, card payment technologies include credit and debit cards that can also be used offline. When used offline, these cards may also include Near-Field Communication (NFC) chips. NFC technology permits connection between two electronic devices over a short distance for touch-free payments. Due to health limitations and safety precautions during the pandemic, this contactless payment has gained increasing traction due to its ease, quickness, and dependability.

Digital payment technologies as shown in Table 8.2 above, are classified into four modes of payment methods: card payments, E-Payments, mobile payments,

TABLE 8.2
Digital Payment Technologies in Various Countries

Digital Payment Technologies	Payment Sources	Countries that have Adopted Digital Payment Services
Bank card payments	Credit card, debit card, prepaid card, NFC	India, Sweden, Denmark, Ukraine, Indonesia
E-Payments	SADAD, e-wallets, e-banking, eCheck, electronic fund transfer, digital cheques, PayCash, OPERA (Google Wallet, Apple Pay, Samsung Pay), OVO, EFTPOS (Khando, Islam and Gao, 2023).	India, Sweden, Italy, Ukraine, Indonesia, Russia, China, UK, Jordan, Zimbabwe
Mobile payments	Mobile Wallets, P2P fund transfer, OPERA (Google Wallet, Apple Pay, Samsung Pay), NFC based PIS mobile app, UPI (Unified Payment Interface)	India, Sweden, Indonesia, USA, 6 GCC
Cryptocurrencies	Bitcoin, Ethereum, Qtum based on blockchain, DCC (Digital Community Cash), Digicash, other blockchain cryptocurrencies	USA, European Union (EU), Russia

Source: Table developed by the authors.

and cryptocurrencies. Table 8.2 shows different emerging digital payment methods adopted by several countries around the world. The main motive of these digital payments is to make the country a paperless, cashless, and digitally empowered economy.

Bank Card Payments

Bank cards such as debit cards, credit cards, and prepaid cards have all gained widespread acceptance in many banks globally. As an alternative to cash payments, many customers often use banking cards, debit cards, credit cards, or prepaid cards. Cards are chosen for a variety of reasons, including ease, portability, protection, security, etc. This is the only digital payment system that is widely used in both online and offline transactions. Compared to other categories of payments like mobile payments, E-Payments, and cryptocurrency, it is a more traditional form of payment. The cardholders can use their bank cards to access their bank accounts and make payments online or at point of sale (POS) terminals. While credit cards enable cardholders to spend money or get cash from ATMs by borrowing a set amount of money from the card service providers, debit cards only let the cardholder pay with money that has already been deposited at the bank. Prepaid cards, on the other hand, are a convenient way to make purchases when you don't have cash with you. A prepaid card is one that has money put onto it so that it can be used to make purchases. Prepaid cards function similarly to debit cards, with the exception that they can be accessed without a bank account.

As we can see in the table, several developed and emerging nations, including Indonesia, Sweden, Denmark, Ukraine, and India, have embraced credit cards as a form of digital payment. Digital payments are accepted broadly across the board, especially in India, as a result of the country's demonetization. The Indian government has actively promoted and implemented digital payments since demonetization in 2016. The idea of "Digital India" served as the foundation for many economic and financial policies that drove Indians to use digital payments. On the other hand, the year 2020, particularly during the COVID-19 pandemic that swept the globe, highlighted the critical need to adapt to new technologies as soon as possible. With the implementation of the lockdown, particularly for digital payments in India, this adaptation happened almost immediately. Many merchants and other small enterprises, including rickshaw drivers, cafes, small restaurants, and shops, began utilizing card payment systems (Thirupathi, Vinayagamoorthi, and Mathiraj, 2019).

Sweden is a nation renowned for having a cashless society. In Sweden, using a card or other digital payment systems to make a purchase is the standard. In daily payment procedures, the use of digital payment technologies, such as card payment transactions, is growing (Dimitrova, Ohman, and Yazdanzar, 2019). Similar to this, as society becomes more digitalized, new opportunities arise for merging card payment data. Denmark is a neighboring country where credit cards are used for the majority of purchases. The card payment information was utilized in their study to calculate consumer spending and consumption patterns' environmental impacts. The economy was also greatly impacted by card payments (Pizzol, Vighi, and Sacchi, 2018).

E-Payments

E-Payments, also known as electronic payments, are commonly understood to be payment methods that don't use actual currency, bank drafts, or checks and instead conduct transactions online. It may also refer to the automated online banking services and products that are provided to consumers (Ankit, 2011). E-Payment and mobile payment technologies are classified differently in this study.

Mobile payments employ mobile phones for transactions, while E-Payment technologies refer to internet payments that may or may not involve mobile devices. A mobile payment technology can be placed on a mobile device as an application and enables "tap to pay" while shopping, frequently using an NFC chip. E-Payments can be accessible online through an E-Payment website or online applications using, for example, a laptop, tablet, or desktop computer. Mobile phones are typically used to scan QR codes or tap POS terminals to make a payment using mobile payment technologies. Mobile payment technologies are often regarded as a subset of E-Payment technology. Certain digital payment systems, such as Google Wallet, Apple Pay, and Samsung Pay, can be categorized as both E-Payments and mobile payments.

Several nations, including India, Sweden, Zimbabwe, Italy, Nigeria, Ukraine, Indonesia, China, Jordan, and the UK, utilize E-Payment systems. SADAD, e-wallets, electronic fund transfers, e-banking, eCheck, OPERA (Google Wallet, Apple Pay, and Samsung Pay), GoPay & OVO (Indonesia), and P2P fund transfers are a few examples of the growing E-Payment technologies found in these studies. The "e-wallet," which utilizes electronic devices like computers, tablets, or mobile phones, is one of the most popular E-Payment technologies.

Due to their relative advantages over debit and credit card payments, e-wallets and mobile wallets are becoming increasingly popular. Although an e-wallet acts similarly to a card for payments, it includes appealing cashback features, a rewards program, and more convenient security features; unlike debit or credit cards, e-wallets don't impose transaction fees. The "digital wallet," which allows users to conduct online transactions by tying their bank accounts together, is another comparable e-payment technology (Kumar, Agarwal, and Mishra, 2020). Digital wallets work with electronic devices; for example, Apple Pay and Samsung Pay both work with Apple devices, but PayPal works with both Apple and Android devices. A customer can easily send money to other users, receive money from other users, and store money in their mobile wallet with the help of a mobile wallet. A mobile wallet can also be used to pay utility bills, purchase tickets, receive incentives, and much more. The use of digital wallets is influenced by a number of factors, such as the government's goal of digitalizing India.

In order to keep the essential characteristics of offline cash payments, OPERA overcomes the shortcomings of previous E-Payment systems. It makes it possible to employ a standard offline digital technology, which is specific to digital cash, by utilizing a "one-time readable memory" and digital token (Park and Baek, 2017). electronic funds transfer at point-of-sale terminal is the name of the electronic equipment. The transaction between a customer's personal bank account and a merchant's account is helped by EFTPOS. EFTPOS usage decreases the need for cash and the total use of currencies.

Mobile Payments

Payments made through mobile devices, such as wireless handsets, PDAs, radio frequency devices, and NFC-based devices, through mobile apps are referred to as mobile payments. Mobile banking enables users to carry out a variety of banking tasks using mobile devices. Most banks now have mobile banking apps that can be accessed via handheld devices such as smartphones and tablets, as well as computers. Thus, customers are finding mobile banking very simple because of its convenience and quick response. Several nations, including India, Sweden, the United States, Indonesia, the six GCC nations (Saudi Arabia, Kuwait, the United Arab Emirates, Qatar, Bahrain, and Oman), Denmark, and the Kyrgyz Republic, are increasingly making use of mobile payments.

Mobile wallets, P2P financial transfers, NFC-based mobile payments, mobile apps (Venmo), MWR apps, OPERA (Google Wallet, Apple Pay, and Samsung Pay), GoPay & OVO (Indonesia), SWIPP, and UPI are among the well-known mobile payment systems. For instance, India is becoming a global competitor in cutting-edge payment systems, and a number of mobile payment technologies, including UPI (Unified Payment Interface), mobile banking, and mobile wallets, have been deployed nationally (Gupta, Kapoor, and Yadav, 2020).

Cryptocurrency

Cryptocurrency, sometimes known as "crypto," is a category of digital assets with several uses that is virtually impossible to forge or double-spend. According to "Crypto," they provide a technique to safeguard data by converting readable information into incomprehensible codes. Since they can be used as a form of payment, they are referred to as "currencies" (Kumari and Farheen, 2020).

The cryptographic methods that allow people to purchase, sell, or exchange cryptocurrencies safely without requiring a third party, like a government or financial institution, to confirm a transaction are what give them their name. There are many types of cryptocurrencies, like Ethereum, Monero, bitcoin, etc.

Adoption of cryptocurrencies has the ability to expedite, improve, and modernize financial services, and numerous recent technological developments have helped allay banks' fears about the risks and allowed them to see the potential benefits instead. Several potential advantages of cryptocurrency include increased speed and efficiency in processing payments and transfers, particularly across borders, and ultimately increased financial inclusion. Cryptocurrency offers peer-to-peer and transparent transaction options.

Bitcoin is the first and most valuable cryptocurrency. In the world of financial markets, bitcoin is a revolutionary new form of digital payment. It enables developers to create automated applications in what has come to be known as decentralized finance, and Tether is a stable coin whose value is tied to the U.S. dollar (Baek et al., 2019).

In the world of cryptocurrencies, Bitcoin is regarded as the "gold standard." While avoiding the majority of the drawbacks of both currencies, it combines the advantages of fiat money with the convenience of commodity-backed money. A central bank or government cannot manipulate the price of bitcoin by inflating, stimulating, or depressing it artificially. One of the key advantages that distinguishes bitcoin from commodity money like gold is this.

Bitcoins, unlike gold, however, offer benefits exclusive to fiat money, such as simpler division. When going to the market, there is no requirement to carry cash or gold bars. There is no requirement for printing, melting, or expensive shipping and security. It's simpler to transfer and store. Bitcoin offers numerous advantages over gold or other commodity-backed money that fiat money does not.

Bitcoin and other cryptocurrencies operate according to a mathematical method that uses blockchain technology. Since bitcoins were first produced, the blockchain has used mathematics to keep track of every bitcoin that has ever existed and where each one is at any given moment. The algorithm is programmed to only produce a predetermined number of bitcoins at a predetermined rate. It would be comparable to attempting to manipulate Y=mx+b or gravity. Therefore, it's impossible to do, and trying to do it makes no sense at all (Rykwalder, 2014).

Bitcoin and blockchain technology: Bitcoin and other cryptocurrencies make use of blockchain technology that was developed from a distributed network database (Hong Kong Monetary Authority, 2017). The blockchain functions as the historical accounting record for all bitcoin transactions. The history of the currency is recorded in an accessible public ledger. The blockchain offers a solution for how to prevent manipulation and duplication of digital currency. The main issue with digital goods is how easy it is to copy items for practically no money: music, articles, books, and films. The capacity for anyone to replicate money without restriction would cause severe inflationary problems for a money system. Because it enables the peer-to-peer, middleman-free exchange of safe, non-repeatable bits of information amongst people all over the world, the blockchain mitigates the "danger of double counting."

The blockchain keeps account of a bitcoin's journey from the time it is mined until the end of time. All transactions' amounts, dates, and account addresses are recorded in the ledger. The world is free to access this material, which is also regularly updated. Information that is personal and private is kept confidential. While many studies also examined the privacy of Bitcoin users, an investigation on the privacy standard of Bitcoin in a university setting found that the privacy protections provided by Bitcoin were insufficient (Androulaki et al., 2013). Table 8.3 shows the difference between cryptocurrency transactions and banking transactions.

8.4.2 REAL-WORLD CASE

Government Initiatives for Digital Payments in India

There are also some new digital payment initiatives launched by the Government to encourage Indians to use digital payments methods.

Bharat QR (Quick response code)

Bharat QR is a QR-based payment solution that can be used to make P2M (Person to Merchant) digital payments. This means that customer can use any

Bharat QR-enabled mobile application to scan the Bharat QR code displayed at a merchant's or seller's location. Bharat QR is a new way to pay using your mobile phone. There's no need to carry any cash. This is an innovative technology that could help millions of small retailers accept electronic payments. All you need is a smartphone with an internet connection and a Bharat QR-compatible mobile app (Rajesh, 2017).

BHARAT BILL PAYMENT SYSTEM

The Bharat Bill Payment System (BBPS) is an online digital platform launched by the Reserve bank of India (RBI). This platform was developed to make paying bills simpler and to increase the reliability and security of bill payments. It is a move towards paperless transactions. The Bharat Bill Payment System (BBPS) is an integrated bill payment system in India that provides customers with an interoperable and open bill payment service through a network of registered members known as Agent Institutions (AI), allowing for multiple payment modes and instant payment confirmation (Shaikh, 2014).

TABLE 8.3
Difference between Cryptocurrency and Banking Transactions

Banking Transaction	Cryptocurrency Transaction
Governments manage and regulate banks worldwide.	Cryptocurrency is decentralized and is not backed by any one country.
Occasionally, a bank experiences a single point of failure.	Cryptocurrencies don't have any single points of failure,
The government has some control over bank transactions to limit certain transactions.	while the peer-to-peer nature of cryptocurrency transactions eliminates the need for middlemen like banks.
Bank transactions are associated with a particular bank account through financial institutions.	Transactions are linked to the transaction ID on the block chain.
Banking transactions maintain privacy and confidentiality.	The privacy of cryptocurrency transactions is not protected.

Source: Table developed by the authors.

8.5   DIGITAL FINANCE SECTOR

With the freedom of digitization, the financial sector worldwide is rapidly expanding. The financial industry includes commercial banks, insurance firms, non-banking financial companies, co-operatives, real estate, pension funds, mutual funds, and other smaller financial institutions. Technology and business model advancements have led to the emergence of DFS (Digital Financial Services), which can provide more specialized financial services at scale while also lowering costs and improving speed, transparency, security, and availability. From opening an account to doing customer due diligence, verifying transactions, and automating other, product-specific activities, such as determining creditworthiness, digitization may minimize friction at every stage along the financial service life cycle. Thus, DFS is known for having low marginal costs per account or transaction, which can result in scale-related cost savings (Phillippon, 2020).

Financial services facilitate investments in people's companies, homes, health, and education, as well as smooth consumption and increase resilience to shocks like illness, losing a job, or a poor harvest, through remittances and basic savings, lending, and insurance products.

What is Digital Finance?

The term "digital finance" is used to describe how emerging technologies are affecting the financial services business. It encompasses a wide range of products, applications, procedures, and business models that have revolutionized the way banking and financial services are delivered.

What is FinTech?

FinTech is defined as "innovation in financial services made possible by technology that could lead to new business models, applications, procedures, or products with a meaningful impact on the provision of financial services" (FSB 2017a).

Figure 8.3 shows different top FinTech companies viz. mobile banking, blockchain, digital KYC process, cross-border remittances, and cryptocurrencies.

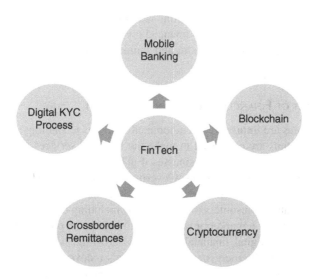

FIGURE 8.3   Top fintech companies.

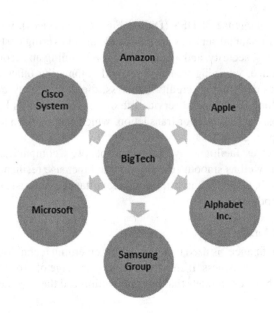

FIGURE 8.4 BigTech technologies.

The continuing wave of new DFS is also generally referred to as "FinTech." Web, mobile, cloud services, machine learning, digital ID, and application programming interfaces (APIs) are a few examples of these technologies.

What is BigTech?

BigTechs are large technology companies that operate on a global or international scale, have a high market capitalization, well-known brands, and a strong market position, and primarily provide non-financial goods and services, both traditional and digital, via digital platforms (Harasim and Janina, 2021). The big tech technologies are shown in Figure 8.4.

8.5.1 Impact of Financial Technology (FinTech)

Financial services are improved and automated with this technology. Advanced software and algorithms are employed to make the financial services process easier for business users, consumers, and businesses. FinTech makes use of technology such as bitcoin and other cryptocurrencies. Governments are using FinTech to rapidly and securely provide cash transfers, other forms of financial aid, and emergency liquidity to enterprises. It enables consumers to send money, including cross-border remittances, and pay bills online, at a market or store, or with little to no physical touch.

Thus, the use of digital financial services is growing, which can help with the settlement of the health emergency, the economy's recovery, and the establishment of economic growth. Long term, it will aid in economic growth and the eradication of poverty.

The following are some examples of how financial technology can be used:

- It is a cutting-edge methodology for the creation of digital currency.
- It can also be used for double-entry accounting.
- As a result of the freedom of digitization, FinTech services save money by combining streamlined solutions with cutting-edge technology.
- With the freedom of digitization, financial services that were formerly limited to branches, desktops, and salesmen are now mobile and may be accessed via laptops and mobile phones.
- FinTech is now being utilized for a variety of financial operations like bank transfers, check deposits via mobile phones, credit applications, and raising capital for business start-ups, among others.

8.5.2 INFLUENCE OF FINTECH ON THE FINANCIAL SECTOR

With the freedom of digitization, FinTech contributes to the financial sector's digital platform activity. FinTech can transform other financial services like insurance, investment, and remittances. FinTech has a great impact on the banking and financial sector in the following ways as a result of the increase of emerging digital technology:

Loans: The way banks operate has undergone a significant change. There is a new market for lending-based markets nowadays. Consumers can readily obtain loans and other types of advances.

Digital payments: The use of Digital payment and mobile wallets worldwide has been steadily expanding over time with the high number of internet users and huge smartphone penetration. Payments may be done quickly and easily over the internet using mobile phones. These days, one of the most important advantages of internet buying is the ability to make payments online. As digital payments are increasing over time, money can also be transferred effortlessly from one bank account to another for a lower transaction cost and with less risk of fraud.

Fund management: With the introduction of advanced and innovative technology, customers' behaviors and methods for saving, investing, and managing their assets have changed dramatically. A company's goal is to provide comprehensive investing and savings alternatives. Fintech software also aids in selecting the best investment.

Remittance: Earlier traditional remittances were more challenging; they were expensive, difficult, and time-consuming. But today in this digital age, inward and outbound transactions are straightforward, efficient, and affordable thanks to Fintech companies.

Insurance/investment services: With the freedom of digitization and e-KYC, Insurance can be purchased online, with all tailored plans and details available. Starting with the application for premium payment, every process is now paperless and cashless. Also, the total amount of money invested in the financial markets is only going to rise.

Equity-funding services: New project ventures and businesses can raise funds in the form of equity from a wide number of people using these technologies.

8.6   CHAPTER CONCLUSION

Thus, the banking sector has emerged as one of the world's fastest-growing sectors. With the help of digitization in the banking sector, banks worldwide are now not only gaining more customers but also providing excellent service to their customers. The main challenges in the banking industry are that, in this digital age, they must ensure that their clients are protected from cybercrime and that the most advanced cybernetic principles are used. The shift to digitalization and its implementation should help the company save money by reducing work and automating the system. Banks have also discovered that advanced and innovative technology will help them gain a competitive advantage. Along with the banking sector, FinTech also contributes to the financial sector's digital platform activity. FinTech can transform other financial services like insurance, investment, and remittances. Fintech has a great future ahead in the financial industries worldwide.

EXERCISES

1. Why do banks invest in digital technologies?
2. What do banks mean by "digital"?
3. What are types of digital payments?
4. What new innovative features have been added to digital payments?
5. What are the main benefits of mobile apps?
6. What is cryptocurrency?
7. What methods are used to record cryptocurrency transactions?
8. What are the biggest cryptocurrency issues?
9. Differentiate between cryptocurrency transactions and banking transactions?
10. How did the COVID-19 pandemic encourage the banking industry to go digital?
11. What is digital finance?
12. What are the financial sectors of a country?
13. What is FinTech? Give examples of FinTech.
14. What are FinTech's effects on the financial sector?

REFERENCES

Adeoti, O. and Osotimehin, K. (2012) 'Adoption of point of sale terminals in Nigeria: assessment of consumers level of satisfaction', *Research Journal Financial Account*, vol. 3, pp. 1–6.

Androulaki, et al. (2013) *'Evaluating user privacy in bitcoin'*, In International Conference on Financial Cryptography and Data Security, Springer: Berlin/Heidelberg, Germany, pp. 34–51.

Ankit, S. (2011) 'Factors influencing online banking customer satisfaction and their importance in improving overall retention levels: An Indian banking perspective', *Informational Knowledge Management*, vol. 1, pp. 45–54.

Baek, H. et al. (2019) *'A Model for detecting cryptocurrency transactions with discernible purpose'*, Eleventh International Conference on Ubiquitous and future Networks (ICUFN), IEEE, pp. 713–717.

Bech, M. and Hancock, J. (2020) *'Innovations in payments'*, BIS Quarterly Review, March.

Consultancy.eu (2022) *'Seven components for building the (digital) bank for tomorrow'*, 20 December, Available at: https:// www.consultancy.eu/news/8053/seven-components-for-building-the-digital-bank-of-the-future (Accessed: 02 January 2023).

Devries, P.D. (2016) *'An analysis of cryptocurrency, bitcoin and the future'*, International Journal Business Management Commerce, pp. 1–9.

Dimitrova, I., Ohman, P. and Yazdanzar, D. (2019) *'Challenges in the limited choice of payment methods in terms of cashless society: bank customers' perspective* (work in progress)', In Proceedings of the 2019, 3rd International Conference on E-commerce, E-Business and E-Government, Lyon, France, June 19–21, pp. 45–48.

FSB. (2017a) *'Financial Stability Implications from FinTech'*, Supervisory and regulatory issues that merit authorities attention, Basel: FSB, June.

Gupta, R., Kapoor, C. and Yadav, J. (2020) *'Acceptance towards digital payments and improvements in cashless payment ecosystem'*, In Proceedings of the 2020 International Conference for Emerging Technology (INCET), Belgaum, India, 5–7 June, pp. 1–9.

Harasim and Janina (2021) 'FinTechs, BigTechs and banks–when cooperation and when competition?' *Journal of Risks and Financial Management* 14: 614, https://doi.org/10.3390/jrfm14120614

Khando, K., Islam, M.S and Gao, S. (2023) *'The emerging technologies of digital payments and associated challenges: a systematic literature review'*, Future Internet, 15. https://doi.org/10.3390/fi150100021

Kumari, S. and Farheen, S. (2020) *'Blockchain based data security for financial transaction system'*, 4th International Conference on Intelligent Computing and Control Systems (ICICCS), IEEE, pp. 829–833.

Kumar, M., Agarwal, S. and Mishra, R. (2020) 'User behaviour and digital payment ecosystem: an audit of connections between usage attributes and demographic profile', *International Journal of Emerging Technology*, vol. 11, pp. 935–938.

Park, K.W., and Baek, S.H. (2017) 'OPERA: a complete offline and anonymous digital cash transaction system with a one-time readable memory', *IEICI Transformation Informational System*, 100, pp. 2348–2356.

Phillippon, T. (2020) *'On Fintech and financial inclusion'*, BIS Working Paper 841, Bank for International Settlements, www.bis.org/publ/work841.pdf.

Pizzol, M. Vighi, E. and Sacchi, R. (2018) 'Challenges in coupling digital payments data and input-output data to change consumption patterns', *Procedia CIRP*, 69, 633–637.

Rajesh, R. (2017) 'Bharat OR code: an insight', *Paripex, Indian Journal of Research*, May 01, vol. 6, no. 5.

Rykwalder, E. (2014) *'The math behind Bitcoin'*, October 19. Available at: www.coindesk.com/math-behind-botcoin/ (Accessed: 03 January 2021).

Shaikh, M. (2014) *'BHARAT BILL PAYMENT SYSTEM (BPS)'*, December 08, Available at: https://moinshaikhwordpress.com/2014/12/08/bharat-bill-payment-system-bpps (Accessed: 03 January 2020).

Thirupathi, M., Vinayagamoorthi, G., and Mathiraj, S.P. (2019) 'Effect of cashless payment methods: a case study', Perspective Analysis, *International Journal of Science Technology Resource*, vol. 8, pp. 394–397.

9 Digital Logistics

SUMMARY

This chapter will examine the value of digitalization and its necessity for the expansion of the logistics sector. This chapter also covers the significance of a variety of cost-effective digital technologies utilized in the logistics industry for enhancing service to maintain the supply chain's resilience and deliver items on schedule. We'll also concentrate on the real-world case of India where various initiatives, such as the introduction of the GST, Make in India, DFC, and others, have improved the Indian logistics industry and the government of India's investments. The chapter also discusses the region's enormous economic and social impact from the government's ambitions to transform the country into a digitally empowered society.

9.1 INTRODUCTION

The logistics industry is the backbone of every economy. Transportation and logistics, like most other sectors, are undergoing significant change, which, like all change, brings both risk and opportunity. The modern world's economy is being shaped by new business models, digital networks, new customer demands, and data-based services.

In almost every field, the world is rapidly digitizing. Many developed and developing countries around the world are examining their options for becoming truly digital economies in the twenty-first century. As evidenced by the countless new startups, governments worldwide are taking numerous steps to encourage economic digitalization. India's government has agreed to invest heavily in internet accessibility and digital development as it faces growing pressure from strong digital economies such as the United States and China.

WHAT IS DIGITAL LOGISTICS?

The term "digital logistics" is defined as the automation and digitization of processes involved in the transfer of products and goods.

Each link in a company's supply chain could be impacted by digital logistics, including:

- inventory control
- transportation administration
- warehouse management systems and warehousing (WMS)

DOI: 10.1201/9781003403784-9

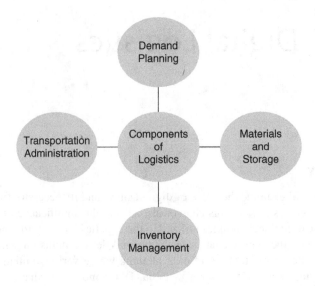

FIGURE 9.1   Components of logistics.

- forecasting and analytics for the supply chain
- notifications to customers and live shipping tracking

9.1.1 Components of Logistics

There are four important components of logistics as shown in Figure 9.1.

Demand planning: It is an important task that ensures client order fulfillment. Customer demands are met, profits are increased, and goods are ordered in the proper quantities, at the proper price, and with reliable transit.

Inventory control: The movement of items into and out of a warehouse is regulated by inventory management. Utilizing targeted data to forecast consumer demand determines how much inventory to keep on hand and where to place it.

Transportation administration uses various forms of transportation to carry goods from one supply chain to the next. For long-distance supply chains, merchandise may need to go by road transport, freight trains, shipping, or even by air transport.

Warehouse management: As demand can be erratic, it is essential to keep extra products until customers need them. The storage, handling, retrieval, and packaging of goods are all handled by warehouses. Therefore, a warehouse management system improves storage capabilities, machinery, retrieval times, and warehouse procedures.

9.2 NEED FOR DIGITALIZATION IN LOGISTICS

The need for digitalization in the logistics industry is very important, as it will increase working capacity and transportation quality. There was a disturbance in the supply chain due to the movement of truck drivers during the COVID-19 pandemic, but other ways of transition were addressed in the best possible way due to the adoption and implementation of digitalization in logistics. This pandemic has compelled the world to shift far faster than anticipated toward an important bouquet of digitally activated, dependable, and scalable services.

Across the world, advanced technological advances are transforming the traditional transportation and logistics industries. As a result, traditional players in the logistics and transportation systems are devising new strategies to survive and thrive. Advances in emerging technology, changing customer preferences as a result of e-commerce, government initiatives, and a change in service sourcing strategies are all expected to drive the global logistics ecosystem's transformation.

Digitalization of logistics is the need of the hour and will enhance working capacity and transportation efficiency. As the logistics and transportation industry undergoes technological transformations, transportation companies must be prepared to adapt by developing new business models. With real-time data and a clear supply chain, digital platforms have increased competition and reduced costs. To keep up with the changing logistics world, logistics service providers must evolve and adapt to modern digital technologies.

The industry is today confronted with many challenges, and there is a need for the adoption of innovation and advanced technology to boost growth. Therefore, the digitalization of the logistics industry will have a significant impact on supply chain effectiveness, resulting in a decrease in operational costs.

9.3 IMPACT OF DIGITALIZATION ON THE LOGISTICS INDUSTRY

As a result of increased digital freedom, increased use of innovative digital technologies will support a significant portion of the logistics industry. A successful logistics organization will digitally automate all supply chain functions, making it easier to monitor orders, equipment, and deliveries for increased quality and productivity. With the help of digital freedom, the logistics sector has a lot of room to develop.

In the logistics industry, the use of innovative and advanced digital technology has brought refreshing changes and growth, which have had a direct effect on the industry. In this industry, digitization has the potential to bring about transformative changes.

Major factors that have led to transformative changes in the logistics industry are:

- With the effect of digital freedom, logistics has evolved into a third-party service provider with major companies as clients. Established businesses are now hiring third-party logistics for transportation, resulting in a double profit.
- As a result of innovations and advancements in digital technologies such as GPS monitoring, real-time surveillance, and real-time temperature feed, all these factors have improved customer services. Market standards, on the other hand, have risen as a result. On-time delivery, high-quality deliveries, immediate returns, and versatility have all become important aspects of logistics.
- In response to technological advancements, the logistics industry has developed new performance, security, and safety standards. Automated networks and data exchanges have increased the industry's reliability ratio.

9.3.1 The Impact of Digital Technologies on Logistics

The adoption of digital technologies in the logistics industry aims to boost the country's growth by creating new investment opportunities and promoting globalization. The logistics industry has been dramatically transformed as a result of the adoption of digital technology.

It has provided end-to-end lean and smart logistics solutions that improve quality, cut costs, and minimize human intervention through the adoption and implementation of advanced digital technology in this industry, such as the Internet of Things (IoT), automation technology, blockchain technology, cloud computing, advanced/big data analysis, artificial intelligence (AI), and robotics. Also, many advanced technologies, such as RFID, FASTag, and IoT, are now playing an important role in the logistics industry. These technologies have not only enhanced operational efficiencies and cargo safety, but they have also assisted in lowering transportation costs by increasing freight movement speed.

Several industries, including automotive, retail, and manufacturing, are now adopting digital technologies that are available to the logistics industry and are being utilized to re-invent their supply chains to cut logistical costs and boost company efficiencies.

Digitalization has allowed systems to connect through the internet, resulting in a significant improvement in the ease with which the sector's communications and transactions are conducted. As a result, a global infrastructure of reliable networking has emerged. It has proven to be more effective than any other method in increasing productivity while streamlining the operations of the logistics sector.

IoT and Logistics Industry

The logistics industry is experimenting with IoT technology to streamline its business processes and reduce visibility. With the help of analytics, mobile computing, and cloud services, all of which are powered by the Internet of Things, the logistics industry's delivery and fulfillment processes are undergoing rapid change.

Benefits of IoT in the Logistics Industry

Location management system: In the logistics industry, IoT aids in the creation of a smart location management system that allows businesses to easily monitor driver activities, vehicle location, and delivery status. A push message can be sent to the manager when the items are shipped or arrive at a specific location. All changes are immediately observed and mirrored. As a result, Internet of Things (IoT) technology can be used to enhance location management and business processes.

Inventory tracking and warehousing: One of the most important aspects of the logistics ecosystem is inventory management and warehousing. Companies can easily track inventory items, monitor their status, and create a smart warehouse system by making use of sensors in different locations. Employees can successfully prevent any type of loss by utilizing IoT technology, ensuring safe storage of goods, and quickly locating a required item. IoT can help reduce human error (Kalaivani and Indumathi, 2018).

IoT and predictive analysis: Internet-connected devices gather a vast volume of data and send it to a central location for further study. IoT and predictive analysis can be used for distribution routes and preparation as well as the detection of various defects before they cause problems. These outcomes include the timely replacement of machinery components, the avoidance of any kind of collision, and effective vehicle or equipment maintenance.

IoT and blockchain for supply chain: Many IoT security problems can be solved with blockchain technology, which can also add significant value to supply chains. When these two technologies are combined, they will meet the requirements for supply chain protection, accountability, and traceability.

Self-driving vehicles: The logistics industry will be the first to incorporate self-driving cars into their business processes in the future. The IoT devices will collect a huge amount of data, which will be transformed into smarter driving routes and directions by the analytics system. As a result, the industry will lower the number of automobile accidents, lower maintenance costs, and improve traffic on the road.

IoT technology helps the warehouse industry in the following ways: This industry is seeing a lot of investment, and as a result of the transformations and improvements brought on by these investments, this industry is employing a large number of jobless people. The rapid growth of the E-Commerce and manufacturing sectors has fueled the rise of the warehousing market. Additionally, technical improvements like warehouse automation and robotic mechanization are projected to transform the market.

Security: In warehouse management, security is also an important factor. The Internet of Things contributes to the warehouse's defense. For example, IoT technology is used by video surveillance cameras and sensors in the warehouse to detect some types of theft. Remote alarm monitoring allows you to keep track of video data from several locations at any time. Text message warning systems may also be used to warn whether entry to restricted areas has been gained. The Internet of Things (IoT) could help with this.

Safety: Employee protection and safety are also critical considerations in warehouse management. Companies, on the other hand, are using IoT to protect their employees and have been able to eliminate injuries to a greater degree. The use of IoT can assist warehouse owners in detecting any defects before human contact. This has decreased the risk of injuries and, as a result, increased the safety of staff in the warehouse.

Improved performance: IoT makes it possible for equipment to be connected, and connected systems enable improved warehouse management, which is essential for corporate expansion. Due to their ability to see their entire business, companies employing IoT have better control over their warehouses. With the use of technology, one can readily observe the inventory that is on hand as well as other activities going on in the warehouse. IoT makes sure that resources and equipment are used properly in the warehouse, which ultimately helps the company increase warehouse productivity.

Consumer Benefits from IoT

Improved efficiency: The Internet of Things (IoT) aids in business growth by increasing customer productivity. Customers place orders and pay with their mobile devices. This type of technology makes it easier for consumers to conduct their business, resulting in more repeat purchases.

Transparency is also an important factor in the development of trust, which improves business relationships. Customers can track the movement of their goods using IoT from the time they purchase to the time they receive their products. Real details about the customer's delivery without any involvement of workers build trust in the services provided, eventually leading to satisfaction.

AI in Shipping and Logistics

Artificial intelligence is useful for saving time, lowering costs, increasing efficiency, and improving accuracy. It helps us save time and money by automating a variety of time-consuming procedures and assisting with demand forecasting. Artificial intelligence allows computers to compile, analyze, and make important decisions in a matter of seconds, saving humans time and money by automating a variety of time-consuming procedures and assisting with demand forecasting. Artificial intelligence allows computers to compile, analyze, and make important decisions in a matter of seconds, saving humans time. Robots are now commonly used in warehouses, for example, to drive, monitor, and locate inventory.

Demand forecasting: Historical data is used in demand forecasting, and AI can improve the analysis of historical and real-time data to provide more accurate demand forecasts. Shippers can improve inventory control, dispatches, and staff planning by using more reliable demand forecasts, resulting in higher service levels. AI-powered forecasting methods could reduce supply chain network errors by 30 to 50 percent (Kudtarkar and Shaikh, 2021).

Supply planning: The logistics industry is incomplete without supply preparation. Artificial intelligence can help with real-time demand analysis. Businesses may increase supply chain flow, improve efficiencies, and increase profitability by continuously adjusting supply planning parameters.

Automation in warehousing: The increased demand for contactless processes in supply chains, owing to current global events, appears to have pushed the need for advanced automated business processes. In the warehousing case, AI can revolutionize automation. Combining robotics and artificial intelligence, robots can monitor and locate inventory as well as perform picking, sorting, and packing tasks that would normally require an additional workforce.

Predictive logistics: Better machine learning algorithms can derive critical logistical insights that can help with decision-making. Artificial intelligence can help with capacity planning, forecasting, and network management, allowing operations to run more smoothly and improving overall supply chain efficiency.

Back-office automation: Workflow automation is the use of artificial intelligence to automate complex and time-consuming back-office processes. Documentation in freight forwarding is a time-consuming operation that can be greatly simplified by using robotic process automation (RPA) and optical character recognition (OCR). Since shipping documents aren't always in the same format, innovations like these may help simplify the reading and interpretation of documents that are printed or handwritten with pinpoint accuracy. This type of process automation will free up a large amount of time for logistics staff, allowing them to focus on more value-added tasks.

AUTONOMOUS TECHNOLOGY

Dynamic AI technology is now driving numerous autonomous car systems. Self-driving cars, robots, and drones, for example, can help with labor-intensive occupations in manufacturing and logistics. Self-driving cars can dramatically reduce reliance on human drivers, and technologies like platooning can help drivers' health and safety by lowering vehicle fuel consumption and carbon emissions.

APPLICATIONS OF MACHINE LEARNING IN THE LOGISTICS INDUSTRY

Machine learning, likewise, is gaining popularity in every industry and dimension of our lives, including logistics. Machine learning also helps in avoiding common human errors, saving time, and anticipating future opportunities and difficulties. Its algorithm, as well as the logistics companies that use it, can quickly analyze massive, diversified data sets, enhancing demand forecasting accuracy. In the collaborative supply chain and logistics market, machine learning helps to reduce freight costs, increase supplier delivery performance, and reduce supplier risk.

In the logistics business, machine learning replaces the time-consuming tasks of planning and scheduling, allowing for greater accuracy and efficiency and therefore streamlining the processes. Machine learning also assists logistics service providers in analyzing massive amounts of data and improving the logistics management system. Predicting future results and demands is a challenging and vital task throughout delivery and management. Machine learning assists businesses in predicting and tracking future production demands, such as projecting demand for new items. Machine learning is an extremely efficient technique because it combines the strengths of supervised, unsupervised, and rewarded learning.

CLOUD COMPUTING IN LOGISTICS

Over the past few years, the logistics industry has had a positive effect on the world's economy. According to a recent survey by many professionals, cloud solutions have proven to be a "game changer" in the logistics industry. Cloud-based apps are more agile, quicker, and more powerful than any other technology.

The logistics sector today, in the age of digitalization, has a lot of scope for transformation, and cloud computing is a key component. The standard by which logistical activities are judged has risen in response to factors such as rising customer expectations, price pressure, rising fuel costs, E-Commerce, and environmental concern. Process and resource efficiency are essential in today's world.

Scalability: Cloud computing technologies' inherent scalability features can be immensely advantageous to the logistics industry. It's simple to scale up with cloud computing solutions without losing time, money, or resources. This makes it simple and quick for logistics companies to enter new markets or introduce new services. Cloud scalability aids in the development of flexible supply networks.

Cost efficiency: Cloud-based logistics systems aid in the real-time management of various parts of operations, making pricing scalable and thus lowering costs. Cloud-based logistics save money on software maintenance and upgrades because it is based on a pay-per-use model. Capital expenditures are significantly reduced due to a lack of demand for on-site resources.

Flexibility: The decision to shift to the cloud in the logistics industry is usually driven by financial considerations. There are fewer upfront costs because there is no need to spend much on IT infrastructure, upgrades, or support. It is also simple and quick to add users to the online environment, regardless of their location.

Onboarding: Using cloud technologies, new trading partners can be on boarded in days rather than weeks. By allowing any-to-any interfaces and maintaining flexible protocol connections, the cloud allows shippers, carriers, freight brokerages, and 3PLs to meet a variety of client requests or requirements.

9.4   LOGISTICS USING FLEET TELEMATICS

Telematics is a technology that uses telecommunication components, vehicle sensors, wireless networking, and data dashboards to enable the long-distance transmission of data from moving transportation devices (Basu Mallick, 2020).

The landscape of the logistics industry has changed due to the merits of video telematics. It has resulted in a positive shift that has resulted in significant growth and development. The primary goal of introducing fleet telematics into the logistics arena was to improve organization. Telematics has a lot of potential for organizing this disjointed economy.

ADVANTAGES OF FLEET TELEMATICS IN THE LOGISTICS INDUSTRY (SHAIKH, 2022)

Real-time fleet tracking: Using a mobile logistic solution, you can constantly monitor the status of your vehicle. It allows fleet owners to monitor their fleet in real-time, ensuring speed, efficiency, and safety for their customers.

Easy monitoring of the logistics industry benefits from fleet telematics because it allows for easy monitoring of fleet details such as engine activity, tire conditions, mileage, and so on.

Automation: It addresses the problem of manpower shortages. As a result of video telematics, driver education, behavior tracking, and performance-based incentives have become commonplace.

Solves problems: It solves transportation puzzles like route planning, demand forecasting, vehicle efficiency analysis, and goal-oriented achievements.

Easily accessible data: Thanks to fleet telematics, complex data as well as simple details such as driver hours per day, distance traveled per day, maximum and average speed, harsh braking, and so on, can now be easily accessed, maintained, and analyzed.

Saves time: Managers, administrators, drivers, and mechanics all benefit from the time savings provided by fleet management software.

Tracking option: There are fleet tracking options available to improve the sector's visibility of driver and vehicle performance. With the various data streams that software offers, fleet managers have greatly benefited from this economical technique.

9.5 EFFICIENCY IN LOGISTICS' EFFECT ON ECONOMIC DEVELOPMENT

Economic development can be viewed as the outcome of improvements in an economy's well-being, which were made possible because growth rates were high, the procedures for accumulating capital were enhanced, and social-economic prosperity continued to rise. It has been amply demonstrated in development economics that such qualitative jumps are not brought about by quantitative advancements in a single variable. The levels of social and economic well-being are instead affected by several variables, and these variables can be influenced by both internal and external forces.

Currently, logistics has a significant impact on the economies of most developing nations, having an impact on many areas including transport networks, storage systems, information and communication technology, packaging services, supply chain management, industry and products, exports and imports of services, and more. Logistics is now a significant component of trade and is actively contributing to this development. As a result, the growth of the logistics industry is important, offering benefits for development and growth. Logistical expenditures also alter how businesses and nations operate as a whole.

For the ultimate in customer satisfaction, cost reduction, and general prosperity, the economics of logistics functions in the business include incoming flows of material resources from suppliers, producing goods, handling them in the warehouse, internal transportation, and then moving finished goods to the customer through external transport.

The cost structure of businesses, productivity-related issues, connection and accessibility, and population welfare are all impacted by infrastructure services, which also help to increase the nation's gross domestic product. Costs decrease as investment increases market accessibility for inputs and services, as well as the effectiveness of input supply chains and the storage and marketing of commodities, or logistics.

The interaction of the main market elements, physical infrastructure, conditions brought about by sectoral policies and regulations, and market characteristics— determine the availability, effectiveness, and efficiency of infrastructure services. When it comes to efficiently providing inventories, "logistics" is the term that comes to mind. This concept is linked to two basic ideas: (a) that it is supported by infrastructure and transport services, and (b) that such conception implies the idea of integration, allowing an efficient disposition of transport infrastructure and related services, maximizing their contribution to the improvement of economic growth (Easterly, 2005).

9.5.1 THE VALUE OF TRANSPORTATION INFRASTRUCTURE TO THE ECONOMY

The foundation and growth of a country are based on transportation, and economic development depends heavily on the transportation infrastructure. Transportation system development occurs in a socioeconomic setting. While physical capital is the emphasis of development plans and initiatives, recent years have seen a better balance by integrating human capital challenges. Infrastructures cannot function efficiently without proper operation and maintenance. At the same time, a solid infrastructure is necessary for economic activity. The fact that many transportation-related operations are very transactional and service-oriented emphasizes the complicated relationship between the sector's needs for physical and human resources. For instance, efficient logistics depend on management skills and infrastructure (Rodrigue, 2020).

In every nation, transportation continues to be crucial to development. Inadequate transportation infrastructure has an influence on productivity by encouraging poor market integration and lowering export levels (Fink, 2002).

Infrastructure investments could increase economic growth by lowering enterprise transportation costs (Jacoby and Minten, 2009). The roads in the United States affect both domestic and foreign trade, and good transportation infrastructure can have a favorable impact on the economy by promoting market integration and regional trade (Duranton, 2014). Thus, the transport industry is a significant part of the economy and an important tool for development because it makes extensive use of infrastructure. This is especially true in the context of a global economy where employment prospects are more closely linked to the movement of people, goods, and information and communication technologies. There is a clear correlation between the amount and caliber of transportation infrastructure and the degree of economic development. High growth is generally related to a proper transportation network and solid infrastructure. An effective transportation network can lead to the benefits of economic and social development such as increased job opportunities, global market accessibility, and investments.

9.5.2 DRIVING FORCES FOR THE DEVELOPMENT OF TRANSPORTATION SYSTEMS

Transportation systems grow to interact at various scales that play a significant role at the national level under the impact of many causes such as environmental, historical, technological, political, and economic factors. Environmental factors include hydrography, geomorphology, climate and oceanic masses. Historical factors include cultural and settlement patterns, urban system, Colonialism/Imperialism and globalization. Technological factors consist of roads, railways and canals, corridors and sea routes, and air transport and telecommunications. Whereas, political factors consist of taxations and regulations, trade agreements and multilateral agreements (WTO). And finally, economic factors are responsible for employment and distributions, modal competitions markets and interdependency and comparative advantages (Rodrigue, 2020).

ROAD INFRASTRUCTURE

Solid road infrastructure is very important for commerce and businesses, as better road infrastructure helps the country export more commodities and save on transportation expenses, especially when it comes to getting cargo to ports and airports on schedule.

Inland freight routes are used to transport cargo to seaports and airports, and their efficiency is important for timely deliveries, particularly of sensitive commodities. Roads have developed into an essential form of transportation that goes beyond a nation's socioeconomic needs, particularly for nations that rely heavily on trade agreements, like Mexico. The risk of transporting products to ports and borders for extra-regional trade also exists in other regions, such as Central America (Carballo, Schaur, and Volpe, 2017). Low-quality roads could result in greater fuel prices and longer travel times, which would increase the cost of transportation (Celbis, Nijkamp, and Poot, 2014).

AIRPORT INFRASTRUCTURE

Airport infrastructure includes all facilities, including runways, terminals, aprons, taxiways, centralized ground handling infrastructure, and any other structures that directly support the supply of airport services by the airport to airlines and other service providers. Therefore, airport infrastructure must be secure, useful, and reasonably priced for airlines, travelers, and cargo to operate profitably in every country. Airport infrastructure in emerging markets is different from that in developed nations. While there are many airports in developing nations, they also have problems with poor quality, a lack of commercial services, and a skilled labor force. These elements, according to the WB, have an impact on the exportation of time-sensitive goods and the flow of intermediate inputs between production networks.

The role of air transport infrastructure in the transfer of products has increased. Airport extensions have been directly linked to various economic growth factors, such as on-time delivery and changes in production networks (Button et al., 2010), bolstering the relationship between airport extensions and economic development.

RAILWAY INFRASTRUCTURE

Long-term economic growth is positively impacted by railway infrastructure. Rail modes are one of the most effective means to move huge quantities of manufactured goods and commodities and provide economies of scale for passenger transport. Railroads are an effective inland transportation method for moving large freight over long distances. Railroads provide more advantages due to economies of scale that facilitate producers' easier access to inputs, raw materials, and intermediate goods (Aritua, 2019).

Investing in rapid rail transit infrastructure is crucial for expanding public transportation options and lowering costs. Also, it creates additionally connected enterprises through interregional connectivity, which adds value. This encourages the creation of new jobs and opportunities, which improves interregional development and the general expansion of the national economy.

9.5.3 THE EFFECT OF TRANSPORTATION COSTS ON ECONOMIC GROWTH

International trade, as well as the organization of economic development, are both significantly impacted by transportation expenses. A 10% increase in transport costs results in a more than 20% decrease in trade volumes, according to empirical data.

Half of the variance in transportation costs may be attributed to the overall caliber of transportation infrastructure. In a market where transportation is a service that may be bid on, transportation prices are impacted by the individual rates of transportation providers or the percentage of the transportation expenses that are passed on to customers (Rodrigue, 2020).

In general, cost-effective transportation lowers expenses across various economic sectors, whereas ineffective transportation raises these expenses. In addition, the effects of transportation may occur unexpectedly or without any predetermined outcome. For instance, providing customers with free or inexpensive transportation infrastructure frequently has unintended consequences, such as congestion. Congestion, however, is also a sign of an expanding economy as infrastructure and capacity struggle to keep up with the escalating transportation needs. It is impossible to ignore the significant social and environmental strain that transportation bears.

9.5.4 Cost-effective Transportation Management

Costs associated with transportation include depreciation of transportation equipment, warehouse costs, material, and energy use costs, employee salaries associated with transportation operations, and expenses associated with outside services like transportation, loading, replacement, taxes, and transport fees. 40% to 50% of the entire transportation expenditures go toward energy costs, 25% go toward maintenance, and 20% go toward personnel pay for transport operations (Krakowiak-Bal et al., 2016).

Several categories can be used to categorize transportation costs. The fixed expenses have the distinctive property of remaining constant in a total volume regardless of the level of activity (Chivu et al., 2015). The costs of insurance and registration of transport means are also included in the fixed costs of transportation. Depreciation is determined using time-based depreciation methods. Understanding fixed expenses is crucial for calculating the viability threshold, or the least amount of activity (or revenue) required to turn a profit for the business. The costs of gasoline, lubricants, and other supplies necessary to maintain vehicles are included in the variable transport costs, together with toll prices and the wages of the staff members responsible for loading, unloading, monitoring, and transporting goods. When there are additional alternatives, it's critical to consider the variable costs (Nielsen et al., 2015).

The Transport Costing Method, which is based on daily cost inclusion for each vehicle, is one of the available strategies for paying for transportation expenses. The number of cost units in transportation is determined by multiplying four variables: the quantity being transported, the number of vehicles, the distance being traveled, and the number of days. The following can be noted as potential targets for determining transport costs:

- control of operating and running costs, as well as a reduction in fuel and other resource waste;
- compared the expense of operating personal vehicles to other modes of transportation;
- enables providing hiring rate quotations to third parties who request transportation services;
- the calculation of idle vehicle costs and wasted running time

Two factors affect the cost of transportation:
- Total distribution capacity: The number and size of the available transportation options are referred to as the capacity, which directly affects the fixed costs.
- Distance traveled: The number of vehicles that will be used for transportation depends on the overall distance (expressed in kilometers) (Abdallah, 2004).

In addition, there are two categories of characteristics that affect transport costs:
- Those that are connected to the product itself (such as weight, size, and value).
- Those that are related to the market (such as clients' locations, such as whether they are in a rural area or next to a traffic port).

9.5.5 REAL-WORLD CASES

GOVERNMENT INITIATIVES FOR THE LOGISTICS INDUSTRY

Digitalization in India has gotten a big boost thanks to the government's "Digital India" initiatives and its policies. Due to government programs such as the "Make in India" campaign and the "Digital India" program, the logistics sector in India is developing at a very rapid rate.

MULTI-MODAL LOGISTICS PARKS (MMLPS)

Multi-Modal Logistics Parks (MMLPs) are an initiative by the Government of India that aims at improving the country's logistics industry by lowering total freight costs, reducing vehicle pollution and congestion, and lowering warehousing expenses. An MMLP, according to the government, is a freight-handling facility that has access to multiple modes of transportation and includes automated warehouses, specialized storage solutions like cold storage, facilities for mechanical material handling and inter-modal transfer container terminals, and bulk and break-bulk cargo terminals. MMLPs contain inter-modal connectivity, such as a dedicated rail line, access from notable highways or expressways to provide commercial vehicle mobility, and connectivity to an airport or a port (or inland waterway terminal). Customs clearance with bonded storage yards, quarantine zones, testing facilities, and warehousing management services will also be available in logistics parks (Kumar, 2022).

DEDICATED FREIGHT CORRIDOR (DFC)

The Dedicated Freight Corridor Corporation of India was launched in 2006 under the Indian Companies Act 1956. DFCCIL is a Special Purpose Vehicle created under the administrative control of the Ministry of Railways to plan and build dedicated freight corridors and raise funds for their construction, maintenance, and operation. The Dedicated Freight Corridor Corporation of India Limited (DFCC) is responsible for the construction of two world-class freight corridors: the Western Dedicated Freight Corridor and the Eastern Dedicated

Freight Corridor. This will help in the reduction of greenhouse gas (GHG) emissions connected with vehicle transport, as well as cost savings and the ability to travel more quickly (Banerjee, 2022).

INCREASED USE OF DFC ON INDIAN RAILWAYS

The DFC's long-term goal is to run longer, heavier trains. To accomplish this, the sections were planned with a long-term outlook in mind, and the foundation can support a 32-ton axle load while the tracks and sleeper density were intended for a 25-ton axle load. The DFC will benefit the rail sector as well as the economy and the environment (Banerjee, 2022).

MAKE IN INDIA

Make in India is an initiative established by the Indian government on September 25, 2014, to encourage enterprises to produce their products in India. With programs like Make in India, India's logistics industry is playing a larger role in overall growth. This has the potential to dramatically increase the country's economy. India is attracting large-scale manufacturing investments. Over the next five years, Make in India will add more than $20 billion to the Indian logistics sector, because 20 of the 25 key industries in Make in India are heavily reliant on logistics (Syal, 2016).

These government efforts have the potential to revolutionize the logistics industry in India. As a result, international investors are now aware of the benefits of funding Indian logistics companies, networks, and infrastructure.

9.6   CHAPTER CONCLUSION

The future of the logistics industry is being aided by advancements in digital technology and numerous global government initiatives. Thus, the adoption of advanced digital technologies in logistics will need strong implementation and coordination, high levels of engagement from various actors and rivals along the supply chain, as well as a shared willingness to invest. Additionally, logistics is a vast and difficult industry that needs a great deal of accurate data to be successful. To keep the operations on schedule, forecasting demand, shipping schedules, and inventory should be managed efficiently.

EXERCISES

1. What part does digitalization play in the logistics sector?
2. What are the applications of AI in the logistics industry?
3. Define the term "Telematics." What are its benefits for the logistics industry?
4. What are important digital technologies used in the logistics industry?
5. What are the factors responsible for the economic growth of the logistics industry?

6. Why is it vital to develop the transportation infrastructure?
7. What would happen if transportation costs rose in the logistics sector?
8. What benefits are there for the economy from low transportation costs?

REFERENCES

Abdallah, H. (2004) *Guidelines for accessing costs in logistics system: an example of transport cost analysis*, Arlington, John Snow, Inc.

Aritua, B. (2019) *The retail challenge for emerging economies: how to regain modal share*, Washington, DC: World Bank, https://doi.org.10.1596/978-1-4648-1381-8

Banerjee, Dr. Kallal (2022) 'Dedicated Freight Corridor (DFC): current scenario and social economic benefit-an analytical study', July 20, http://dx.doi.org/10.2139/ssrn4168041

BasuMallick, C. (2020) *'What is telematics? Meaning, working, types, benefits and applications in 2022'*, (Last updated: 20 August 2022) Available at:www.spiceworks.com/tech/iot/articles/what-is-telematics/ (Accessed: 02 November 2022).

Button, K., Doh, S., and Yuan, J. (2010) 'The role of small airports in economic development', *Journal of Airport Management*, 4(2), pp. 125–136, ISSN: 1750–1938.

Carballo, J., Schaur, G., and Volpe, C. (2017) *'Transportation and trade interactions: A trade facilitation perspective'*, In B.A. Blonigen and W.W. Wilson (Eds.), Handbook of International trade and transportation, pp. 422–450, Elgar Publishing.

Celbis, M., Nijkamp, P. and Poot, J. (2014) *'Infrastructure and trade: A meta-analysis'*, *Region*, 1(1), pp. 25–65, https://doi.org.10.18335/region.v1i1.25

Chiv, L. Ciutacu, C. and Georgescu, L. (2015) 'Household income in Romania. A challenge to economic and social cohesion', *Procedia Economics and Finance*, 22, pp. 398–401. https://doi.org/10.1016/s2212-5671(15)00310-X

Duranton, G., Morrow, P.M. and Turner, MA. (2014) 'Roads and trade: evidence from the US', *Journal of Review of Economic Studies*, vol. 81, p. 681.

Easterly, W. (2005) 'National policies and economic growth', *Handbook of Economic Growth*, vol. 1. A, Edited by P. Aghion and S. Durlauf.

Fink, C. (2002) *'Transport services: reducing barriers to trade'*, Global economic prospects and the developing countries, International Bank for Reconstruction and Development, The World Bank, pp. 97–127, ISBN 0-8213-4996-1.

Jacoby, H.G. and Minten, B. (2009) 'On measuring the benefits of lower transport costs', January, *Journal of Development Economics*, vol. 89, pp. 28–38, 724.

Kalaivani, C. and Indumathi, G. (2018) 'Applications of Internet of Things (IoT) in logistics industry', *International Journal of Research and Analytical Review*, vol. 5, no. 3, (E-ISSN 2348-1269 P-ISSN 2349-5138).

Kudtarkar, A and Shaikh, D. (2021) 'Application of machine learning techniques in supply chain management', *International Journal of Creative Research Thoughts*, vol. 9, no. 7, July, ISSN: 2320-2882.

Krakowiak-Bal, A. and Sokora, J. (2016) *'The Logistic Cost Analysis in Agribusiness- Case Study of Food Sector Company'*, vol. 4(3), pp. 1535–1545, doi: https://dx.medra.org/10.14597/infraeco.2016.4.3.11

Kumar, N. (2022) *'Multi-modal logistic park set to reduce cost of logistics in India'*, (Updated on 03 December 2022), Available at: www.sundayguardianlive.com/business/multi-modal-logistics-parks-set-reduce-cost-logistics-india (Accessed: 17 December 2022).

Nielsen, L. Mitchell, F. and Norreklit, H. (2015) *'Management accounting and decision making'*, Two case studies of outsourcing, Accounting Forum, pp. 64–83, https://doi.org/10.1016/j.accfor.2014.10.005

Rodrigue, J.P. (2020) *The geography of transport systems*, 5th Edition, New York: Routledge, ISBN 978-00367-36463-2, https://doi.org/10.4324/9780429346323

Shaikh, N. (2022) *'Significance of fleet management in logistic industry'*, Last updated (May 20, 2022). Available at: www.peerbits.com/blogs/signigicance-of-fleet-managemnet-solutions-for-logistics-indutry.htm (Accessed: 02 November 2022).

Syal, A. (2016) *'Six government initiative that have major impact on Indian logistics sector'*, July 16. Available at: www.business-standard.com/content/manufacturing-industry/six-government-initiatives-that-have-major-impact-on-indian-logistic-sector-116071600466_1.html (Accessed: 10 December 2022).

10 E-Commerce Digitalization

SUMMARY

In this chapter, we will discuss the impact of digitization on economic growth and its potential for creating employment opportunities in the country. We will also study the importance of digitization in the present digital world responsible to integrate the economy by creating digital markets. The chapter also focuses on real-world case of developing country India, how internet and smartphone penetration in India has played a significant role in the growth of the E-Commerce market in a country. In addition, we'll look at how advances in digital technology contributed significantly to the global E-Commerce industry's expansion and how the COVID-19 pandemic has shown that these businesses must digitize their sectors if they are to face the problems of the global market going forward. Readers will also comprehend the effect of logistics on the growth of E-Commerce. Also, the idea of mobile commerce will be covered, along with its benefits and drawbacks.

10.1 INTRODUCTION

"Digital shopping," also known as online shopping, is a form of electronic commerce that enables customers to purchase products or services directly from a seller over the internet using a web browser or by using digital networks or mobile applications from anywhere at any time. Shoppers may typically use "search" features to locate unique models, brands, or products in online stores. As a result of digital freedom in the shopping industry, Customers can shop on the website using a variety of computers and devices, including desktop computers, laptops, tablets, and smartphones.

The convenience of not having to go to the store and the time saved bargain seeking are both advantages and crazes for digital shopping. The reason for the acceptance of this technique in many developing and developed countries is that they have developed attractive online websites with user-friendly interfaces, large online stores with new fashion, easy payment methods, cash-on-delivery, no bounds on quantity or quality, and so on.

Digital shopping factors include the following:

- website attractiveness;
- website service quality; and
- website security.

FIGURE 10.1 Best shopping applications.

10.1.1 DIGITAL SHOPPING APPLICATIONS

An application called a "shopping app" enables users to explore and purchase goods or services from a retailer or service provider. There are many shopping apps available today that have a big impact on businesses throughout the world.

Customers now have a wide range of options for product offerings. At the time and location of their choosing, people can purchase whatever they choose. The days when brick-and-mortar retailers created a monopoly on the goods and the consumers suffered are long gone. They are well aware of the abundance of possibilities available today.

The best shopping applications are given in Figure 10.1.

Among other shopping apps, Amazon is one of the largest E-Commerce sites in the sector, and it is also one of the most user-friendly.

10.2 THE CONCEPT OF E-COMMERCE

Business-to-business (B2B), business-to-consumer (B2C), and M-Commerce (mobile commerce) are all terms described as E-Commerce.

The term "E-Commerce" has been defined by numerous academics and researchers explained below:

E-Commerce, is the exchange of money for goods and services over the internet. The four possible definitions of E-Commerce (Kalakota and Whintons, 1997):

- E-Commerce is the transmission of goods, services, or money via computer networks, communication channels, or any other kind of electronic communication.
- The use of technology to automate work and business transactions is known as E-Commerce.

- A tool that responds to the need for businesses, customers, and management to reduce service costs while enhancing the quality of goods and services and speeding up service delivery.
- The capacity to buy and sell goods and data over the internet and through other online services.

Rahman, M. et al. (2017) found that individuals in India are most likely to buy and sell goods and services online, or, to put it another way, we can say that people in Indian society are now modernized through the use of secure and convenient E-Commerce.

All forms of economic transactions involving both organizations and individuals, that are dependent upon the electronic processing and transmission of data, including text, voice, and visual image, are referred to as "e-commerce" (Diwan and Sharma, 2000).

10.2.1 Types of E-Commerce

There are four types of E-Commerce—B2B E-Commerce, B2C E-Commerce, B2G E-Commerce, and G2B E-Commerce—as shown in Figure 10.2.

B2B E-Commerce: E-Commerce between businesses, such as between a manufacturer and a wholesaler or a wholesaler and a retailer, is known as B2B E-Commerce. Most analysts believe that B2B E-Commerce will continue to expand more quickly than other categories.

B2C E-Commerce: It is defined as commerce where there is a transaction between the business and the customer. Similar to when you purchase things from an online retailer.

B2G E-Commerce: This term is used to describe trade between businesses and the government. It is based on the usage of the internet for government-related tasks including licensing and public procurement.

G2B E-Commerce: Instead of private persons, government-to-business (G2B) interactions take place online between local and central government and the commercial business sector (G2C).

10.2.2 Role of Digitalization in E-Commerce Markets

The twenty-first century has been dubbed the "golden age of technology." Smartphones and computers are undeniably the most significant assets that the present generation

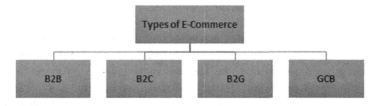

FIGURE 10.2 Types of E-Commerce.

owns, with significant advancements occurring every year. Furthermore, it has resulted in the formation of important markets, commonly referred to as E-Commerce, in nearly every developed and emerging region of the world. E-Commerce's contribution to fast-emerging regions like India has been a hot topic of debate around the world, with India being regarded as one of the most potential markets in the future. E-Commerce has grown in importance as a platform for small and major businesses throughout the world to sell their products to new markets.

Increased internet penetration, rapid technology adoption, and high sales of technical gadgets such as smartphones and tablets globally have resulted in a large online client base and an unparalleled E-Commerce boom. People are now using the internet and their smartphones to order groceries, clothing, jewelry, furniture, and ordering food by just sitting in their homes.

The use of information and technology has become very important to stay ahead in today's highly competitive market. The younger generation around the world is increasingly using the internet, which presents the potential for online shops. Therefore, most businesses have begun to use the internet to reduce marketing costs and, as a result, lower the price of their products and services on the market. Thanks to the freedom of digitization, consumers save time and effort by buying online because of the cheap internet connections. Many companies are also making use of the internet to convey, communicate, and disseminate information, as well as to sell products, solicit feedback, and run customer satisfaction surveys.

10.2.3 THE WORLD'S FASTEST-GROWING DIGITAL MARKET

Due to the growth in internet usage and increase in smartphone penetration, many countries around the world are adopting advanced digital technology for economic growth. ICT has proven to be a general-purpose technology that has grown integral to the business models of companies operating across the economy as technology has developed and costs of ICT have continued to decline. Today, companies from many industries may design and construct their operational models around technological capabilities to increase flexibility and efficiency and broaden their market reach. Companies in various industries have altered the way they conduct their operations by utilizing improvements in communications and data processing to reduce transaction costs and broaden their reach to international markets (OECD, 2014). Additionally, adoption of innovative digital technologies and acceleration of digitization has allowed for the introduction of the digital goods in the global E-Commerce markets.

China dominated the global E-Commerce sector in 2019. With a market size of 738 billion USD, China was in first place. In second position with a $542 billion E-Commerce market was the United States. One of the largest B2C E-Commerce marketplaces was the United States. Cross-border E-Commerce has increased in the United States, and many companies use this global channel to entice new customers and sales. Japan made an $89 billion contribution to global E-Commerce. With E-Commerce worth $79 billion, the UK was ranked fourth. In the E-Commerce market, Germany, South Korea, France, and India ranked fifth, sixth, seventh, and eighth, respectively. The Indian market is the largest emerging E-Commerce market in developing nations. High internet and smartphone penetration, as well as the majority of payments being made through mobile devices, are the primary drivers of the nation's E-Commerce growth (Merzlyakova, Ershova, and Bridskiy, 2021).

10.2.4 FACTORS FOR E-COMMERCE GROWTH

The following factors have contributed significantly to the growth of digital shopping in the country:

Faster and cheap internet: Better broadband connections, such as 3G and 4G, have offered consumers better internet access and also cheaper data tariff plans. All these factors have compelled people to spend more time online. A significant portion of people have broadband internet subscriptions, and the number of users of 3G and 4G is growing across the nation.

Increased smartphone users in many developed and developing countries around the world. There has been a drastic increase in the number of smartphone users and this is quickly expanding due to the cheaper and more affordable data internet plans.

Time saver: Unlike markets, there is no need to run around searching over the city and spend hours doing so. With just a few clicks, one may save time and order your favorite goods anytime.

Cheaper rates and discounts: In online shopping, customers who are on a tight budget will benefit from the exciting discounted rates (for e.g. free shipping), exciting offers and year-end sales, greatest deals on a variety of products, especially during festival seasons.

Cash on delivery (COD): This service is only offered in India, and it has proven to be convenient. This service means that a customer can pay their bill at the time of receiving their products. Customers who are hesitant to use debit or credit cards have a free choice to use this service.

Home delivery and return policies: Convenient choices such as faster delivery and return policies are also available within a particular timeframe and have been well received by customers if there is a damaged product issued.

Growth of warehousing and logistics infrastructure: The warehouse and logistical infrastructure have significantly improved over the past few years as a result of innovative digital technologies implemented in these sectors. The expansion of these sectors is likewise being encouraged by the government with numerous incentives.

Increased mobile applications: Today almost all E-Commerce sites now have mobile apps through which customers may quickly and easily visit the company's website for quick and easy service at any time anywhere.

Emergence of M-Commerce: Mobile device use is rising daily, and customers are starting to pay attention to mobile financial services at a slow but steady rate. Globally, the use of mobile technology, mobile internet connectivity, and M-Commerce is expanding quickly; nevertheless, growth rates differ greatly by economic region.

Internet content accessible in local languages: With the freedom of digitization, content on the internet is accessible in many local languages; as a result, there are no language barriers to accessing the internet. This makes it simple for individuals to access the internet in their native tongue.

Digital freedom helps in innovation, the convenience of working, new career prospects, and economic growth across the world. It also contributes to system transparency and thus the E-Commerce industry is transforming the business across the world. The rapid digital transformation of businesses and trades has not spared the sector.

Because of the superior capital and innovative digital technology used, a digitally empowered economy develops considerably more quickly, effectively, and efficiently. And as a digitally empowered country, it may attain massive growth rates and compete with developed countries if used properly and skillfully.

10.3   CURRENT TRENDS AND FUTURE PROSPECTS OF E-COMMERCE

With the freedom of digitization today, advanced digital technologies used in e-commerce, such as big data, robotics, 3D printing, blockchain technologies, and artificial intelligence have a significant impact on its development.

The growth of E-Commerce has been greatly done by the digitalization process. Only having a connection to the internet is required to use e-services and make purchases at any time of day or night from anywhere in the world. Websites are increasingly becoming crucial avenues for retailers around the world, and through them, online merchants offer accurate and current information while also launching dependable and secure information systems to guarantee good service provision and delivery (Kalia and Prateek, 2017).

10.3.1   DIGITAL PLATFORMS IN E-COMMERCE

The software and technology used to synchronize and streamline IT systems and company activities are known as a "digital platform." The operational and consumer engagement backbone of a firm is its digital platform.

A digital platform is composed of several elements, typically a data-ingestion engine, a machine-learning transactional engine to perform tasks or rule-based activities, an analytical engine, and increasingly, an AI engine, APIs, or tools that allow digital platforms to talk to other software, and tools monitoring regulatory compliance. To improve user experiences, these elements must be merged and coordinated (Bendor-Samuel, 2018).

Instead of a world driven by processes, digital platforms enable a data-driven world. The end-to-end business process is managed by the digital platform in order to provide partners, customers, and workers with an enhanced experience.

A digital platform is essentially a cloud-based implementation that uses AI and machine learning to contextualize and personalize each action a user takes on the platform. Big data technologies are used to store a variety of real-time data, and APIs are used to "converse" with this vast, heterogeneous big data.

Although the internet itself serves as the basis for designing and launching platforms for all E-Commerce websites, a number of technology companies also known as "BigTech giants" in spoken language are now emerging as infrastructure providers, enabling other businesses to build their own company portals and deliver services and goods using cloud infrastructure. As an illustration, Amazon Web Services (AWS) offers the digital infrastructure and resources on which other platforms are developed. The Google Cloud Platform (GCP), which is likewise one of the market's fastest-growing cloud computing platforms, is similar. Other noteworthy participants in the market for "platforms for platforms" are IBM Cloud and Alibaba Cloud.

Types of Platforms and Business Models

Based on the services provided, various researchers have divided digital platforms into a number of categories, including (Wirtz, 2019):

- Platforms for search (e.g., Google, Bing, and Yahoo)
- Platforms for payments Platforms (e.g., Alipay, Visa, and PayPal)
- Platforms for development (e.g., app stores and gaming consoles)
- Platforms for retail (e.g., Amazon, eBay)
- Platforms for communication (e.g., WhatsApp, Skype, WeChat)
- Platforms for social networking (e.g., Facebook, Twitter, Pinterest)
- Platforms for matching (e.g., Tinder, e-Harmony, and Task Rabbit)
- Platforms for content and reviews (e.g., YouTube, TripAdvisor)
- Platform for booking (e.g., booking.com, Expedia, and Pagoda)

10.3.2   DIGITAL TECHNOLOGIES IN E-COMMERCE GROWTH

Digitalization has now transformed how firms transact internationally and how resources are allocated to the production of goods and services. The growth rate of the economy has increased dramatically as a result of advanced digital technologies. Economic growth is being driven by the internet and digital devices. Today in this digital world, there are a large number of small- and medium-sized businesses that offer E-Commerce and e-services (SMEs).

Worldwide, the E-Commerce industry is developing as a result of the country's fast-expanding smartphone and internet user populations. Nowadays, E-Commerce traders offer a wide range of services, from everyday essentials to logistics, which aids in the expansion of the E-Commerce industry throughout the world. Figure 10.3 shows the advance digital technologies used in E-Commerce industries worldwide.

Big Data Applications in E-Commerce

Online shops must fully utilize technology to attract, keep, and grow their consumer base. By creating plans through big data analytics, they may give customers a sense of exclusivity and foster brand loyalty (Wu and Lin, 2018). Businesses are now able to gather a lot of consumer data thanks to the growing acceptance and use of smartphones, which can then be used to conduct advertising and marketing campaigns that are specifically targeted at the right customers.

Companies in the E-Commerce industry have to manage a huge volume of data in their databases. Therefore, volume, velocity, variety, and veracity are a combination of the four Vs that best describe big data. Big data technologies not only process

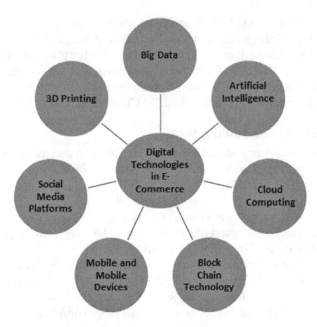

FIGURE 10.3   Digital technologies in E-Commerce.

massive amounts of data in various forms, but they also accelerate the process. Every second, more and more data is produced by the diverse E-Commerce components; in order to get the most value out of this data, it must also be analyzed holistically. Data regarding consumers, suppliers, retailers, goods, procedures, costs, logistics, and many other aspects of enterprises are expanding more quickly than ever. In such a scenario, using big data and big data analytics to store, update, use, process, and distribute these expanding business insights becomes relevant.

Big data analytics is the act of looking through huge and diverse data sets to find hidden patterns, undiscovered connections, and other valuable information that can aid organizations in making better business decisions and predicting future trends. Predictive analytics, data mining, statistics, artificial intelligence, and other types of tools are all included in big data analytics. The science of big data analytics, in conjunction with intelligent and predictive processing made possible by AI and ML algorithms, enables the complicated study of big data.

Artificial Intelligence in E-Commerce

Artificial intelligence is widely used in almost every sector worldwide for its development and increasing productivity. Artificial intelligence has the potential to gather and process vast amounts of data to make actionable decisions. This technology is also being used in E-Commerce to detect trends based on browsing, order background, credit checks, account records, and other factors.

Artificial intelligence is allowing E-Commerce platforms to use vast datasets about customer purchase behavior and product search trends, which is allowing

E-Commerce enterprises to become closer to their customers. Online shoppers can enjoy tailored purchasing experiences thanks to self-learning AI algorithms.

Life experiences, from daily activities to important decision-making, are being rapidly transformed by AI and its key component, ML. Rule-based extractions on heterogeneous, multidisciplinary data gathered across the whole value chain of enterprises are made possible by AI and ML.

Impact of Artificial Intelligence in E-Commerce

The growth of every business now depends heavily on its customer service. While businesses can now offer quicker sales, they also do not offer 24/7 customer support. A chatbot is an artificial intelligence assistant (AIA) whose main function is to use a NLP system to automatically respond to customer queries, carry out simple speech instructions, and offer products. Chatbots can help customers find the right products, check if they're available, compare them, and eventually make purchases. If a customer has any issues or queries, they may also use the Chatbot to get in touch with the right support staff. Even in the absence of a person to handle client concerns, AI is helping organizations provide proactive customer care across numerous outlets (Song et al., 2019).

A recommendation system is based on a platform for machine learning algorithms known as a recommendation engine. AI algorithms can be used to implement deep learning, mathematical programming, consumer behavior modeling and interpretation, analysis of big data sets, and prediction of which products are most likely to attract buyers.

A logistics production method is known as "intelligent logistics." It uses information technology to make machinery and controls intelligent, enabling mechanical equipment to take the position of people. Intelligent logistics improve operational performance and service quality compared to traditional techniques of logistics.

AI in E-Commerce is currently transforming how small businesses run their warehouses. Automated commodity pick-and-pack activities that don't need any breaks between works. Robots powered by AI can work around the clock, every day of the week. Because AI robots can position and retrieve them as needed because they can identify their location, using AI solutions in the warehouse helps reduce errors. Robots may also perform dangerous tasks for the safety of warehouse workers to protect from the risks.

AI in E-Commerce has improved visual search capabilities and helps you find products that are related to what you're looking for.

Blockchain Technology

Since it was created to store transactional data, blockchain technology fits in well with E-Commerce. Any distinguishing action that necessitates a fixed record, such as those connected to payment and order fulfillment, can be included in this data; it is not necessary that it be financial. Blockchain technology can benefit E-Commerce in the following ways:

- helps in the decision-making process
- promoting openness and reliable data

- reducing blind spots in the distribution of goods
- accessing the suppliers' inventory: understanding the flow of work between businesses
- providing real-time data accessibility
- synchronizing demand planning and forecasting along the supply chains
- increasing traceability and standard compliance
- facilitating billing management

Cloud Computing in E-Commerce

Cloud computing benefits E-Commerce by giving the business a large, robust digital presence. The following are its benefits (Aydin, N., 2015):

Scalability: Such cloud services, which are commonly referred to as "elastic," enable a business to quickly scale up and satisfy seasonal or promotional demand spikes. An E-Commerce business may respond to changing consumer demands and conditions thanks to cloud computing.

Trust: In the early days of the internet, one of the biggest issues facing early adopters of E-Commerce turned out to be a human problem: trust. It required time for them to construct a collection of online credentials and gain customers' trust before they could start an online buying experience.

Speed: For the growth of an E-Commerce business, speed is crucial to keeping clients interested. Greater bandwidth, storage, and computational capacity are provided through cloud computing.

Use of Mobile Phones and Mobile Devices

In this present age of digitization, everyone has smartphones, and anyone who lives a busy life today wants to be able to access services quickly. These services might be as commonplace as buying groceries or clothing online, paying utility bills, or even purchasing and investing in fixed and moveable assets using smartphones and other portable devices. The importance of smartphones and mobile devices and the convenience they provide in our daily lives cannot be understated. Mobile-based solutions have increased and grown as a result of increasing internet usage and the widespread acceptance of mobile devices.

Brands that have opted for mobile advertising are gaining attention. Online merchants have taken note of the potential growth in future mobile phone online buyers. Additionally, as customers become more accustomed to browsing and purchasing on mobile devices, they are now more receptive to receiving messages from companies on their phones. Businesses are putting strategies into place to incorporate mobile into their marketing campaigns, but first, they must work to optimize their legacy websites for mobile to better serve their customers.

Use of Social Media Platforms

E-Commerce and social media have a significant impact on the company. In this digital age, the amount of time spent on various social networking platforms like Twitter, Facebook, etc. is increasing day by day, and approximately 80% of people utilize social media. Social networking platforms have been developed to advertise various brands. Today, popular social networks like Facebook, Twitter, Instagram, and others have proliferated on the internet, opening up new opportunities for customer and consumer connection.

Today, almost all big corporations have a social media presence. Today, both established and startup businesses use social networking sites to market their brands, goods, and services, as well as collect vital customer feedback. In fact, social media interaction has almost entirely replaced traditional metrics for measuring how well a corporation treats its customers. Small or home-based enterprises that just use their Facebook or Instagram pages to do business are already very prevalent. Also, social media makes it simple for companies to give value to customers before asking for anything in return.

Typically, businesses apply different marketing tactics to increase their social media presence and to continuously promote their goods and services, which aids in turning visitors into followers and subsequently into customers. Additionally, social media platforms have the potential to have material or advertising spread more quickly than any other platform and influence individuals to act in ways that are advantageous to business owners. Social media, however, has an impact on users of all ages and races. For instance, while it is successful with various demographics, it is particularly successful with younger generations (Felix, Rauschnabel and Hinsch, 2016).

Due to the popularity of social media, marketing and advertising tactics have changed from relying on mass-market media like radio and television to the social platform. Today, every big company and brand boasts of having a sizable fan base and following across the majority of social media platforms, including Facebook, Twitter, YouTube, Instagram, etc. Platforms for social media not only save money but also bring producers and consumers closer together.

Marketers and advertisers are constantly searching for various methods to better understand clients and determine their propensity toward various products. To do this, a lot of data on the clients and their preferred method of product purchase must be obtained. Social media could be used to acquire data on online users that could then be further examined to track consumer behavior. To increase sales of their goods and services, numerous businesses use social media sites like Twitter and Facebook. Using social media in E-Commerce has emerged as a popular strategy for businesses looking to capitalize on the social interactions that take place online between customers.

As a result, social media contributes to the expansion of the E-Commerce sector in a number of ways:

Helps in the creation of brand communication: The different communication channels that social media platforms offer for users to interact with one another and a brand are covered, including chat, messaging, video, email, voice chat, file-sharing, blogging, and discussion groups. The marketing messages are evolving to be more sociable, entertaining, and individualized.

Popularity of blogs and social media activity: Brands have the chance to use social media on a worldwide scale as an efficient medium for marketing their goods and services. Yet, the ROI (return on investment), a crucial factor, heavily influences how well any marketing channel performs. When evaluating the efficacy of any marketing channel, the majority of marketers focus on ROI. So, the study looked at the return on investment for weblogs and how advertising through two extremely famous social networking sites, namely Facebook and Twitter, impacts their popularity and consequently raises their revenue from advertisements (Bhat, 2012).

Builds communication between business and customers: The way that businesses and their customers communicate has changed as a result of the rise of social media. Instead of communicating to each other through the media, businesses now listen to each other and engage in conversation. All businesses need to stop talking and start paying attention to how people are perceiving them online since the online consumer is also a commentator, reviewer, and publisher (Smith, 2010).

Aids in the development of brand communication: The different communication channels that social media platforms offer for users to interact with one another and a brand are covered, including chat, messaging, video, email, voice chat, file-sharing, blogging, and discussion groups. The marketing messages are evolving to be more sociable, entertaining, and individualized.

Popularity of blogs and social media activity: Brands have the chance to use social media on a worldwide scale as an efficient medium for marketing their goods and services. Yet, the ROI (return on investment), a crucial factor, heavily influences how well any marketing channel performs. When evaluating the efficacy of any marketing channel, the majority of marketers focus on ROI. So, the study looked at the return on investment for weblogs and how advertising through two extremely famous social networking sites, namely Facebook and Twitter, impacts their popularity and consequently raises their revenue from advertisements (Bhat, 2012).

Builds communication between businesses and customers: The way that businesses and their customers communicate has changed as a result of the rise of social media. Instead of communicating with each other through the media, businesses now listen to each other and engage in conversation. All businesses need to stop talking and start paying attention to how people are perceiving them online since the online consumer is also a commentator, reviewer, and publisher (Smith, 2010).

Use of 3D Printing and Additive Manufacturing

Additive manufacturing (AM) and 3D printing are two distinct phenomena. AM is a broad category of technologies rather than a single technology. Similar terminology is used to describe 3D printing, which is also known as a method that combines additive manufacturing with stereo lithography, fused deposition modeling, and selective laser sintering (Gibson, Rosen, and Stucker, 2010).

AM, also known as 3D printing technology, can benefit E-Commerce businesses in various ways by increasing production, lowering costs and inventory waste, enabling highly customized and individualized product design, etc. As an illustration, prominent shoe companies like Adidas, Nike, New Balance, and Under Armor already include AM in their business plans (Mellor, Hao, and Zhang, 2014).

AM is a promising technology as a result of the quick advancement of modern manufacturing technologies. Similar to AM, 3D printing also involves the production of actual items based on digital files that reflect their design.

10.3.3 Impact of E-Payment on E-Commerce Growth

The foundation of international E-Commerce is electronic payment services. An electronic payment system or E-Payment, commonly referred to as an E-Commerce payment system, is one that allows customers to make digital purchases without using cash or cheques. Owing to the widespread use of internet-based activities like online buying and baking, an electronic payment system is a widely used payment method. Smart cards, electronic wallet bank transfers, credit cards, bitcoin wallets, and other payment methods are available online. In contrast, there are two categories for e-payments: credit payment systems and cash payment systems.

Payment companies have become some of the fastest-growing and most valuable businesses throughout the world as digital transactions have replaced cash. All these companies are gradually moving toward cashless and paperless transactions.

Advantages of E-Payment Systems for the E-Commerce Industry

Business dynamics have altered in the digitized world where technology is continually emerging and evolving. For payers, payees, E-Commerce, banks, organizations, and governments, using the E-Payment system has several advantages. These advantages may encourage the global adoption of electronic payment systems. Faster payouts, better tracking, transparent transactions, less time spent, cost savings, and enhanced trust between vendors and purchasers are all made possible by an effective and dependable E-Payment system. Financial transactions, assimilated users, and high-quality E-Payment technology all play a role in the development and adoption of technology in the E-Payment system, which in turn shapes users' views and expectations.

The traditional payment system has been replaced with an electronic payment system that can help businesses expand successfully thanks to ongoing technological advancements. Due to their simplicity and ease of use, electronic payments have revolutionized the payment process. Also, they no longer require customers to visit banks to conduct transactions or engage in other activities. A few advantages of an electronic payment system are listed below.

Quick payments: Today everyone is busy with their jobs, relationships, finances, health, and a variety of other issues. The conventional approach is a time-consuming and stressful process because it is frequently slow and time-consuming. Due to its speed and simplicity, such as credit cards, e-cash, etc., the electronic payment system minimizes worries. By eliminating the need to visit banks and saving time and energy, electronic payments can be made through an electronic payment app from anywhere.

Increased payment security: One of any company's top priorities now that more enterprises are operating online is security. Payment security is a company's top priority in order to safeguard customer data and information from fraud and other problems. Security is one of the primary reasons why the electronic payment system is the best in the world. By offering numerous encryptions, SSL, tokenization, and other payment security measures, it offers clients a higher level of payment protection. Customers can save card information using a one-time password to avoid having to swipe their cards multiple times.

Savings on processing costs: In cost accounting, the term "processing cost" is used in industrial units to assign and collect costs. It averages the process' overall cost across all of the production branches. For instance, you require a card processor when you offer payment services to customers. This processor permits payment transactions in exchange for a high cost.

Ease and convenience: Offering ease to a customer is crucial for business since it influences whether a client chooses to interact with a brand. Experts assert that ease plays a key role in a company's expansion. Electronic payments give more security, but more crucially, they also improve customer convenience.

Lower chance of theft: It enables customers to make good purchases using card facilities and make payments afterwards. Also, it automatically collects the designated money in accordance with the regulations without bothering customers with repeated reminders and notifications for payments.

The company's finances and daily operations depend on its capital. Therefore, collecting payments in cash is extremely hazardous and unsafe. Due to the steadily rising crime rate, there are many risks associated with being stolen and even depositing money into a bank account. Due to the safe and secure nature of electronic payment systems, the risk of theft has decreased. Moreover, it provides all transaction data by day's end.

Transparency is a crucial component for any business; customers are more concerned with and eager to preserve their privacy. Customers will stop being interested in them and go on to another business where they feel more comfortable disclosing their personal information. For a better user experience, the electronic payment system offers you data on transactions to enhance transparency.

Improved user experience: A company must provide a better user experience to draw in customers. Electronic payment is the cutting-edge technology that provides a superior user experience in terms of a seamless transaction, eliminates barriers to purchase like long lines or a limited quantity, incurs no additional costs, and more.

10.3.4 REAL-WORLD CASES (1–2)

REAL-WORLD CASE 1

E-COMMERCE IN INDIA

The global E-Commerce market continues to grow and expand. Several innovative digital technologies have altered E-Commerce for more than a decade in India. Indian E-Commerce startups like Flipkart, Amazon India, Reliance, Jabong, Snapdeal, and Myntra have produced a new success story among global players like eBay and Amazon.

Customers' increased use of smartphones and similar gadgets has been one of the main causes of growth in E-Commerce shopping activity. As a result, many enterprises have started E-Commerce operations and are doing well in the market.

POPULAR E-COMMERCE COMPANIES IN INDIA

- Amazon India
- Flipkart
- Paytm
- Myntra
- Zomato
- Alibaba
- Sanpdeal
- IndiaMART
- Book My Show

E-COMMERCE MARKET SIZE IN INDIA

India is projected to experience a surge in the E-Commerce market. Also, India is a rapidly expanding E-Commerce sector in Asia. Increased internet and smartphone usage have fueled most of the industry's growth. The major drivers of this industry include a young demographic profile, increased internet usage, and relatively stronger economic performance.

In addition to this, the government of India's policies and regulatory frameworks, such as 100% foreign direct investment (FDI) in B2B E-Commerce and 100% FDI via the automatic route in the marketplace model of B2C E-Commerce, are projected to boost growth in the sectors even more.

The introduction of 4G and 5G networks, as well as an increase in consumer wealth, have all contributed to the expansion of smartphone users. In 2014, total E-Commerce retail sales were estimated at $7 billion (US $), $13 billion in 2015, $ 15 billion in 2016 increasing to $17 billion (US $) in June 2017 which gives strong support to the government. (Mann and Rana, 2019).

REAL-WORLD CASE 2

Government Initiatives for Growth of the E-Commerce Market

E-Commerce markets are one of the world's fastest-growing sectors in India. E-Commerce is an economic key driver of every country around the world. The Indian government is working hard to transform India into a trillion-dollar internet economy by 2025 (Babli, 2021).

Government e-marketplace (GeM)

The Government of India and the Union Bank of India signed a Memorandum of Understanding (MoU) in October 2019 to promote a cashless, paperless, and transparent payment system for a variety of services. Purchases with a threshold limit of more than Rs. 50,000 will be made based on criteria such as lowest price bidding, quality standards, specifications, and delivery time requirements. The platform will host the most often utilized items and services for government workers (Government E-Marketplace, 2019).

Bharat Net

The BharatNet Project, also known as Bharat Broadband Network Services, is the largest optical fiber-based rural broadband access scheme in the world. This major project was carried out by Bharat Broadband Network Ltd (BBNL).

A Special Purpose Vehicle (SPV), BBNL was established by the Government of India under the Companies Act, 1956. The purpose is to make it easier for rural Indians to access internet, e-banking, e-health, and other services (BharatNet Project, 2021).

Digital India Program

The Digital India movement also saw the debut of many government projects such as Udaan, Umang, and the Start-up India Portal. Bharat Interface for Money (BHIM), a basic mobile-based platform for digital payments, was also established by the government.

Mahila e-haat

The Indian government's Ministry of Women and Child Development developed Mahila e-haat, an E-Commerce portal for women entrepreneurs. This E-Commerce marketplace platform allows women to register and display their products online for free (PIB, 2021).

10.4 CONNECTIVES OF LOGISTICS AND E-COMMERCE

The E-Commerce industry has seen a lot of progress in logistics. The development of the E-Commerce industry is supported by logistics, which is a significant component of it. The integration of logistics into the E-Commerce sector is significant for a country's economic growth. The E-Commerce industry has developed to compete in today's digital age in numerous ways. In the past, shops used to purchase products directly from suppliers and manufacturers. Currently, the products are distributed through E-Commerce fulfillment facilities. Warehouse management, inventory control, billing, packaging, labeling, shipping, cash on delivery, payment, product return and exchange, and many other features are all included in logistics. Logistics companies use specialized business mobility software to streamline the process because they handle most of the problems, including tracking, managing stock levels and locations, packing, and fulfillment (Chavaralakshmi and Srivani, 2017).

To help businesses develop a global sales network and logistics infrastructure that supports effective online order fulfillment, E-Commerce includes: providing enterprises with information and data on various business activities, production, and sales information to solve the challenging problem of collection; reducing market entry links that help businesses open up the market to minimize the circulation of goods; and reducing business costs (Yang, 2012).

Thus, the primary responsibility of logistics is to provide prompt and effective product delivery so that consumers are happy and return as well as refer you to others.

In today's competitive world, retailers are working hard to satisfy customer demand. Many e-retailers have started offering same-day delivery or same-day dispatch of products to entice customers who can't or won't wait for even next-day service. For many things, some retailers provide free or low shipping charges for their customers. Online shoppers seek competitive pricing and hassle-free product delivery. In order to not only acquire but also keep customers, a superior product delivery experience is essential. So, it is in the best interest of E-Commerce players to enlist expert logistics services, as doing so would lead to the firm growing, succeeding, and becoming more dynamic more quickly.

10.4.1 E-Commerce and Logistics Management System

Logistics management is known as the process of planning, implementing, monitoring, and controlling the effective flow and storage of products, goods, and services from the point of origin to the site of consumption in order to satisfy customers' needs. Logistics is becoming more and more important for the E-Commerce industry because businesses are going global in order to access new markets, increase production efficiency, and leverage technology capabilities outside of their own national borders (Cooper, 1998). In recent years, there has been a lot of interest in logistics due to the lowering of trade barriers and the development of cutting-edge technologies. The current scope of logistics operations extends to client services, packaging, production, distribution, and inventory management.

To increase consumer happiness and E-Commerce trade, there must be a strong management interaction and correlation between E-Commerce and logistics. The effectiveness of an E-Commerce company's distribution systems and logistical performance are closely correlated with one another. The performance of a business can be improved through superior E-Commerce logistics management. Different logistical activities are more likely to be prompted by the characteristics of distinct global contexts, such as the logistical capabilities of various nations. Nonetheless, only a small number of studies have thoroughly examined global E-Commerce logistics business models. The study found that important elements influencing people's intentions to transact online include their level of perceptions of internet safety, acceptability of E-Commerce, privacy concerns, and personal interests (Antwi, A.O., and Agyeman, A.O., 2020).

In order to manage logistics effectively, it is necessary to have excellent delivery services, ideal logistics information systems, secure e-procurement procedures, inter-organizational collaboration, convenient mobile banking, an effective mobile channel, and appropriate collaboration tools. A company's financial performance can be improved with improved E-Commerce logistics management (Yu et al., 2016). E-Commerce investments need to take a variety of conceivable configurations, including insourcing and outsourcing, into account. E-Commerce investments must take into account sources for a wide range of potential configurations, including insourcing and outsourcing.

An institution called the distribution center gathers and distributes products for customers. Manufacturers, warehouse service providers, domestic freighters, and international freighters are the major actors in a highly specialized global logistics environment. Moreover, distributors and wholesalers combine their jobs to market and distribute products from several manufacturers to clients abroad via a single channel. Global logistics services enable the transportation of goods between numerous businesses that are geographically dispersed through a variety of distribution methods. The main concerns for the effective functioning of a distribution center are logistics management and distribution services (Huang et al., 2001). Businesses and individuals can get systematic transportation management, demand forecasting, information management, warehousing, inventory control, and distribution services from logistic service providers like UPS and FedEx.

10.4.2   E-Commerce Impact in Logistics

The role of logistics is important to E-Commerce because if you want your online store to succeed, logistics is essential. There are five pillars of E-Commerce:

Infrastructure: Even if the business is fairly large, a solid infrastructure is important. It must be able to quickly and effectively address the needs of the business.

Marketing and promotion: For a greater impact, businesses need to combine offline and internet marketing strategies. Marketing is essential for attracting the attention of potential customers.

Payment procedures: Given that they meet the needs of the users, the most payment options, or at least some, must be available.

Security: Customers must feel secure in order to earn their loyalty. An online store needs to build trust and have the capacity to respond. With your customers, you must be open and work to address their concerns.

Logistics is the foundation of E-Commerce industry. The company won't be successful, and the customers won't be happy, if the logistics of E-Commerce fail. Maintaining effective logistics will guarantee that deliveries are made on schedule and that returns or adjustments are managed.

10.5   E-COMMERCE CHALLENGES

Due to widespread internet use and advanced electronic devices, India's E-Commerce sector is expanding at a rapid rate. In today's digital world the biggest concern is the safety and security of online financial transactions. There is occasional news of online fraud, contact thieves, spam emails, and an increase in credit card information theft frauds. As a result, there are numerous difficulties and problems with E-Commerce, which are described below.

Security and privacy concerns: Lack of security and privacy is a major problem for Indian E-Commerce companies. To sustain a reliable business relationship, the buyer and trader's privacy and information must be safe. Because data can occasionally be exploited by criminal organizations to steal customers' and traders' money, decreasing the trust in E-Commerce businesses.

Low infrastructure is an important component of the E-Commerce industry, hence poor infrastructure issues are problematic. Without a solid infrastructure, the firm cannot continue. The infrastructure of E-Commerce depends on the internet.

Because E-Commerce requires constant, uninterrupted internet, it is essential to guarantee it. Not only is infrastructure important for the trader, but it is also important for the consumer. The main E-Commerce infrastructures are the availability of computers, buyers' and sellers' mobile and electronic devices, internet service providers' availability and internet penetration rates, the caliber and speed of internet connectivity, internet security, and online payment gateways (Hajli and Featherman, 2017).

Online payment system: As the number of fraudulent cases is increasing in online shopping, to prevent such fraud, people prefer not to make online purchases with their credit cards.

Cash on delivery (COD): To overcome the issue of online transaction security, not all but some of the E-Commerce platforms have included the cash-on-delivery (COD) option, which allows a customer to pay for their product at the time of delivery. But sometimes the problem with this type of system is that many of the consumers refused to pay for them, which led to significant losses in product transit and ultimately lost sales and revenue.

Lack of digital illiteracy: One of the main prerequisites for an E-Commerce system is a lack of digital illiteracy. However, India's low level of digital literacy poses a challenge to the country's successful E-Commerce development. Though software development for E-Commerce calls for a team of top IT professionals. Infrastructure development and software adaptation by customs by negotiations with international E-Commerce service providers are all important, yet top-tier IT specialists are interested in leaving the country for personal benefit, which is a form of brain drain (Sarkar, Sulatana, and Prodhan, 2017).

Absence of adequate cyber laws: Cybersecurity is a key instrument for preserving consumer confidence in the E-Commerce industry. To protect the nation's cyber security, proper cyber law should be implemented. Therefore, it is impossible to do E-Commerce business successfully in any part of country without enacting timely and suitable cyber law. However, cyber law in some countries is not up to the mark; it requires reform and establishes laws by the code to ensure correct application. Cyber law would be uniform such that personal property rights, content and data privacy, and data protection should be reserved with its criminal and commercial legal frameworks (Micheal, Arunachalam, and Srigowthem, 2017).

Views of the consumer: Consumer impression is a crucial factor in the E-Commerce industry. In comparison to conventional service processing methods, e-service substitutes may appear strange, unnatural, and unauthentic (Devaraju, 2016). Consumers can think that new internet-based processing techniques expose them to new threats. The risks of online fraud, identity theft, and phishing scams have made it usual for people to utilize faked websites to obtain personal information, which is likely to worry and frighten customers.

Shipping and logistics: Shipping and courier services needed a lot of upgrading. One of the main factors in the success of any online business is a strong and flawless logistics service, but India is facing difficulties in this area as the majority of towns and small villages are still outside of the serviceable areas of many courier and logistic businesses. E-Commerce is severely affected due to the limited services provided by courier services firms.

Language and location localization: Due to transportation costs, delivery times, and other connected concerns, an E-Commerce business in one province cannot adequately transport its goods to other places. To deliver the product on time and easily boost E-Commerce, localization is therefore required. In addition to its many benefits, online commerce is facing danger due to its so-called "faceless and borderless" nature (Islam et al., 2017).

10.6 M-COMMERCE

M-Commerce is also known as mobile commerce. It is an emerging trend as the demand for smartphone users and internet users are increasing rapidly globally. The term "m-commerce," or "mobile commerce" is known as the exchange of products and services using wireless handheld devices like cellular phones and PDA. Products and services offered by M-Commerce are:

Mobile banking: Mobile banking, or m-banking, is a common name for this service. Banks and other financial organizations utilize mobile commerce to let their customer access account information and other transactions like buying stocks or sending money.

Mobile ticketing: Several technologies send tickets to mobile devices. By showing their phones at the venue, users can then use their tickets right away. With the aid of straightforward application downloads or by logging into the WAP sites of various travel agencies or direct service providers, tickets can be purchased and canceled on a mobile device.

Mobile brokerage: This refers to the stock market services that are currently increasingly popular and are provided via mobile devices. They enable the subscriber to respond to market developments without regard to their physical location and promptly.

Merits of M-Commerce

With the freedom of digitalization in today's digital age, more people are utilizing mobile commerce. Additionally, the availability of data packs at cheaper prices and the development of 4G smartphones have made it simpler for the general public to utilize the internet. In countries worldwide nearly all of the population now use smartphones for many different purposes other than making calls. This includes utilizing apps for grocery shopping, ordering food through various restaurant apps, and financial applications to access banking and other financial services, using apps for educational purposes, booking cabs, booking tickets for traveling, and so on. This ongoing rise in reliance on mobile apps can be attributed to their usability, reach, portability, accessibility, and ability to provide several benefits.

Seamless shopping: Visiting stores physically to shop is a waste of both time and money. Through M-Commerce, businesses can connect with customers directly. Therefore customers may now simply shop with just one phone click thanks to the capabilities that many E-Commerce companies have included. In reality, the transactional side of shopping has improved as well. Today, shops provide services like e-wallets, instant on-site payment choices, discount coupons, etc.

Social media M-Commerce: It is an efficient way for businesses to increase their sales. For instance, social media advertising on sites like Facebook and Twitter raises public awareness and highlights the advantages of using mobile apps. Nowadays, a lot of businesses launch social media campaigns to reach a broad audience and lower their marketing expenses.

Simple and convenient: A trained consumer is not necessary. Customers do not need to complete the online checkout process because they can browse thousands of things on their mobile devices. It is very convenient because customers can already shop, conduct financial transactions, download media files, and more using mobile devices with just a few clicks.

Simple connectivity: Mobile devices can connect and conduct business transactions not just between themselves but also with other mobile devices as long as there is a network signal. There is no need to set up a modem or Wi-Fi connection.

Time-saving: Users don't have to wait for their laptops or personal computers (PC) to load or plug anything in when doing M-Commerce transactions.

Quickly purchasing: It's been discovered that mobile apps perform 1.5 times faster when loading data, allowing users to browse and make purchases more quickly.

Direct communication with customers: Sending push alerts or notifications about new products or rewards to customers' phones is simpler for businesses than sending emails, which take time and frequently go unread.

Demerits of M-Commerce

Every technology has its benefits and drawbacks. It is also applicable to this M-Commerce company. Despite a rise in smartphone users, the majority of people in rural areas still do not use smartphones or mobile apps for the several reasons mentioned below:

Lack of technological skills: In a developing nation like India, where more than half of the population is illiterate, it is evident that they are unable to utilize mobile apps for shopping since they are unable to operate their phones. Additionally, as these apps are majorly connected to the internet, there is always a level of risk involved with using these applications to make payments (Bansal, Kadian, and Garg, 2018).

Poor internet connections: Mobile commerce demands 3G's high-speed connectivity. Even though 4G is already accessible, only a few cities and regions have it. In India, few phones have 4G and 3G capabilities, and the few that do cost too much for the majority of people.

Security and privacy concern: because mobile phone security software is still in its starting stage, there is always a chance of hacking, phishing, and other fraudsters when they use smartphones to do business. Indeed, a lot of apps have been known to improperly access users' personal information, including passwords and bank details.

Language issues: The majority of mobile commerce company's favor using English rather than a local language for their apps. As a result, especially in the case of banking and shopping apps, this causes issues for app users.

10.7   CHAPTER CONCLUSION

Despite its drawbacks, both E-Commerce and M-Commerce are dominating not only in Asian markets but also in many other international markets as well. Smartphones and rising internet data usage around the world have contributed to the rapid growth of E-Commerce and M-Commerce businesses by giving consumers the freedom to access every aspect of the business. Many developing countries like India, Indonesia and others has emerged as the global E-Commerce market with the fastest rate of growth. As the number of people using mobile devices is rising daily, the future of M-Commerce also appears to be quite promising.

EXERCISES

1. What are the various reasons people opt for digital shopping?
2. What are the types of E-Commerce?
3. Which is the leading online shopping app in the world?
4. What are two major factors responsible for E-Commerce growth in India?
5. What are two main factors responsible for growth in digital payments?
6. What are the benefits of E-Payment system in E-Commerce?
7. According to your opinion, which technology has proven to be a promising for E-Commerce development around the world?
8. What is the role of social media platforms in E-Commerce industry?
9. How are logistics important for E-Commerce growth?
10. What are five pillars of E-Commerce?
11. How do privacy and security affect the E-Commerce industry?
12. Define the term "M-Commerce"?
13. What are the merits and demerits of M-Commerce?

REFERENCES

Antwi, A.O. and Agyeman, A.O. (2020) 'The impact of e-commerce adoption on logistics companies', *European Journal of Economics, Business and Accountancy*, vol. 8, no. 1, ISSN 2056-6018.

Aydin, N. (2015) 'Cloud computing for e-commerce', ISOR, *Journal of Mobile Computing and Applications*, vol. 2.

Babli (2021) 'Digital economy: impact and challenges on Indian economy', vol. 20, no. 5, pp. 8148–8154, DOI: 10.17051/ilkonline.2021.05.914.

Bendor-Samuel, P. (2018) *'What is a digital platform?'* December 27. Available at: https://enterprisesproject.com/article/2018/12/what-digital-platform (Accessed: 03 March 2020).

Bhat, A. (2012) 'Blog popularity and activity on social media: an explanatory research', *Indian Journal of Marketing*.

BharatNet Project (2021) July, Available at: www.drishtiias.com/daily-updates/daily-news-anaylsis/bharatnet-project-1 (Accessed: 07 December 2021).

Bansal, P., Kadian, P and Garg, M. (2018) 'Emerging trends of m-commerce in India', *Journal of Emerging Technologies and Innovative Research*, May, vol. 5, no. 5, ISSN: 2349-5162.

Chavaralakshmi, and N. Srivani. (2017) 'Role of logistics in e-commerce', *International Journal of Advanced Research,* DOI: 10.21474/IJAR01/5935

Cooper, L.C. (1998) 'Logistics strategies for global businesses', *International Journal of Physical Distribution & Logistics Management*, 23 (4), pp. 12–23.

Diwan, Parag and Sharma, S. (2000) *'Electronic commerce: a manager's guide to e-business',* New Delhi: Vanity Books International, pp. 31–32.

Devaraju, D.P. (2016) 'The challenges and opportunities of e-commerce in India: future prospective', *International Journal of Engineering, Computer Science,* vol. 5, no. 11, pp. 19065–19069.

Felix, R. Rauschnabel, P.A. and Hinsch, C. (2016) 'Elements of strategic social media marketing; a holistic framework', *Journal of Business Research,* https://dx.doi.org/10.1016/j.jbusres.2016.05.001

Gibson, I., Rosen, D.W., and Stucker, B. (2010) *Additive Manufacturing Technologies,* New York, Springer, https://doi.org/10.1007/978-1-4419-1120

Government E-Marketplace (2019) 'A Gem of an Idea', 19 April, *International Journal of Emerging Technologies and Innovative Research,* ISSN: 2349–5162, vol. 6, no. 4, pp. 192–196.

Hajli, N. and Featherman, M.S. (2017) 'Social commerce and new development in e-commerce technologies', *International Journal of Information Management,* vol. 37, no. 3, pp. 177–178.

Huang et al. (2001) 'Planning enterprise resource by use of a reengineering approach to build a global logistics management system', *Industrial Management & Data system,* 101(9), pp. 483–491.

Islam et al. (2017) 'Determinants of profitability of commercial banks in Bangladesh', *International Journal of Banking Financial Law,* vol. 1, no. 1, pp. 1–11.

Kalia and Parteek, (2017) 'Service quality scales in online retail: methodological issues', *International Journal of Operations & Production Management* 37 (5), pp. 630–663.

Mann, P.K. and Rana, R.K. (2019) 'E-commerce: fueling the dream of digital India', *Inspira-Journal of Commerce, Economics and Computer Science,* vol. 5, no. 03, ISSN: 2395-7069, pp- 71–79.

Mellor, S., Hao, L., and Zhang, D. (2014) 'Additive manufacturing: a framework for implementation', *International Journal of Production Economics,* 149, pp. 194–201, https://doi.org/10.1016/j/ijpe.2013.07.008

Merzlyakova, E., Ershova, I. and Bridskiy, E. (2021) 'Main trends in the development of the global e-commerce market', *SHS Web of Conference* 110, 01035, DOI: https://doi.org/10.1051/shsconf/202111001035

Micheal, G., Arunachalam, A.R., and Srigowthem, S. (2017) 'E-commerce transaction security challenges and prevention methods new approach', *International Journal of Pure Applied Mathematics,* vol. 116, No. 13, pp. 285–289.

OECD (2014) 'The digital economy, new business models and key features in addressing the Tax Challenges of the Digital Economy', OECD Publishing, Paris, https://doi.org/10.1787/9789264218789-7-en

PIB (2021) *'Mahila E-Haats: Ministry of Women and Child Development',* 05, February. Available at: www.pib.gov.in/PressReleasePage.aspx?PRID=1695509#:~:text="Mahila%20E-haat"%2C,NSIC)%20to%20support%20the%20entrepreneurs. (Accessed: 03 May 2021).

Rahman, M. et al. (2017) 'Problems and prospects of electronic banking in Bangladesh: A case study on Dutch-Bangla Bank Limited', Am. *Journal of Operational Management Information System,* vol. 2, no. 1, pp. 42–53.

Sarkar, M.N.I., Sulatana, A. and Prodhan, A.S. (2017) 'Financial performance analysis of Islamic Bank in Bangladesh: A case study on AI-Arafah Islamic Bank Limited', *World Journal of Economics Finance*, vol. 3, no. 1, pp. 52–60.

Smith, T. (2010) 'The social media revolution', *International Journal of Market Research*, vol. 51, no. 4.

Song et al. (2019) 'The Aaplication of artificial intelligence in electronic commerce', *Journal of Physics: Conference Series* (3), 1302–1302.

Wirtz, J. et al. (2019) *Journal of Service Management*, vol. 30, no. 4, pp. 452–483, Emerald Publishing Limited 1757-5818, DOI: 10.1108/JOSM-11-2018-0369.

Wu, P.J. and Lin, K.C. (2018) 'Unstructured big data analytics for retrieving e-commerce logistics knowledge', *Telematics and Informatics*, vol. 35, pp. 237–244.

Yang, G. (2012) 'Relationships between e-commerce and supply chain management', In K. Haenakon (Ed.), *Advances in Technology and Management: Advances in intelligent and soft computing*, Berlin, pp. 653–658, Springer. DOI: 10.1007/978-3-642-29637-6_87

Yu et al. (2016) 'E-commerce logistics in supply chain management: Practice perspective', *Procedia CIRP*, vol. 52, pp. 179–185.

Index

Printed in the United States
by Baker & Taylor Publisher Services